# A WOMAN'S WEAPON

DORIS G. BARGEN

# A WOMAN'S

# WEAPON

## SPIRIT POSSESSION IN
## *THE TALE OF GENJI*

UNIVERSITY OF HAWAI'I PRESS ![HAWAI]

HONOLULU

02 01 00 99 98 97   5 4 3 2 1


**Library of Congress Cataloging-in-Publication Data**
Bargen, Doris G.
   A woman's weapon : spirit possession in the Tale of Genji / Doris
G. Bargen.
   p.    cm.
   Includes bibliographical references and index.
   ISBN 0–8248–1801–6 (cloth : alk. paper). — ISBN 0–8248–1858–X
(pbk. : alk. paper)
   1. Murasaki Shikibu, b. 978? Genji monogatari.   2. Murasaki
Shikibu, b. 978?—Characters—Women.   3. Spirit possession in
literature.   I. Murasaki Shikibu, b. 978? Genji monogatari.
English.   Selections.   II. Title.
PL788.4.G43B37   1996
895.6'31—dc20                    96–25663
                         CIP

Book design by Kenneth Miyamoto

*For Allen Guttmann*

# Contents

# Acknowledgments

A MILLENNIUM after Murasaki Shikibu created her magnificent *Genji monogatari,* scholars produce ever more critical studies from a growing variety of perspectives. William J. Tyler's extraordinary class on classical Japanese literature first inspired me to study the masterpiece of Japanese literature. Melinda Takeuchi's lectures on Japanese art prepared me for my first journey to Japan in 1980. On my return I was privileged to study Japanese language under Hirota Akiko, also at Amherst College, and have had many teachers of modern and classical Japanese language since. I am deeply indebted to all of them.

I discovered that *The Tale of Genji* contained more *mono no ke,* or possessing spirits, than I was prepared to handle when I first presented a comparative paper on Murasaki Shikibu's classic and Marcel Proust's *A la recherche du temps perdu* at the international "World of Genji" conference at Indiana University at Bloomington in August 1982. My paper sparked a controversy about spirit possession and related issues that called for interdisciplinary inquiry into the phenomenon, applying the findings of anthropology and psychology in addition to the insights of literary criticism. I am grateful to the conference organizers Eugene Eoyang and Sumie Jones for inviting me, then a novice in the field, as well as to Earl Miner and Janet A. Walker, for their early encouragement and continuing support.

In addition to the scholars and the institutions named above I received the help of more scholars than I can name. Sei Shōnagon's brilliant technique of capturing in starkly simple lists what might have overwhelmed her in fleshed-out detail offers me an appropriate solution. I am grateful to these specialists in anthropology, art, history, literature, medicine, psychoanalysis, and religion: Gridth and Steven L. Ablon, Arima Teruomi, Klara Bargen, Camille and Gwendolynne

Barr, Alice S. and Otis Cary, Frederick K. Errington, Bettina and Herwig Friedl, Fujii Sadakazu, Norma Field, Deborah B. Gewertz, Maribeth Graybill, Howard Hibbett, Higuchi Jō, Hirokawa Katsumi, Edward Kamens, Kojima Shigekazu, Takie Sugiyama Lebra, Ioan M. Lewis, Martha McClintock, Matsuyama Nobunao, Julia Meech, Miyeko Murase, William E. Naff, Denise O'Brien, Thomas P. Rohlen, Betty Romer, Paul B. Roscoe, Stephanie Sandler, Sasaki Takashi and Noriko, Hiroaki Sato, Shimozato Shigeru, Charlotte and Bardwell L. Smith, Robert J. Smith, Uda Yoshitada.

Librarians at Amherst College and the University of Massachusetts deserve much credit for their astonishing ability to provide me with the books I needed when I needed them. Dōshisha University and the Stanford Japan Center in Kyoto generously opened their doors to me.

My research on "Spirit Possession in *The Tale of Genji*" was assisted by a 1989 summer stipend from the National Endowment for the Humanities, a grant for the following two summers from the Joint Committee on Japanese Studies of the American Council of Learned Societies and the Social Science Research Council, with funds provided by the Ford Foundation and the National Endowment for the Humanities. And I most gratefully acknowledge receiving a National Endowment for the Humanities Fellowship for 1991–1992.

Toward the end of any research project, spouses can be unusually useful. Allen Guttmann, who became positively familiar with *mono no ke* as he labored through many drafts, encouraged me with his unwavering faith in the value of my project. My colleague in Japanese history, Richard H. Minear, generously agreed to read the penultimate draft. I am also indebted to the readers for the University of Hawai'i Press, especially to Paul G. Schalow for his perceptive reading and constructive criticism. From the beginning, my editor, Patricia Crosby, understood me in such uncanny ways that I wonder whether I am acting as a medium for her own passionate interest in this particular *Genji* topic. Finally, the managing editor, Cheri Dunn, made everything fall into place.

An earlier version of my "Aoi" chapter appeared as "Spirit Possession in the Context of Dramatic Expressions of Gender Conflict: The Aoi Episode of the *Genji monogatari*," in the *Harvard Journal of Asiatic Studies* (June 1988). I am grateful to the editors for permission to use this material. The illustrations for *A Woman's Weapon* were provided through the cooperation of museum curators and directors, librarians and private collectors, book publishers and the Kongō School of Nō. Obtaining permissions is an arduous process. Baba Minako provided a helping hand, and her friendship has been invaluable to me. Higuchi Hideo and Fusako did what seemed humanly impossible. I cannot find words adequate to express my gratitude to both of them and the extended Higuchi family of Matsumoto and Kyoto.

Just as my first *Genji* mentor, William J. Tyler, opened up a whole new world for me, so my Japanese Sensei, Hirota Osamu, guided me with incredible patience and sensitivity to my needs through the maze of Japanese scholarship on *mono no ke*. Without his expertise, I could never have completed this project.

# Emblems

THE DECORATIVE DEVICES heading the five cases of spirit posses-sion analyzed in this study are emblems from the *Genji* incense game *(Genji-kō)* that denote the *Genji* chapters in which the five women become possessed: Yūgao in "Yūgao" ("Evening Faces"), Aoi in "Aoi" ("Heartvine"), Murasaki in "Wakana ge" ("New Herbs: Part Two"), the Third Princess in "Kashiwagi" ("The Oak Tree"), and Ukifune in "Tenarai" ("At Writing Practice"). Each emblem consists of five vertical lines recording (from right to left) the experience of incense on five occasions. The aim of the contest is to distinguish the fragrances. Intently "listening" to incense *(monkō)*, the connoisseur leans over the incense burner *(kiki kōro)* with head cocked to the side as if to recover a sensual memory matching the present fragrance. If a fragrance is unmatched, it stands alone as a vertical bar; if it matches one or more fragrances, it is linked by a horizontal bar. The "Tenarai" emblem, for example, indicates that the five successive incense experi-ences are of the same fragrance. It is a fortuitous coincidence that one goal of the present study is similarly to differentiate between the pos-session experiences of five female *Genji* protagonists. The *Genji-kō* emblems are not meant to be interpretive but merely to serve as a reminder of this goal. Widely appreciated for their aesthetic appeal outside incense-listening circles, the striking geometric patterns can be found in kimono designs, woodblock prints, lacquerware, pottery, even confectionery. In returning the *Genji-kō* emblems to their origi-nal source by suggesting the power of incense to evoke spirits, I hope that they will be conducive to the pacification of *mono no ke*.

# Introduction

MURASAKI SHIKIBU is to Japan what Homer is to Greece, Shakespeare to England, Dante to Italy, Goethe to Germany, and the T'ang poets to China. Her *Genji monogatari* (The Tale of Genji; 1001?–1014?) is, moreover, the only national classic written by a woman. Why is it important to make a point of this departure from the expected relationship of gender to literary production? And what does it have to do with the representation of spirit possession and possessing spirits *(mono no ke)*,[1] a psychic phenomenon so integral to the text that it seems almost to structure the entire narrative?

To arrive at an answer, one must consider both the place of women in the elite courtly society of the Heian period (794–1186) and the status of the fictional narratives *(tsukuri monogatari)* that were their chief and unsurpassed mode of literary expression. Despite their considerable economic independence, aristocratic women were expected not only to concede political power to men—hardly unusual in any time or place—but also to grant men precedence in the realm of culture. Women were encouraged to show their sophistication by playing the koto and other musical instruments, by practicing calligraphy in the "woman's hand" *(onna-de)*, and by composing thirty-one-syllable poems *(waka)*. Their penchant for composing vernacular narratives was tolerated. No matter how exciting contemporary Heian readers may have found these products of the imagination, the Confucian notion that prose fiction was synonymous with lies demoted women's *tsukuri monogatari* to the lower rungs of a male–constructed artistic ladder.[2] Meanwhile, men, writing in classical Chinese *(kanbun)*, followed literary conventions imported from the continent. Since poetry was a literary form approved by the Chinese literati,[3] men felt free to write poetry not only in Chinese but also in the vernacular.

The boundary between the genres of men's and women's writing was occasionally transgressed. Ki no Tsurayuki (869–945) crossed the line into women's future literary territory by posing as the female author of an intensely personal diary, the *Tosa nikki* (The Tosa Diary; ca. 935).[4] Other men, writing anonymously, produced fictional narratives such as the *Taketori monogatari* (The Tale of the Bamboo Cutter; ca. 960), the *Ochikubo monogatari* (The Tale of the Lower Room; late tenth century), and the *Utsubo monogatari* (The Tale of the Hollow Tree; late tenth century). (When women, writing in an animated style quite unlike men's stilted historiography, collaborated in historical narratives [*rekishi monogatari*], such as the *Eiga monogatari* [A Tale of Flowering Fortunes; ca. 1092], they too effaced themselves.)[5] Despite these sorties into unfamiliar territory, Heian female writers of vernacular prose fiction found themselves engaged in an undeclared contest with male scholars who—officially—had mere contempt for the "lies" *(soragoto)* of fiction. The struggle over "truth" became a gender issue. It is, therefore, especially ironic that, with the exception of the men who ventured into women's territory, the mid-Heian literature best remembered and most admired today consists precisely of these women's narratives.

Representing her male-dominated society through a female literary medium, Murasaki Shikibu (973?–1014?) dramatized spirit possession in ways that subtly subverted the structure of domination and significantly altered the construction of gender in Heian times. As John J. Winkler has noted about Sappho (late seventh century B.C.E.), "In distinguishing women's perspective from men's she necessarily shows a double consciousness of the two systems and their putative relation to one another as dominant to submissive. But, like linguistic minorities forced to be bilingual, Sappho understands more about the 'dominant' practices of men than they do about the 'submission' of women."[6] A reading of the *Genji,* as of Sappho's lyrics, calls for the recognition of such a "double consciousness." Even though Murasaki Shikibu may appear to present the mostly female phenomenon of spirit possession as perceived through the eyes of the male hero, the facts of female authorship and a largely female audience leave indelible traces in the text—traces that entice the reader to ask questions about the perceptions and the motivations of the possessed women.

In attempting some answers to these questions, I mean to address not only *Genji* specialists but also scholars from the fields of anthropology and gender studies who are curious about the complex phenomenon of spirit possession as it is reflected in the mirror of a major literary work. It may seem absurd, in an age that some have character-ized as "postmodern," for European and American scholars to attempt persuasive interpretations of the *Genji monogatari,* written a millennium ago in a culture other than their own. Even if we were privy to all the customs and conventions of that temporally and cultur-ally distant society, what must we fail to hear in its courtly discourse? To begin with, we do not even know the author's full name, only the sobriquet by which she was known at the imperial court.[7] There is no holograph. Despite its fame the *Genji* began to elude the Japanese themselves as the culture of the Heian aristocracy fell into decline, overwhelmed by the thrust of a newly emerging warrior culture. The acknowledged difficulties of historical reconstruction can, however, be exaggerated. On the basis of the written, visual, and archaeological evidence that has been preserved from Heian times, scholars have done a great deal to suggest how Murasaki Shikibu's world might have looked to her. I have, in turn, benefited from their efforts. There are skeptics who believe that all such efforts are futile because we must inevitably imagine the past from the perspective of our own time and with its conceptual instruments. These skeptics ignore the fact that even a minimally sophisticated twentieth-century approach can ac-knowledge otherness and adjust its angle of vision in order to avoid the temptations of narrowly ethnocentric interpretation.

The Japanese themselves have, necessarily, scrutinized the *Genji* from the perspective of their own time and place. Was Motoori Nori-naga's (1730–1801) emphasis on the *Genji*'s hitherto neglected mood of elegiac sensibility *(mono no aware)* in his *Genji monogatari Tama no ogushi* (A Small Jeweled Comb of the *Genji monogatari;* 1793–1796) not a product of his culture—an insight born from the need to revise radically the traditional approach of gauging literature solely for its didactic value? Contemporary Japanese scholarship no longer restricts itself to the critical tools handed down by *kokubun-gakusha,* itself a conservative term for Japanologists, but has boldly crossed boundaries to enrich the field with Western methods—struc-turalism, postmodernism, narratology, deconstruction, and finally, with some hesitation, feminist criticism. Ironically, the erroneous notion that twentieth-century Western scholarship must limit itself to the cultural perspective of Heian times is itself a Western construct.

Just as some scholars have worried about "imposing our ideas on them," others have pointed to the dangers of taking literature as a

mirror of social reality. Michele Marra warns: "To take courtly refinement as the paradigm of the historical Heian court is to present fiction
as reality."[8] Similarly, writing about the complex interplay between
kinship and power, Peter Nickerson notes that, "as a work of fiction,
the *Genji* is likely to narrate events that are interesting precisely
because they are unusual; what the *Genji* characters do, including
especially how they love and marry, may not have been typical of mid-
Heian men and women. Thus, when we wish to assess the meaning of
*Genji* characters marrying in certain ways, or finding certain types of
matches exciting and others dull, we must do so, not reading the
*Genji* as a kind of fictional ethnography, but instead assessing state-
ments in terms of the larger structural and symbolic context within
which the narrative operates."[9] The "larger structural and symbolic
context" includes the courtiers' diaries and chronicles composed in
Heian times. As Mimi Hall Yiengpruksawan has provocatively argued,
they provide a corrective to the refined cultural construct eagerly
gleaned from selected works of art and literature.[10] They also provide
us with a great deal of useful information but, as Helen C. and William H. McCullough have noted, they have their shortcomings.[11]
Even if the imaginary "reality" reflected in the *Genji* cannot be veri-
fied, neither can the politically colored "reality" of the chronicles.
Where Murasaki Shikibu used the phenomenon of spirit possession to
probe deeply into gender relations in her polygynous society, the
chroniclers blamed rampant *mono no ke* for political strife and for inexplicable or untreatable diseases, both physical and mental. In addition
to the problem of historicity—the reliability of *any* historical document—there is the inability of "objective" information to capture the
feel of life as it is lived. As the McCulloughs have observed, fiction is
often our best guide to experienced reality: "Although official chronicles may have their uses in government, we must turn to tales if we
want to know how people have actually lived, and what they have felt
and thought."[12] Scholars who are nervous about this use of literary
texts can be reassured by no less an authority than Claude Lévi-
Strauss. He begins his discussion of the *Genji* by asserting that "this
dense, slow narrative, attentive to the finest details of Japanese court
life during the Heian period, also offers a mass of precise anthropological data, especially about a social change that certainly took place
elsewhere, too, but about which we have little information outside of
this invaluable source."[13]

   Although it cannot be my aim to reconstruct Heian historic "reality" from the pages of the *Genji monogatari,* there is much to be learned about Heian *mentalité* from Murasaki Shikibu. Fujimoto Katsuyoshi's recent comparative study of *mono no ke* in the *Genji* and in historical narratives demonstrates that the brief scenes of spirit possession interspersed in the chronicles of courtly life fall far short of the psychological depth of Murasaki Shikibu's literary masterpiece.[14] The chroniclers' intermittent flashes of insight became an explosive force in Murasaki Shikibu's dazzling spectrum of the possessed, their spirits, and their targeted witnesses.

Besides gleaning information about *mono no ke* from a variety of sources and from the techniques of Western and Japanese literary scholarship—obviously a sine qua non—I have, like the classicists who have recently enlivened the study of Greek and Roman antiquity, drawn upon the methods and insights of modern cultural anthropology. This cross-cultural discipline can "raise questions and provide comparisons that illuminate much of the ancient material, letting us see much more clearly just how familiar and how strange it really is."[15] In this spirit, I locate *mono no ke* within the politics of Heian polygynous society and interpret spirit possession as a predominantly female strategy adopted to counter male strategies of empowerment such as incestuous transgressions and *kaimami* ("peeping through a hole in the fence"), a custom that inspired Heian noblemen not only to compose poetry but to take physical possession of the glimpsed woman. I have also drawn, cautiously, upon modern psychoanalytical theory (with the modifications necessary to adjust for cultural differences). Freud's notion of the uncanny (1919), for instance, is useful in understanding certain aspects of the *mono no ke* crowding the Heian unconscious and the *Genji monogatari.*

In addition to contemporary Japanese scholarship, there is now an impressive body of Western *Genji* scholarship that simply did not exist as recently as twenty years ago. Virtually all *Genji* scholars on both sides of the Pacific preface their efforts with modest remarks about the astronomical number of books and articles devoted to Murasaki Shikibu's classic. I too am awed by the sheer magnitude of the critical task.[16] To limit the focus, as I have, to spirit possession reduces the vast amount of scholarship somewhat, but it is still a mountain that one cannot climb from all sides. I am greatly indebted to the Japanese and American guides—mentioned in the acknowledgments—to my chosen mountain path. Since the *mono no ke* path is a particularly dangerous one, I have tried to cut through the underbrush to find an alternate route that avoids some of the stumbling blocks which impeded earlier scholars.

The organization of my chapters is simple. Since spirit possession expresses not merely the conflict of an individual but a larger crisis generally not acknowledged by society, the individual case studies of possessed women in the *Genji* are embedded in ritual drama staging *mono no ke* who enter and exit like dramatis personae.[17] Thus my chapter, entitled "Enter *mono no ke*," emphasizes some of the salient aspects of the *Genji* within the context of Heian culture and defines the flickering contours of *mono no ke* against the backdrop of related psychic phenomena. Since the ancient custom of illustrating copies of *monogatari* allows us valuable insights into the text, I end this chapter by exploring the relationship of *monogatari* conventions to the representation of *mono no ke* within the iconography of *Genji* art. Yet it is the rare *Genji* picture *(Genji-e)* that focuses directly on the central drama of trance and exorcism. Since *mono no ke* can startle through their absence in traditional iconography, I have also explored the artistic displacements of *mono no ke* in the triggering, foreshadowing, or analogous incident for each spirit possession, as well as in tentative resolutions, such as religious vows or poetic compositions. I then discuss, in chronological order, each of the *Genji*'s five important cases of spirit possession. In addition to showing how visual artists have perceived all five cases of spirit possession, I have, with one exception, concluded my chapters by commenting on spirit possession in the *Genji* as it was centuries later refracted through the lenses of *nō* playwrights.[18] In "Exit *mono no ke*," the final chapter, I assess the efficacy of spirit possession as a woman's weapon and suggest that possessing spirits may seem to vanish only to reappear in different form—not only in the pages of the *Genji* but throughout Japanese culture, down to the present day. Finally, my study contains two appendices. Appendix A places the emergence of possessing spirits within the chronology of major *Genji* events. Appendix B provides genealogical charts that locate characters implicated in cases of spirit possession within the complex kinship structure of the *Genji*.[19]

# Enter *mono no ke*
## Spirit Possession in Cultural Context

THE *Genji monogatari* was written at the peak of the Heian period (794–1186), an age celebrated for its stylized decorum and elegant refinement.[1] It was an age in which highborn men as well as women lived by the famous "rule of taste" and enjoyed the gratifications derived from an "infinite ingenuity in matters of personal adornment."[2] The Heian court's highly stylized way of life demanded a ceremonial approach to the emotions. The court's sumptuous style required not only the submission, voluntary or coerced, of the lower classes but also the repression of the courtier's own impulsive behavior. The men and women of the court were not, however, always successful in the exercise of rigid self-control. Anger was expressed.

## Aestheticism and Discontent

Aggression, which seems to be an integral part of human nature that can never be entirely eliminated, emerged most dramatically in the private lives of the Heian aristocracy, especially in gender relations. That aggression was an element of Heian courtship is easy to overlook because violent acts took place within an elegantly mannered social context. Aggressive acts were concealed in a courtship ritual so refined as to almost elude us.

In order to reach a noblewoman hidden in multilayered robes behind curtains, screens, and fences, the nobleman first had to discover her through a peculiar Heian courtship custom known as *kaimami*—literally, peeping through a gap in the fence. The courtier would be dressed in careful disguise, often a rough outdoor garment to suggest a rank lower than his true status or a hunting robe to pretend another than his actual purpose. In the first episode of the *Ise mono-*

1

*gatari* (Tales of Ise; 905), a poem-tale *(uta monogatari)* that greatly influenced Murasaki Shikibu, a man of exemplary courtly sensitivity is hunting near the ruined old capital of Nara when he catches a glimpse of two beautiful sisters through a gap in their hedge. Courtship is here analogous to the hunt, or an extension of it, with the women as the symbolic prey and the hedge as the enclosing wilderness. Following this *homo necans* paradigm, the man is compelled to aggression; but instead of killing the prey, he sublimates his violence by tearing a strip from his hunting robe to dash off an elegantly allusive poem about the fabric's random design and his amorous confusion. The poem suggests that the forceful rubbing of a moss-fern pattern onto the cloth reflects the sisters' powerful imprint on the poet's heart.

In a myth recorded in the *Kojiki* (Record of Ancient Matters; 712), male desire and longing lead to the violation of taboo and to pursuit by female furies.[3] In the archetypal hunt, life requires killing and killing necessitates sacrificial ritual. By retaining the hunt as an aristocratic pastime and sacrifice as an aesthetic gesture, the opening episode from the *Ise monogatari* signals the transition to the prevalent form of Heian courtship ritual, in which the aggressive gesture of *kaimami* seems totally absorbed into aesthetic pleasure. While the *kaimami* courtship ritual in the *Ise* episode still reflects elements of the underlying archetypal pattern of raw force and the confrontation with death in the hunt, *kaimami* in the *Genji* is almost entirely dissociated from this pragmatic primary function. Only the occasional hunting disguise remains. In the *Genji,* the raw violence of hunting is reduced to a male social discourse of cunning necessitated by the sequestering of women.

In endogamous Heian aristocracy, however, the cunning of *kaimami* can involve a violation of the incest taboo when the woman is forbidden by kinship rules. The Heian aristocracy's polygyny created a complicated kinship structure with a large number of half-siblings and step-relationships. Within this complex structure, the incest taboo, which plays a crucial role in the *Genji,* took forms that are often unfamiliar to Western eyes and even to modern Japanese eyes. Moreover, incest in the *Genji* may not always be defined as in Heian society—especially since the definition of incest appears to be, except for parent-child and sibling relationships, as unclear as Heian descent reckoning and as vague as the concepts of marriage and divorce.[4] Since Murasaki Shikibu often created anomalous situations based on forms of love and marriage that were clearly a departure from the norm, her

*Genji* may inevitably describe incestuous relations for which there may or may not have been historic precedents. Although anthropologists know relatively little about incest regulations in Heian society, scholars of the *Genji* may assume the author's knowledge of whatever restrictions there may have been on sexual relations in her time.[5] Since Murasaki Shikibu was free to manipulate Heian rules concerning the incest prohibition in creating the fictional world of the *Genji,* the literary context dictates what constitutes incest. For the purposes of my study, incest consists of those sexual acts that the *characters* believe to have been especially transgressive and forbidden because of a kin link, whether that link was confined to blood relationships or extended to in-laws.[6]

In the *Genji,* incest and *kaimami* appear as alternate and sometimes intertwining strategies of taboo violation for the sake of male empowerment; spirit possession is a counteracting female strategy of breaking the behavioral code for the same purpose of empowerment. The hole in the fence not only serves men to access their power over women; it is also the site of women's *mono no ke*—the spirits who intimidate their audience and aim to correct men's excessive vision. (It is interesting to note that the activity of *kaimami,* despite its violent implications, was couched in aesthetic terms while the ritualized dramatic spectacle of spirit possession was considered indecorously unaesthetic.)

Another reason why instances of male aggression in Heian Japan have been largely ignored is that aristocratic women were socialized from a very young age to comply with the prevailing code of behavior and to remain silent even when they felt preyed upon. In a society that was both patriarchal and polygynous, various complex forms of marriage practices forced women, even more than men, to disguise their grievances, to suppress their angry impulses, and to repress the very thought of open rebellion.[7] Polygyny as a social structure dictated that a wife be a faithful spouse and accept her status as one of several women among whom her husband divided his amorous attention. In fact, polygyny allows men sexual privileges, expects women meekly to acquiesce in their inferior sexual status, and—as a result of this unrealistic expectation—produces endemic female jealousy.[8] Men then condemn this emotion as a form of deviance. Married and unmarried women were expected to respond to their lovers with the same docile acceptance of the double standard. In male-dominated Heian society, men might be rivals in their pursuit of the same woman, but they considered themselves immune to jealousy; allegedly, only the weaker sex could be affected by this disease. Only women faced legal penalties for this reaction to men's exclusive right to more than one spouse. Under the Taihō Code (702) a woman's jealousy was grounds for divorce. Popular Buddhist and Confucian views of the time adduced jealousy as one of woman's evil attributes (see S:805; 5:172).[9] The result of these attitudes is that women who have no other options repress their emotions—if they can. As more than one modern feminist has pointed out, "muteness is the condition of the silent, uncomplaining woman—an ideal of patriarchal culture."[10] Yet women did protest, and they did have means to inflict their own version of aggression on men from their side of the fence. Whether men could recognize female aggression for what it was is another matter.

For Heian aristocratic women, a milder form of expressing discontent than the unsightly exposure of spirit possession was the diary (nikki).[11] Heian society produced a profusion of public and private diaries, nearly all of the latter type written by women. The author of the Kagerō nikki (The Gossamer Years; 954–974), known as the Mother of Michitsuna (Michitsuna no haha; dates uncertain), was the secondary wife of Fujiwara Kaneie (929–990), a high-ranking, influential man who had some eight or nine other wives and mistresses. Although she herself boldly attempted to usurp the place of Tokihime (d. 980), Kaneie's principal wife (kitamandokoro),[12] she was emphatic in her outraged comments about her husband's continual neglect of her in favor of his lesser women (and about the psychic hardships of women in a polygynous society).[13] Her articulation of her sense of purposelessness and helplessness is poignant: "This was for me a melancholy period. Life seemed pointless, the monotony was unbroken: a listless rising and going to bed, no variation for twenty days on end. What had brought me to this, I wondered. But there was, after all, nothing to be done about it."[14] That this autobiographical account, despite its intimate content, was not meant to be kept under lock and key, like the traditional Western diary, is evident from the author's opening statement. She expresses her hope that "the story of her own dreary life, set down in a journal, might be of interest."[15] At times, even that prospect seems a will-o'-the-wisp: "As I think of the unsatisfying events I have recorded here, I wonder whether I have been describing anything of substance. Call it, this journal of mine, a shimmering of the summer sky."[16] She continued nonetheless to write, taking comfort in the hope of literary bonding with a predominantly female readership.

Although the Mother of Michitsuna denigrated popular *mono-gatari* as "masses of the rankest fabrication,"[17] other women, the most eloquent of whom was surely Murasaki Shikibu, resorted to fiction *(tsukuri monogatari)* as a coping strategy.[18] In fact, the *Genji mono-gatari* includes among its many themes complex and profound dramatizations of the kinds of frustration and despair that the Mother of Michitsuna confided to her diary.[19] These subtle forms of protest have often been overlooked. The *Genji* is famed for its delicately drawn characterizations and for its detailed realistic scenes of tenth-century court life rather than for its numerous, highly dramatic, violently animated, narratively important episodes of female discontent. Charmed by the overwhelming force of fictionalized aestheticism, *Genji* scholars have been reluctant to decode the covert forms of aggression that Murasaki Shikibu was too good a psychologist to deny.

It is easy to understand why most critics prefer to revel in the splendid surface of the *Genji* rather than probe beneath it. Murasaki Shikibu seems so wholeheartedly to endorse an idealized Heian world and a Shining Prince that many readers have overlooked her sometimes subtle and sometimes blatant disagreements with the aesthetic code and its complex political implications. What reader is not struck by the extreme aestheticism of Murasaki Shikibu's tale of love, courtship, and devotion to the arts at the aristocratic court of Heian-kyō (modern Kyoto)? In the fictional world depicted by Murasaki Shikibu, all but a few of the characters—and *they* are ridiculed for their choppy, garbled speech and outlandish attire—belong to the closed society of the Heian court. For that society, it was poor form for a love poem to come straight from the heart. After all, it was not the poem's unique content but rather the correct performance of a poetic ritual that made the beloved quiver. In *The Bridge of Dreams*, aptly subtitled *A Poetics of "The Tale of Genji"*, Haruo Shirane describes the elegance and sensitivity at the heart of this exquisite society:

> In the *Genji* it is not the fulfillment or frustration of desire that becomes the focus of the narrative so much as the elegant and elaborate process of courtship: the poetry, the carefully chosen words, the calligraphy, the choice of paper, the evocative scent, the overheard music.[20]

To think that one's sexual appeal might ultimately depend on one's choice of paper! In this ritual exchange of poetic emotion, frequently mediated by a male or female attendant, what could possibly be revealed of the hopeful lovers' innermost feelings? Very little indeed; but then, less seemed more: a tantalizing glimpse, a mere trace of individual emotion or desire, sufficed. Never "I love you" in the unmistakably direct emotional cascade of Romantic Love that flooded through the courts of Europe several hundreds of years later; but, above all, never "I hate you."

The literary critics who have quite rightly marveled at a world where life seems to have become art have seldom commented on the fact that decorum is preserved by severe and often unbearable constraints on individual expressiveness. The frisson of pleasure evoked by the *Genji*'s smoothly aesthetic surface has often distracted critical attention from the *monogatari*'s troubled depths. Despite her culture's prohibition of overt expressions of personal hostility, Murasaki Shikibu articulated both civilization and its discontents. Of the many modes by which Heian female discontent with *kaimami* and other insults to their integrity was expressed, she chose to emphasize the most complex: spirit possession. "In Murasaki Shikibu's hands," writes Shirane, "evil spirits, or *mono no ke,* become a dramatic means of expressing a woman's repressed or unconscious emotions."[21] They are a way of telling what cannot be told.[22]

## Spirit Possession as Oblique Aggressive Strategy

The courtier who witnessed a possession experienced a startling contrast to incense games, picture and poetry competitions, debates about fashion, and meditations on the right kind of paper for a love letter. Afflicted persons—or their mediums—twisted, turned, cried out in strange voices, tore their hair, rent their clothing. As a mode of expression the experience of spirit possession was diametrically opposed to quiet artistic pastimes; but it too had a recurrent pattern, a strangely ambiguous, even contradictory pattern that sent out conflicting messages as well as a message of conflict. It sprang from a destructive impulse directed against male dominance. At the same time, spirit possession was a constructive phenomenon that engaged women in female bonding and in collective self-assertion. The *mono no ke* acted as the apparent victim's vehicle for dramatically calling attention to otherwise inexpressible grievances. Despite its extraordinary aspects, spirit possession was an integral part of Heian culture. As Susan Bordo has pointed out, "the psychopathologies that develop within a culture, far from being anomalies or aberrations, [are] charac-

teristic expressions of that culture; [they are], indeed, the crystalliza-
tion of much that is wrong with it."[23]

Appearing suddenly in a culture normally characterized by gentleness and indirection, the disturbingly violent phenomenon of spirit
possession can best be understood as a disguised form of female protest triggered by the psychological hardships of Heian polygyny.[24] As
Ioan M. Lewis has shown, in many quite different cultures women
who feel themselves to be oppressed have vented their tensions and
frustrations in the form of spirit possession.[25] Their expression of protest is not, however, directed openly and straightforwardly at the men
responsible for the oppression. Aggrieved women resort instead to the
mysterious esoteric language of spirit possession. Specifically, although
Heian women were generally conditioned to tolerate rival concubines,
individual temperament, aggravated by somatic crises such as illness or
a difficult pregnancy, made spirit possession a ritual resort for the
rehabilitation of a wounded psyche. In this sense, the woman who fell
"victim" to possession was actually resisting the constraints and injus-
tices of a male-dominated culture. Lewis has aptly characterized this
indirect protest as "oblique aggressive strategy."[26]

In terms of its effect on the social structure, the putatively supernatural event of spirit possession momentarily inverts traditional roles
and upsets the normal order of values so that possessed women temporarily assert control over men without overtly claiming any kind of
authority. In this sense, spirit possession is what Victor Turner refers
to as a "liminal state," one that simultaneously challenges and reaf-
firms the normative order and its customary set of social relationships.[27] Deviant behavior establishes boundaries and clarifies, perhaps
even transforms, relationships, but the kind of deviance associated
with liminality is—finally—normative.[28]

From an anthropological viewpoint like Turner's, spirit possession
can be understood as two phases of a single process that begins as a
dramatic, subversive response to the social injustice and psychic
repression of women;[29] the process culminates in the attempt of exorcists *(genja; genza)* to pacify female frustration and prevent social
restructuring. When it is concluded, the liminal phenomenon of spirit
possession seems to leave no mark, or at most a healing "scar," on the
received hegemonic order of the society.[30] Nonetheless, the possessed
person experiences a significant personality change because spirit possession is, like all ritual, "transformative."[31]

For spirit possession to be effectively transformative, it must be clearly distinguished in the minds of everyone involved from physical and mental illness.[32] Some *Genji* scholars, however, have blurred this crucial distinction between the extraordinary occurrence of spirit possession and the mundane manifestations of poor health. In his classic background study to the *Genji*, Ivan Morris, citing Arthur Waley's translation of *mono no ke* as "infection," followed in his mentor's footsteps and likened spirit possession to contagious physical illness: "For people spoke of 'catching' an evil influence *(mono no ke)* in much the same way as we refer to catching a germ."[33] The damage done by this misleading analogy has been considerable. Ironically it was Waley who, in a review of Morris' work, became the first to point it out.[34] Although Morris made a sophisticated argument about the "spiritual and mental factors" underlying a decline in physical health, he failed to see that the healing methods of Heian times were more comparable to modern psychoanalytic treatment than to the ministrations of a medical expert.[35] Instead, he wrote condescendingly that Heian "methods of cure were based squarely on primitive shamanistic superstition."[36]

More recently than Morris, William H. McCullough, the pioneering Western scholar of the Heian marital system, has reflected on Chinese influences on the "illness" of spirit possession. He notes that Ch'ao Yüan-fang's *Chu-ping yüan-hou tsung-lun* (ca. 610) was brought to the attention of the Heian court by Tanba Yasuyori's (912–995) *Ishinhō* (982–984). This "medical encyclopedia" contained descriptions of the symptoms and pathology of spirit possession.[37] W. H. McCullough maintains that "the etiological [disease-related] variety was the basic form" of Heian spirit possession, a form that did not become prominent until the tenth century.[38] He stresses that etiological forms of spirit possession are not recorded in the earliest Japanese chronicles, the *Kojiki* (Record of Ancient Matters; 712) and *Nihon shoki* (*Nihongi*, Chronicles of Japan; 720).[39] Chinese influence on Heian culture can scarcely be overstated. And although the argument that spirit possession was sometimes thought of as an illness is undeniable, the effort to conceptualize this complex psychic and somatic phenomenon as an essentially *physical* event diverts attention from an important fact about the *Genji:* in every one of its five major cases of spirit possession, the mind, in the last analysis, dictates what the body does.

Lewis' reconceptualization of spirit possession in psychological rather than physiological terms has not escaped criticism. Some feminist scholars have faulted him because his emphasis on indirection and

obliqueness seems to be "a classic but unhappily androcentric portrayal of women, who are forever seen as *re*acting to men rather than
acting for themselves within a specific cultural context."[40] This criticism misses the mark. All social relationships are *interactive*. When
Heian women became possessed, they were undeniably reacting to
men, but their strategy was articulated in a predominantly female
idiom to which men, in turn, were forced to react. Lewis has also been
criticized on the grounds that Japanese women are more restrained,
even in the throes of spirit possession, than are the women of other
cultures.[41] How valid is this criticism? It is true that anthropological
studies of possession in a number of cultures have shown that the
experience can be so intense that it borders on death. In Bali, for
instance, the entranced "victims" of spirit possession seem on the
verge of stabbing themselves with the Balinese kris.[42] Compared to
such frenzy, Japanese spirit possession is indeed, for the most part, a
relatively pacific phenomenon, but criticism of Lewis on this score
obscures the point, which is the necessity of the possessed to disguise
the nature of their protest. In a culture that prizes decorum and self-
control, spirit possession need not take the extreme forms familiar in
cultures where violent emotions are more freely expressed. In Heian
Japan, a little seizure went a long way.

## The Paradigmatic Form of Spirit Possession

It is essential, if one is to understand the oblique aggressive strategy of spirit possession in Japanese culture and in the *Genji*, to distinguish it not only from physical illness but also from two psychic
phenomena with which it can easily be confused: witchcraft, which has
been relatively unimportant in Japanese culture, and shamanism,
which has a long Japanese tradition. The important difference
between spirit possession and witchcraft is one that anthropologists
have clarified. Lewis has defined this difference as one of degree of
severity: spirit possession constitutes a "milder and less radically challenging assault than that conveyed by charges of witchcraft and sor-
cery."[43] Lewis also distinguishes between the indirect "devious
manoeuvre" of spirit possession and witchcraft's "direct strategy of
mystical assault."[44]

There are also very important cultural differences in the responses
to witchcraft and spirit possession. In the comparatively recent witch
hunts and trials of medieval Europe and colonial America, spells and

"demonic possession" were attributed to the actions of persons who were diabolically empowered to do evil. After their confession, often obtained by torture, witches were condemned to death. In contrast, Japanese practices were relatively benign. Buddhist exorcist rituals allowed *mono no ke* to reveal themselves and disperse. The evil spirits were immune to prosecution because they, as a rule, belonged to the dead. Thus, unlike persons accused at European and American witchcraft trials, those thought to be the source of *mono no ke* were not blamed for the harm and pain they caused the possessed. Furthermore, of the Japanese thought to suffer from the afflictions of witchcraft, Carmen Blacker writes: "Only rarely...were the unhappy victims condemned to death, and never, as far as I can discover, death by burning."[45]

The mildness of the response can be attributed to the belief that neither the spirits of the living *(ikisudama; ikiryō)* nor the spirits of the dead *(shiryō)* were thought to form the kind of intentionally evil alliance that the witch forms with the devil. If the *mono no ke* is said to act independently of the possessor, who has no control over it, then that person cannot be held responsible for the possession.[46] On the contrary, possessors are exempt from responsibility for the destructive acts their spirits allegedly commit. This logic springs from the belief that the living themselves are to blame if they are haunted by spirits, especially those of the dead, for they must have harmed them in their lifetime.

It is relatively easy to distinguish spirit possession from witchcraft. It is much more difficult, although equally necessary, to understand the difference between shamanism, which was already a familiar phenomenon in pre-Buddhist Japan, and spirit possession, which evolved during the syncretistic Heian period into a more complex and differently valenced form of human interaction with the realm of spirit. Some anthropologists, among them Mircea Eliade and Luc de Heusch, see spirit possession and shamanism as mutually exclusive phenomena. Carmen Blacker, on the other hand, tends to discuss spirit possession as if it were one kind of shamanism.[47] A shaman, in her view, is anyone who has acquired or is endowed with the gift of bridging the gap between this and another world. Ioan M. Lewis takes the middle ground. He acknowledges the differences but emphasizes the shared characteristics of shamanism and spirit possession, both of which he sees as varieties of "ecstatic religion."[48]

The prototypical shaman is a special kind of Siberian medium who suffers an initiation sickness known as "arctic hysteria"—an "out-of-body" experience culminating in a mantic flight that transforms him into a communicator with other worlds. He then becomes a communal healer. Once initiated, the shaman has the ability to induce altered states of consciousness. His role as charismatic intermediary between two worlds must, however, be carefully distinguished from the roles of the exorcist and the medium who are summoned to deal with the affliction of spirit possession. Unlike the exorcist and the medium, who work in tandem to *expel* evil spirits from other persons, the shaman traditionally acts as one who *summons* spirits into himself for the benefit of his tribe or community. In shamanism, the shaman himself is the center of attention. In spirit possession, by contrast, the focus is, or should be, on the possessed person rather than on the exorcist and medium.

Although men are in general much more likely than women to be shamans, pre-Buddhist Japan was an exception to the rule. There were Japanese women whose role approximated the ritual function of the Siberian shaman. The "shamanesses" *(kamnagi; miko)* of pre-Heian Japan were communicators with the dead.[49] Their most important appearances were on the occasion of the otherwise male-dominated rituals for a dead sovereign's temporary interment *(mogari no miya)*. At the liminal moment of the imperial succession, women who had been sexually intimate with the emperor—or, alternately perhaps, the virginal Ise Priestess *(saigū)*—presided over spirit-summoning or spirit-recalling rituals *(tamafuri)* in which they exercised their power to transfer the imperial spirit to his successor.[50] From the ancient and nearly divine *miko* descended her somewhat less powerful sisters, the Ryukyu *yuta* and the blind medium found in northern Honshū, the *itako*.[51] At the time of the *Genji,* the female role in Shinto rituals still retained some of its shamanistic importance, but Buddhism allotted men the greater authority in the drama of religious life.[52] As shamanism declined in importance in Japanese culture, spirit possession became more salient.

Like other common cultural phenomena that occur in many guises, spirit possession has been studied cross-culturally. Beginning with the pioneering work of Traugott Konstantin Oesterreich in 1921,[53] modern scholars have endeavored to decipher what has always been a mysterious phenomenon. While spirit possession is almost always associated with, if not motivated by, grave psychic disturbances or conflicts, it is often triggered by purely physical causes, such as the hardships of pregnancy, nutritional deficiencies, or the use, intentional or unintentional, of drugs.[54] (The *Genji*'s three middle cases of spirit possession, involving Aoi, Murasaki, and the Third Princess, all begin with reproduction crises, perhaps the most commonly recognized and socially sanctioned triggers of spirit possession.)

Although fictional episodes of spirit possession tend to emphasize the inner turmoil of the persons undergoing possession, it is clear that the individual's seizure relates to the concerns and pursuits of the immediate community and reflects upon the larger culture. In this sense, spirit possession is not merely a conflict between the possessed and the possessor; it also tests the values of the whole society. In other words, the intensely private experience of spirit possession makes a public statement. The spirits' complaints and wishes, voiced directly through the possessed or indirectly through a medium, are a challenge to the social order. In the terms popularized by the followers of Michel Foucault, the body of the possessed person is a "site of contestation," a site of resistance to physically "inscribed" social power.[55]

When someone is seized, the family or friends of the possessed call upon an exorcist, without whose help the possessed person may die (which is exactly what happens in the *Genji* in the case of Yūgao [S: Evening Faces]).[56] Exorcists, who act for the community and represent its male values, frequently employ a medium (usually female) to assist them in approaching the possessed, identifying the possessing spirit, and driving it out. It is universally assumed—by practitioners of and believers in spirit possession—that the naming of the spirit is a magical act that will expel it from the body of the victim as effectively as physical ailments respond to medical treatment.[57]

Since spirit possession is a social phenomenon,[58] even when its manifestation is localized to a single person, its sudden occurrence usually generates an audience as well as an exorcist and a medium. When there is no audience to witness the ritual drama of exorcism,[59] the possessed person's effort to communicate his or her distress is only partially successful. The audience, like the medium and the exorcist, is likely to be more concerned with the identity of the possessing spirit than with the motivations of the possessed person. Indeed, spirit possession is a psychological strategy so oblique that questions about the motivations of the possessed are hardly ever asked. What makes the ritual drama of spirit possession and exorcism so powerful is that it is periodically repeated and "left undiscussed."[60]

Although my main purpose here is to shift the focus of attention

from the identity of the possessing spirit to the motivations of the possessed person, I do not mean to imply that the exorcism is insignifi-
cant. Exorcism is a ritualization of individual conflict and a form of
therapy for the whole community. When exorcists are present (as they
are in all but the first of the *Genji* episodes of spirit possession), the
psychic drama of spirit possession intensifies until, with the identification of the spirit and a promise to answer its wishes, the spell is broken
and communal life resumes its customary course. Exorcism is important, and exciting, but I wish nonetheless to insist that the drama that
is overtly staged and brought to resolution is a refraction of the sub-
liminal psychic conflict that initiated the sequence of dramatic events.
Conflict has been expressed but not resolved.

   This, then, in paradigmatic form, is the most common pattern of
spirit possession as a cross-cultural phenomenon: a distressed person,
usually a woman, is possessed by a malign spirit; the concerned witnesses summon an exorcist who, with the aid of a medium, identifies
and expels the spirit. The phenomenon of spirit possession sends
shock waves through the audience and the ritual of exorcism restores
society to equilibrium—until the next seizure occurs. How then do
these various actors—the medium, the exorcist, and the *mono no ke*
itself—appear in Heian culture?

### Mediums and Exorcists

   The *Eiga monogatari* (A Tale of Flowering Fortunes; ca. 1092)
records a case of spontaneous enactment of the roles of exorcist and
medium by amateurs who respond to a crisis of spirit possession after
professional incantations had failed. The prominent statesman Fujiwara Michinaga (966–1027), father of the possessed Yorimichi (992–
1074), started to pray in the manner of an exorcist "with frantic
energy, the tears streaming from his eyes, and the possessing spirit fled
to a nearby lady-in-waiting [*nyōbō*], someone who had never acted as a
medium before. As the lady began to weep, looking extremely dignified and awe-inspiring, the monks fell silent."[61] Generally, however,
the male exorcist was a professional whose prominence tended to
obscure the role of the medium. Unlike women's fictional narratives,
which focused on gender relations by expressing mainly female grievances, historical reports of spirit possession revealed a political purpose
and featured members of both sexes possessed by either male or
female spirits. For example, Yorimichi's female medium addresses

Michinaga by incorporating the wraith of Prince Tomohira, who is anxious about the possibility of his daughter Takahime's replacement by Emperor Sanjō's daughter Shishi as Yorimichi's favorite wife.

In Heian times, the mediums through whom the spirits spoke were usually female. They were often described as girls whose hair in wild disorder signaled that they were in a trance.[62] (In the possessions of Aoi and Ukifune, they are merely referred to as "person" [2:26; 6:262: *hito*], but it was clear from their hairstyle that they were female.[63] In the case of Murasaki's possession, there is a specific reference to a "small child" [4:222: *chiisai warawa*], also presumed to be female.)[64] In episodes dramatizing gender conflict rather than political strife, mediums were especially effective mouthpieces because they symbolized the vicissitudes of the female condition in polygynous society, even if the mediums were sometimes too young wholly to have experienced them. Not only did they sense the psychic conflict of the possessed, they articulated it in an awe-inspiring theatrical manner. Already initiated into spirit mediumship, they had become adepts at a rough idiom that high-ranking possessed women would not learn to speak and had therefore delegated to mediums. Thus it was rare in Heian society for the possessed noblewoman to take over the role of medium—and when it did happen the audience was shocked. The *Eiga monogatari* records the case of Norimichi's wife who became possessed in 1024, shortly after the safe delivery of her sixth or seventh child: "One spirit after another made its presence known through the lady herself. Such a thing had never happened before, and Norimichi found the sight unbearable. 'If only we could transfer them to someone else!' he said."[65] In the major possession cases of the *Genji,* only Aoi eventually eliminates her medium.

While the possessed woman absented herself in deep trance, the medium responded with an altered state of her own; this psychic transference effected the possessed woman's dissociation from the medium's wild, aggressive gestures and unfamiliar speech. The transference also reinforced—through repetition—the belief in the centripetal movement of the spirit from an external source into the possessed woman. At the same time, however, the transference from the possessed to the medium erased the original centripetal movement by replacing it with the spirit's centrifugal movement from inside the possessed person to an outside host, the medium.[66] No doubt the self-erasing traces of the *mono no ke* contributed to its mysterious power.

As the focal point of the exorcist ritual, the medium not only shielded the possessed from expressing aggressive and erotic feelings but also functioned to deceive the audience about the possessed as the true source—the playwright—of her performance. The medium furthermore functioned as a female receptacle, most strikingly at the moment when the possessing spirit was channeled out of the possessed individual and into what might be called—without necessarily adopting Jungian theory—a female collective unconscious.[67] Interacting in this manner, the possessed, the possessing spirit, and the medium formed a powerful female triad engaged in resolving gender-related conflict.[68]

The more closely one looks at the Japanese exorcist, the more problematic is the notion that he played the leading role in the psychic drama. If one were to extend the metaphoric role assignment in the ritual drama of spirit possession to the exorcist, he might more accurately be seen as the director of the performance. Although he is a highly visible male presence, his influence on the course of the drama is secondary. In fact, the exorcist deflects attention from the addressed male spectator, just as the medium deflects attention from the possessed.

Lewis has pointed to "the fundamentally ambiguous status of exorcists" in his important cross-cultural study of "Exorcism and Male Control of Religious Experience."[69] His analysis can readily be supported by examples drawn from women writers of Heian literature. Sei Shōnagon (966?–1017?), the author of the *Makura no sōshi* (The Pillow Book; ca. 1000–1010), and Murasaki Shikibu were two women writers who used the covert male-female conflict of spirit possession as an opportunity for overt criticism of male exorcists and implied criticism of the entire male-dominated society. Sei Shōnagon, not known for embellishing unpleasant truths, brings her skepticism about the efficacy of professional exorcists to the seething point of ridicule. In section 7 of her *Makura no sōshi*, "That Parents Should Bring Up Some Beloved Son" *(omowan ko o)*,[70] she begins by seeming to sympathize with the lot of a young exorcist who, treated as a mere "piece of wood," cannot help having shamefully carnal thoughts which distract him from his healing task. In another blend of pity and contempt, she portrays an exorcist who is unable to expel the evil spirits from his patients. Oblivious to the public outrage over his shortcomings, he dozes off. In section 24, "Depressing Things" *(susamajiki mono)*,[71] her derisive tone satirizes an exorcist's grinding cicada voice and all his magic paraphernalia that ultimately accomplish nothing. Here the exorcist's obvious boredom with his failed mission, expressed in his yawns and his napping, earns the proverbially sharp-tongued author's contempt.[72] This incompetent exorcist fails to exert control over his female medium *(yorimashi)*, who was supposed to become possessed through his magic spells and incantations *(kaji; darani)*.

This last case is especially interesting because Sei Shōnagon names the benign spirit that was supposed to enter the medium. It was a *gohō dōji*,[73] a Buddhist boy-guardian spirit who was expected to aid the exorcist in forcing the evil spirits to flee from the possessed to the medium.[74] By introducing a *gohō dōji*, the almost comically inept exorcist sought, unsuccessfully, to alter the gender configuration created by the female triad of host, spirit, and medium.[75] He attempted, as it were, to gain a male ally in his confrontation with an array of women. Sei Shōnagon takes pleasure in noting this exorcist's discomfiture.

In section 322, "The House Had a Spacious Courtyard" *(matsu no kodachi takaki tokoro no higashi)*,[76] Sei Shōnagon portrays a young, handsome priest who succeeds in expelling a *mono no ke* from a female patient. What entices this exorcist not to doze off is the voluptuous trance behavior of the medium, whose spectacular tossing about had exposed her to a degree requiring a sympathetic bystander to rear-range her clothing. Sei Shōnagon implies that one can forgive an exorcist who, upon the medium's innocent awakening from trance, cannot restrain himself from confusing her by welcoming her back with a seductive smile.[77]

Murasaki Shikibu shared Sei Shōnagon's predominantly scornful response to male exorcists. Her critique appears in her diary, known as the *Murasaki Shikibu nikki* (The Diary of Murasaki Shikibu; ca. 1010), as well as in the *Genji*. In the diary, Murasaki Shikibu recorded the lying-in of Empress Shōshi (Akiko, 988–1074), in whose entourage she served as lady-in-waiting. The long-awaited birth of Atsuhira in 1008 is made difficult by the evil spirits who inevitably emerge at politically significant events such as this one.[78] To combat them, exorcists and *yin-yang* diviners *(onyōji)* have been carefully chosen to augment the ranks of the regular priests *(sō)*. With impressive incanta-tions, the exorcists try to assure a safe delivery by transferring the evil spirits *(onmono no ke)* from the empress to mediums.[79] Instead of the ritual solemnity that one might expect, however, Murasaki Shikibu describes pandemonium. The high drama of possession, exorcism, and childbirth degenerates into farce as the members of the audience quite literally let themselves go in a manner diametrically opposed to stiff Heian court etiquette: the women in dishabille, with eyes swollen from unrestrained tears; the men casting uninhibited lustful glances at those so scandalously exposed. For the longest time, the spirits stubbornly refuse to enter the mediums, and when they do, they make an "uproar" *(onmono no ke utsure)* and send an exorcist sprawling to the ground.[80]

In the *Genji,* too, exorcists make a mostly pathetic spectacle of themselves. In the ritual during Aoi's lying-in, they are only partially effective in transferring the possessing spirits to a medium, leaving Genji to deal all by himself with the most stubborn of these spirits. In the end, however, they hypocritically claim credit for the safe delivery. Their self-congratulatory pose (see S:169; 2:35) stands in sharp contrast to their actual incompetence.[81] In portraying exorcists as a rather sorry lot, Murasaki Shikibu encourages us to turn our attention elsewhere.

### The Possessing Spirits

In early Japan there was a widespread belief, rooted in the indigenous animistic religion of Shinto, that human life was influenced by the spirits of both the living and the dead. These spirits were thought to emanate from rocks, trees, plants, and animals as well as from humans. According to the "Way of the Gods," a person's spirit *(tama; tamashii)* was not private but shared property and, upon death, was cared for by the community in a prescribed manner that eventually led to deification. Dead spirits who achieved this divine status were protective gods *(kami)* of the Japanese people; but when offended they could, as angry spirits *(onryō; goryō),* turn against individuals, groups, or the entire nation. Anger was activated by a number of causes, including various forms of pollution that had to be counteracted by purification rituals. Neglect of an obligatory purification ritual seriously jeopardized the peaceful equilibrium between nature and humankind. It is important to realize, however, that in early Japan harmful spirits were not feared to the degree they were in China, where they struck terror in the hearts of people. In pre-Buddhist Japan, faithful observance of the proper rituals was sufficient to preserve or restore harmony. Dutifully acting upon the Shinto imperative to purify pollution and pacify wronged spirits, people were reassured that they exercised a degree of control over the invisible world.

With the arrival of Buddhism in 538, mainland cultural lore about the spirit world greatly complicated indigenous Japanese views. As early as the third century C.E., the Chinese had developed an elaborate demonology.[82] The Japanese appropriated elements of this systematic approach to the art of controlling resentful and harmful spirits through "exorcistic weapons," "magical binding," and "oaths and spells,"[83] but the Japanese also contributed to the syncretic result. Even as the imported religion of Buddhism with its impressive paraphernalia threatened to dominate native Shinto, the Buddhist clergy began to adopt non-Buddhist rituals of purification and pacification. By the mid-Heian period, when all manner of spirits were rampant, religious exorcisms associated with Shinto were performed by Buddhist priests, contrary to earlier Buddhist doctrine. Underlining this syncretism, William H. McCullough maintains that even "the use of mediums in the exorcism rites [of spirit possession] came apparently not from Shintō, but, as Shimazu Hisamoto has shown, from the Āvesa Ritual of esoteric Buddhism."[84]

The story of the brilliant scholar-statesman Sugawara Michizane (845–903) exemplifies the curious blend of culturally diverse beliefs about the spirit world. As the ambassador to China, he was well versed in Chinese learning. He was also resented by his rivals from the Fujiwara clan for his superior influence at the Heian court. In time, his opponents won the upper hand and Michizane was exiled to Tsukushi (Kyūshū), where he died. When calamities subsequently struck Heian-kyō, afflicting even the imperial court, people high and low attributed their troubles to Michizane's angry spirit (*goryō*).[85] This fear of an "avenging ghost" who punished not only individuals but sometimes whole families or communities was a part of Chinese spectral culture borrowed by the Japanese.[86] In order to pacify the restless spirit of the unjustly banished sinophile Michizane, the Kitano *jinja,* a Shinto shrine, was erected in the capital in 947—with the apparent approval of Heian-kyō's Buddhist clergy.[87]

One may detect a note of annoyance in Ivan Morris' description of a religious syncretism pushed to what seems to him the point of absurdity:

> It will be noticed that . . . the [Heian] exorcists were members of the Buddhist clergy. This was normal in the period and represents one of the many anomalies of Heian religious-superstitious practice. Shamanism and the idea of possession by evil spirits formed no part of Buddhist doctrine; and, if logic played any role, we

should expect Shintoist priests to officiate on occasions of this kind. . . . Not only did the various religious functions overlap, but the religions themselves blended imperceptibly with the vast network of superstitions.[88]

The dismissive description of spirit possession as "superstition," which pervades Morris' pioneer study, is outdated. Carmen Blacker, the prominent scholar of shamanism in Japan, has a more sophisticated view of syncretism:

> The large area of religious practice common to the two [Shinto and Buddhism], in which the worshipper is scarcely aware whether the deity he is addressing is a Shinto *kami* or a bodhisattva, has been either ignored or relegated to various snail patches with pejorative labels such as superstition, syncretism or magic.[89]

The important point is that Shinto and Buddhist beliefs and practices combined in a way that made spirit possession a familiar phenomenon in Murasaki Shikibu's Japan.

It should be noted that the term *"mono no ke"* was used neither for the protective nor for the vengeful spirits of pre-Heian Japan. The latter in particular, like the avenging ghosts of ancient China, had a strong moral impact as they straightforwardly acted out their vengeance for the atrocities committed against them. There was little doubt even in the minds of rational Chinese literati, much less the general population, that those with some evil deed on their conscience had, when they fell sick or died under strange circumstances, undergone retribution at the hands of *goei* (ghosts), *suey* (evil emanations), or *lih* (vicious specters).[90] Heian *mono no ke* were quite a different kettle of fish. Anything but straightforward, they commanded respect precisely through their inscrutability. They did not appear as such until the ninth and tenth centuries[91] when women developed an indigenous style of writing and created, almost single-handedly, an intense interest in private matters of the psyche that supplemented when it did not replace political and religious concerns.

The term *"mono no ke"* is etymologically rooted in the vexingly obscure concept of *mono*—not the tangible "thing" it means in modern Japanese but its very opposite in ancient usage: something unspecifiable, without a clear form, and therefore extraordinary, strange, to be feared as an outside force. In early Japan, the *mono no be*, thought to be "a guild of specialists of the sacred whose duties involved pacifying and controlling *mono*,"[92] may be regarded as the indigenous

ancestors of Buddhist exorcists. During this chaotic but highly forma-
tive stage, the notion of the supernatural was rendered in various Chinese characters suggesting visual and moral aspects such as the
demonic *(oni)* or the awesome unknown spirits *(seirei)* in contrast to
the more familiar spirits *(tama; tamashii)* of great importance in Japanese ancestral cults.[93] The demonic *oni* are first recorded in the *Fudoki*
(Topographies; 713) and spelled with the characters for the syn-
onymic goblins *(chimi); oni* become associated with hell since their
appearance in the Izanami–Izanagi story as told in the *Nihongi,* where
*oni* is written with the character now commonly used.[94] At the same
time, in the earliest extant poetry collection of the *Man'yōshū* (Collection of Ten Thousand Leaves; compiled in the mid-eighth century),
the character for *oni* was read as *mono,* suggesting that, in its earliest
forms, *oni* spanned the entire range from the visible *(chimi; yōkai)* to
the invisible *(mono).* As *mono no ke* began to take over the branch of
the invisible, however, *oni* and *yōkai* were increasingly perceived as visible fantastic creatures, sometimes half human, sometimes more
closely resembling animals.[95] These protean creatures were rampant in
the *Konjaku monogatari shū* (Tales of Times Now Past; compiled no
later than the early twelfth century).[96] In medieval anecdotal tales *(setsuwa),* these *oni* would frequently embody women's uncontrolled
jealousy and not hesitate to eat husband and children.[97] They can be
physically distinguished from *mono no ke,* which, in Murasaki
Shikibu's masterpiece, always take an invisible form imagined to signify human spirits.

In the *Genji,* the imagined form can be male or female, but it
almost always emanates from a woman, usually the female medium
but sometimes the possessed herself. Since the *monogatari* was a literary genre especially favored by female authors, specialists in narrative
theory have asked about the relationship between *mono no ke* and
*monogatari.* What exactly constitutes the *mono* of *mono no ke* and the
*mono* of *monogatari* (literally the telling of *mono,* or matters)? The
first thing to be noticed is that the world described in *monogatari*
goes far beyond the domain of Heian material culture. It includes also
the realm of fears, dreams, fantasies, and secret passions. From this
realm of the uncanny, the phenomenon called *mono no ke*—"mystery
matter"—emerges. Arriving from the world of the uncanny, the *mono
no ke* have their own perspective on the ordinary. The narratologist
Takahashi Tōru has compared the radically different perspective of the
*mono no ke* to the unconventional viewpoint of the (mostly female)

"omniscient" authors of *monogatari*. Thus author and *mono no ke* are analogous figures ("mono no ke no yō na sakusha").[98] The *mono no ke* are tropes to express emotions that the authors, like their female characters, dare not articulate even in indirect discourse. In other words, it is through *mono no ke* that the female author and her possessed female characters can articulate their "double consciousness."

Similar to Takahashi's suggested analogy between the *mono no ke* and the "omniscient" *monogatari* author is a theory put forth by the scholar-poet Fujii Sadakazu. He has likened the *mono no ke* to the Japanese gods. Since *monogatari* have evolved from myths never completely discarded by the largely secular world of romance, *monogatari* characters "are being watched intently from some place outside the work [and] *from the outside of its pages, the Other World makes a forceful appearance.*" These watchful agents of the Other World can be either gods or *mono no ke,* the "low-ranking . . . 'fallen' members of the Other World."[99] In either case, they come to the fore in a religious context, drawn to the sacred space designated for rituals such as festivals *(matsuri)*, purification *(harae)* or pacification *(chinkon)* ceremonies, and, not infrequently, exorcism. One might think, then, of the startling phenomenon of *mono no ke* as a figment of the female imagination, a religious sign, a figure of speech, or, quite literally, a metafictional character. Although the *mono no ke*'s appearance is fleeting, its impact on the story is lasting.

*Mono no ke* have very important messages to deliver from the realm of the uncanny. In his attempt to come to grips with the slippery concept of the uncanny, Sigmund Freud (1856–1939) used the definition of Friedrich Wilhelm Schelling (1775–1854): " *'Unheimlich'* [uncanny] *is the name for everything that ought to have remained . . . secret and hidden but has come to light.*"[100] On the basis of this and other definitions, Freud developed the idea that the uncanny arouses anxiety because the familiar and the unfamiliar appear in inextricable conjunction. In his psychoanalytic reflections he associated the uncanny with a repeated "doubling, dividing, and interchanging of the self" ("Ich-Verdoppelung, Ich-Teilung, Ich-Vertauschung").[101] Thus, although *mono no ke* spoke in intelligible, lucid language, more often through a medium than the possessed person directly, they nonetheless produced a ciphered text.[102] The audience was bewildered, but not because of any mumbo jumbo or magical formulas. The *mono no ke* text became esoteric because of its uncertain authorship. What the speech meant was a function of the identity of the speaker, but the speaker's identity had itself become mysterious. The possessed person had become other. For this to happen, for the possessed person to adopt and maintain—for the duration of trance—the normally untenable position of the other, it was necessary to draw upon the transformative power of dramatic performance to suspend the audience's disbelief. This staging created the paradox that the possessed person, virtually absent in trance, was present in the *mono no ke*—an idea confounding enough to stretch logic, challenge the imagination, and render the *mono no ke*'s text nearly undecipherable.

The simultaneous presence in a single physical body of self and other resembles the kind of alienation from the self that is experienced in hysteria—which is, like spirit possession, a psychic and somatic phenomenon. William H. McCullough, in addition to discussing the etiological form of spirit possession derived from China, argues that an "inspirational form of possession," namely "hysterical possession," was not altogether absent from Heian life.[103] In fact, McCullough contends that an unspecified illness, diagnosed as spirit possession, was expelled in exorcistic rites "through the induction of a state of hysterical possession,"[104] either in the patient or a medium.

It is, however, important to distinguish between hysteria and the phenomenologically related trance behavior of spirit possession. Jean-Michel Oughourlian describes hysteria as an altered state of consciousness that can lead to spirit possession.[105] Janice Boddy, however, argues that the two phenomena tend to occur in different personalities that, in turn, are characteristic of "disparate cultural contexts." According to her, hysteria is a disorder in which the boundaries of the self become too definite and rigid. The hysteric becomes entrapped by the self's separateness from the other. This disorder is obviously not unique to our own culture, which celebrates manifestations of individualism, but it does seem to express "an overdetermination of selfhood"[106] more typical of modernity than of Heian Japan, where the self was far more diffuse than in the modern West.

Boddy's analysis is persuasive and helps clarify the relation of gender to spirit possession. Gender differentiated the relatively amorphous character of the Heian self. To the extent that Heian aristocratic men, under normal conditions, enjoyed greater power than women, they were able to perceive themselves as more clearly defined than women. This gender difference in the conception of the self helps to explain why men experienced spirit possession less frequently than women. Murasaki Shikibu sharpens gender conflict to the point where only women become possessed. Men's greater power and autonomy also gives the male protagonists of the *Genji* what seems to us an uncanny ability to substitute one loved woman for another. Heian women were not in a position to substitute—or appropriate—others with the same facility. Instead, by resorting to spirit possession, they, like the marginalized or severely stressed men in the histories, made an advantage of the disadvantage of less potent, precisely defined selves—by merging with the other, incorporating the other, or becoming the other.[107]

## Murasaki Shikibu's Demons in the Heart

Does the *mono* of *mono no ke* refer to the stuff of which the material world is made or is it im-material? Physics or metaphysics? If we rephrase the question in terms favored in Heian times, is the *mono* reality or dream? To these questions there are no simple answers. Possessing spirits, whether they appear in fictional or in historical narratives, can be "real" in the sense of an actual presence, natural or supernatural, external to the possessed character. They can also be as imaginary as Lady Macbeth's "dagger of the mind, a false creation, / Proceeding from the heat-oppressèd brain" (II.i.38–39). The ontological differences, reflected in the beliefs of the fictional or historic characters, are determined by the author, who is, of course, influenced by his or her cultural construct of spirit possession. Although one must bear in mind that the *Genji monogatari* is not a historical document, it is reasonable to assume that it is Murasaki Shikibu's creative rendition of Heian realities.

Murasaki Shikibu's dramatization of spirit possession in her *monogatari,* widely regarded as "realistic," raises an ontological question for many readers, especially modern critics: did the author's skepticism vis-à-vis exorcists mean that she doubted the reality of *mono no ke*? Despite its unverifiability as an autobiographical document,[108] the *Murasaki Shikibu shū* (Murasaki Shikibu's Poetry Collection; ca. 1014) is frequently cited to prove her skepticism about the common folk belief in spirits, demons, and such. In the prose-poetry sections 44–45, Murasaki Shikibu appears strongly to favor a psychological approach to allegedly supernatural phenomena.

In these sections, the unspecified narrator meditates upon a scroll painting in which the husband of a possessed woman is attempting to exorcize the demon, presumably the man's former wife.[109] In this pictorial representation of spirit possession, the possessed woman is meant to be perceived as a "repulsive figure" or "grotesque form" (*minikuki kata*).[110] In the painter's arrangement of the scene, the possessed woman's unsightly appearance is attributed solely to the suffering inflicted on her by the possessing spirit *(mono no ke)* of her husband's former wife, who is pictorially rendered as demonic *(oni ni naritaru moto no me)*. Counteracting this demonic force are a priest, who literally is subduing the dead wife in the guise of *oni*, and the husband whose sutra chanting is intended to make the raging spirit wince and depart. The painter thus places the blame entirely on the former wife's resentful spirit and portrays priest and husband absorbed in the admirable role of healer.

This painting, possibly illustrating a *monogatari*, provides the occasion for an analytical poem in which Murasaki Shikibu startles her audience by referring to the dead woman *(naki hito)* as a mere pretext *(kagoto)*. The pretext is usually taken to be the exorcizing man's, but it could as easily be the possessed woman's. Whereas the painter had depicted priest and husband as having no doubts about blaming the dead wife turned *oni* for the tormented state of the present wife, the author-poet challenges this dominant male perspective on woman in distress by introducing a feminine viewpoint. In her poetic response to the visual image, she suggests that the source of the conflict may lie in the witnessing husband's own troubled psyche projecting the demon in *his* heart *(kokoro no oni)* onto the dead wife's possessing spirit. In addition to the critics' standard interpretation of Murasaki Shikibu's reading of the painting, the latter half of her poem may also refer to the possessed woman, who appears entirely capable of expressing the demon of *her* heart in a performative dynamic completely disguised as that of other (the dead wife). Spirit possession thus requires a coordinated reading involving the perspectives of all the actors implicated in the drama. The poet's provocative questioning of the referent commonly associated with *"kokoro no oni"* undermines and corrects the painter's and, presumably, the ordinary viewer's unreflective assumptions.

The identity of the poet who composes a reply (section 45) is as difficult to grasp with certainty as the subject of *"kokoro no oni."*[111] At first glance, the speaker of this poem enthusiastically endorses the woman author's unorthodox, ambiguous positioning of the demon in the heart. Yet the speaker of this poem appears to do so only to revert to the orthodox view that a person in the darkness of his heart will invariably locate demonic forms outside himself. Between the lines one may detect the teasing idea that those who perceive demons in the hearts of others must have experienced them in their own hearts. If, as Norma Field has speculated, the reply is Murasaki Shikibu's own,[112] then the author doubly endorses her own unorthodox view by demonstrating the clever readiness with which one projects the inner demons outside oneself; furthermore, she also humbly includes herself among those susceptible to the darkness breeding demons in the heart. There is a suggestion that the audience's degree of involvement to some extent determines the perception of the phenomenon.

### *Mono no ke* and the Critics

Like the scroll painter of the *Murasaki Shikibu shū* 44, who translates invisible *mono no ke* into visible *oni*, most literary critics of the *Genji* seem to be prisoners of conventions defined by folk belief in their interpretation of spirit possession. While it is important to recognize the existence of such beliefs and to gauge their meaning, it is equally important to explore other venues for understanding the phenomenon. To clarify my own view of *mono no ke,* I must comment on the critical tradition.

Marian Ury calls for understanding *mono no ke* strictly within the context of Heian folk beliefs:

> Reading the *Genji* . . . we are so well satisfied with interpreting the mononoke who afflict its heroines as "a dramatic means of expressing a woman's repressed or unconscious emotions" . . . that we are apt to stop there, overlooking the fact that, on a literal level, the mononoke belong to a class of beings which Murasaki Shikibu's original audience thought of as actually existing and of which many of those readers must have had explicit conceptions.[113]

Ury has a point, but hypothesizing a belief in *mono no ke* in the minds of Heian people does not preclude or invalidate questions about the affective impact of *mono no ke.* It is precisely *because* Murasaki Shikibu's original audience believed to varying degrees in the existence of *mono no ke* that she was able to involve them, as readers, in her amazingly subtle psychological exploration of the "demons" in the hearts of the actors in the drama of spirit possession.[114] In the last analysis, whether or not all Heian Japanese believed in the literal existence of *mono no ke* is a secondary and insoluble question.[115] Suffice it to say here that *Genji* characters vary both in their conceptualization of *mono no ke* and in their skepticism.

In short, we can resolve with certainty neither the question of Murasaki Shikibu's private beliefs nor that of the Heian audience's beliefs. What we can do, however, is retrace the author's literary process in constructing *mono no ke*. Surely it is no accident that she repeatedly situates the phenomenon of spirit possession at crucial moments in her narrative and elaborates on variations of the phenomenon with a psychological complexity and sophistication unprecedented in her day. Nonetheless, *mono no ke* exist in the *Genji* only to the extent that they serve Murasaki Shikibu's literary purposes. In other words, the author is the explicit agent who constructs spirit possession discursively in her narrative. Insofar as Murasaki Shikibu is a product of her culture, her literary construction of spirit possession grew out of the social manifestations of spirit possession. Thus there is both an intimate relationship and a pronounced difference between spirit possession as Murasaki Shikibu's fictional reality and as an actual historical reality (not to be confused with the politically biased rendering in chronicles). Which of the two realities comes closer to the "truth" is, I am afraid, as insoluble a question as the verifiability of *mono no ke*.

Confronted with the extremely complicated drama of spirit possession, critics have placed themselves among the audience.[116] To be more precise, they have adopted the perspective of Genji, the most prominent spectator. The danger of this commitment should be immediately apparent. Genji never pretends to be an unbiased observer (as the critic should be); he is an emotionally involved participant in the performance. His preoccupation with identifying the possessing spirit has led critics to be as preoccupied as he is, but Genji's identification of the *mono no ke* is important only to the extent that it reveals Genji's involved assessment of the phenomenon. Genji seems to have but one identifiable source for the *mono no ke* that plague his wives: Rokujō (Rokujō no miyasudokoro). Consequently, the critics' Genji-centric view has led to the demonization of this formidable woman whom Genji, through his identification, makes responsible for the possession of his wives. The critics conclude with Genji that Rokujō is the incarnation of female jealousy.

My study presents a radical reassessment of this traditional approach—including a debunking of Rokujō's demonization. By shifting the focus from the *mono no ke,* as interpreted by Genji, to the possessed person I am hoping to restore the forgotten presence of the true agent of spirit possession. It is important to remind ourselves that Murasaki Shikibu dramatizes exclusively *women's* possessions, a literary fact significant in itself and made even more important by the *Genji*'s female authorship. It appears that this female author wanted to articulate precisely that which her female characters were forbidden to articulate. The literary form she has chosen for the unspeakable in women's lives is *mono no ke*. Just as Murasaki Shikibu uses *mono no ke* as a literary trope, so her possessed female protagonists employ *mono no ke* as a creative device to express the otherwise inexpressible. Since the possessed women in the *Genji* cannot openly verbalize grievances they are not supposed to hold, a number of them—Yūgao, Aoi, Murasaki, the Third Princess, Ukifune—stage their social and psychological conflicts as performances in which possessing spirits give voice to their anguish and their anger. My departure from the traditional critical approach allows me to suggest that the possessed woman is not a passive victim but an active agent who uses—subconsciously, surreptitiously, subversively—the charisma of others in the guise of *mono no ke* to empower herself. In contrast to the traditional approach to *mono no ke,* my study proposes an entirely different dynamic between the possessed woman and her charismatic, empowering spirit—a dynamic that is no longer defined as an antagonism (the male viewpoint) but as an alliance (the female viewpoint).

Although one must examine the spirits as noisily acclaimed points of attention, it is essential to retrieve the lost voices of the possessed. After all, it is the possessed, not the spirits, who are the true agents of "oblique aggression." It is they who stage the highly encoded conflict. Their performative strategy is not so much consciously contrived as intuitively conceived to have a powerful effect on the audience and—if all goes well—to be beneficial to the sufferer at least in some measure and for some time. Since we cannot determine to what degree Murasaki Shikibu's dramatization of spirit possession in the *Genji* mirrored historical realities, our findings derived from her *monogatari* can only suggest the larger historical picture. It is nonetheless clear that her genius opened a window into the subtleties of gender conflict through spirit possession that seemed shut to most of her contemporaries. My focus is on exploring the complexities associated with the psychological state of virtually voiceless women for whom spirit possession was a last desperate effort to be heard.

## Text and Picture: *emakimono*

While it is possible to examine Murasaki Shikibu's literary construction of spirit possession from her text, it is impossible to know
how she would have wanted *mono no ke,* the unspeakable in Heian
noblewomen's lives, to be rendered by illustrators of her *monogatari.*
From the *Murasaki Shikibu shū* 44–45, one senses a certain dissatisfaction with the illustrated narrative *(emakimono)* that provoked her
reflections on *kokoro no oni.* If the painter's concrete visualization of
an unsightly jealous woman distorted the author's conception of
*kokoro no oni,* then the *Genji monogatari* required an iconography of
invisible *mono no ke.* I will try to show in my discussion of the major
possession cases how this hypothesis fares in *Genji* pictures *(Genji-e)*
through the centuries. To understand the creative tensions between
author and illustrator, however, it is first necessary to examine the production and reception of Heian illustrated narratives. This was, after
all, an enormously complex process engaging authors, painters, calligraphers, readers, and listeners.

The first extant *Genji* picture handscroll is the artistically influential twelfth-century *Genji monogatari emaki.* In the "Azumaya I" (S:
"The Eastern Cottage") scene, Ukon, a lady-in-waiting *(nyōbō),* is
reading aloud a text, presumably a courtly tale.[117] Her audience consists of no fewer than five court ladies. Closest to her is a princess
(Nakanokimi) whose deep concentration on listening is pictorially
rendered by showing only her long trailing hair, gently pressed against
her back and combed by another attentive *nyōbō* (Plate 2.1). A reading
of the relevant portion of Murasaki Shikibu's *Genji* text (S:958–959;
6:66–67), however, corrects this visual impression of exemplary
behavior. It reveals that Nakanokimi, no longer immersed in the tale,
is absentmindedly noting a resemblance between Ukifune, the newly
discovered half-sister facing her, and Ōigimi, her recently deceased
older sister. One wonders what motivated dreamy reflections such as
these. Is Nakanokimi bored by the narrative, or does some element of
the unidentified *monogatari* speak with unexpected power to the sisters' own melancholy condition? Could it possibly be that the Uji sisters are here listening to an earlier chapter of the *Genji* itself?[118] These
rhetorical questions are prompted by the fact that Nakanokimi's
absentmindedness hints at a profoundly uncertain existential state. A
Heian noblewoman's hair, always indicative of mental and physical
health, is here in need of cosmetic attention. The silent figure shielded

by hair seems sunk in an elegiac mood, but this pose veils a still more disturbing realization. Ironically, Nakanokimi's preoccupation with washing her hair at a propitious time had led her husband Niou to the discovery of the unknown beauty who is now innocently facing her sister-in-law. Confronted with frighteningly scandalous possibilities, Nakanokimi seems to ask about a pair of opposites that particularly fascinated the Heian psyche: dream or reality ("yume ka utsutsu ka"— *Ise monogatari,* episode 69)?

Meanwhile, the scroll fragment reveals that Ukifune is absorbed in visualizing the story by means of its colorful illustrations—pictures within a picture. (Interestingly, the *Genji monogatari emaki,* which actually alternates text and paintings, shows Ukon reading the text and Ukifune looking at the paintings, each woman holding a separate album.) Murasaki Shikibu's text gives no clue about Ukifune's innermost thoughts, but she—like her lost-in-thought sister—may be trying to unpeel the layers of pigments to find a hidden "text" she can "read" as her own story. Although the sisters are seen sharing a *monogatari,* they are in fact reading different texts. The painting that Ukifune's gaze is penetrating was executed in the technique called *tsukuri-e.* Layers of pictures, with sketches and notations underlying them, refer back to skeleton outlines now fleshed out in luxurious color. To the pigments, silhouettes in ink were restored as a final touch. By compilation, erasure, and restoration, the *tsukuri-e* technique results in a picture whose complexity parallels that of the *Genji* it illustrates.

This intimate scene from the *Genji monogatari emaki* includes two prominently featured *nyōbō,* straining from behind a curtain *(kichō)* to catch the words and glimpse the paintings. Like courtiers peeping through crevices and cracks in fences, shutters, and other dividing walls, in the amorous pastime of *kaimami,* these women are removed by a flimsy partition from the *monogatari* illustrations, but their separation can be seen as a different mode of engagement. In this female version of *kaimami,* the unseen spectators' detachment liberates their capacity for fantasy. These women have their own texts to decipher. After all, they are ladies-in-waiting—as Murasaki Shikibu herself was—and they know something of the tensions between Nakanokimi and her sisters, indeed, they may have been accomplices in producing them. As intermediaries *nyōbō* played a political role, and within Murasaki Shikibu's work their impact on the action is reflected in their frequent assignment of reporting or narrating the story.[119]

Moreover, *nyōbō* participated not only in women's writing *(onna-de)* but in women's painting *(onna-e)*.[120] Their prominence in the painting at hand suggests their control over both the action and its artistic reproduction.

It is taken for granted that writers and poets are sometimes able to reach into the innermost recesses of consciousness and make lucid what renders the rest of us inarticulate. But how did the illustrators of *monogatari* convey with a palette of colors and the stroke of a brush what went on inside the courtly structures in which they placed their enigmatic figures? As in all forms of aesthetic communication, it seems that barriers had to be surmounted, fences had to be peeked through. The subtle intimacies in the *Genji* must have posed a challenge to illustrators that could be met only by a drastic measure—by a painterly innovation that literally blew the roofs off the aristocratic mansion *(shinden)* by means of a technique called *fukinuki-yatai*. The viewers themselves are thus implicated in the process of *kaimami*, all the while realizing that the roof is only the first thing that must be removed in the unpacking of texts and the unpeeling of layers of paint to approach the invisible and sense the unspeakable.

The ingenious team of artists in this segment of the *Genji monogatari emaki* mirrored in their art the very activity their audience was engaged in.[121] Murasaki Shikibu would have been the first to take delight in such self-reflective meta-*emakimono* scenes, as is amply evident from her own meta-*monogatari* and meta-*emaki* treatises in "Hotaru" (S: "Fireflies") and "Eawase" (S: "A Picture Contest"). In fact, reflections about the arts in general as well as art appreciation and appraisal are well-known and much extolled aspects of her *Genji*. Not only that but the author attributes to her last female protagonist Ukifune an authorship that appears to step outside the boundaries of the *monogatari*; unlike the artistic efforts of other *Genji* characters, Ukifune's poetry is not instrumentalized as part of the plot.[122] Ukifune must, however, undergo a long arduous journey from the reception of illustrated *monogatari* to the creation of her own autonomous texts.

As the "Azumaya I" scene demonstrates, reading was not an individualistic silent experience in Heian aristocratic life but rather a communal aesthetic event. Since the event encompassed a variety of artistic media, there was always the possibility of fragmentation: those who heard were not always in a position to see, and those who could see may have missed some of what they heard. The depiction of Nakanokimi, Ukifune, and their eavesdropping ladies-in-waiting was in accord with the Heian aesthetic that prized the partially revealed and partially hidden: the crack in the fence to excite curiosity, the hidden text to tease the imagination.

In the cooperative venture of *emakimono* production, artists interpreted the literature they were instructed to embellish. Limitations of space imposed by costs forced them to interpret concisely. Just as the dialogues in foreign movies are reduced to brief subtitles, much to the detriment of nuances, *Genji-e* were a highly selective synopsis of representative moments chosen from a myriad of possible *monogatari* scenes.[123] Like a film-maker, the illustrator had to scroll the text and arrest the viewer's eye—and perhaps distract the listener's ear—at exactly the right places.

This was not an easy task. Since the ability to read the *Genji monogatari* began to fade seriously within a couple of centuries after its composition, post-Heian artists increasingly relied on *Genji* synopses and manuals not only for their knowledge of the content of this nearly inaccessible work but also for guidance to what could be properly transformed into other artistic media. As artists lost the ability to work directly from the text, their slavish adherence to manuals meant that "the central iconographic program . . . has remained largely unchanged through the centuries."[124] Nonetheless, nagging questions about how to represent in picture the elusive *mono no ke* of Murasaki Shikibu's text were occasionally transformed into new artistic challenges. Could the visual arts make visible the invisible, just as the *Genji monogatari* succeeded in expressing the unspeakable?

# Yūgao

To UNDERSTAND the meaning of *mono no ke* in the *Genji monoga-tari* it is important to recognize that readers have been influenced by artistic conceptions of *mono no ke* scenes. Since Murasaki Shikibu's text did not always serve as the blueprint for these creative artists, their visualizations of *mono no ke* constitute period interpretations. The "Yūgao" (S: "Evening Faces") chapter of the *Genji monogatari* features just one of Genji's many love affairs, yet it has received more than its share of painterly attention. Unfortunately, we have neither Murasaki Shikibu's holograph nor a contemporary copy nor any of the contemporary illustrations.[1] Since none of the twenty extant paintings of the earliest depictions—the unsurpassed *Genji monoga-tari emaki*—is devoted to this chapter, we are left to wonder how that illustrious atelier dealt with the challenge of the "Yūgao" chapter. We do, however, have the results of an interpretive tradition established by subsequent generations of artists. The specific scene most frequently illustrated in later *Genji-e* captures the moment that precipitated the fleeting love affair between Genji and Yūgao: a white gourd flower *(yūgao: Lagenaria siceraria)* is passed over on a fan that, according to the text, is embellished by a *waka*, a thirty-one-syllable poem in the phonetic *kana* script known in Heian times as *onna-de,* literally, woman's hand (Plate 1.1).[2]

## Pictorial Representations

The "gourd flower presented on a *waka*-inscribed fan" became part of an established iconography documented in the earliest extant manual, the sixteenth-century *Genji monogatari ekotoba*.[3] In this manner *the* representative image of the Yūgao affair was visually transmitted over the centuries. The detachment of illustration from text and the narrow artistic focus on aesthetic elements, such as the flower and the poem-fan, may have fixed the attention of many readers in such a way that crucial aspects of the chapter have gone unnoticed.

Some artists seem, furthermore, to have been unaware of the subversiveness of the text they illustrated. Perhaps because the moment of passing the fan is frozen in art an ambiguity arises that may confuse the identities of giver and recipient. It is frequently difficult to tell from their rendering of the scene whether the fan, the gourd flower, and the poem are presented *by* the hero, which would have been expected of a Heian courtier, or *to* him, which would have been a breach of etiquette. What seems to be, on the surface, a stereotypical episode from aristocratic court life is in fact a disturbing departure from Heian courtship conventions. It is clear from Murasaki Shikibu's text that it is not Genji who courts Yūgao with a poem, elegantly written on a fan and accompanied by a beautiful flower, but rather the conventionally reticent woman who, although unintentionally, makes the first move. In Murasaki Shikibu's text, traditional gender roles are reversed because intermediaries act for the main protagonists whose intentions are not necessarily represented accurately. Although only a sophisticated grasp of the text can reveal this, Genji and Yūgao have blundered unwittingly into an unconventional scenario. The subtle subversiveness of the episode, in which courtly etiquette is violated, calls into question the moral basis of a society that claims to be aesthetically oriented almost to the exclusion of everything else.

The selectivity of artistic tradition has also influenced responses to the most problematic aspect of the Yūgao episode. At the dramatic highpoint of the tragic affair—at the moment of Yūgao's death in the presence of her lover Genji and her lady-in-waiting Ukon[4]—there appears a *mono,* something frightful.[5] The apparently inexplicable arrival of the *mono no ke* is as important as the delivery of Yūgao's unconventional fan, but it was far less easily rendered in the painterly medium.

One suspects that the earliest manuals did not record or approve of *mono no ke* scenes. Whether any such scene was included in the twelfth-century *Genji monogatari emaki* will remain forever unknown unless more precious fragments of this spectacular picture scroll are unearthed. We do know that many of its paintings conformed to iconographic code but that some compositions, like the "Azumaya I" scene, "never reappear in later works, including the Osaka manual [*Genji monogatari ekotoba*]."[6] A painterly idiom was found in the post-Heian medieval age to express the supernatural, especially the frightful ghosts and unpredictable demons [*yōkai; oni*] that came to haunt the medieval imagination,[7] but the *mono no ke* described in the *Genji* must not be confused with these grotesque folkloric monsters. The *yōkai* of medieval picture scrolls, conceptually different from *mono no ke*,[8] are not to be found in traditional *Genji-e*. Whether of their own accord or because of their patrons' tastes, the artists who chose *Genji* scenes for their picture hanging scrolls, illustrated hand-scrolls, albums, folding screens, small squares of paper, fans, and a whole variety of smaller art objects refrained from associating ugly specters with the courtly classic. For these artists, *mono no ke* were simply not presentable.

For his English translation of the *Genji* Edward G. Seidensticker chose illustrations by the Kyoto lacquer artist Yamamoto Shunshō (1610–1682), whose woodcuts for the *Eiri Genji Monogatari* (Illustrated Tale of Genji; 1650) portray anthropomorphic *mono no ke* (Plate 1.2). Thus Yamamoto Shunshō represents a painterly propensity to bridge the gap between *mono no ke* as invisible abstractions, sometimes metaphorically suggested by an ominous wind, and *mono no ke* as fantastic creatures. A more iconoclastic approach than that of the traditional *Genji* images became a possibility in the late Edo period, when artists who were much less dependent on artistic manuals favored *hon'an*, a technique of "imaginative recasting,"[9] sometimes with a touch of parody, perhaps as a clever way of escaping censorship. Writers of popular literature *(gesaku)* and woodblock artists were freer than their predecessors in their approach to classics like the *Genji* and the *Ise monogatari*.[10] Artists boldly created fascinating fake *(nise)* tales spun with original threads, like Ryūtei Tanehiko's *Nise Murasaki Inaka Genji* (Impostor Murasaki and Rustic Genji; 1829), illustrated by Utagawa Kunisada in 1842.[11] Yet, unlike the anthropomorphic ghosts depicted by woodblock print artists such as Yamamoto Shunshō and Okumura Masanobu, the team of Tanehiko and Kunisada presented the demonic threat as a fully human Edo woman.[12] Their bestselling joint venture of *Nise Murasaki Inaka Genji* inspired a whole new genre of *Genji-e* woodblock prints.[13] Furthermore, it became possible in the late Edo period for woodblock print artists to ignore the iconographic canon and begin to develop *Genji-e* in the fashion of the floating world *(ukiyo)*, sometimes inspired by the craze for erotica *(shunga)*,[14] sometimes by Edo-period *kabuki* actors.[15] These full-fledged human conceptualizations of the demonic turned surreal and fantastic toward the end of the nineteenth century when *nō* theater conventions, which flourished in the fifteenth and sixteenth centuries, were revived. Powerfully drawn to *nō,* Tsukioka Yoshitoshi (1839–1992), one of the so-called *ukiyo-e* decadents, placed the possession scene at the deserted temple on the *nō* stage: the frightened characters (Mitsuuji alias Genji and Tasogare alias Yūgao) are in the center of his triptych and the demonic aggressor, wearing the jealous woman's *nō* mask Hannya (see Plate 1.6),[16] is approaching from the right (Plate 1.3).[17]

Inevitably, departure from the iconographic canon involved the artist in acts of interpretation. In Yamamoto Shunshō's depiction of the "Yūgao" chapter's *mono no ke* scene, Genji observes a woman with frazzled hair who has entered the room thanks to the conventionally blown-off roof (Plate 1.2). Threateningly, she hovers directly over Yūgao. In this portrayal we can detect the beginnings of an important—and ultimately misleading—interpretive tradition that identifies the possessing spirit as a jealous female rival or, as in the recastings of Tanehiko and others, a wronged woman who seeks revenge.

In the twentieth century, when translations of the *Genji* into modern Japanese made the text widely available, artists have varied greatly in their approach to the subject of *mono no ke*. A print by Ebina Masao (b. 1913) places a prostrate Yūgao on the lap of an alert Genji whose sword lies as a protective barrier in front of the lovers.[18] An ominous wind sweeps the curtains at them from behind, threatening to snuff out the flickering candle that Genji's eyes are fixed upon as if it were the life of his beloved. It seems that invisibility rather becomes the *mono no ke*. In Ebina's print, there is no effort to explain the possession through supernatural elements. Other artists have followed the pictorial tradition of representing the demonic in distinctly ghostly contours. The genre of Japanese comics, which sees itself in the tradition of narrative picture scrolls, does not hesitate to make blatant the supernatural hints of early *Genji* woodcut illustrations, such as the Yamamoto Shunshō print of 1650. For example, the *manga* artist Tsuboi Kou (b. 1951) renders the same Yūgao episode as sheer melodrama (Plate 1.4). Ebina's suggestively moving curtains are replaced by the ghost of a larger-than-life woman with menacingly blank eyes, an all too obvious allegory of Jealousy.

## Nine Topoi

Like the multimedia production and fragmented reception of illustrated *monogatari, mono no ke* appear multifaceted and elusive. Thus any single perspective on the phenomenon, traditionally that of the male protagonist, is insufficient and a wider vision, including the female viewpoint, must be restored to complete our grasp of what cannot unambiguously be put into word or picture.

### The Court

Yūgao's story is extremely complicated. In order not to lose our way, topography shall be our guide. We can follow the path marked by the various highly symbolic settings. The Heian court forms the background, but most of the settings of the "Yūgao" chapter lie outside the court's immediate perimeter. Each of the settings is associated with social status of one kind or another, reflecting the courtly emphasis on hierarchy and rank. The Yūgao story is spun from men's tales about women of different ranks. Whenever Genji misconstrues a woman's rank or causes her displacement, the nature of their relationship is fundamentally distorted.

Genji falls in love with a mysterious woman whom Murasaki Shikibu never named. She is traditionally referred to as Yūgao by Japanese readers, and she has the frail beauty of the ephemeral flower that is her eponym. As the orphaned daughter of a Middle Captain of the Third Rank (Sanmi no Chūjō), Yūgao belongs to the middle rank within the hierarchy of the Heian court aristocracy.[19] Genji, himself demoted to "commoner" rank by his imperial father, falls in love with her, but he loses her when she dies suddenly, in the middle of a spirit possession. The episode has furnished popular material for linked verse *(renga)* and *nō* drama as well as for the visual arts.[20] Often anthologized and used to give Japanese schoolchildren an initial (and sometimes a last) impression of classical Japanese literature, this episode, abstracted from its context, has become famous as a poignant story in its own right. Its transformation into other literary genres and its existence in isolation testify to its significance, but the decontextualization of the episode has inevitably distorted it.

Genji's affair with Yūgao (fig. 1 in App. B) occurs during a time of painful confusion. The seventeen-year-old Genji has been married to Aoi, the sister of his friend Tō no Chūjō, for five years, but he remains preoccupied with the memory of his late mother Kiritsubo, a woman who did not fit the courtly stereotype. An outstanding beauty but not of the highest courtly rank, she had been envied by her female rivals and ultimately victimized because of the favor she received from Genji's father, the Kiritsubo Emperor. Genji was only three years old (two by the Western count) when his mother died. Although Genji cannot remember her, his father helps him imagine Kiritsubo by keeping her memory alive. For almost eight years, Genji cherishes his mother as the archetypal woman. When his father marries Fujitsubo because she, the fourth daughter of a former emperor, has an uncanny physical resemblance to Kiritsubo, Genji's longing takes on a new reality. Seeking in his father's wife the reincarnation of his lost mother and simultaneously realizing that his desire violates a taboo, Genji behaves irrationally in ways that can be seen as an effort to stifle his illicit passion.[21] He engages in the minor affairs of amorous conquest that in Heian times were not only sanctioned but encouraged. Genji's visits to his various women may seem highly erratic, but there is an underlying pattern to them: they function as a smokescreen for Genji's clandestine pursuit of Fujitsubo. To what extent Genji has already approached Fujitsubo at the time of the Yūgao affair is unclear.[22] It is clear, however, that Genji is trying to free himself from his obsessive memory of Kiritsubo and to deflect his impulses away from the unattainable and the forbidden.

It is in the spring preceding Genji's affair with Yūgao that the author first hints at Genji's daydreaming of Fujitsubo (see S:38; 1:166). He is unintentionally encouraged in this reverie by tales told by his more experienced male companions in the "Rainy Night Discussion of Women's Ranks" *(ama yo no shinasadame)* in "Hahakigi" (S: "The Broom Tree"). Their stories intimate that women of the middle ranks are the most interesting while the ideal woman is an almost unattainable rarity. The challenge of finding the most fascinating woman, if not the ideal one, impresses Genji as he, depicted in the passive, languishing pose of a Heian woman (see S:24; 1:137), pretends to be absorbed in dreamy slumber.

Fujitsubo is on Genji's mind, but he must hide this passion and look for diversion. Of the stories discussed that rainy night—about jealous, unfaithful, unassertive, and wise women—the one told by Genji's best friend, Tō no Chūjō, has the greatest impact. This story takes the form of a doleful complaint about a woman, whom he characterizes as quite unassertive, who inexplicably disappeared along with the daughter she had borne him. Tō no Chūjō calls his unassertive woman "Tokonatsu," or fringed pink *(Dianthus superbus)*. Their daughter is referred to as "Nadeshiko," a synonym for the same flower. This daughter was the subject of a troubled poem that "Tokonatsu" had sent Tō no Chūjō. In his callous reply, he made sport of her concern and referred to her, in a suggestive pun on "Tokonatsu," as a "summer bed." Tō no Chūjō not only underestimated the depth of his beloved's anxiety; he also overestimated her submissiveness. Instead of bringing a knowing smile to her lips, the pun hit a raw nerve. Having been made thoroughly uncomfortable by his jealous principal wife, she took her "Nadeshiko" and quietly disappeared from sight.[23] When she reemerges, it is as another flower: Yūgao.

Since in polygynous Heian society concubines *(shō)*, secondary wives *(shōsai)*, and principal wives *(kita no kata)* were expected to tolerate each other, "Tokonatsu's" withdrawal was an unusual act. Tō no Chūjō's self-pitying and defensive depiction of her as an unassertive woman falsifies her character. After all, it takes quite a bit of self-assertion for a woman with a child to pack up and leave the man she loves and on whom she is wholly dependent. As Tō no Chūjō fully realizes: "I was all she had" (S:33; 1:157). Her departure is an unmistakable criticism: a slap in the face to the complacent male. More than that, Yūgao's quiet escape and her wordless defiance of convention are a form of self-sacrifice: she elects to undergo the hardship of raising Tō no Chūjō's child without his material or emotional support. Her self-imposed marginalization is all the more daring because she herself is an orphan and cannot rely on parental backing.

Ironically, Tō no Chūjō scolds Genji during the rainy night discussion for neglecting Aoi—Tō no Chūjō's sister, Genji's principal wife, and the "victim" of a future occurrence of spirit possession (fig. 2 in App. B). The man who is baffled by the severe consequences of his neglect of Yūgao anticipates the aggressive reaction by his proud sister to similar stress. Later events show that Tō no Chūjō's fears about the consequences of politically arranged marriages—like Genji's and Aoi's—were well founded.[24]

### The Inner River Mansion

A tempestuous sexual adventure immediately following the "Rainy Night Discussion" contributes to the complexity of the Yūgao story. Because of a directional taboo *(katatagae)*, Genji cannot spend the night at his principal wife's residence at Sanjō ("Third Avenue"). As a place to rest, he accepts the water-cooled gardens of the Inner

River Mansion of the Governor of Kii, one of his gentlemen-in-waiting. It happens that others have also taken shelter there for the sake of "ritual purification" (S:38–39; 1:169), among them the Lady of the Locust Shell (Utsusemi), the young stepmother of the governor (fig. 1 in App. B). Genji is immediately fascinated by this woman whose attractiveness seems to result more from her familial relationship than from her intrinsic merits. The Governor of Kii's incestuous longing for Utsusemi parallels the hero's secret infatuation with his own stepmother, Fujitsubo. By courting Utsusemi, Genji distracts himself from his desire for his father's young wife, but he also suspects that his secret obsession with her has been detected by Utsusemi's ladies-in-waiting. Genji's extreme fear of their gossip (see S:40; 1:171) betrays the fact that his desire has gone beyond mere fantasy.[25] Nonetheless, it is impossible to tell how far Genji's courtship of Fujitsubo has actually progressed. His original love for his mother, transferred to the stepmother who physically resembles her, is now deflected toward Utsusemi and then, through an amorous episode of mistaken identity, toward her stepdaughter (Nokiba no ogi). In assuming the governor's role, Genji calls the reader's attention to the author's creation of incestuous tangles. Utsusemi serves Genji as the "first *fictive* model of incestuous desire" for Fujitsubo.[26]

The comic element in a night of mistaken identities foregrounds tragic episodes to follow. Although Genji's amorous escapades up and down the hierarchical ladder may seem random and whimsical, they have a purpose and a pattern. In vainly attempting to be recognized by Utsusemi as her lover, he experiences the romantic attraction of inaccessibility. In mistakenly seducing her listlessly consenting stepdaughter, whom he then discards, he realizes that love easily attained is easily forgotten. The brief encounter has distracted him from his longing for Fujitsubo, but the entire episode leaves him with a strong sense of unfulfillment and just a trace of remorse for his callous treatment of Utsusemi's stepdaughter.

## Rokujō

The chapter entitled "Yūgao" begins harmlessly enough with a realistic setting and a hero engaged in the typical courtier's pastime of visiting his women. According to the given chapter order,[27] young Genji is on his way to the lady of the sixth ward (Rokujō watari), who is seven or eight years his senior and had only reluctantly yielded to his passionate courtship. Rokujō no miyasudokoro, as she is elsewhere called, is the widow of Crown Prince Zenbō, the younger brother of the Kiritsubo Emperor, Genji's father (fig. 1 in App. B). Her father, an important minister, died without realizing his ambition to see his daughter or his granddaughter (later known as Akikonomu) become empress.

Like Fujitsubo, Rokujō is surrounded by a mysterious aura that is due partly to Murasaki Shikibu's narrative technique.[28] Such an episodic structure and elliptic style should not come as a surprise in a writer many of whose most complex and important characters are introduced as if the reader ought to have known them already.[29] Major actors in the author's drama enter and exit as if they were ancillary figures: the most startling and unforgettable examples are the laconic account of Genji's affair with Fujitsubo and the cryptic announcement of his death. The literary tendency *not* to describe events of supreme significance in detail is analogous to an established feature of the Japanese visual arts—the aesthetics of blank space. Within the context of Murasaki Shikibu's *monogatari*, such blanks can signal the presence of the uncanny, which in turn may emerge in the guise of *mono no ke*.

When Genji finally arrives at Rokujō's mansion, he finds her "cold and withdrawn" (S:61; 1:216). It is as if she intuitively knew and resented that her young lover had strayed from the direct path to her. In fact, Genji's relationship with Rokujō seemed beset with problems from the moment he first conquered her and she first claimed to take possession of him. Rokujō's instinctive coldness at the beginning of "Yūgao" seems due to seething jealousy at his neglect of her during those days of high summer when the *yūgao* flower is at its best. Later in the story, when Yūgao becomes possessed and dies, Genji interprets the possession simply as the result of regrettable female jealousy. In assuming that one of his women must be to blame, Genji behaves conventionally. Jealousy, after all, was as common as concubines in the polygynous marital system of Heian society. There is, however, a rather obvious, if frequently overlooked, difficulty with Genji's interpretation. For his other women to have been jealous of the new mistress would require their knowledge of her existence. Since the affair had been kept a secret, none of them knew of it, and each of them had reason to attribute Genji's neglect to attentions paid to a known rival rather than to the unknown Yūgao. Despite this fact, critics have frequently taken at face value Genji's assumption of jealousy on the part of these other women. In their almost exclusive focus on Rokujō as the culprit, many critics have been even more definite than the hero

himself. Unfortunately, the narrow focus on Rokujō has inhibited serious consideration of female jealousy in Heian culture and its relation
to spirit possession.

### Gojō

Genji's visits do not give Rokujō priority. Before seeing her, he
makes a courtesy call at Gojō ("Fifth Avenue"), where his nurse (Daini
no menoto), an important mother figure, is ill. Since Genji is struggling
psychologically to cut childhood dependency ties, he is less than fully
committed to paying the obligatory visit. While the modern concept of
adolescence does not apply without modification to Heian society, it is
undeniable that in the fictional world of *Genji* intimate relations with
mother figures become problematical with the onset of puberty.

The nurse's house is located on a "dirty, cluttered street" (S:57;
1:209) in a run-down neighborhood. Illness may have forced this
mother figure to remove herself not only from Genji but also, in a
religious response to her imminent death, from the amenities of this
world. She has become a nun, and this austere location is an expression of her physical inaccessibility. When Genji arrives at Gojō, the
nurse's gate is locked, as if to indicate that Genji must now go elsewhere. Although this rebuff irritates Genji, he comes upon a "new
fence" (S:57; 1:209) next door that is also a "strange fence" (my
translation for "shabby place" [S:58; 1:210: *ayashiki kakine*]). The
quarters protected by this fence are as unpretentious as the flower
with a "very human sort of name" (S:58; 1:210), that is, the *yūgao*
flower whose eerie beauty catches Genji's eye.[30] Like the lotus heavy
with Buddhist symbolism, this flower grows from the mud. Its fresh-
ness contrasts almost grotesquely with the dilapidated state of the
neighborhood. Genji might not normally have been so completely
arrested by what he sees, but he is in a state of unusual anxiety. The
lowly flower gives him aesthetic delight, and the signs of domestic
inelegance induce a more energetic pulse.[31]

To my knowledge, it has not been emphasized that the psychological context of Genji's exceptional interest in a house this "tiny and
flimsy" (S:57; 1:210) is his anxiety over his nurse's illness and impending death. Under such stress, the absolutes of Heian cultural values,
especially the hierarchical order and the canon of aesthetic taste,
become relative. Death inspires thoughts of mutability: the grave idea
that we are here for mere "temporary shelter" (S:57; 1:210). To the
extent that Genji's sensibilities are jarred loose from the strictures of

courtly etiquette, his emotional horizon widens. It is almost as if he were preparing to enter a different world. Thus Norma Field stresses that "from Genji's point of view, the Yūgao episode represents an excursion into foreign territory—foreign . . . for its unaristocratic realism as well as its supernaturalism."[32]

The setting, juxtaposing two houses, encourages Genji's passage into the dark unknown. On the one side, there is the nurse's house, its locked gate announcing her resignation from sexuality and her preparation for death; on the other side is Yūgao's refuge, promising the efflorescence of "vulgar" (S:60; 1:215) love. Much has been made of the whiteness of the blinds in the openings of Yūgao's raised latticed shutters (hajitomi),[33] as well as the whiteness of the flower blossoming on its green vines.[34] According to Japanese convention, the color white unites the incompatible concepts of purification and pollution, innocence and defilement. Symbolizing the transcendence of quotidian reality, whiteness assumes ritual significance in diametrically opposite birth and death ceremonies.[35]

Genji is captivated by the symbolic implications of the ephemeral blossom, a thralldom intensified by the mysterious delivery of the poem on the fan that also carries the emblematic flower.[36] Koremitsu, the ill nurse's son (menotogo), Genji's "breast brother" and attendant,[37] remarks on the inappropriateness of the moment for amorous pursuits, but Koremitsu is unaware of the full extent of the moral danger in Genji's cupidity. Only after Genji has had the flower picked, only after he has seduced the woman who had it presented on a poem-fan, does Genji realize what he had merely suspected: that he had coveted his best friend's lost love—"Tokonatsu." Dimly aware of withholding information from Tō no Chūjō concerning his lost love, Genji will nonetheless repress the guilt his covetousness arouses. Eventually he will appropriate Yūgao's infant daughter, Tō no Chūjō's "Nadeshiko" or "wild carnation" (S:33; 1:158). These rash acts set off a veritable chain reaction. This daughter, first seized by Genji and then raised in distant Tsukushi (Kyūshū), returns many years later as Tamakazura. She becomes entangled in incestuous conflicts with both her ascribed father (Genji) and her biological father (Tō no Chūjō). All this, however, lies in the future.

Genji does not react immediately to the puzzling delivery of an intimate poem from a mysterious woman he has yet to meet. Enough time elapses during Genji's pursuit of the "strangely cold and withdrawn" (S:61; 1:216) Rokujō for Koremitsu to peep in (kaimami) on the beautiful Yūgao. It is interesting to note that this kaimami is at

Genji's behest, making it a mediated *kaimami* in the wake of a mediated *waka* offering.[38] On the basis of his assigned *kaimami*, Koremitsu reports to Genji that Yūgao is a young woman of higher rank than initially assumed from the dismal setting. The house belongs to "a certain honorary vice-governor" (S:60; 1:214: *yōmei no suke*). Although Koremitsu cannot explain her presence in this decayed neighborhood, Genji learns later that she came there only because a directional taboo (see S:79; 1:260) prevented her from leaving for some mountain village from her first refuge, her nurse's "wretched little hovel" in the western part of the city, to which she had fled after ill treatment from Tō no Chūjō and his principal wife. For the first time, Genji is attracted to a woman not for her maternal attributes but for her strangely childlike qualities.

Meanwhile, at Gojō, Yūgao's women are all astir over unconfirmed rumors that their former provider, Tō no Chūjō, had passed by their humble quarters in his carriage. When Koremitsu reports this commotion, an ominous thought crosses Genji's mind: "Might she be the lady of whom Tō no Chūjō had spoken that rainy night?" (S:64–65; 1:224). Genji had earlier imagined this "Tokonatsu" in his friend's distinguished household, but her extraordinary disappearance left him with the vague idea of an orphan dislodged and homeless. Has Tō no Chūjō's lost loved one undergone a floral metamorphosis? At this stage of the nascent affair, Genji's romantic speculation about Yūgao's identity can be dismissed as the improbable product of his excitable youthful imagination. The thought is not pursued.

By itself, however, improbability is too neat and plausible an explanation for Genji's failure to make the necessary connections. The psychologically subtle scene places Genji precisely on the threshold of knowledge. Here he denies what he intuitively knows to be the truth: that Yūgao is none other than the "Tokonatsu" of the "Rainy Night Discussion" and that she belongs to another. In a fairly blunt manner, Genji is practicing for the first time the combined techniques of betrayal and self-deception. In denying his own suspicion of Yūgao's identity, he also betrays Tō no Chūjō's trust. Nonetheless, momentary qualms reveal that Genji has not yet mastered the complicated strategy of disguise and deceit. This dubious feat he will achieve in the ultimate betrayal of his imperial father with Fujitsubo. For the time being, Genji manages to repress the suspicion that Yūgao is Tō no Chūjō's unassertive woman: "Genji did not know who the lady was and he did not want her to know who he was" (S:65; 1:225).

Since Yūgao conceals her identity, she collaborates unwittingly in

Genji's willed unawareness. Concealment was not her original intention. When she, in accidental reversal of proper female etiquette, first
reached out to him with an intimate poem on a mysteriously white
fan, she seems merely to have mistaken a stranger for the lover she had
left in despair rather than from lack of love (1:214; S:59):

> kokoroate ni    sore ka to zo miru    shiratsuyu no
> hikari soetaru    yūgao no hana

> I think I need not ask whose face it is,
> So bright, this evening face, in the shining dew.

According to Kurosu Shigehiko's hotly debated theory, Yūgao acted
on the basis of mistaken identity when she sent to Genji the poem-fan
meant for Tō no Chūjō. Kurosu's argument is supported by Yūgao's
images of an ephemeral white flower and the even more fleeting
dew,[39] two images of impermanence more appropriate at the sad end
than at the hopeful beginning of a relationship. Some scholars, noting
that Genji seems mildly taken aback at this "vulgar" (S:60; 1:215) ini-
tiative, have associated Yūgao, driven from shelter to shelter in the
company of her women, with the archetypal homeless courtesan
(yūjo),[40] a descendant of the wandering shamaness (miko).[41] But
Genji's view of the matter is not condescendingly to classify the
author of the poem among the courtesans; he is rather appreciative of
the "easy familiarity of the poem [that] had not been at all unpleasant,
not something to be pushed away in disdain" (S:60–61; 1:215).

Genji's poem in response indicates that he correctly attributes her
forwardness to mistaken identity. He encourages her to acknowledge
her error in perception (1:215; S:61):

> yorite koso    sore ka to mo mime    tasokare ni
> honobono mitsuru    hana no yūgao

> Come a bit nearer, please. Then might you know
> Whose was the evening face so dim in the twilight.

Shocked by the realization of her embarrassing mistake, Yūgao is
unable to send a reply. Before Genji had an opportunity to look at her
poem, she had excitedly dashed off a "letter" (S:61; 1:215)—which
he never sees because it was sent to Tō no Chūjō, the man addressed

in her poem. It is, therefore, only when Yūgao receives Genji's reply that she realizes the full extent of her mistake and lowers her shutters as a barrier to further contact.

Genji would not be Genji if Yūgao's demonstrative seclusion were enough to keep him away. For a while, he continues to associate erotic diversion and contemplation of mortality with the adjacent but symbolically opposed houses on Gojō. Thinking of Yūgao and of his ailing nurse, he says to Koremitsu: "Let me have a peep for myself when I call on your mother" (S:65; 1:225). Then, suddenly, thoughts of the younger woman overwhelm the sense of obligation to the older one, and Genji becomes obsessed with the pursuit of pleasure. Rushing to Yūgao in "very shabby disguise," Genji "did not stop to see his nurse" (S:65; 1:225–226). His incognito hardly obliges Yūgao to reveal her identity. Scholars have noted the playful hide-and-seek quality of the lovers' approach to each other,[42] but their secretiveness goes beyond the tantalizing play of young lovers uncertain of each other's rank. The affair becomes quite irrational because the lovers cannot admit—even to themselves—that the other is not the truly longed-for person.

As his visits at Gojō become more frequent and his love more like "madness," Genji grows increasingly introspective about his fascination with this unknown woman: "What was there about her, he asked himself over and over again, that drew him to her?" (S:65; 1:227). The heroine, too, displays a curious blend of awareness and denial. Her anxiety indicates that she is experiencing this relationship in the traumatic context of a previous affair: "She was frightened, as if he were an apparition from an old story" (S:65; 1:227). Rather than explaining her apprehensiveness by the bitter frustration with Tō no Chūjō, some Japanese critics claim that her fears of the "apparition" (henge) derive from the Miwayama myth.[43] In the more widely known of the two variants of this story, the "odamaki or hemp-thread type,"[44] a woman receives exclusively nocturnal visits from a spectral lover. When she demands to know his identity, she confronts a god (Ōmononushi no kami).[45] (In the other version of the legend, the apparition materializes as a snake.) In his role as henge, Genji evokes for Yūgao the painful past with Tō no Chūjō that she is attempting to forget by losing herself in this new love.

To spin the thread of the Miwayama myth further, the product of the mythic union is a divine child (kami no ko).[46] Although Yūgao does not bear Genji a child, his forced appropriation of "Nadeshiko" (that is, Tamakazura) puts Genji in the role of father to the child she has already. In that sense, this variation on the Miwayama myth shows us a man in pursuit of political power through symbolically rather than biologically engendered offspring. At the same time, it is no accident that the Yūgao affair serves as a foil for the tabooed Fujitsubo affair, which involves the biological procreation of an emperor. Thus, in the two superimposed affairs, Genji obtains a politically valuable daughter not biologically his while fathering a future emperor whose parentage he must hide.

In the initial phases of courtship at Gojō, the lovers suffer from mutual fears of losing each other. The affair becomes so intense that Genji contemplates securing their love by moving Yūgao to the Nijō-in, his main residence. Yet he rejects the plan almost as quickly as he conceives it. The move might come to the attention of the public and mean a formal commitment to the lower-ranking Yūgao. The political repercussions might injure both of them. If the initial impulse to install a mistress in Kiritsubo's quarters reflects Genji's desire to replace his late mother with another woman, rejection of the idea reflects his intuition that the childlike Yūgao cannot be the one.

Genji alludes to the uncanny mystery of his bond to Yūgao by lightheartedly echoing the bantering tone used in the *Ise monogatari* (episode 58) for the topos of the ruined house and its demons. Genji employs the specific metaphor of the fox for their reciprocal seductive-ness: "Which of us is the mischievous fox spirit?" (S:67; 1:228). Clearly, something stands between them, not only as a theriomorphic barrier but also as a force of animal attraction. The fox is also a playful acknowledgment of their incognito—which, in their case, means not so much being someone else as not being one's own self. Like the god or the snake in the Miwayama myth, their incognito is a version of the role playing so fundamental to spirit possession. Furthermore, since the fox in Japanese folklore induces sexual passion by taking either male or female shape,[47] the image helps to visualize ineffable fears about character transformation. Nonetheless, it is important to note that possessed characters in the *Genji* are without exception afflicted by *mono no ke,* an anthropomorphic species quite distinct from foxes and other animal spirits.

Having consummated his love with a woman whose identity he still does not know, Genji is once again reminded of Tō no Chūjō's unassertive woman (see S:67; 1:229). Although he intuitively recog-nizes a strong resemblance between his friend's lost love and Yūgao, his purposefully unquestioning behavior indicates that he still resists equating the two. He seems determined to linger on the threshold of knowledge, thereby creating a metaphorical gap in the fence that facilitates the appearance of *mono no ke*. That Yūgao maintains her secretiveness about the past makes Genji's evasiveness easier. Gazing at her mysterious new lover, she is painfully reminded of the rupture between her past and her present lives. The tension shows in both their invisibly masked faces. In the Freudian sense of the uncanny, their anxiety stems from being both familiar and unfamiliar toward each other. In Yūgao's case, the frighteningly unfamiliar seems to recall something vaguely familiar. Genji experiences the uncanny as the inexplicably powerful attraction to an unknown woman whom he seems somehow to recognize. His refusal to acknowledge Yūgao's true identity as Tō no Chūjō's lost love points to his repression of awareness of the more important link between Yūgao and the forbidden Fujitsubo.

At this point of mutual denial, the first crisis in the fragile love affair occurs. Initially, the strangeness of the Gojō environment had excited Genji. Unfamiliarity heightened sensual perceptions and inspired a love so intense as to be almost stifling. Dark romantic passion overpowered conventional Heian court etiquette and hierarchical differences. During their lovemaking at the time of the harvest moon,[48] Genji was fascinated by the novelty of lower-class life in the vicinity of Yūgao's Gojō residence. In time, however, he is exasperated by the "plebeian voices in the shabby houses down the street," sounds that he finds "genuinely earsplitting" (S:67; 1:230). The noise grates on his courtier's sensibility: " 'Let's go off somewhere and enjoy the rest of the night. This is too much' " (S:68; 1:231).

## The Villa

Genji is not only irritated; he is also fearful. The realm into which he entered almost as a lark now threatens to overwhelm him. Incognito is becoming the gradual loss of self. He is aware enough of this process to save himself in time. With another woman, he might have forestalled this experience by installing her at his Nijō ("Second Avenue") residence, but—as we have seen—he had rejected the idea on political grounds. Now he is desperate for a neutral territory where neither has to adapt to the other's domain, where love alone determines who is who. The idea is religiously inspired. At the end of the eerie night at Gojō, the lovers witness a pious old man invoking the Buddha of the Future (Tōrai Dōshi or Miroku Bosatsu). Genji seizes the opportunity to think ahead and vow to Yūgao that their love will survive this world (see S:68; 1:232), but it is the wrong moment for such a vow. Lovers' pledges were considered inauspicious when made during the night of the harvest moon.

The woman (*onna*), as she is referred to in the classical text, has hardly said a word to her lover beyond her initial, intimate, misdirected *waka*. Her few comments so far have served to express her doubts about his plans or her fright about the discrepancy between Genji's words and his actions. His recklessly inauspicious harvest-moon pledge is now too much for her.[49] She expresses her anxiety in a new *waka* that uses overtones of the Buddhist doctrine of karma to sound a secular theme: the past inhibits the future (1:233; S:68):

> saki no yo no    chigiri shiraruru    mi no usa ni
> yukusue kanete    tanomigatasa yo

> So heavy the burden I bring with me from the past,
> I doubt that I should make these vows for the future.

Ignoring such indications of apprehension, risking discovery and scandal, Genji nonetheless deems it wise to move Yūgao from the Gojō territory that has begun to threaten him to an uninhabited villa associated with a formidable minister and a remarkable emperor. Many scholars hold that this isolated villa (1:233: *nanigashi no in*) refers to the Kawara-in. This once beautiful setting, nostalgically celebrated in the *Ise monogatari* (episode 81), is haunted by the ghost of Minamoto Tōru (822–895), its former owner, believed to have been one of Murasaki Shikibu's models for Genji.[50] Zeami's *nō* play *Tōru* (also known as *Shiogama*) explores the elegant minister's obsession with creating in the capital a landscape replica of Shiogama at Chika in Michinoku.[51] Murasaki Shikibu mirrors the technique of replication. As the Kawara-in duplicates Shiogama, the "Inner River Mansion" (Nakagawa) duplicates the Kawara-in. A replicated landscape is an ideal symbolic site for the human substitution of Utsusemi (Nakagawa) and Yūgao (Kawara-in) for Fujitsubo (Shiogama).

There may be an additional parallel. Tōru's spirit appeared at the villa after it was taken over by Retired Emperor Uda (867–931; r. 887–898).[52] According to some sources, such as Ōe Masafusa's (1041–1111) *Gōdanshō* (The Ōe Conversations; 1111), the retired emperor's consort, Kyōgoku no miyasudokoro (Fujiwara Hōshi) was with him when Tōru's angry spirit tried unsuccessfully to reclaim his magnificent territory from the ailing Uda.[53] If Murasaki Shikibu was aware of these sources, then she placed Yūgao in a position to play Kyōgoku no miyasudokoro to Genji's Retired Emperor Uda, with Tō no Chūjō in the offstage role of Minamoto Tōru.

Genji's choice of this "forbidding place" (S:69; 1:235) accentuates his inability to cross the threshold of knowledge, thereby not only postponing responsibility and avoiding guilt but inviting catastrophe in the form of *mono no ke*. For Yūgao, the precipitous move to the desolate villa is an ambiguous act that threatens, elates, and ultimately kills her. On the one hand, Genji's rejection of his earlier plan to establish her at the Nijō-in is a token of his desire to avoid all risk of public scandal. In this sense, Yūgao can interpret the physical isolation of the villa as a sign of her lover's refusal to acknowledge her and as an omen of inevitable disavowal. On the other hand, "memories of past wrongs quite left her" (S:70; 1:237) when she considers how much she must mean to a disguised lover if he is willing to sacrifice his own peace of mind at a neglected residence where "devils" (S:69; 1:235: *oni*) might come forth. Each of the disguised lovers is teetering on the edge of conscious realization of the other's true identity. They oscillate between psychic stress and the joys of passion, but the trauma of her first love intensifies Yūgao's conflicts to a degree not experienced by Genji.

Yūgao may consider herself fortunate to be favored by a courtier, which is what she now assumes the still-disguised Genji to be, but the flattering thought that she has attracted a man of high rank triggers further thoughts about social status that leave her insecure, "frightened, and bewildered" (S:69; 1:234). Although her father had ranked higher than Tō no Chūjō at the time of her concubinage,[54] his position did not protect her when she was humiliated by Tō no Chūjō's jealous principal wife (Shi no kimi). Her father's death left her entirely dependent on Tō no Chūjō. Her status plummeted when she decided to leave him for the precarious life of a single mother. In her own eyes, she was reduced, metaphorically, to the level of a "fisherman's daughter" (S:70; 1:236: *ama no ko nareba*). In this second affair, Yūgao's impaired self-confidence is undermined further by anxiety about a second abrupt end to passionate love. How can she have confidence in a disguised lover acquired when he blundered into the role of the man who had already hurt her and damaged her self-esteem?

Yūgao is right to be distrustful. In his pledge to her, given in response to psychological pressure, Genji had fallen short of the intensely passionate vows alluded to by mention of the Chinese legend of Hsüan Tsung and Yang Kuei-fei. Genji's consciousness is divided between Yūgao and the ideal, forbidden figure of Fujitsubo. Through the clandestine adventure of the present affair, Genji can anticipate the dangerous, pleasurable frisson promised by his affair with his stepmother.

Instead of giving the details for the Genji–Fujitsubo affair, Murasaki Shikibu chooses to narrate Yūgao's story at great length and thus to suggest the extreme pleasures and pains of a secret forbidden love. The Yūgao affair can therefore be seen as an extended prelude that provides the hero with valuable experiences that can be acted upon in the momentous drama gradually taking shape behind the scene. In other words, the Yūgao plot, complex as it is, stands in for the incestuous affair with Fujitsubo,[55] which is, quite literally, unspeakable and must therefore be kept secret from most characters within the narrative and remain largely untold even to the author's audience.[56] The experiment that situates Yūgao and Genji in direct (though hidden) rivalry with Rokujō and Tō no Chūjō is a trial for Genji's secret, forbidden, and intense relationship with Fujitsubo. Literally and metaphorically, the Yūgao affair is both "pretext" and "subtext" for the Fujitsubo affair.

Another way to describe the immensely complicated relationships among the characters is to resort to a traditional geometric metaphor. Quite apart from Genji's dalliance with Utsusemi and his seduction of her stepdaughter, Genji is involved in no fewer than four love triangles. The first is formed when Genji neglects his principal wife Aoi in favor of Rokujō. The contours of this particular triangle are obscured so long as the two women do not know of each other, but Genji is concerned about the possible hurt to Aoi's pride should she learn of this affair. Never one to simplify a situation where complication is possible, Genji forms a second triangle involving himself, Rokujō, and Yūgao. As in the first triangle, the two female rivals for Genji's love know nothing of each other. Insofar as Yūgao is Tō no Chūjō's lost mistress, a third triangle is formed. In this constellation Tō no Chūjō cannot play the role of an active rival because Genji misleads him about the affair, but he is a powerful presence in Yūgao's consciousness and a repressed one in Genji's.

The fourth triangle is the least obvious and the most intriguing. It is actually a series of imaginary triangles each of which consists of

Genji, the woman with whom he is sexually involved, and the unnamed forbidden woman for whom he longs in violation of the incest taboo. Genji's restlessness in his marriage with Aoi, his affair with Rokujō, and his frustration in the Utsusemi affair indicate his longing for this forbidden woman. Yūgao can approximate Genji's ideal only to the extent that he suspects Yūgao to be Tō no Chūjō's lost love, but this hardly makes her taboo in the terms of a polygynous society. At most, Genji can be accused of committing adultery and repressing the realization that he is deceiving his best friend. The real taboo figure lurking behind Genji's apparently aimless promiscuity is Genji's stepmother Fujitsubo. The most psychologically consequential of the imaginary triangles is the one formed by Genji, Yūgao, and Fujitsubo. The affair with Yūgao is narrated in the language of mystery; the affair with Fujitsubo cannot be fully narrated—it appears as a fait accompli. Since the details of this taboo story cannot be told, the Yūgao episode constitutes a substitute narrative.[57]

Throughout the Yūgao episode, Genji is seemingly more in control of events than the passive, dependent Yūgao. Yet he is hardly a paragon of moral self-scrutiny. Genji has a conscience, but it is remarkably selective. Shortly before Yūgao's possession at the deserted villa, he is "sure that whatever devils [*oni nado*] emerge will pass me by" (S:69; 1:235). When he lies awake the night of Yūgao's sudden possession and death, he still appears to have repressed his incipient awareness of having stolen his best friend's lost mistress. He also appears insensitive to Koremitsu's interest in Yūgao, a woman who, by all appearances, better matches the social status of Genji's nurse's son.

In his waking state, before the disaster, Genji does feel oppressed by his obligations to the court (see S:70; 1:237). What particularly fills him with unease is his imperial father's worries about his whereabouts. Underlying this particular fear of a court rumor is Genji's realization that an affair with his stepmother could not only undermine his father's power but also, if there were offspring, ruin the pure imperial descent line from the sun goddess Amaterasu. Genji assumes that there will be a search for him. Although his shirking of responsibility brings no reprimand from his imperial father, Genji's sense of oppression while at the villa may signal a guilty conscience about the anticipated transgression with Fujitsubo.

Whether or not his affair with Fujitsubo has advanced into the first stage beyond pure fantasy, in his reflections immediately before

Yūgao's possession, Genji is concerned about the other women he has betrayed or neglected. Especially apprehensive about the demanding Rokujō, he realizes that women become dangerous when men cause them to become jealous. At the deserted villa, in the dead of night, just before Yūgao becomes possessed, a worried Genji is thinking of a court search for him and the threat posed by Rokujō's jealousy. When he slips from his agitated, waking state into sleep, he sees the mysterious image of a woman whom many readers have identified as Rokujō. Since, at this early stage of the crisis, Rokujō weighs most heavily on him, "it was that sad lady to whom his thoughts first turned" (S:70; 1:237) when he ponders the meaning of his dream. Yet it is important to note that the woman is presented in nightmarish anonymity. The abstract description of "an exceedingly beautiful woman" (S:71; 1:238: *ito okashige naru onna*) who is trying to snatch Yūgao away from his bedside also fits women other than Rokujō. Genji's thoughts might have turned to any one of the other women he slighted for the sake of his secret love. Aoi, his principal wife, is perhaps the most obvious. She has been neglected and Tō no Chūjō has recently scolded Genji for this neglect. In fact, he does evince fears concerning her. These fears surface when he asks one of his father-in-law's stewards "not to tell a soul" (S:69; 1:234) of the amorous retreat. There is also the young hero's lingering attachment to the nurse from whom he received early intimate physical contact and perhaps even erotic experience. His bad conscience concerning her, now seriously ill and withdrawn into the religious life, is not revealed until after Yūgao's death, when he gives instructions to Koremitsu not to let his mother know, for "she does not approve of this sort of adventure" (S:72; 1:242).

While Rokujō, Aoi, and the nurse weigh more or less heavily on the hero's conscience, there is yet another factor responsible for his nightmarish vision of the possessing spirit. This is of course the image of the ideal woman: the one who can replace his mother, Kiritsubo. It is Fujitsubo who best fits Genji's vision of the ideal woman. The charges of neglect brought forth by this "exceedingly beautiful woman" can emanate from Genji's betrayal of her as well as from his neglect of Rokujō and Aoi. During the "Rainy Night Discussion," that vision had stimulated Genji's fantasies of his stepmother, Fujitsubo.[58] Genji had pursued the ideal in the substitute figure of another stepmother, Utsusemi, but that adventure had ended in frustration and farce. Now that the affair with Yūgao—a very different kind of woman—arouses in him "an infatuation such as he had not known before" (S:66; 1:228), he may well be haunted, for the first time seriously, by the betrayal of his ideal.

In other words, if the visionary beauty is a composite made up of all the women Genji has neglected in his pursuit of Yūgao, there is nonetheless reason to believe that thoughts of Fujitsubo have caused the most profound mental disturbance. After all, Genji's treatment of Rokujō and Aoi is not at all unusual for a Heian courtier. Genji quite conventionally attributes their jealousy to a character fault. His active courtship of his stepmother and simultaneous betrayal of her with Yūgao are, however, derelictions unacceptable even by the permissive canons of his polygynous society. He keeps both of these affairs locked in his heart, safely secluded from the public eye and half hidden from his own. Yūgao's sudden spirit possession breaks the lock.

While Genji is half-asleep, Yūgao is seized by a *mono no ke*. Just as the specter of the beauty is turning to snatch his beloved away from his bedside, Genji is jolted awake by the possessed Yūgao's violent trembling. He begins to act as if he too were possessed. His first thought is for himself: he does not at once conclude that Yūgao is possessed. Momentarily at least, Genji fears that he himself may be the one possessed: "He awoke, feeling as if he were in the power of some malign being" (S:71; 1:238: *mono*).[59] Genji overcomes this sensation of vulnerability through a gendered reflex: he reaches for his sword, symbolic of male power, and quickly dispels all fears for himself. By the time Genji realizes that it is Yūgao who is possessed, it is too late for him to help her. She dies.

The drama of Yūgao's possession and sudden death is so powerful that he feels compelled to share her altered state and will continue to do so, in a kind of deferred possession (see S:78, 83; 1:257, 268), even after her death. This violent denouement of the love affair forces the hero into the role of interpreter. Since it is from Genji's perspective that Yūgao's precipitous mental and physical decline are first assessed, his frame of mind continues to be as pertinent to our understanding of Yūgao's tragedy as her own history of anxieties. In his first frantic attempts to explain the cause of Yūgao's death, he suspects magically unrealistic, dreamlike forces: "fox spirits" (S:71; 1:240: *kitsune nado*); "some evil power" (S:72; 1:240: *mono*); "the woman in his dream" (S:72; 1:241: *yume ni mietsuru katachi shitaru onna*); a legendary "devil" (S:72; 1:242: *oni*). But these vague agents represent an intermediary phase of explanation. Neither his descriptions to attendants of "a very strange seizure" (S:72; 1:242: *ito ayashū, mono ni osowaretaru hito*) nor his search for a natural cause in "a strange, hollow call of a bird" (S:72; 1:242: *keshiki aru tori no karakoe*) can provide a satisfactory explanation for the possession.

Because of the suddenness of Yūgao's possession and death and the absence of an exorcist who might have familiarized the mysterious, Genji must master the crisis without the aid of ritual. In search of an alternative remedy, Genji meditates on the symbolism of his first encounter with Yūgao: in one house, a young woman, the promise of a new love; in the other, an older, ailing woman, the reminder of an old dependence. The two represented the contrast between amorous adventure and a kind of filial obligation. Before the fatal move to the villa, Genji had straddled the fence, as it were. As soon as he lost sight of his nurse's house and removed Yūgao from her quarters to a new location, matters started to go wrong. Indeed, the villa seemed ominously to bring the two Gojō houses together, without any fence to mark the division between love and death, eros and thanatos. Having chosen the first and watched it become the second, Genji now selfishly calls for Koremitsu's older brother, a "holy man" (S:72; 1:242: *azari*) who had been commissioned by Genji to pray for his critically ill nurse. Too traumatized to be aware of the ruthlessness displayed by his request, Genji asks the *azari* to abandon his own mother in her crisis. Genji's sole reflex is to keep the affair with Yūgao concealed from his dying nurse, for fear of her disapproval.

Genji is torn between the conflicting emotions of grief for his lost love and terror akin to that of a murderer who must dispose of a dead body. Genji's breakdown seems inevitable. That Yūgao should have died so suddenly from fright arouses the suspicions of Genji's confidant Koremitsu, now a rather detached observer, who is called to the scene for help. Genji's suffering does not end when Koremitsu takes care of practical matters. When Koremitsu inquires about Yūgao in medical terms, wondering whether there had been "anything wrong with her" (S:74; 1:245), Genji tells him, truthfully, that physical illness was not the cause of the tragedy; but Genji further burdens his conscience by lying to the suspicious Tō no Chūjō about the cause of his absence from court. Not surprisingly, emotional distress is accompanied by psychosomatic symptoms: headaches, lack of appetite, and fever. Only his confidant can help him to stop "torturing" (S:75; 1:250) himself. This Koremitsu does by suggesting penance, which implies the recognition of wrongdoing.

It is only when Genji, "the only rational one present" (S:72;

1:243) at the scene of the tragedy, can come off his high horse—and he is about to take such a fall quite literally—that he can accept Koremitsu's advice and come to terms with Yūgao's tragedy and his role in it. He acknowledges a degree of complicity: "He was being punished for a guilty love, his fault and no one else's" (S:73; 1:243). If it was indeed a guilty love, a love that should not have been (1:243: *ōkenaku arumajiki kokoro*), the reason has less to do with the Yūgao affair per se than with the affair in relation to Genji's other loves. Genji seems at this point to feel that Yūgao's death is a punishment for his betrayal of his imagined ideal woman.[60] Norma Field hardly overstates the case when she concludes that "Yūgao's corpse becomes a symbol for the absent Fujitsubo."[61]

If the closest approximation of the ideal is Fujitsubo, which does seem to be the case, then Yūgao's death can be seen as retribution (1:243: *mukui*) for this illicit desire.[62] Has Genji's affair with Fujitsubo already progressed beyond mere fantasy? Murasaki Shikibu is conspicuously silent on the issue, but it is possible that Genji's eventual recovery from the lethal outcome of his inappropriate liaison with his friend's lost love and his successful cover-up of her demise may be what emboldens him to push ahead to the ultimate taboo violation with his stepmother. It is ironic that Genji, whose erotic adventures cause so much distress, emerges from the trauma of the Yūgao affair energized rather than sexually intimidated or spiritually reformed.

While Genji's waking, dozing, and sleeping states are minutely described in the text, the heroine's point of view is dramatized in far less detail.[63] This near omission is remarkable because the author of the *Genji*, many of her narrators, and most of her Heian audience were women. For them, Yūgao's largely unheard voice may have been nonetheless audible, her unrecorded thoughts and feelings palpable. Proficient in excercising their double consciousness, the female audience could "read" the female author's unwritten or faintly spelled-out text about this and other female protagonists trapped in gender conflict. Nor is it unreasonable to assume that the imbalance of voice and vision reflects a gender-bound imbalance of power. Genji certainly plays a domineering and directive role. By contrast, Yūgao is a much more ambiguous character. On the one hand, she is bold enough to have taken her daughter and left Tō no Chūjō because of his disagreeable principal wife; on the other hand, Genji perceives her to be timid and helpless. Her essential ambiguity emerges in their first encounter when she allows the *yūgao* flower to be passed on to Genji on her fan.

Whether the accompanying *waka* was written by her or by one of her ladies-in-waiting is debatable; but, according to courtly convention, the lady bears responsibility even if she had no hand in the actual composition or was completely ignorant of her entourage's activities. As a result of this initial uncertainty, Yūgao's own will in the initiation of the affair is a matter of speculation. Did she mistake Genji for Tō no Chūjō? Is her poem merely a polite greeting, as some have argued, or is it an improperly lewd pass at a noble courtier?[64] Yūgao herself provides almost no verbal clues. When she does express herself, her voice is faint, lyric, or mediated, yet her silence has its own eloquence.

Yūgao's tensest moments are the result of her traumatic experience of the past and her fear of a repetition in the present. Not surprisingly, her terror increases when Genji removes her from her refuge at Gojō to the deserted villa. The first eerie night at the villa is filled with ominous sounds instead of the familiar street noises at Gojō. Time and place together produce Yūgao's extreme mental and physical agitation: "The girl was trembling violently" (S:71; 1:238). She falls into a "trance" (S:71; 1:238: *ware ka no keshiki nari*). The question of the cause and the purpose of this trance goes unasked because the story's largely female Heian audience was encouraged—like Yūgao—to hold its breath for the hero's sake. We accompany the Shining Genji (Hikaru Genji) on his nocturnal visits; we do not wander with Yūgao nor are we made impatiently to wait with her for her lover. More than anything else, the sudden appearance of *mono no ke* should alert us to her underrepresented state of mind, but the *mono no ke* has been treated as a phenomenon separate from her psyche.[65]

The point I wish most emphatically to stress is that the psychology of the person perceived as the "victim" of spirit possession has been neglected because the entire episode is seen through Genji's eyes and from his angle of perception. Genji's initial interpretation of the nightmare and the possession and his subsequent guilt about his betrayal of Tō no Chūjō ignore Yūgao, the crucial figure in the drama; yet she has her own perspective, which is not expressed through words so much as through gestures culminating in her possession trance and death. The ultimate symbol of both Genji's and Yūgao's conflicts combined is the *mono no ke*, which lies outside the realm of rationality and ordinary communication. In order to be understood, this symbol—of fear itself—has to be translated, as it were, into intelligible forms of discourse. Genji's translations are derived from legend (the haunting spirits of deserted houses [*hai-in no yōbutsu*]), from myth (*Miwayama densetsu*), or from the folk beliefs (fox [*kitsune*], demon [*oni*]) expressed in Heian literature and the oral tradition of ghost tales *(kaiitan)*.[66] At times, he diagnoses the *mono no ke* as an instrument of jealousy: the stock explanation for female hysteria, especially in polygynous societies.

Naturally, Yūgao never perceives any *mono no ke*.[67] She is in a trance—an altered state of consciousness that suspends individuality and allows the self to incorporate otherness. What propels a person to enter into such an altered state of consciousness is an extreme conflict, a traumatic dilemma. Yūgao makes no secret of her extreme fears even if she speaks them in a shy whisper. Genji listens but does not hear what she says. A man of his time, he finds her fearfulness charming, even seductive: "Yes, she might well be frightened. Something child-like in her fright brought a smile to his lips" (S:67; 1:228). After the unwanted move to the villa, she reiterates her terror of continuing displacements in a *waka* (1:234; S:69):

> *yama no ha no   kokoro mo shirade   yuku tsuki wa*
> *uwanosora nite   kage ya taenamu*

> And is the moon, unsure of the hills it approaches,
> Foredoomed to lose its way in the empty skies?

To this, which ought to be plain enough, she adds: "I am afraid" (S:69; 1:234).

She feels quite literally lost, dispersed into several directions at once, and about to dissolve into the thin air of the "empty skies."[68] Her misdirected poem-fan and the realization of mistaken identities had first trapped her in an unnatural incognito. Since her incognito was much less part of a strategy than Genji's, she faces more of an identity crisis than he. Who was she and who has she become? The unbearable tension between her past persona as "Tokonatsu" and her present incognito, associated with the white gourd flower, impels her to burst the confines of a single self. In her trance she transcends the deep split dividing her former and present selves. To narrate this psychic event, Murasaki Shikibu abandons the realistic mode of the previous chapters and introduces the concept of a strange thing *(ayashiki mono* or *mono no ke)*. Yoshitoshi captured this vision of Yūgao's elusive self in a trance fading into death. His hauntingly beautiful print shows the dim shape of a frail woman suspended in midair; the light of the full moon seems to drain the lifeblood from her lips as she is ensnared by the gourd vine forming a Pre-Raphaelite-style frame (Plate 2.2).[69] Yūgao's spirit possession expresses her liminality, between her past and present selves, between eros and thanatos. It is what one authority on altered states of consciousness has called the "fear of life and the longing for death."[70]

In the frightening spectacle of spirit possession, Yūgao also breaks Genji's control over her. Suddenly it is she who briefly and dramatically appears on center stage. To Genji she appears both as the woman he thinks he knows and as a very frightful other (1:242: *ito ayashū, mono*). As we have seen, that "other," condensed in the uncanny phenomenon known as *mono no ke*, he interprets in various self-centered ways, none of which allows for Yūgao as subject rather than object.

In other words, the *mono no ke* is best understood as neither the living spirit of the jealous Rokujō, nor the spirit of the villa, nor a demon, monster, or *evil* spirit. The *mono no ke* is the deadly discrepancy between Yūgao and the selves that others forced her to be. While Genji manages to contain the structural autonomy of his self despite severe bouts of confusion and disorientation, Yūgao breaks in two, as it were, under the stress of dissimulation. Her *mono no ke*, occupying the breathing space between face and mask, manifests itself in the spectral beauty at her side. Although Genji is too self-centered to understand what he sees, the *mono no ke* demarcates the split between her past persona as "Tokonatsu" and her present one as "Yūgao." In his vision Genji sees the possessed Yūgao literally split between the creature he loves and the alter ego represented by "an exceedingly beautiful woman."

Throughout the affair, Genji continues ostensibly in control. He speculates, dreams, fantasizes. Meanwhile, Yūgao acts in the only manner available to her. An otherwise helpless woman who has been victimized once and is fearful of a second victimization by a second lover, she seizes a defensive weapon. Sometimes, when the suffering became unbearable, Heian women took the tonsure to escape the world of male sexuality. This may originally have been Yūgao's wish when she left her nurse's inadequate dwelling to seek refuge in a mountain village *(yamazato)* frequently associated with religious retreats. Other women sought relief from extreme stress in anorexia nervosa, which sometimes led to death. Spirit possession was yet another way to criticize and perhaps to lessen male dominance. Yūgao's possession has no explicit political dimension, but it is a typical phenomenon in every polygynous social system because such societies severely limit women's control over their sexual lives. Dis-embodiment is, paradoxically, a way to reclaim one's own body. Spirit possession is not a feminist protest in the modern sense of the term; but neither is it "profound passivity" in the presence of social injustice.[71] Nor is Yūgao's possession the product of a deviant or disordered personality: it is an unusual but nonetheless socially sanctioned response to conventional assumptions about the inappropriateness of direct female self-assertion, especially verbal complaints. At critical times such as severe illness and childbirth, Heian culture permitted physical forms of self-expression within a strictly controlled ritual context. Yūgao is neither physically ill nor pregnant, but she does realize that neither her explicit references to her fears nor the allusive warnings of her *waka* elicited anything more than a conventional male response. With her ecstatic trance, she tries to say all she has no words for. Unfortunately for Yūgao, her last effort to communicate, her feverish attempt at spirit possession, fails because Genji is simply unable to realize that she, made vulnerable by her rank and gender, has used the only psychological weapon available to her. Failure is fatal.

Ordinarily, spirit possession is ritually supervised, and a significant segment of society participates in the ritual, either as exorcists, mediums, or witnesses, to assure healing. It is therefore rare indeed that spirit possession and trance culminate in death. Here, however, events move too quickly and the religious machinery to ensure Yūgao's survival is missing, making the Yūgao case unique in the *Genji*. The vain exertion proves so strenuous that Yūgao, unaided by the communal comforts of ritual, dies.

### Toribeno

Although Genji risks discovery of his involvement in Yūgao's fate, he feels compelled to pay his last respects to her. At a mountain temple he expresses his grief by commiserating with Ukon, Yūgao's lady-in-waiting.[72] As he departs from the temple, exhausted from guilt and shame, he falls from his horse. To look like a fool is no small matter in a culture that emphasizes poise. Having lost control, Genji falls outside the approved norm. Tumbling from his mount is not the worst fate to afflict a courtier who has been romantically involved with a woman fallen from rank by her efforts to maintain her pride, but it is an indignity and perhaps an omen.

From the outset, the illicit and secretive Genji–Yūgao relationship was acted out against a backdrop of fear. This fear amounts to nothing less than the fear of death itself. Put differently, the idea of *mono no ke* reflects the disturbing conflation of two irreconcilables: love and death. In the death of his mother Genji had experienced the two phenomena as separate and consecutive. In the "Yūgao" chapter, Genji experiences the close juxtaposition of eros and thanatos in the two houses at Gojō. Yūgao's mysterious demise constitutes Genji's first confrontation with eros and thanatos in dramatic simultaneity.

At that moment, as we have seen, Genji experiences the bifurcation of the beloved into two images: the still recognizable Yūgao and a hauntingly unidentifiable beauty. The effects of this "double exposure" linger on as Genji contemplates Yūgao's corpse. At the mountain temple, just before Yūgao's cremation, Genji's emotions are like those of a necrophiliac who cannot accept the reality of his beloved's death. As he reflects on his last glimpse of her in front of her dead body, Genji seems more dead than alive. He is deeply confused about their separated identities: "He scarcely knew where he was. The girl was exactly as she had been that night. They had exchanged robes and she had on a red singlet of his" (S:77; 1:254).

By implication, the robe Genji wears beneath his "travel robes" (S:76; 1:251) is Yūgao's "white robe" (S:67; 1:231). Their identities, like their robes, have become interchangeable. This confusion of dead and living identities is a grotesque variation on the theme of their mutual incognito. Clearly, identification with the other beyond death constitutes the ultimate attachment and, as such, the classic Buddhist impediment to enlightenment. Although the identification is a mere illusion, it is a powerful one. Just as they merged briefly into one as lovers, denying their distinct selves, so they now appear, for a similarly short while, to merge in the experience of death. Their brief encounters in moments of eros and thanatos are both intense and illusory, but they suffice for Genji to become aware of the intimate connection between love and death. He has also become aware, through the spectacle of Yūgao's dead body clad in his red robe, of his own mortality. The ambiguous imagery of the robe, with its intense connotations of love and death, is brought back with great poignancy at the end of the "Yūgao" chapter. It is transmitted obliquely through a reference to Utsusemi's robe, left behind as she slipped away from Genji's grasp. This robe is Genji's keepsake of Utsusemi (lit. the "shell of the locust"), of the woman who did not die but merely went away. At the end of the "Yūgao" chapter, this robe, like the shell of a locust, becomes emblematic of the loss of life and love.

## Nijō

Considering the deeply symbolic settings, from Gojō and the villa to Toribeno, the reader is hardly surprised that Genji seeks refuge and a chance to recover from the trauma of death at the Nijō-in, his most intimately familiar residence. There the aftereffects of stress bring on a twenty-day crisis from which recovery is slow and painful: "For a time he felt out of things, as if he had come back to a strange new world. . . . He spent a great deal of time gazing into space [*nagamega-chi ni*], and sometimes he would weep aloud" (S:78; 1:257). Since "gazing into space" was a common fictional expression of Heian women's "immobile existence,"[73] Genji's behavior arouses comment. Experiencing a version of Yūgao's trauma, he appears to others as if he were a woman possessed, and the women at court, despite their ignorance of Yūgao's tragedy, diagnose his condition in terms of spirit possession: "He must be in the clutches of some malign spirit [*onmono no ke*], thought the women" (S:78; 1:257). The assessment of a man's possession state is relatively rare in Murasaki Shikibu's work. It reflects a reality more commonly noted in those Heian chronicles in which spirit possession is the reaction of emperors and high-ranking political figures to succession disputes and other power struggles.[74] Genji's state of mind, evidenced by his behavior, is clearly extraordinary, but it is not alarming enough to call for treatment by exorcists.

One way for Genji to deal with his grief is to appropriate Yūgao in the form of her daughter. In the immediate wake of Yūgao's death, Genji claims to be doing penance by caring for Yūgao's child. But his apparently charitable intentions are actually quite selfish because Tamakazura is also the child of Tō no Chūjō, a fact that Genji can no longer repress after a confidential talk with Ukon about Yūgao's history.[75] Genji continues to avoid responsibility for the tragedy. He barely manages to acknowledge that his and Yūgao's deception—the disguise that enabled them to conceal their mutual betrayal of Tō no Chūjō—lies at the root of their love's failure. He is wholly unable at this point to acknowledge that the betrayal of his ideal woman—Fuji-tsubo—is even more serious than his half-conscious deception of his best friend. Put differently, Genji's affair with Yūgao constitutes a dress rehearsal—incognito—of Genji's affair with his stepmother and their joint betrayal of the Kiritsubo Emperor. Even if this affair has not yet been consummated, Genji has already, in the deep recesses of his subconscious, violated the taboo: the impregnation of his father's wife. It is only in this larger context that Genji's shocking trivialization of the "Yūgao" incognito as an "unfortunate contest of wills" (S:78; 1:258) can be understood.

### Hiei-zan

After the forty-ninth-day memorial services for Yūgao, Genji continues to be bothered by a bad conscience: "His heart raced each time he saw Tō no Chūjō" (S:82; 1:266). While Yūgao's ritually appeased spirit resides in limbo *(chū-u),* Genji experiences another nightmare "of the woman who had appeared that fatal night" (S:83; 1:268). As Taya Raishun has pointed out,[76] it is significant that Genji's second vision of the mysterious "beauty" occurs immediately following the important Buddhist ritual for the pacification of the dead. Taya concludes that Genji's experience is analogous to the later nightmares suffered by women formerly in Yūgao's service. At the beginning of the "Tamakazura" chapter (S: "The Jeweled Chaplet"), these women, now acting as guardians of Yūgao's daughter in faraway Tsukushi (Kyūshū), have rare "twin" dream visions of their lady who had disappeared so mysteriously (see S:388; 3:84). The dream brings them to conclude, while lacking all empirical evidence, that Yūgao must be dead.

Although Japanese scholars frequently treat spirit possession and dream visitations as the same phenomenon, it is important to distinguish between them.[77] Tamakazura's women suspect that Yūgao has died, and thoughts of their beloved lady's unresolved end trouble their sleep. They are haunted by a dream in which Yūgao appears split, in the form of liminal twins, neither dead nor alive. Normally, dreams are experienced by a single person and can be shared with others only in retrospect. In the case of Tamakazura's women, one dreamer's suggestively narrated account of the twinned Yūgao evokes the same dream in others. Although it is true that this dream is ominous (because Heian culture considered multiple births, such as twins, to be unnatural for humans), the difference between an eerie dream and spirit possession is important. In spirit possession, the possessed person behaves in such a manner that he or she generates a dream*like* spectacle experienced immediately by others who are awake rather than asleep.

No more than Tamakazura's women is Genji possessed. He knows, of course, that Yūgao is dead, and his second vision of the mysterious beauty is born of his desire to dream of Yūgao and thereby to recover her. Apparently his desire is not gratified. Instead, the dream recreates for him the most horrifying moment of all—namely, the moment during the possession when the beauty hovering next to Yūgao berated him. Since this spectral woman no longer menaces him, he does not associate her with the idea of jealousy. Upon waking from his dream, he concludes that the spirit of the villa lies behind the mysterious events. This seems to settle the matter and to exculpate him, but in fact it does not. Was it not he, after all, who brought Yūgao to this demon-infested place? Considering all the other places he might have taken her, even in secret, had he not taken her to this wilderness in order to enjoy the vertiginous thrill of eros and thanatos? Grieving for Yūgao, longing for Fujitsubo, nagged by apprehension, vaguely guilty about his disloyalty to Tō no Chūjō, haunted by his dream of the spectral woman, Genji continues to hesitate on the verge of insight into Yūgao's motivation, but he cannot seem to understand that Yūgao's possession was a "natural" result of his own selfishly exploitative behavior.

The Yūgao episode is rounded off by the formal conclusion of the affair with Utsusemi and her stepdaughter. Genji lies to the stepdaughter's new husband as he had to Tō no Chūjō, but his respectful treatment of Utsusemi now shows a more enlightened attitude toward this particularly adamant woman who had managed to set clearly defined limits to Genji's sexuality. On a different level of discourse—the level of the *mono no ke* in Yūgao's case—the narrator passes judgment on the hero in a direct appeal (narrator's commentary, *sōshiji*) to the reader.[78] *Monogatari* conventions, which called for an idealized prince as the hero, are flouted. Although praise of Genji runs through the first part of the "Yūgao" chapter, the bright thread of this theme gradually thins until it becomes totally frazzled in the final, devastating comments that make no concessions to Heian conventions of male heroism: "I had hoped, out of deference to [Genji], to conceal these difficult matters; but I have been accused of romancing, of pretending that because he was the son of an emperor he had no faults. Now, perhaps, I shall be accused of having revealed too much" (S:83; 1:269).

### Off the Court Record

The Yūgao affair is framed by Genji's unsuccessful courtship and symbolic loss of Utsusemi. The Utsusemi and Yūgao affairs are more or less synchronic: both end with Genji contemplating a literal or a figurative memento mori, a human corpse in one instance and the shell of a locust in the other. The psychic energy behind both of these affairs is Fujitsubo. She is, in fact, the driving force behind all of

Genji's relationships with women—and she too is thought to be possessed. To fully appreciate Fujitsubo's role as the ideal lurking behind Yūgao (as well as Murasaki and the Third Princess), Murasaki Shikibu's readers must unroll her text scroll in both directions. Thus the intricate role *mono no ke* plays in the Fujitsubo incident can be uncovered only by a clear grasp of physical and psychic circumstances that also relate to the Yūgao tragedy.

Unique in its high degree of taboo violation, the Genji–Fujitsubo affair testifies to the intensity of the lovers' passion. Relatively little is said about this mysterious affair. Nonetheless, Tamagami Takuya claims that its "bedscene" is unsurpassed in the entire *Genji*.[79] Although the term "bedscene" (which Tamagami gives in English) may arouse expectations of a graphic description of the sexual act, Murasaki Shikibu chooses not to narrate what her characters cannot confront. A metaphysical dimension replaces the physical dimension. The author manages to convey the erotic passion of this taboo violation by leaving it a blank to be filled by the reader's imagination. At no place in the *Genji* does she describe the sexual act, preferring to use her very finest brush to record erotic moments in her lovers' innermost feelings and thoughts. Not surprisingly, then, for *this* "bedscene," the painter's brush must also rest altogether, according to the Osaka manual.[80]

This virtual blank in the narrative is erotically charged by the taboo of incest. Although H. Richard Okada, a deconstructionist critic who correctly stresses the importance of "Narrating the Private" and "Substitutions and Incidental Narrating," acknowledges that the Genji–Fujitsubo affair goes largely unnarrated, he does not link the author's narrative strategy to the exceptionally forbidden nature of this affair. Quite the contrary. Okada repeatedly proposes that the Kiritsubo Emperor actually encouraged his wife's intimacy with his son.[81] Okada stresses the emperor's political motivation, which is to compensate for demoting his favorite son by offering him his own imperial consort (whom he advises to be Genji's mother surrogate because her features are virtually interchangeable with Kiritsubo's). In my view, however, the Kiritsubo Emperor's words to the sixteen-year-old Fujitsubo strongly underline rather than eliminate the incest taboo (S:16; 1:120):

> "Do not be unfriendly," said the emperor to Fujitsubo. "Sometimes it almost seems to me too that you are his mother. Do not

think him forward, be kind to him. Your eyes, your expression: you are really so uncommonly like her that you could pass for his mother."

Okada argues that the "emperor's counsel thus brings together the rhetorical and the political in a configuration of mutual complicity."[82] Although Okada recognizes complicity, he does not define it. He denies the seriousness of the lovers' taboo violation.[83] Norma Field's view of the affair stresses Fujitsubo's youth rather than her role of stepmother. After first recognizing incest in the Genji–Fujitsubo relationship, she reexamines the problem after Fujitsubo has taken religious vows and arrives at the hypothesis that "Genji and Fujitsubo represent a mildly parodic version of brother-sister rule (*hiko-himesei*)."[84] Yet the phenomenon of royal incest seems to belong to archaic myths; it is inapplicable to Genji because he has lost his claim to the throne and to Fujitsubo because she is already married to the emperor. More important, the two never behave as if they were indeed entitled to exercise the privilege of royal incest. Not only do they have indisputable feelings of guilt, they take great care in keeping their dark secret from the world.

The moment of Fujitsubo's conception at age twenty-three signals a high degree of interiority. Yet the supremely intimate moment is marred by a dark secret that allows everyone—except the lovers and Ōmyōbu (Fujitsubo's attendant)—to assume that the child is the Kiritsubo Emperor's.[85] The public's initial pleasure at the prospect of an imperial child gives way to mounting anxiety when Fujitsubo fails to come to term. Her failure to deliver in the Twelfth Month causes panic about the possible death of the mother, the child, or both. Heian belief leads immediately to the suspicion that malevolent forces are at work. There are rumors of spirit possession. At the same time, Murasaki Shikibu has carefully prepared the reader, through her revelations concerning the truth about Fujitsubo's time of conception and the identity of the child's father, to be skeptical of such beliefs. While the characters within the narrative suspect *mono no ke,* the author asks the reader to contemplate the rift between true and false perceptions based on complete and incomplete information.

In other words, the omniscient author must mediate between the initiated protagonists and the other characters, who have but limited knowledge of the situation. The pivotal point of knowledge versus ignorance is *mono no ke,* which becomes, in Murasaki Shikibu's woman's hand *(onna-de)*, a literary trope. The author employs *mono no ke* to define the border between what can and cannot be narrated, what is and is not imaginable. To understand the role of *mono no ke* as situated in this explosive interstice, we must examine closely the Fuji-tsubo affair, which, even before it has actually occurred, drives the Yūgao affair.

Insight into these two affairs and their connectedness hinges on the complex issue of time. Since Murasaki Shikibu frequently gives precise dates for much less important events, the mystery at the core of her entire narrative is deliberately reinforced by her conspicuous vagueness about when things happened. Information about the tim-ing of Genji's encounters with Fujitsubo is especially sparse. It seems befitting that details of the incestuous transgression be presented as a riddle of nearly oedipal dimensions. There is, however, general schol-arly agreement that there were at least two intimate "secret meet-ings." In the *Genji* text the first meeting is not described. Instead it is forcefully implied in the description of Fujitsubo's anxiety before the second meeting, which takes place late in the Fourth Month (see S:98; 1:306).

The first meeting had triggered a panic so severe that it may have caused Fujitsubo to suspect conception, plead "illness," and withdraw from court to her family's Sanjō palace. Since in Heian times (and until recently) the term of pregnancy was ten lunar months (280 days) from last menses, she calculated that her child was due in the Twelfth Month. In other words, Fujitsubo convinced herself that she had con-ceived during the first meeting, which must therefore have taken place in the Third Month, before Genji left for the Kitayama retreat toward the end of that month. At the beginning of the second meeting, Fuji-tsubo is terrified of the possible consequences of a discovery of her clandestine encounters with her stepson.[86] She recalls, in a terror exceeding even Yūgao's fears of a repetition of her traumatic past, that something similarly horrible had happened to her before (see S:98; 1:305: *miya mo asamashikarishi o oboshiizuru dani*). It is the terrified Fujitsubo's inability to prevent a second dangerous meeting that brings about the conception she mistakenly assumed to have happened already. Her fearful conviction to the contrary, Fujitsubo cannot have conceived in the Third Month (unless Murasaki Shikibu indulged in an uncharacteristic departure from the known facts of physiology). The medical facts, even considering postmature birth, do not bear out Fujitsubo's initial calculations. In the Sixth Month she quietly announces that she is three months pregnant (see S:99; 1:307). Since she gives birth to a healthy baby (Reizei) either after the tenth day or at the end of the Second Month of the next year (here too the text is tantalizingly ambiguous; see S:138; 1:397 and n. 19), she must have conceived no earlier than the Fourth Month. At some point between her return to court in the Seventh Month and her failure to deliver in the Twelfth Month, Fujitsubo realizes the truth—namely, that she conceived in the Fourth rather than the Third Month.

For Fujitsubo, this realization brings a real fear. What if the Kiritsubo Emperor discovers that he could not have fathered this child? As long as Fujitsubo believed that she conceived at court in the Third Month, she could attribute the child's paternity to the emperor. In the Fourth Month, however, Fujitsubo had retired to her own residence, not returning to court until the Seventh Month.[87] During this period the emperor did not see her at his palace. (Of all Heian men the emperor alone did not visit his women but received them.) In order now not to arouse suspicion Fujitsubo must maintain the fiction of conception in the Third Month. Fujitsubo knows that her pregnancy is within the normal range, but the public is quite naturally concerned about her health when the delivery is, in its eyes, delayed beyond human limits. Popular opinion, which is totally in the dark about Fujitsubo's forbidden affair and her misrepresentation of chronology, attributes the dangerously late delivery to *mono no ke*. Intentionally or not, Fujitsubo contributes to the fiction that the public reads as if it were a text of its own making. The fact that she made the customary announcement of being three months pregnant not from the imperial palace but from her own residence raised eyebrows because of her apparent disregard for the Kiritsubo Emperor's feelings. It triggered the first wave of rumors about *mono no ke* as the cause of Fujitsubo's indisposal and hasty withdrawal from court (see S:99–100; 1:307). The public's original suspicion that something was seriously wrong with Fujitsubo's account is erased through the concept of *mono no ke* and replaced with a false explanation of her distress. A formal report to the emperor only makes him adore Fujitsubo more for her suffering on his behalf. It is perhaps because of his acquiescence that these early rumors of *mono no ke* die down until the critical stage of Fujitsubo's pregnancy is reached.

Genji knows what the emperor and the public do not. For him, the later the delivery the more inescapable the truth that the child was fathered—by him—during their second secret meeting in the Fourth

Month, when Fujitsubo had removed herself from the reach of the emperor. How can he prevent others from coming to the same disastrous conclusion? The fact that Genji orders religious services not in Fujitsubo's delivery room at her Sanjō palace but at various temples proves that he worries more about the discovery of their secret than about Fujitsubo's health.

Although Fujitsubo feels that her death would be appropriate retribution for her sin,[88] she cannot hope to die in childbirth, for such a death would give a political advantage to her female rival Kokiden, who is already gloating behind the screens. Such a death would also, according to Heian beliefs, create a new sin.[89] Why does she not consider the option of entering into a trance and acquiring the charisma of another, disguised as *mono no ke?* Why does Fujitsubo not take up the woman's weapon of spirit possession? Here a comparative analysis with Yūgao's case is instructive. To begin with, Fujitsubo is, unlike Yūgao, neither vulnerable in her social position nor uncertain of her place in Genji's heart. Fujitsubo is Genji's ideal woman. She feels no need to empower herself by seizing the woman's weapon of spirit possession: her complicity in incest is itself a form of empowerment that cancels out the need for *mono no ke.* Unlike Yūgao, she has no grievance. Indeed, she is an active agent in the cuckolding of her unwitting husband; she is neither his nor Genji's nor anyone else's passive victim. After she has overcome her deep fears about the discovery of the transgression against the Kiritsubo Emperor, she accepts responsibility for the affair with Genji—not by revealing the secret of her son's paternity but by containing her despair within herself. She has her own charisma and need not borrow that of another through spirit possession. She is willing to bear the consequences of her excruciatingly passionate and painful love. Moreover, she is never alone even in her darkest moments, for she can trust Genji to share the burden of their love.

After her healthy son is born without the appearance of a single *mono no ke,* the public readily drops the issue of spirit possession as if it had never existed. Fujitsubo and Genji have no reason to be astonished by the failure of *mono no ke* to materialize. They know, after all, that the dreadful rumors were based on ignorance of a truth too horrible for the public to have imagined. If anything, Fujitsubo, inasmuch as she created apprehension about the time of both her conception and delivery, can claim *mono no ke* as her own fabrication. As a weapon, however, the hypothesized *mono no ke* was entirely unnecessary for her.

Nonetheless, not long after her successful childbirth Fujitsubo fears that the infant's resemblance to Genji constitutes a potential threat to her secret. Her anxiety generates a brilliant insight: others may suspect *mono no ke* where she situates her tormented conscience (see S:139; 1:398)—a perception that mirrors in its very terminology Murasaki Shikibu's analysis in her poetry collection (*Murasaki Shikibu shū* 44–45) of *mono no ke* as the projection of demons in the heart *(kokoro no oni)*. Fujitsubo knows that the conscious recognition of one's own demons eliminates the tendency to project them onto others defined as *mono no ke*.

After the affair, Fujitsubo's most difficult problem is to guard the dark secret of her son's paternity. She can derive some comfort from the fact that Genji shares the responsibility for keeping the secret. Still, she must, like Genji, live a lie. For this shadow on her radiance she later atones by taking religious vows, at a politically opportune time, after her son's political future has been secured and the Kiritsubo Emperor has died. Ironically, these events in turn propel Genji, now twenty-four, to renew their passionate affair, but transgression has lost most of its earlier thrill. Nonetheless, this last encounter, precipitating as it does Fujitsubo's religious vows, is intensely moving despite the fact that Genji's pathetically absurd, even clownish, fumbling is narrated in embarrassing detail (see S:195–198; 2:99–105). In her handling of tabooed relations Fujitsubo invites comparison with Utsusemi, who, at the mere threat of her true stepson's advances, takes the tonsure. Although Utsusemi played it safe where Fujitsubo did not, one's admiration of Utsusemi's moral resolve cannot match the undefinable but profoundly moving emotions *(aware)* evoked by Fujitsubo's transgression.

There is, in short, something that sets Fujitsubo apart. Not only is she Genji's ideal; his longing for his lost mother comes to fruition in Fujitsubo, the only "original substitute" among his women.[90] She can reside in a privileged zone free of *mono no ke* because she alone among all the women in the *Genji* seems to achieve at least a measure of control over her own life. All she has to do is to protect her secret. In her control over what can and cannot be told—*mono no ke* territory—she commands an almost authorial authority. Despite her fears of discovery, she is able to keep her dark secret until she dies. Within the constraints of a male-dominated polygynous society, she attains a degree of autonomy that is equaled only by Ukifune, the last *Genji* heroine, who must first lay down the woman's weapon of spirit possession before she can

obtain a similar grasp on her fate. Meanwhile, at the beginning of
Murasaki Shikibu's narrative stands Yūgao, the woman who prefigures
Fujitsubo in both her mysterious attraction and her most vulnerable
points. Yūgao's brave attempt to wield the weapon of spirit possession
is a remarkable achievement, but her fleeting moment of triumph ends
in death. For Fujitsubo to become a woman made of flesh and blood
and still remain Genji's ideal, Yūgao must first be sacrificed.


## Theories

A frequent critical response to the psychological complexity of the
"Yūgao" chapter has been to treat the text as a detective story (*suiri
shōsetsu*) in which the discovery of a culprit automatically exonerates all
the other suspects.[91] For centuries a debate has raged about the identity of this culprit. Among the various theories, two have been especially prominent.[92] The first, known as the *"Rokujō Miyasudokoro no rei
setsu,"* holds that Rokujō's living spirit *(ikisudama)* is Yūgao's possessing spirit. This tradition can be traced back to Ichijō Kanera's (1402–
1481) *Kachō yojō* (Aesthetic Impressions; 1472) and Sanjōnishi
Kin'eda's (1487–1563) *Sairyūshō* (Small Stream Notes; 1528).[93] Some
proponents of this theory have been quite dogmatic.

If Yūgao's possessing spirit is not Rokujō's living spirit, maintains
Taya Raishun, the chapter is "chaotic" *(shiri metsuretsu)* and the
revered author of the *Genji monogatari* must be seen as "clumsy" *(se-
tsuretsu).*[94] The Rokujō theory is well represented in the West, albeit
without Taya's cocksureness. Arthur Waley, Ivan Morris, Edwin A.
Cranston, Earl Miner, and Richard Bowring form an impressive group
of critics who subscribe to it without much comment.[95] A new generation of critics is more hesitant. Haruo Shirane refuses to take sides,[96]
and Norma Field seems to want to have it both ways. Field is strongly
drawn to the Rokujō theory because it "seems inefficient and uneco-
nomical not to identify this murderous spirit with the Rokujō Lady."[97]
Yet for reasons of "aesthetic tact," Field, following Saigō Nobutsuna's
argument, prefers not to tarnish the image of a sophisticated woman
with accusations of murder.[98] In the end, Field concludes that the
"Rokujō Lady-like spirit" remains "unidentified" because of Yūgao's
relatively low status.[99] In Field's judgment, Yūgao simply does not
belong in the same category as Rokujō's other targets: Aoi, Murasaki,
and the Third Princess.

In sum, although Murasaki Shikibu never names the possessing spirit, most critics have identified Genji's hallucination of an "exceedingly beautiful woman" as Rokujō. To single out Rokujō, "whose sense of rivalry" (S:166; 2:27) becomes a serious threat only in the second possession case,[100] is, however, to limit unnecessarily the sources of Genji's unease. If we consider the state of Genji's mind as he wrestles with a number of conflicting emotions, as I have done in some detail, we can see the vision as a projection of Genji's troubled psyche, a collective image, a composite of his betrayed women. Takahashi Tōru approaches this conclusion when he argues that the *mono no ke* others have perceived as Rokujō actually represents the "dark side" of Genji's love for Fujitsubo and the decadence of imperial rule *(ōken no yami)*.[101] While this interpretation is an improvement on the theories blaming Rokujō alone, it ignores altogether Yūgao's desperate contribution to the tragedy that culminates in her possession and death.

The second major theory shifts the focus from actors to the scene of the action. This theory, known as the *"Kawara-in densetsu,"* is based on the legendary encounter of 926 between the ghost of Minamoto Tōru and Retired Emperor Uda. In modern *Genji* scholarship this latter theory seems to be favored by Japanese critics.[102] Adherents of this tradition argue on the basis of Genji's interpretation of his second dream vision of the ghostly beauty that the spirit of the deserted villa must have been responsible for Yūgao's possession and death. Although originally based on a specific legend, the *Kawara-in densetsu* refers more generally to the rich lore about haunted houses and murderous demons. Proponents of this approach have assiduously mined literary sources of folk beliefs such as the *Nihon ryōiki, Ise monogatari, Konjaku monogatari-shū,* and *Uji shūi monogatari*.[103] As one Jungian critic has argued, the Kawara-in is meant as a generic setting for Minamoto Tōru's angry spirit, a prominent part of the Heian collective unconscious.[104]

There is certainly some support in the text for the Kawara-in theory. Waley and Seidensticker both translate the "fleeting dream" passage at the end of the "Yūgao" chapter in a way that emphasizes the shift from Yūgao to Genji: "He was dismayed at the thought that some demon which haunted the desolate spot might on the occasion when it did that terrible thing, also have entered into him and possessed him" (W:79–80); "he concluded, and the thought filled him with horror, that he had attracted the attention of an evil spirit haunting the neglected villa" (S:83; 1:267). The passage suggests that Genji, while beginning to acknowledge his responsibility for

Yūgao's death by causally connecting it to his haunted villa, indulges in self-pity as he portrays himself as a secondary victim of the tragic incident.

The parallels between the Kawara-in legend and Yūgao's demise at the villa are, however, quite imperfect. Tōru is often considered as one of the literary models for Genji, yet the legendary Minister of the Left corresponds in the Yūgao episode not to Genji but to the *mono no ke* that Genji perceived in his dream to be a woman,[105] and then a fox or other demons, and finally, as if to close the circular argument, the spirit of the villa itself.[106] If the *Kawara-in densetsu* is to make sense in terms of the plot, Genji ought to play the role of the Retired Emperor Uda, whose intercession saved his beloved; but Genji fails where Uda succeeded. Furthermore, Kurosu has recently argued that Yūgao's *mono no ke* must be a dead spirit *(shiryō)*; it therefore cannot be Rokujō's or Tō no Chūjō's principal wife's. Kurosu believes that a dead spirit, unlike a living spirit, does harm at the request of the person who wants to send a curse.[107] In addition, it is important to note that Genji, who is otherwise given to comments on literature and legend, does not make any explicit reference to the *Kawara-in densetsu* at the height of his crisis over Yūgao. The closest he comes to the allusive reference is at the end of the chapter, just after the last rites for his departed love, when he has his "fleeting dream" of the beauty he saw earlier at Yūgao's side.[108]

Both the Rokujō theory and the Kawara-in theory seem flawed, but another critical tradition, that of Hagiwara Hiromichi (1813–1863), has attempted a compromise. In his *Genji monogatari hyōshaku* (Annotated *Genji*; 1861), Hiromichi sought to refute the persistent notion that Rokujō's spirit is Yūgao's *mono no ke*. He proposed instead that the mysterious beauty in Genji's dreams reflects Rokujō's shadow on Genji's conscience, which is then darkened further by the evil spirit of the villa.[109] Hiromichi's compromise theory has led some modern critics, like Fujii Sadakazu and Hirokawa Katsumi, to develop innovative variants by drawing on folk beliefs about angry spirits *(onryō)*. Although it must be remembered that the actual location and name of "a certain villa" *(nanigashi no in)* are never revealed,[110] there have been speculations since Yotsutsuji Yoshinari's *Kakaishō* (Rivers into Ocean Notes; 1364), a *Genji* commentary, that the villa stood on the site of the Kawara-in and was later rebuilt as Genji's Rokujō-in. Hirokawa further argues that the sites of the Kawara-in and Rokujō watari,[111] with which Rokujō no miyasudokoro is closely associated, are interchangeable.[112] Fujii's contribution is to see Rokujō's spirit as expressing not her individual jealousy but rather her family's grudge.[113] Her late husband, Crown Prince Zenbō, was either deposed or failed for some other reason to become emperor. Her father, disappointed in not having a grandson to become emperor, died unfulfilled in his ambitions to see at least his daughter become empress. To pacify their angry spirits, the Rokujō lineage's living and dead spirits roam restlessly, disguised as *mono no ke*. Genji later builds the Rokujō-in not only to pacify these *onryō* on Rokujō's behalf but also to oppose the court.[114] After all, Minamoto Tōru's failure to become emperor serves as the historical model for Crown Prince Zenbō no less than for Genji himself.[115] In this way, the Kawara-in, Rokujō watari, and *"nanigashi no in"* combine to symbolize frustrated ambitions and lost splendor. Thus Genji, in the effort to reconstruct the magnificence of the past, builds the Rokujō-in on the site of dark historical and personal memories.

In none of these three theories, or clusters of theories, has Yūgao's perspective received more than minimal critical reflection. In other words, few critics have asked how the situation expresses Yūgao's conflict. She had sacrificed her unhappy existence as Tō no Chūjō's concubine for the unhappy but independent life of a homeless wanderer. Genji, however, soon catches her in his snares and forces her back into the traditional Heian female role. She had escaped from the threats of Tō no Chūjō's principal wife Shi no kimi, but she cannot so easily extricate herself from the villa's weedy labyrinth.[116] Her installation there must be classified as an abduction that puts an end to her autonomy. She is Genji's prisoner of love.[117] Her last option is to abandon herself to a place rife with an atmosphere of frustration and death in order to roam the "empty skies" (S:69; 1:234). None of these aspects of her story is taken seriously into consideration by theories that focus only on Genji and his concerns and his susceptibility to the spirit of the place. The critical debate has never included the possibility that Yūgao's possession is an expression of *her* desperation as well as the outcome of Genji's transgressions. In other words, critics have not asked if the spirit that possesses her might not be a separate *mono* from the "exceedingly beautiful woman" whose sudden appearance activates Genji's guilty conscience and speculations. Who the possessing spirit was meant to be from Yūgao's perspective—as a woman fearing others, seeking an ally, trying desperately to shake her lover from his complacency—we cannot know. One is tempted to conclude with some chagrin that not only Genji and Yūgao but also the *mono no ke* is incognito. As such, it points to the uncanny. The concept of *mono no ke* expresses the woman's bold reappropriation of self-determination through the construction of a dream self.

### Yūgao in the *nō*

Yūgao's spirit possession is reflected not only in *Genji* paintings (*Genji-e*), as shown at the beginning of this chapter, but also in *nō* drama created four to five hundred years after the *Genji monogatari*. In this form of theater, a priest in the role of *waki*, or secondary actor, usually encounters the *shite*, or principal actor, who appears first in disguise and then in his or her true form.[118] The transformation is brought about by the *waki*'s questions, sometimes reinforced by professional exorcists who help reveal the *shite*'s identity and bring him or her to confession. The true self is often the spirit of an aggrieved dead person who sheds all grief, resentment, or lingering attachment in a dance intriguingly like the trance of spirit possession. In fact, *nō* drama—especially the category of "two-part dream *nō*" (*fukushiki mugen nō*)—has many affinities, structurally and thematically, to the phenomenon of spirit possession.

Zeami (Kanze Motokiyo, 1363–1443), the most eloquent theorist of *nō*, stressed the importance of spirit possession scenes from *Genji* as an "elegant source" for *nō* playwrights: "In addition to the ineffable beauty of such court ladies visually, Lady Rokujō's possession of Lady Aoi, Yūgao's possession by an evil spirit, and the spirit haunting Ukifune provide an elegant source, while at the same time serving as a means for creating the high point in a play. One rarely comes upon such a valuable source."[119]

There are two *nō* plays based on Yūgao's story: *Hajitomi* by Naitō Tōzaemon (n. d.) and *Yūgao*, attributed to Zeami himself.[120] It must be remembered that *Genji* themes in painting, linked verse, or *nō* do not precisely reflect the *Genji monogatari*, which by the Muromachi period (1336–1573) had become inaccessible except to specialists. Not unlike *Genji* illustrators and enthusiastic *renga* poets, the *nō* playwrights "read" the *Genji* by means of manuals and digests originally designed to establish a *Genji* iconography and help *renga* poets with the art of literary allusion.[121] At times the discrepancy between the *Genji* and a corresponding *nō* play can be radical. Zeami's *Yūgao*, for instance, dramatizes the heroine's "attachment to the villa" as an impediment to her religious enlightenment.[122] In each play, the spirit of the dead Yūgao appears to the *waki* at the site of its most intensely passionate attachment. In *Yūgao*, the original spirit possession is especially prominent as it eerily passes through the filter of the *shite*'s posthumous memory. In both plays, Yūgao's spirit overcomes the worldly attachments, and the old resentments, that are the obstacles to final enlightenment.

Between the *Genji* and the *nō* plays, the emphasis has shifted from Genji to Yūgao—from spirit possession as present-tense experience to the transcendental (that is, posthumous) memory of spirit possession. In an important change of perspective, neither *Yūgao* nor *Hajitomi* dramatizes the possession as it was seen through Genji's eyes.[123] Unless one wanted to associate him with the *waki*, Genji is significantly absent from the *nō* stage as a distinct character. The main viewpoint is Yūgao's.

Despite the shift in emphasis from Genji to Yūgao in *nō*, the basic construct in these two plays is similar to Genji's consecutive dream visitations by the spectral beauty before and after Yūgao's death. If we take advantage of the structural affinity of *nō* and spirit possession, we can see the *monogatari* in a new light. We can interpret Genji's first vision as the equivalent of an encounter with a *maeshite*, a spirit in disguise. In the absence of an exorcist ritual, his multiplying speculations are never confirmed, and the spirit does not—or cannot—reveal its identity. The cathartic moment is postponed until the proper rituals for Yūgao's dead spirit have been performed. Yet in his second dream, corresponding to the self-revelatory appearance of the *nochishite* in *nō*, Genji still does not see what he wishes to see—namely, the Yūgao he knew when she was alive. He encounters an abstraction of her dead body at Toribeno, but, still traumatized, he is unable to understand clearly the meaning of this vision. His instant waking speculation about an evil spirit at the villa functions merely to transpose the intensely personal vision into the impersonal realm of legend and folk belief associated with harmful spirits haunting deserted houses. This diversionary technique helps to relieve Genji of the task of questioning the identity of the beauty and her relation to him. The Genji of the *monogatari* stops short of the enlightenment achieved by Yūgao at the end of the two *nō* dramas that carry her story to a religious resolution.

# Aoi

LESS MYSTERIOUS than Yūgao's case of spirit possession, but by no means less complex, is the possession of Genji's principal wife, Aoi.[1] Whereas the first case is seen mostly through Genji's eyes, the second is perceived through the various perspectives of the possessed, the alleged possessor, the most immediate witness, the medium, the exorcists, and the audience at large. Whereas Yūgao's possession is private and brief, Aoi's prolonged state of mental dissociation is recognized as a public affair. Even the Retired Kiritsubo Emperor expresses great concern for his favorite son's wife. Indeed, of all the possession cases dramatized in the *Genji monogatari,* this is the most detailed—approaching the scope of an anthropological case study. Because of the exceptionally elaborate and subtle portrayal of Rokujō's reaction to the rumors of her implication in Aoi's possession, this case has greatly influenced the critics' understanding of Rokujō as the possessing spirit in this and other incidents of possession in the *Genji.*

As in any case study, causal relationships and the various perspectives of all the major participants must be carefully examined. When we are introduced to her, Aoi seems secure in her status as Genji's principal wife (fig. 2 in App. B). She is the daughter of the powerful Minister of the Left and Ōmiya, a first-generation princess *(nai-shinnō).* Since Ōmiya is the younger sister of Genji's father, the Kiritsubo Emperor, the arranged match between Aoi and Genji was clearly intended to strengthen both parties. Although first-cousin marriages were desirable as political alliances, they were entirely unsuited to generate the romance characteristic of Heian narrative. It has frequently been noted that the Aoi–Genji relationship is "emotionally impoverished."[2] A "cold intellectual" (S:608; 4:200), Aoi intimidates rather than encourages her young husband. Indeed,

Genji's immaturity repels her. And yet the carriage quarrel on the Day of Lustration *(gokei no hi)* of the Kamo Priestess *(saiin)* proves that, for all her aloofness in her quarters, she desperately needs a public demonstration of his loyalty and respect.[3] Unlike Rokujō's jealousy, Aoi's discontent is associated less with sexual possessiveness than with status anxiety.[4] She is less secure than she seems.

At the beginning of the "Aoi" (S: "Heartvine") chapter, the twenty-two-year-old Genji is dividing his time among a growing number of women, the most important of whom is now Rokujō. She, like Aoi, is the daughter of a powerful minister, but she is related to the imperial house merely as an affine (fig. 2 in App. B). Her marriage to Crown Prince Zenbō failed to blossom into imperial status because of his unfortunate political career and premature death. After the death of her husband and her father, she was left behind with her daughter (Akikonomu). Genji was attracted to this proud and ambitious widow, but his amorous interest vanished after his successful seduction of her, just before the Yūgao affair. One reason for his sudden loss of interest in Rokujō may be precisely what dulled his interest in Aoi, namely, his father's interference. Because Genji feels pressured to give support to Rokujō, perhaps even by marrying her, he begins to shun her. He has no desire to complicate relations with Aoi by calling her attention to a glamorous and forceful rival. His caution goes for naught when Rokujō's presence at the Day of Lustration procession precipitates the famous carriage quarrel *(kuruma arasoi)*.

## The Carriage Quarrel

To understand the carriage quarrel and its relation to the spirit possession that follows, it is helpful to look closely at Genji's, Aoi's, and Rokujō's frames of mind in the period before the quarrel. How do their mental states illuminate the outbreak of animosities? In the four chapters preceding the crucial "Aoi" chapter, Aoi feels mounting resentment occasioned by rumors of her young husband's growing number of mistresses. Having been designated "the first lady in his life" (S:135; 1:388) at the time of her arranged marriage to the twelve-year-old bridegroom, she is aware, after almost a decade of marriage, that her status as *kita no kata* has been strengthened neither by the power of romance nor by the birth of an heir (although she is, at last, pregnant). Genji is hardly less dissatisfied, but he is infinitely freer to seek his happiness elsewhere. Aoi's father and brother occasionally rebuke Genji for his neglect of her, but they both adore Genji and cannot bring themselves to be severe with him. Even the Kiri-tsubo Emperor, who is afraid that Genji may have insulted his in-laws, expresses sympathy for his son. Clearly, most of the blame for the lack of passion in this arranged marriage rests on Aoi. No attempt is made by the other characters to explain, let alone excuse, her sullenness, remoteness, and jealousy as the results of a mismatch that has left the couple "completely at cross purposes" (S:138; 1:395).

Genji handles marital strife by acting defensively. Sensing that the wrath of a principal wife can be formidable, he warns his newest love, young Murasaki, of Aoi's jealousy.[5] This warning demonstrates Genji's sensitivity to the small but significant age difference between him and his older wife, who can be assumed to resent the budding charms of a girl on the verge of womanhood. Painfully ironic from Aoi's perspec-tive is the fact that Genji is attracted to women even older than she is. When criticized by his in-laws for his eagerness to visit Fujitsubo, who is about two years older than Aoi, he self-righteously blames his wife for not directly discussing these rumors with him. "If she had com-plained to him openly, as most women would have done, he might have told her everything, and no doubt eased her jealousy. It was her arbitrary judgments that sent him wandering" (S:135; 1:388). He cannot imagine her humiliation, indeed the "terrifying sense of anni-hilation" caused by jealousy,[6] were she to voice such complaints. It is apparent from Genji's comment that "most women" did indeed suffer from neglect, but they were culturally conditioned to endure the pangs of jealousy silently. The prouder the woman—and Aoi is very proud—the more humiliating the suggestion that she confess her jeal-ousy to her husband.

In the crucial "Aoi" chapter, the focus shifts from Genji's relations with Aoi to the resumption of his tense and somewhat soured affair with Rokujō. Despite her different role, Rokujō—like Aoi—withdraws in hurt response to the Shining Prince's youthful desire for a number of simultaneous affairs. In introverted and extroverted manifestations of aggression, Aoi withdraws spiritually and emotionally while Rokujō threatens to withdraw physically as soon as her daughter is appointed high priestess *(saigū)* of the Ise Shrine. "No longer trusting Genji's affections, the Rokujō lady had been thinking that, making the girl's youth her excuse, she too would go to Ise" (S:158; 2:12). Her resolve is not only historically unprecedented[7] but as startling as Yūgao's deci-sion to leave Tō no Chūjō with their daughter and as unexpected as

Fujitsubo's withdrawal from court to her own residence after her first secret meeting with Genji.

As if his mounting emotional problems with Aoi and Rokujō were not enough, Genji's political vulnerability increases when his father, the Kiritsubo Emperor, abdicates and power is transferred into the hands of the Kokiden faction, archenemies of Genji's late mother Kiritsubo.[8] To make matters worse, his father, now retired, expects Genji to assume the guardianship of the crown prince, Genji's illegitimate son by his stepmother Fujitsubo. Genji admits to himself that his behavior toward Rokujō has been "a scandal" (S:159; 2:13), but he shudders even more at the thought of his father's discovery of the forbidden affair with Fujitsubo. Genji's worries over his other women— such as his cousin Asagao and his pregnant wife—seem ordinary by comparison.

The carriage quarrel, which initiates open hostilities between Aoi and Rokujō, occurs on the Day of Lustration before the Kamo Festival. In Heian times, the celebrants' ox-drawn carriages were important status symbols, and the drovers were anxious to avoid mishaps during their torturously slow movement. Reserving space for the carriages at the site of the festival required much scheming in advance. Brawls among menservants of different parties were a common sight and are often featured in illustrations and paintings (Plate 2.3). One important literary forerunner of the *Genji monogatari,* the *Ochikubo monogatari* (The Tale of the Lower Room; ca. 980), describes graphically two carriage quarrels that are designed unambiguously to humiliate to the utmost the wicked stepmother of the beautiful, compassionate, forgiving—in short, the flawless—heroine.[9] By contrast, the far more subtle conflict between Aoi and Rokujō is not a simple allegory of the struggle between Good and Evil. Neither party sets out self-righteously intending to "slay" the other, as happens in the *Ochikubo monogatari.* The *Genji*'s carriage quarrel is more subtle and complex because Murasaki Shikibu allows her readers to become aware of the ambivalences, misgivings, grievances, and unacknowledged fears of both women, neither of whom is consciously malicious or completely innocent.

Rokujō goes to the festival to "forget her unhappiness" (S:160; 2:16), but her self-administered therapy is made ineffective by the behavior of others and by her inability to overlook a slight: "[Genji] passed without stopping his horse or looking her way; and the unhappiness was greater than if she had stayed at home" (S:161; 2:17). Her first reaction is to feel "utterly defeated" (S:161; 2:18). Aoi, for her part, has been ambivalent from the start of the day. Her pregnancy leaves her with little desire to attend the festivities, but she capitulates to pressure from her women and her mother. The most significant factor in Aoi's reluctance may be her unspoken fear of confronting her rivals. Just such a situation arises: while it is Aoi's menservants who are responsible for blocking Rokujō's view and entrapping her carriage, and the rudeness is properly blamed on them, it is Aoi who worsens the situation by not calling her men to order: "It was under her influence that the men in her service flung themselves so violently about" (S:163; 2:20–21). And when respectfully greeted by her Shining Prince, Aoi is gratified by a victory over Rokujō.

While Aoi first savors her triumph and then awakens to its illusory nature, Rokujō comes to see in her humiliation something less than total failure. Albeit slow as the axle of an ox-drawn carriage, the wheels of fortune are about to turn, but with no happy issue for anyone. This outcome echoes both women's initial ambivalence and premonitions about attending the festival. Clearly, it is a simplification to declare one of them a winner and the other a loser in the contest of carriages. Rokujō's defeat is as inconclusive as Aoi's triumph.

In fact, Aoi pays dearly for Genji's public recognition of her status as his principal wife: "He was sorry for the Rokujō lady and angry at his wife" (S:163; 2:20). His unsuccessful attempt to mollify the hurt Rokujō initiates an interlude within the narrative, as though the author wanted to distract him, and us, from his intractable troubles. These brief digressive scenes involve three women: Asagao, who is known for her restraint and who stands in sharp contrast to the choleric chief contenders; young Murasaki, who drives Genji to distraction with her abundant hair, the traditional marker of youthful vitality; and old Naishi (Gen no naishi), whose unbecoming forwardness is mitigated by her cleverness and wit. These more or less amusing episodes increase the suspense. The three main protagonists have yet to resolve the issues that are the crux of the carriage quarrel. The stage is set for the climax of the drama.

## Spirit Possession

The first to show symptoms of severe psychic distress is Rokujō. Having earlier declined to see Genji—using the pretense of her daughter's sacred mission—at last she relents and discusses with him whether she should go into self-imposed "exile" at Ise or remain behind and expose herself to further scandal. In her state of unrelieved "anger" and "indecision," she falls "physically ill" (S:165; 2:25). She is unable to respond positively to Genji's conciliatory gestures, obsessed as she is with the unforgivable "violence" done her, ironically, at the "river of lustration" (S:165; 2:25).

Aoi too shows signs of emotional disturbance—weeping "in loud wailing sobs" and feeling "tormented by nausea and shortness of breath" (S:165; 2:26–27). It is a time of great anxiety because a pregnant woman, after her fifth month, was in a state of defilement *(kegare)* and liable to pollute others with the blood of a miscarriage, stillbirth, or regular delivery. If she died in pregnancy or in childbirth, she carried a heavy burden of sin *(tsumi)* and acquired adverse karma for the next life.[10] These beliefs cause much speculation at court about Aoi's pain. The weakening effect of pregnancy is thought to make her especially susceptible to psychic influences. And these are surmised to be, without exception, various spirits *(mono no ke; ikisudama)*, some malign and others not. Exorcists *(genza)* go to work. While they succeed in transferring most of these troublesome spirits to a medium *(yorimashi)*, one of the *mono no ke* continues to bother Aoi. Everyone assumes that this spirit's motive is jealousy. Hence a meticulous and systematic search is directed to find the jealous woman: "The Sanjō people went over the list of Genji's ladies one by one" (S:165; 2:26). They conclude that the stubborn malign spirit must be either Rokujō or young Murasaki, for "no doubt they were jealous" (S:165; 2:26: *urami*). Thanks to the presumed innocence of her youth, Murasaki is, by common consent, tacitly eliminated as a possible assailant. By acting as interpreter, Aoi's social circle participates not only in the identification of the spirit but also in the explanation of motives.

The reason for narrowing the focus to Rokujō as the culprit is the carriage quarrel. This distasteful event, still vivid in public consciousness, has transformed a mere "sense of rivalry" (S:166; 2:27) into excessive emotions quite beyond rational control.[11] Genji feels once again compelled to soothe Rokujō's anger. For selfish reasons, he would rather not see her isolated from courtly activities and immersed in the ascetic Buddhist rites she is now conducting—at a ritually safe distance from her daughter's purified Shinto residence—to exonerate her from the charges of possessing Aoi. He is touchingly sympathetic: "He knew why she was unwell, and pitied her" (S:166; 2:28). That he comes to spend the night with her despite his wife's severe condition raises new hopes in Rokujō's heart that are, however, shattered at the moment of his leavetaking. Thus Genji's intention of pacifying Rokujō and making amends for the wrong done by his wife backfires: the discrepancy between Rokujō's desire for Genji and her disappointment in him increases the emotional tension.

In perfect unison with Aoi's steady approach to the dramatic climax of spirit possession, Rokujō agonizes over her lack of self-control. In the imagery of self-estrangement, she is, literally, beside herself: she is "not at all herself" (S:166; 2:27). Rumors have reached her that the responsibility for Aoi's suffering lies either with her—Rokujō's *living* spirit—or with the dead spirit of her father come to avenge his daughter. In the highly self-reflexive form of an interior monologue, she searches her conscience for signs of her possible culpability in Aoi's possession by a malign spirit. Sorrowfully, she interrogates herself, considering the possible truth of the devastating allegations: "Might it be that the soul of one so lost in sad thoughts went wandering off by itself?" (S:167; 2:29–30). At this point, although not possessed, she is, in anthropological terms, approaching a state complementary to spirit possession, namely, "introspective witchcraft."[12] Her defensive rationalization in response to these thoughts of possible culpability is that her conscious purpose is not to harm Aoi but merely to use her rival as a way to get at her real tormentor, Genji.

This rationalization does not save her from repeated nightmares in which she encounters her own spectral being. As a cultured and sophisticated woman, she recoils in horror at the *Traumbild* of herself as an uninhibited virago: in her dreams "she would push and shake the lady [Aoi], and flail at her blindly and savagely. It was too terrible" (S:167; 2:30). Rokujō's plight is not unlike that of a prophet who foresees his fate but is helpless to alter it. As a consequence of her inability not to feel like an angry "hateful" (S:167; 2:30) spirit, she fears that her reputation will be still further tarnished by the impact of more unpleasant rumors: "She would be notorious" (S:167; 2:30). She is caught in a vicious circle that is defined by the futile attempt to cure herself—she realizes that even in attempting to forget Genji, the ultimate cause of her conflict with Aoi, she has him very much on her mind: "She must think no more about the man who had been so cruel to her. But so to think was, after all, to think" (S:167; 2:31). It is the disparity between her usual willpower and her present inability to act and be effective that makes Rokujō such a tragic figure—the embodiment of mystery and profound depth *(yūgen)*.[13] It is symptomatic of her total absorption in rumors and nightmarish thoughts that Rokujō loses sight of her daughter's urgent religious preparations for her departure for Ise in the Ninth Month.

At this point in Rokujō's state of mental paralysis, Aoi, still possessed, goes into premature labor. Genji is summoned to her bedside according to the possessing spirit's wishes (Plate 1.5). As he takes pains to comfort his wife, she seems strangely altered: "Usually so haughty and forbidding, she now gazed up at him with languid eyes that were presently filled with tears" (S:168; 2:32–33). The tone of her voice has changed as well. Most eerie, however, is the effect on Genji of hearing his usually unpoetic wife recite a *waka*. That she had previously been poetically reticent was understandable because she had not experienced the kind of romantic courtship in which *waka* were invariably exchanged after *kaimami*. That she now speaks poetry convinces Genji that the voice he hears is actually someone else's.

In truth, Aoi's crisis reveals that she may not be cold and unpoetic. She has, after all, been trapped in an arranged marriage that has left her emotionally unsatisfied. Her unexpected pregnancy is evidence that she was not totally neglected by her errant husband, but it is doubtful that Genji fulfilled more than his duty by having sexual intercourse with her. Moreover, to her it must have seemed an abrupt physical invasion that was not preceded by *kaimami*. Nonetheless, is it not possible that the sudden change in her physical condition is accompanied by an unexpected flickering of repressed passion and poetic sensibility? As if in passing, Norma Field has suggested that although "the Rokujō's Lady's spirit is speaking through Aoi's person, [the poem might be] read as Aoi's."[14] Critics have not pursued this intriguing possibility because Genji's perception of his women tends to prevail even beyond the boundaries of the *monogatari*—and Genji, stubbornly refusing to concede positive character traits to Aoi,[15] believes that the voice must be somebody else's. His inflexibility is particularly ironic since he himself deserves some credit for the change wrought in Aoi. After all, it is the pregnancy that triggers the spirit possession that releases her latent emotions.

Since traditionally *mono no ke* and *waka* represent the apparently irreconcilable opposites of aggression and love, and are therefore difficult to imagine in conjunction, the *mono no ke*'s *waka* deserves close scrutiny.[16] The voice coming directly from Aoi, rather than through a medium, recites these words (2:33; my translation):

| *nageki wabi* | cries of sorrow |
| *sora ni midaruru* | errant in the sky: |
| *waga tama o* | my spirit— |
| *musubi todomeyo* | secure it inside |
| *shitagai no tsuma* | the hem of my robe |

If one interprets the *waka* as most readers have, as emanating from Rokujō's living spirit, then it appears that awareness of her female passion has driven the tearfully depressed Rokujō to appeal to her neglectful lover to catch her errant "soul" (S:168; 2:33: *tama*) and keep it from wandering the skies and straying into her female rival's body. The crucial words seem to be the last. *"Tsuma"* is a homonym for "robe" and "spouse." The robe imagery, based on the folk belief that errant spirits can be summoned back by tying the inside hem of a robe, is entirely appropriate. Yet it is Aoi, not Rokujō, who has the tied hem (Plate 1.5). Since the possession primarily expresses Aoi's state of dissociation, the *waka* demonstrates Aoi's anxiety about losing control over her own spirit. But matters are complicated by the fact that Aoi herself is responsible for incorporating Rokujō as a factor in her marital crisis, first at the carriage quarrel and then during child labor. Thus most readers, sympathizing with Genji, follow his biased perspective inspired by his fear of Rokujō's vengeance and his complicity in Aoi's endangered pregnancy. Although it is certainly to Genji's advantage to see the possession scene exclusively as an expression of the jealous Rokujō's wandering living spirit, his male viewpoint does not do justice to the female perspective.

Reading *"tsuma"* as "spouse" introduces an additional ambiguity. Since *"shitagai"* refers to the "corner of the *inner* hem" (my emphasis), some have interpreted the "spouse" to be a "secret . . . husband."[17] Such a reading, by identifying Rokujō rather than Aoi as the speaker of the poem, hinders us from imagining that Aoi is referring to her own robe and to her acknowledged husband, in which case *"shitagai no tsuma"* might then refer to Aoi in her self-denigration as Genji's largely invisible female spouse.[18]

The rare *waka* associated with *mono no ke*, however, represent not merely one voice, as is usual in *waka* discourse, but two voices in one. Since Aoi has adopted Rokujō's voice, the words can be read overtly as Rokujō's and covertly as Aoi's. After all, it is Aoi who expresses herself through spirit possession; Rokujō merely reacts to the notion of her implication. Yet Genji, convinced that the *mono no ke* is

Rokujō, the woman most famous for her *waka,* hears her voice and fails to hear Aoi's.

Like members of a theater audience who recognize the role an actor is playing by the familiar actor's altered appearance, Genji correctly identifies Rokujō as Aoi's possessing spirit: "It was not Aoi's voice, nor was the manner hers. Extraordinary—and then he knew that it was the voice of the Rokujō lady" (S:168; 2:34). Yet Genji's recognition is limited. Satisfied to attribute the possessing spirit to Rokujō, he fails to ask what motivates Aoi's role playing. In short, Genji sees the possessing spirit as an antagonistic force hostile to the victim rather than seeing possessor and possessed as complementary social actors.[19]

As the formerly alienated husband is drawn into the spectacle of spirit possession, birth, and death, he is first of all terrified by encountering his wife and his mistress in one body, one voice. In their "striving toward fusion with powerful fantasy figures,"[20] Aoi and Rokujō have—in the ecstatic state of possession—each managed to merge with her worst rival in love who becomes, ironically, her best ally in revenge. When Aoi speaks to Genji in the voice of her enemy, she is appropriating a power and charm that she herself does not possess. The possessing spirit (Rokujō) is the possessed person's (Aoi's) "mystical power, or 'charisma.' "[21] At the same time, Rokujō, perceived to usurp the body of the woman who humiliated her physically by pushing her aside during the carriage quarrel, achieves an impressive supernatural presence.

Finally, the identification of the spirit is made not by the noisy incantations of the swarming band of exorcists, even though they congratulate themselves undeservedly "as they mopped their foreheads" (S:169; 2:35). It is made by Genji. Unlike the exorcists, attendants, and other family members, he is an immediate witness of Aoi's transformed appearance. He is drawn into the innermost circle of Aoi's possession. Whereas the more distant bystanders assume the possessed to be a blameless victim—just as they assume the possessor to be an involuntary aggressor—Genji's closeness to the event places him in all of its emotional crosscurrents.[22] He feels not only intimately addressed but appealed to by the raving woman. In no position to analyze coolly the drama he has been drawn into, he is pulled toward and yet instinctively shies away from Aoi's enigmatic performance. Thus he comes tantalizingly close and yet fails to probe to the core of spirit possession. Whether inhibited by despair or by self-defense, Genji senses rather than understands the aggressiveness of the possessed. Finally, the obliqueness of spirit possession eludes him.

What unites Rokujō and Aoi in spirit possession is aggression—revengeful on Rokujō's part, defensive on Aoi's. An unexamined use of the term "jealousy" obscures rather than differentiates among the very complex emotions that make carriages clash and then—through spirit possession—weld together two seemingly irreconcilable personalities. If we attend equally to everyone involved and to the dynamics of interaction, we realize that aggression (on the part of both the possessing spirit and the possessed) and remorse (on the part of the witness) emerge as the two conflicting emotional forces of spirit possession.[23] What begins as a physically violent women's quarrel is transformed into an esoteric spiritual rite in which the psychologically allied women vent their repressed anger at a third party—Genji—and at the polygynous society that allows men to neglect their women with near impunity.

What are we to make of the notion that the spirit of a living person (Rokujō) has detached itself from its body and entered that of another person (Aoi)? In a thorough study of Heian literature, Fujimoto Katsuyoshi has found no precedent for possession by living spirits *(ikisudama; ikiryō)* in extant *monogatari;* there are merely scattered references to *ikiryō* in chronicles and brief narratives *(setsuwa).*[24] According to Fujimoto, the full-blown phenomenon of *mono no ke* as a living rather than as a dead spirit *(shiryō)* is Murasaki Shikibu's invention, replacing the traditional quarrel between a new wife and the spirit of her deceased predecessor.[25] Fujimoto argues that Murasaki Shikibu's innovation requires us to focus on the possessor ("tsuku ningen ni shōten o ate").[26]

Excitement over Murasaki Shikibu's originality in emphasizing Rokujō's role as living possessing spirit can become a distraction. It can draw readers and critics so deeply into the psychology of the *ikiryō* that the possessed person is all but forgotten.[27] If that happens, the reader has ironically repeated the neglect that motivated Aoi to seize the woman's weapon of spirit possession. By becoming possessed, Aoi hopes to be seen and heard and no longer neglected by Genji. It is understandable that Genji, feeling the need to defend himself against charges of neglect, fixes his attention on Rokujō's jealous possessing spirit, but it would be a mistake for us to do the same. If we look at the possession solely through Genji's eyes, we will fail to understand Aoi's strategy. In the Aoi case, Murasaki Shikibu shows us the pos-

sessed person and the possessing spirit as parties of equal weight oper-
ating within the same phenomenological framework, a shared reality.
It is therefore important to refrain from demonizing this exceptional
*ikiryō* as if it were merely another vengeful *shiryō*.

As the carriage quarrel develops into spirit possession, the war
among women becomes a war between the sexes. In other words, the
two female rivals' physical and psychic violence toward each other is
also aimed at their common male oppressor. Both women score.
Rokujō successfully rekindles Genji's old admiration, mixed with new
apprehension about her powers. Meanwhile, Aoi flourishes emotionally, not only basking in the Kiritsubo Emperor's "august attentions"
(S:165; 2:27) but also quite literally spellbinding the entire court. The
women's "oblique aggressive strategy" proves—at least for a time—
effective. Their common target, Genji, never quite understands what
is happening, but he does sense that both women are slipping from his
control.

## Childbirth and Possession

It is no accident that Aoi's crisis erupts in the ritual context of the
Kamo or Aoi Festival. Belonging to the category of *goryō-e*, or gather-
ings to pacify spirits, this festival *(matsuri)* was created to counteract
the transgressions that resulted in the disastrous famine occurring
under Emperor Yōmei (540–587).[28] Although the symbolism of this
festival's emblematic heartvine *(aoi)* is here deprived of its romantic
aura (because of the clashing carriages),[29] the association of the festival
with the Kamo Shrine legend of Tamayorihime bears directly on Aoi's
condition. Touched by an arrow floating down the river, the daughter
of Taketsunumi conceived a son, Wake Ikazuchi. The image of the
impregnating crimson arrow suggests violence done by an objectified
lover. In the *Genji,* Aoi's drama parallels Tamayorihime's mythic tale;
she too experiences involuntary conception, a difficult pregnancy,
spirit possession, and the birth of a son.

The carriage quarrel can be seen as an entirely realistic event.
Aoi's childbearing scene is also depicted in realistic terms but has
superimposed upon it the supernaturalism of spirit possession. What
does the pregnancy mean to Aoi? Her arranged marriage is commonly known to be a mismatch. That she should, after nine years of
neglect, conceive and carry the child of the husband she has come to
resent makes her pregnancy especially poignant. Her reluctance to

appear in public on the Day of Lustration is a symptom of her ambivalence. When her mother Ōmiya and her women force her to appear, her condition, although doubtlessly well concealed beneath her robes, is tantamount to an admission—to herself if not to others—of sexual intercourse with the husband who had so flagrantly neglected to visit her at her family's residence. That conception occurred during a merely physical act preceded by neither love nor courtship is humiliating. Heretofore Aoi had been able to maintain an air of independence vis-à-vis Genji, to whom she condescended as a way of counteracting his indifference. Now she knows that she is henceforth tied to him. In other words, the pregnancy does not transform her aloofness into love; it merely binds her to her husband in a sadly mechanical fashion.

As a prelude to spirit possession, Aoi's pregnancy is especially appropriate because, as Hilary Graham has shown, pregnancy is also a condition of "biological ambiguity" in which two are one.[30] That pregnancy was in the Heian era recognized as a time of susceptibility to spirit possession can be seen in the *Eiga monogatari* (ca. 1092), attributed to Akazome Emon (fl. 976–1041). In this historical narrative *(rekishi monogatari)* of the reign of the Emperor Murakami (926–967; r. 946–967), the Empress Anshi (927–964) is afflicted by spirit possession at the height of her pregnancy.[31] Like Aoi, Anshi is seized by an exceptionally stubborn spirit who refuses to yield to the exorcist rites ordered by her deeply worried consort.[32]

Compared to Emperor Murakami, Genji plays a far more active part in the spectacle of his wife's possession. During Aoi's pregnancy, her psychological suffering is intensified by physical pain. Her conflict with Genji culminates when the child, the pitiful fruit of their loveless marriage, rankles within her and clamors to be born. In the final phase of Aoi's labor the child symbolizes her ambivalence about her marriage. But as a *symbol* the child is opaque, precisely because of the naturalistic context of childbirth. The symbol becomes transparent only through the inscription of the supernatural; the *mono no ke* that possesses Aoi is an analogy to the infant inside her.[33] And while Rokujō's possessing spirit highlights both the tensions and the alliance between the two rival women, there is also symbolic meaning in the double exposure, as it were, of spirit and child—the formal alliance and also the tensions between its parents. Aoi's pregnancy is therefore a perfect metaphor for the weight she has been carrying with her.[34] The burden is lifted from her in childbirth, when Murasaki Shikibu arranges for the inexpressible conflict to be articulated through the intervention of the supernatural.

The two strands of action, the realistic and the supernatural, merge. Rather than perceiving Aoi as victimized by the possessing spirit of Rokujō, it is more fitting to see Aoi in the role of aggressor. Although Rokujō is, as I have indicated, unwittingly allied with Aoi in their shared anger against Genji, she is nonetheless the woman who, like the child, stands between husband and wife. The child will not come into the world unless Rokujō is banished from it. To achieve this goal Aoi first resorts to blunt violence against Rokujō and her carriage. When her triumph at the carriage quarrel proves to be illusory and Genji once again favors Rokujō, Aoi subconsciously resorts to the more sophisticated strategy of spirit possession. She intuits that she, instead of merely shoving Rokujō aside, must be like her to win over Genji. Aoi's aggression toward her rival may actually screen her admiration of her.[35] For that reason, Aoi's voice becomes an impersonation of Rokujō's. The combination of spirit possession and premature labor brings Genji rushing to her side in a way incomparably more satisfying than the token ceremonial respect she received from him on the Day of Lustration. By allowing Genji to recognize the spirit, she simultaneously entices him to exorcise the shadow on their marriage. Thus spirit possession is an extension of the carriage quarrel: it is Aoi's ingenious elaboration of her strategy to "win over" Genji while at the same time commanding his respect by frightening him. When Genji manages to banish Rokujō's spirit by means of a lover's response to Aoi, Aoi responds in kind: by giving birth, she liberates their fettered relationship from its sterility and obsessions.

Spirit possession transforms the conjugal relationship between Aoi and Genji.[36] Aoi's former air of cool reserve has changed drastically in the physical ordeal of childbirth and the psychic stress of possession. What had been a marriage of convenience characterized by her frigid unapproachability is now unexpectedly charged with eroticism. Her dishevelled hair, her rotundity, her tossing supple limbs, and her heaving breasts fill Genji with an unprecedented sexual desire for her.[37] Her voluptuousness is compelling and temporarily overrides all other concerns, including his fear of her death in childbirth. The sensual overtones of Aoi's behavior while possessed are suggestive of an ecstasy that is, in tune with Genji's sensual response, not unlike an orgasmic experience.[38]

To complicate matters further, there may be yet another component to the erotic overtones in Aoi's possession. Aoi's cool reserve has usually been attributed to her arranged marriage and to the fact that she is older than her husband. Beneath the surface, however, may be hidden her jealousy of her brother Tō no Chūjō and her father, two men whom Genji finds quite attractive. It can hardly be a coincidence that her death threatens to come just as Genji once again forsakes her in their company. According to Freud's classic study of *Affektverkehrung* (affect reversal), his patient "Dora's" coldness toward the man who courted her and her fits of jealous revenge were caused by her attraction to the wife of her rejected lover.[39] Aoi's jealousy of the stereotypical "other woman" may actually screen her resentment of Genji's homosocial interest in her male relatives.

By giving Genji a son, Aoi triumphs; the formerly neglected wife is now entitled to her husband's gratitude if not his love. Momentarily, the child is the center of attention, and Genji is grateful to its mother, but the flame of his passion proves short-lived. Ironically, what stands in the way of enduring romantic feelings is the experience of spirit possession, the altered state that seemed to force his love. Although he is moved as never before to tend to Aoi's needs as recompense for the pains of childbirth, the memory of the possessed woman's changed appearance now gives him a "shudder of revulsion" (S:170; 2:38) rather than the frisson of sexual desire. Her captivating sexuality overwhelmed him for the moment, but it is mysterious, suspicious, unaccountable. Finally, Aoi cannot reach Genji except in an altered state of consciousness that incorporates the spirit, and usurps the charms, of her chief rival. She has not, after all, achieved her highest ambition: Genji's undivided devotion.

Whatever happiness is achieved comes to an abrupt end. Aoi's postpartum gratification may be somewhat less illusory than her "triumph" at the carriage quarrel, but it is nevertheless brief. Once again, the obstacle to a permanent emotional bond is Genji. Although she may be justified in her criticism of him, he is nonetheless horrified by her strategy and instinctively repelled by her subconscious use of Rokujō. He has made a reconciliatory move in her direction, but he feels cheated by her manipulation of him. Although he is captivated by her new charisma, he senses that it is a borrowed charm. Unfortunately, rather than probing into the motivations for her complicated, deviant strategy, he remains content with the stereotype of the possessed person as a passive victim of jealousy.

## Victim and Aggressor

With the notion of the innocent victim and the aggressive victimizer, the matter has been laid to rest by critics who have limited their interpretation of spirit possession to the views held in Heian times and who have therefore implicitly rejected modern insights into the phenomenon of spirit possession and its function in polygynous societies past and present. The author of the *Genji*, however, transcended her time's largely unreflective perceptions. In her sophisticated treatment of the triad of major characters caught in the intricate drama of spirit possession, she anticipated modern anthropological and psychoanalytical discourse.

Victor Turner has written insightfully about the liminality of childbirth and spirit possession as a "venue and occasion for the most radical skepticism . . . about cherished values and rules." What Murasaki Shikibu has done with the material of liminality is to raise it from propositions *in* cultural codes to propositions *about* them. In other words, by providing us with a more complex view of spirit possession than can be had from the vantage point of any of the dramatis personae, the author staged not only the performance of spirit possession but also "a metaperformance, a performance about a performance."[40]

The mechanisms of spirit possession dramatized by Murasaki Shikibu can also be likened to the psychic dynamics of "deep play" as analyzed by Clifford Geertz. In his famous essay with that title, Geertz pointed to the importance of status hierarchy, polite etiquette, and abhorrence of animality in Bali. Balinese culture shares these traits with the Heian court—another hierarchy governed by an apparently single-minded devotion to gentleness and refinement and an absolute loathing of physical violence. In modern Bali, however, the ordinary norms of behavior are momentarily suspended during the brutal spectacle of the cockfight. Geertz' description is compelling:

> The hierarchy of pride is the moral backbone of the society. But only in the cockfight are the sentiments upon which that hierarchy rests revealed in their natural colors. Enveloped elsewhere in a haze of etiquette, a thick cloud of euphemism and ceremony, gesture and allusion, they are here expressed in only the thinnest disguise of an animal mask, a mask which in fact demonstrates them far more effectively than it conceals them. Jealousy is as

much a part of Bali as poise, envy as grace, brutality as charm; but without the cockfight the Balinese would have a much less certain understanding of them, which is, presumably, why they value it so highly.[41]

Spirit possession in Heian-kyō functioned in a similar fashion as an expression of sublimated social conflict. For women immobilized in layer upon layer of exquisitely matched robes and dimly visible through manifold enclosures of screens, the spectacle of spirit possession provided at least a temporary escape. Women like Aoi employ, in Geertz' terms, "emotion for cognitive ends,"[42] even if the cognitive results vary from person to person—from the impassive bystander, to Genji, to the manipulator of this spectrum of cognition, Murasaki Shikibu herself.

That Genji approaches insights denied the exorcists only to fall short of full knowledge is in itself a poignant statement by the author. Spirit possession is traumatic. And when it is over, relief and forgetfulness are overriding emotions that inhibit an intellectual analysis of the causes and the meaning of it all. Aoi has aroused in Genji a moment of passion and a somewhat longer term of tenderness, but his uxorial interests ebb quickly under the attraction of court duties. Along with Aoi's father and all her brothers, Genji departs. The traditional pattern of abandonment is reestablished after its brief suspension during the possession. For Aoi the positive effect of her oblique aggressive strategy begins to fade away. To bring about a lasting change in the order of things seems hopeless.[43]

## In the Wake of the Possession

After Aoi's delivery, the exorcists chant and burn incense to prevent a return of possessing spirits tempted by the polluting afterbirth (atozan).[44] The exorcists' farcical behavior enhances the tragic conflict, much as the kyōgen interlude heightens the nō (another art form preoccupied with spirit possession). The mono no ke they are worried about are minor spirits, not to be confused with the jealous spirit they believed had afflicted Aoi earlier. What of this more stubborn spirit that Genji has identified as Rokujō's living spirit? If my argument that Aoi is the primary agent of spirit possession is correct, then Rokujō cannot be said to target Aoi, much less to kill her.

When Rokujō learns of Genji's identification of her as Aoi's *mono no ke,* her mind is in turmoil. She is deeply disturbed about how to deal with the charge of possession. Despite her sustained struggle to fend off allegations and rumors, she becomes more susceptible to them and begins to show hallucinatory symptoms. She imagines herself to be enveloped by the priests' poppy-seed incense (see S:169; 2:36: *keshi no ka*) and is clearly unable to dissociate herself from the role of possessing spirit. She tries to wash off the incriminating odor but cannot undo the deed attributed to her.

The scene has been compared to the compulsive washing scene of Lady Macbeth.[45] In many ways strikingly similar, the two scenes express significantly different motivations and responses to tragedy and to the supernatural. While Lady Macbeth is a fully conscious instigator and accomplice in the murder of King Duncan, Rokujō is innocent of criminal intent. Instead, Rokujō tortures herself consciously over the ominous permeation of ritual scents into her robes and hair. Assaulted by rumors, she is thoroughly astonished at the erratic and allegedly demonic behavior of her unconscious mind. She searches her conscience and finds evidence in her dreams that she wanted to repay Aoi for the violence done her on the Day of Lustration. Even the imagery was the same: shoving, shaking, and eclipsing the rival. Yet Rokujō continues to be baffled because she wishes not Aoi's destruction[46] but Genji's devotion. Through spirit possession, Aoi has inadvertently become her vehicle, the instrument rather than the direct object of her dreamed revenge. Rokujō, in full control of her senses, attempts to extricate herself from the charge of evil, but without denying her loss of control over the unconscious, which she conceptualizes as the part of her that had gone "wandering off by itself" (S:167; 2:29–30: *akugaru naru tamashii*). By contrast, Lady Macbeth seeks to deny the remorse revealed unconsciously in her sleepwalking state. The difference between the two women is grounded in their moral constitution: the one instigates and the other is involuntarily implicated in a tragedy. What both Lady Macbeth and Lady Rokujō do share is the discovery that they cannot control their unconscious minds.

It must be emphasized that Rokujō is not associated with the ultimate tragedy of Aoi's death.[47] There is no indication that any *mono no ke* is responsible. After Aoi's apparent recovery, the exorcist priests retire into the mountains, and everyone is taken by surprise when her death comes suddenly, days after the exorcism and the delivery of the child. Although Murasaki Shikibu's text does not

mention spirits, some critics have argued that the supernatural must
be the cause of Aoi's final agony. Tamagami Takuya, for instance,
relates Aoi's heaving breasts in the lethal crisis to her symptoms
during pregnancy, symptoms traceable to the possessing spirit of
Rokujō.[48] One problem with this interpretation is that possession
requires an audience to be effective. There is no audience for this
scene, not even the audience of one or two—Genji and Ukon—who
witnessed Yūgao's possession. In fact, to make sure that no *mono no
ke* have taken possession of her, Aoi is left undisturbed until her
death—from natural causes—is established.

Aoi's death distresses Genji, and he behaves "as if in a trance"
(S:171; 2:42: *yume no kokochi*). His pain is tempered by stoicism:
"The regrets were strong, but useless" (S:171; 2:42). He is less
stricken than he had been by the loss of Yūgao when he was driven,
half-demented, to the brink of death. At that time he had been alone
in dealing with the funeral; now he is supported by the whole court.
Going through the funeral ceremony and wearing mourning robes in
public helps to mitigate and dispel his grief. His pain is further eased
because Aoi has left behind an important memento in Yūgiri. As a
true child of Genji and Aoi, Yūgiri is unlike Yūgao's daughter
Tamakazura, whom Genji illicitly appropriated after her mother's
death. Furthermore, it is as if Aoi's tragedy served as retribution not
only for Genji's adulterous affair with Yūgao but for his incestuous
affair with Fujitsubo, which produced Reizei. While Genji appropri-
ates Yūgao's daughter and proudly claims fatherhood of Yūgiri, he
cannot acknowledge Reizei as his son.

The drama of Aoi's spirit possession and death seems to resolve
itself relatively smoothly when compared to the drama of Yūgao, but
Genji must still come to terms with Rokujō. He had—in a mixture of
horror (at Rokujō as the possessing spirit) and sympathy (for Rokujō
as the embodiment of female sophistication)—sent her a note informing her of Aoi's death. He postpones a confrontation, for "he did not
wish to hurt her" (S:169; 2:36). When she replies, he is stunned (as
only a Heian courtier could be) by the exquisite elegance of Rokujō's
poem of condolence. Since Rokujō has admitted responsibility for her
wandering possessing spirit, her condolences appear sincere. Although
he is smitten by the powerful aesthetic effect of the poem, he is still
angered by the memory of her role in the spirit possession. He had
been shocked not only by Aoi's impersonation of Rokujō but also
by Rokujō's appropriation of Aoi. Norma Field has described this

moment in a brilliant insight: "When Aoi's body houses Lady Rokujō's soul, when Lady Rokujō's soul inhabits Aoi's body, a new creature emerges. . . . The phenomenon of spirit possession is another form of juxtaposition, an instance of the continuous exploration of character formation."[49]

In his reaction of confused self-righteousness, Genji does not penetrate beyond what he perceives as mere manipulation by the two women. He cannot—or will not—see their grievances. He does not realize that he has been their target. Only after Aoi's death is he able grudgingly to acknowledge his shortcomings in their failed marriage: "He had let her carry her hostility to the grave" (S:171; 2:42). All he wants now is to put this doubly bewildering experience behind him: "No doubt Aoi had been fated to die. But anger arose again. Why had he seen and heard it all so clearly, why had it been paraded before him? Try though he might, he could not put his feelings toward the woman [Rokujō] in order" (S:173; 2:45). What he cannot accept is his complicity in the outbreak of excessive emotions that began with the untidy carriage quarrel and reached its climax in spirit possession. He still believes that he has been a mere witness to a spectacle not in harmony with the most exquisite of Heian courtly sensibilities. Whatever flash of intuition he may have had about his responsibility for setting these two women against each other is insufficient and has been deflected by the rites of exorcism, birth, and death.

Rokujō expresses her regrets about Aoi's tragic fate. Are they sincere? There would be reason to argue the contrary if Aoi were the sole object of Rokujō's jealousy and revenge—a vehicle for demonstrating her superiority over her rival and rebuking Genji for his weakness in the wake of the carriage quarrel—which is the standard view of the critics, many of whom have attributed Aoi's death to Rokujō's hatred and rage. If she were as evil as alleged, however, then Genji's continued relations with her and his admiration of her "good taste" (S:174; 2:47) would seem almost incomprehensible. In his later recollections, Genji never blames Rokujō for Aoi's death: "He had been fond of her, and it had been wrong to make so much of that one incident" (S:233; 2:186). (The "incident" is presumably Aoi's possession rather than her death.) Despite Genji's forgiveness, Rokujō must pay with a damaged reputation: she is now "marked for notoriety" (S:173; 2:45). This notoriety is particularly painful because of her pride in her cultural refinement. Unlike Aoi, who longed just as much for recognition but was never known for an aesthetic sensibility, Rokujō had relied on artistry to win and hold her lover. She feels herself betrayed by the unaesthetic role she reluctantly accepted in the drama of spirit possession.

### The Sacred Branch of Renunciation

Disappointed in her expectations of taking the late Aoi's place, whether merely in Genji's affections or formally as his *kita no kata*,[50] Rokujō readies herself to accompany her daughter to Ise, stopping first at the temporary Shrine in the Fields (Nonomiya). Ironically, no sooner has Rokujō's austere resolve become clear to Genji than he sets out in pursuit of her. To tell her what she still means to him, even though the matter of Aoi remains unresolved between them, he is willing to risk his reputation by visiting the austere site.

What compels Genji to resume so dangerous a contact as this one? Certainly not a masochistic impulse to provoke once more the vehement protest that he believes to have been mysteriously orchestrated by Rokujō's unconscious in the possession of Aoi. Genji acts from a mixture of curiosity, compassion, and a lingering amorous interest that is revived by her inaccessibility at the sacred Shinto shrine. What makes Rokujō especially alluring is her elegance and refinement. The notion that the sensitive should be pitied more because they suffer more reflects a society that, unlike our own, prized aesthetic qualities without reserve or qualification. Accordingly, Rokujō's cultural sophistication moves Genji to a journey of "melancholy beauty" (S:186; 2:77). The visit at the shrine is also an opportunity for the tumultuous affair to be brought to an aesthetically satisfying conclusion in a style befitting the nature of their love/hate relationship. In the complexity of their encounter, Genji has still other motives. He hopes not to appear insensitive at court, and he wishes to pacify an angry woman who may haunt one much dearer to his heart than Aoi had been—Murasaki, his new young wife.

What compels Rokujō to receive the uninvited, tabooed visitor who has humiliated her through his neglect and unwittingly driven her into religious exile? Presumably the same motives as Genji's: the ones that prompted her poem of condolence. Although the chances of making the visit a lasting or even a partial success are against them, they are irresistibly drawn to one another once Genji arrives on the scene. The magic formula that eradicates all barriers between them, including the bitter memory of *mono no ke*, is the call and response of their good taste. While Rokujō's mind habitually oscillates between the two conflicting extremes of ungovernable passion and absolute mastery of the nuances of artistic and social self-control, at the shrine she is determined to repress her passion. She knows that once the dynamics of elegant communication are set into motion, a dialogue that the two perform with consummate skill, she is in danger of falling once again for the Shining Prince.

What then happens at Nonomiya between the two notoriously passionate and unhappy lovers? Genji gives Rokujō a branch from the sacred *sakaki* tree. Ordinarily this evergreen is used in purification rituals, but Genji uses it here in lieu of a spoken apology. Although Rokujō briefly scolds him for the blasphemous act, she is hardly entitled to find fault with anyone's oblique strategies. She quickly pardons him. Genji's gesture is uncanny in its ambiguity. Overtly a religious symbol of purification, the branch becomes an aid to seduction and is used, or abused, as a secular symbol for the courtier's never-ending love: "With heart unchanging as this evergreen, / This sacred tree, I enter the sacred gate" (S:187; 2:79). Genji's famous *sakaki* gesture is accompanied by words so enticing that Edward G. Seidensticker has chosen to render them as a poem. The incompatible realms of the secular and the sacred expressed in Genji's bold words parallel Rokujō's divided psychological state at the temporary shrine. Psychologically and geographically, she is in a liminal position between renunciation of the world and attachment to it. And, as if to take advantage of this limbo, Genji, by presenting the *sakaki*, pulls Rokujō in both directions.

In addition to expressing nonverbally the two complementary aspects of purification—apology and forgiveness—the *sakaki* also becomes a token of undying spiritual love. Genji's bold use of the *sakaki* brings about a bittersweet moment of intimacy based on the "memories" (S:188; 2:80) of all their trials together. Finally, countering Rokujō's determination to renounce the affair, the evergreen branch is a last manipulative appeal to physical passion. It becomes a phallic symbol as Genji pushes it under Rokujō's blinds. It is a poignant appeal that comes too late. Passions rise; the lovers' control over themselves begins to weaken; but Rokujō resists the erotic appeal. She persuades him that passion must be limited to one last, ceremonial flourish—their aesthetic responsiveness. Temptation is cut short by regrets, a truncation that in the ordinary pattern of Heian courtship serves to tantalize and further entice the lovers. But "this was no ordinary parting" (S:188; 2:82–83); it is the last chance not taken.[51]

The most important outcome of the *sakaki* episode is, in practical terms, the termination of an affair. Rokujō, formerly the neglected one, now rejects Genji. Although she acts more decisively than he, both lovers have contributed to this denouement, and, by making it as painful as possible, neither can dismiss the other's love as a trifle. Yet despite the delicately achieved emotional balance, the past constitutes so heavy and mysterious a burden that the parting cannot ensure the absence of future conflict. After Genji's departure, Rokujō begins almost immediately to reconsider the whole affair. When most inclined toward Genji during his brief visit, she had taken a positive view: Genji broke the religious code to show his never-ending love for her. When she is alone again, however, she ponders Genji's more self-ish motives and is reminded of the times when her feelings were com-pletely at his disposal. When the power of spirit possession ascribed to her by Genji and by the public failed to break his emotional tyranny over her, she had fled to the sacred space of Nonomiya, only to expe-rience his intrusion and feel temptation anew. She must acknowledge to herself her frailty. In spurning Genji's parting gifts, she shows out-ward strength, but she knows that inwardly she will never be able to sever her attachment to him. Her response to all of this becomes a fixed resentment.

The visit leaves her with an awareness that the autumn of her amorous life has come. She also broods about her failure to fulfill the ambitious plans of her father. Indeed, at this decisive turning point she must realize that there may not even be time to rehabilitate her name: "It was as if the thought had only now come to her of the ugly name she seemed fated to leave behind" (S:189; 2:83). The clearing of her name becomes her new obsession. But is this possible? Did the Bud-dhist exorcists not struggle vainly to put her angry living spirit at rest? While the cry of her unconscious has been heard, it is never really answered by Genji, the one person who could satisfy her grievance. In her frustrated goals Rokujō appears to be nearly interchangeable with Aoi. It is as if the two women's shared psychic condition had under-gone a structural reversal after Aoi's possession and death so that Aoi now serves as an uncanny shadow to Rokujō.

Rokujō's daughter the high priestess, later known as Akikonomu, is a cool analyst of the situation. She is detached enough to deal Genji a severe blow when she mocks his "pretense of sorrow" over his "role of rejected suitor" (S:189; 2:84). Yet Genji, while acknowledging that he has been hit by her barbed remark, shrugs it off: "He had to smile, however, at the priestess' rather knowing poem. She was clever for her age, and she interested him. Difficult and unconventional relationships always interested him" (S:189; 2:84–85). Genji is accustomed to difficult and unconventional courtships. Seldom does he worry about the ethics of his behavior.

Does this mean that Genji has completely failed Rokujō? The answer depends not only on his perception of her criticism and of Akikonomu's but, more importantly, on the nature of the response required of the courtier by his society. Rokujō plays by society's rules. By responding as he does to what he believes to be her possession of Aoi, Genji too plays by the rules. While he cannot be accused of hurting Rokujō's feelings with his visit—quite the contrary, it must flatter her—he can be charged with covering up his relief over the termination of the taxing affair. In other words, Genji comes away from Nonomiya as the rejected lover who can pretend that he courted the beloved even when she retreated to a sacred and forbidden place. His schemes are such that he achieves his goal no matter what Rokujō does, and he escapes without a sense of guilt.[52] The affair has gone sour, but appearances are kept.

If the parting leaves Rokujō pleased with herself for having been able to resist Genji's charm, having rejected him as he rejected her in choosing young Murasaki as his new wife to replace Aoi,[53] the parting also means the premature end of her female sexuality and a deep frustration over the unfulfillment of her filial duties. Genji, though he may congratulate himself for his diplomacy, cannot fail to harbor a profound unease about leaving Rokujō behind in lonely melancholy and hurt pride. Murasaki Shikibu seems to be laying the psychological groundwork for a resurfacing—in the displaced form of spirit possession—of the conflict between Genji and Rokujō. She emerges from the *sakaki* episode as a woman who can stand up to him, even though he acknowledges her power only after her death, when he blames her dead spirit for possessing his wives (Murasaki and the Third Princess). Genji never imagines Fujitsubo in Rokujō's role of possessing spirit because he does not think of her as a woman threatening him as his equal but as an adorable ideal. Towering over his unconscious, Fujitsubo affects him directly as an admonishing force in a formidable dream (see S:359; 2:485–486) rather than through the mediated form of spirit possession.[54] That Fujitsubo, the idealized woman, should appear to Genji in the private intimacy of a dream reflects the secrecy of their relationship. That Genji identifies Rokujō as an aggressive agent in the public phenomenon of spirit possession reflects Genji's gender conflict with Rokujō, in particular her ostensible threat to his sexual and political power. Although spirit possession can sometimes alter a troubled male-female relationship to the woman's advantage, isolated instances of protest cannot reform the social order. A woman's dissenting voice can haunt a man for a long time and permanently affect his psyche, but it cannot make itself heard long enough to call male hegemony into question.

In her few remaining years Rokujō continues to sound the somewhat superficial note of reconciliation struck in the *sakaki* episode, hoping thereby to rehabilitate her reputation. She is among the women who express their support of Genji during his voluntary "exile" at Suma. A connection is easily made between Suma and Ise as places of atonement and deprivation, and an old bond is paradoxically reinforced through separation and self-imposed exile. This is maddeningly ironic because one expects her to be foremost among those demanding repentance for his frivolous handling of his affairs. However, she desires not Genji's punishment but his change of heart. She empathizes with the suffering of the courtier in isolated, uncouth Suma. Still, an undertone of complaint remains: his "exile" is temporary whereas her withdrawal is, apparently, permanent. And inasmuch as she has fled to Ise in order to be free of him, he is the cause of her symbolic exile. She, on the other hand, has nothing to do with his departure for Suma.

When the Suzaku Emperor abdicates and Reizei ascends to the throne, Rokujō and her daughter return to the capital after six years at Ise, not long after Genji returns from his briefer stay at Suma. As time has not fully healed the old wounds, the former lovers avoid each other, wary of possible demands, uneasy about their estrangement. It is only when Rokujō falls seriously ill and decides to take the tonsure before the critical age of thirty-seven that Genji hurries to tell her "how fond he had been of her" (S:285; 2:300).[55] Having acknowledged this truth, Genji discovers to his surprise a resurgence of the old feelings.

Taking advantage of his reawakened feelings, the dying Rokujō, like Aoi on her sickbed, voices a last request of him. She entrusts her daughter to Genji with a plea that he renounce a foster father's incestuous thoughts: "Life can be dreadfully complicated when her guardian is found to have thoughts not becoming a parent" (S:285; 2:301). With her end near, Rokujō tries to lighten her psychic burden—the old insinuation that it may have been her wandering spirit that possessed Aoi—by sharing it with Genji: "There is a very strong bond between us—it must be so—that you should have come to me now. I have been able to tell you a little of what has been on my mind, and I am no longer afraid to die" (S:286; 2:303).[56] She dies, but memory of that part of her that Genji never wanted to come to terms with—her resentful pride—remains to remind other women that they are not wholly defenseless in the undeclared war between the sexes.

## Aoi and Rokujō in the *Nō*

Classical *nō* plays dramatize Aoi's spirit possession from the viewpoint of Rokujō no miyasudokoro. Janet Goff has commented that, in a reversal of *Genji* chronology, *Nonomiya* (The Shrine in the Fields)[57] precedes *Aoi no ue* (Lady Aoi)[58] in a same-day *nō* program.[59] Although the titles of the *nō* plays suggest a chronological reversal, particularly through their settings, the events described in the *nō* texts (*yōkyoku*) as the core of the dramatic conflict actually reflect the narrative sequence in the *Genji*. If there is no explicit mention of Aoi's spirit possession in *Nonomiya*, it is because that *nō* focuses on Rokujō's coming to terms with the impact of Aoi's extended possession drama on her own troubled relationship with Genji. *Nonomiya* is ultimately designed for Rokujō to recall the triggering event of the carriage quarrel and lay to rest these painful memories whereas *Aoi no ue* expresses Rokujō's need to relive and overcome her jealousy and rage over having been implicated in Aoi's possession crisis.

Kenneth Yasuda expresses surprise that the *Nonomiya* playwright omitted what he, like other critics, takes to be Murasaki Shikibu's characterization of Rokujō. She is the woman who "caused the deaths of three of Genji's loves—Yūgao, Aoi, and Murasaki. Yet of these most heinous spiritual crimes, there is no mention."[60] It is, however, conceivable that the playwright had a less negative interpretation of Rokujō. Unlike the many playwrights and artists who relied on *Genji* manuals and digests rather than on Murasaki Shikibu's text,[61] the author of *Nonomiya* borrows extensively from the *Genji* and eschews superficial synopses and standardized poetic images.

Generally attributed to Zeami and indeed considered his greatest play,[62] *Nonomiya* is classified as a two-part dream *nō* (*fukushiki mugen nō*). Its lack of dramatic movement and its lyric richness contribute to melancholy elegance, or *yūgen,* the effect most prized in *nō*. In the first part, at this site evocative of her complex emotional history, Rokujō's ghost appears in the form of a beautiful woman. She reveals herself to a traveling Buddhist priest who has been attracted to Nonomiya's famous fall scenery. Drawing upon the *monogatari*'s complex interplay of poetic imagery,[63] Zeami has given Rokujō the *sakaki* branch that Genji took from the evergreen tree used in Shinto ritual. The priest hears that Genji, in an act bordering on blasphemy, had used the sacred *sakaki* to tempt Rokujō into resuming their affair. Although Rokujō chose instead to accompany her daughter to Ise, the memory of this episode continues to trouble her. By reluctantly revealing to the *waki* her identity and her shameful ambivalence about the past, Rokujō moves one step closer to purifying her mind of its obsession with these bittersweet memories.

The sacred *sakaki* branch Rokujō holds in her hand in the first part of the play serves not only as a symbol of her lingering attachment to Genji and this world but also as a highly effective focal point of meditation. When Rokujō reappears in her true form in the second part, the *sakaki* has been replaced by—or transformed into—a fan. The change signals a shift from the specific emotions associated with the *sakaki* to the more conventional emotions of the traditional prop.[64] She has laid aside the "objective correlative" of the most excruciating encounter with Genji because, in this play, the power of memory itself must, as a form of attachment obstructing Buddhist enlightenment, be erased.[65] The *waki* assists Rokujō in this task with his questions, becomes involved in the struggle to detach her from pain and longing, and finally witnesses her progress toward religious salvation.

In this second part of *Nonomiya*, the carriage brawl that triggered Aoi's spirit possession is explored for its traumatic effects on Rokujō. Although Aoi is physically absent, her presence is implied by the carriage imagery (Plate 2.4). On the *nō* stage, the carriage, evoked verbally or by a prop,[66] functions much as the robe does in *Aoi no ue*. Yet more powerfully than the robe, the image of the carriage imprisons Rokujō in her memories, recalling her entrapment and displacement, during the brawl on the Day of Lustration.[67] Although Rokujō has never been possessed by any *mono no ke,* her obsessive memories of the carriage quarrel *(kuruma arasoi)* demonstrate that she knows what it means to be controlled by someone to the point of a radical change in personality. In retelling the story of the *kuruma arasoi,* Rokujō feels as if she were once again amid the carriage wheels that

imprison her as the wheel of karma *(sukuse)* imprisons all unenlightened souls in cycles of endless transmigration *(samsāra)*. *Nonomiya*
shows Rokujō, not Aoi, as a woman humiliated, oppressed, and
reshaped by her female rival.

Realizing now that remembrance of the past has kept her attached
to Genji, she seeks to escape from memory through the shrine's torii.
She remains caught, however, on the liminal threshold of the torii, her
foot withdrawing no sooner than it has inched across the invisible line
demarcating this world from the next. The flame of the Fire Hut
*(hitakiya)*, suggestive of the lingering passion that periodically draws
Rokujō back to Nonomiya, still flickers dimly inside her at the end of
the *nō* play. We never learn whether or not she will ultimately step into
the metaphysical carriage the Buddha promised to those who desire to
leave behind all attachments to this world, characterized as a burning
house *(kataku)*. A definite solution would dampen the emotional
vibrations the *nō* playwright achieved between *shite* and spectators by
relieving the audience of participating in Rokujō's agonizing decision.
It is her unresolved struggle that moves the heart.

The *nō* play *Aoi no ue*, first mentioned in Zeami's treatise *Sarugaku dangi* (Reflections on *Nō;* 1430),[68] is of uncertain authorship. It
stands out among *nō* plays, together with *Funa-Benkei* and *Dōjōji*, as a
meta-*nō*. By this term I mean that the common theme of the appearance of aggrieved spirits (living or dead) and their pacification is itself
thematized through the actual staging of a shamanistic ritual involving
the summoning of the spirit by a medium and its expulsion by an
exorcist. Shinto and Buddhism join forces in their complementary
goals of pacification and enlightenment. Thus, more explicitly than
most plays, *Aoi no ue* points to the "connection between *nō* and shamanistic rituals of possession."[69] As a meta-*nō* about spirit possession
and shamanism, the play can be read on the thematic level of the original narrative of spirit possession and on the theatrical level of shamanism, effecting a collusion of past and present. Its literalistic
conceptualization of the demonic simplifies and distorts the phenomenon of spirit possession as it was dramatized in the *Genji*.[70]

One of the most striking features of this play that bears the name
of Genji's first principal wife is that Aoi never appears as an animated
character. Instead, she is represented by a folded short-sleeved robe
*(kosode)*, placed silently by a stage assistant *(kōken)* on front center
stage. Her presence is an absence. Her personality remains an enigma.
Put differently, Aoi's disembodied appearance as a magnificent outer

shell symbolizes the high social status that caused her dissociation not only from others, including her husband, but from herself. Although the robe lies immobile throughout the play, it is emotionally charged. Aoi is, after all, the central axis around which the action of the play revolves. Represented by her robe, she is the first to enter the stage as a *kosode* in an extreme form of "faceless display... called *uchide* or *idashiginu,* 'putting out one's robes,' "[71] and she is the last to leave.[72] More properly speaking, she is carried in and she is carried out; not only is her objectified appearance forced,[73] making her an involuntary participant in the drama to follow, but she does not—she cannot—exit of her own accord.

The traditional classification of *Aoi no ue* as a contemporary play *(genzainō)* does not do justice to its complex temporal structure.[74] The time scheme is such that the play conforms to the conventions of dream *nō (mugen nō),*[75] in which the *shite* typically personifies the spirit of a dead person who returns to express an unspeakable grievance and to be relieved of it through a theatrical performance of song and dance inspired by ancient shamanistic *kagura.*[76] Seen as *mugen nō,* then, *Aoi no ue* is a play in which Rokujō's *dead* spirit returns to reenact her resentment of Aoi and is pacified (in Shinto terms) and enlightened (in Buddhist terms) only when defeated by the esoteric spells and religious formulas of the Shugendō mountain ascetic *(yamabushi).*[77] The opening lines of the court official to the Shujaku-in *(wakizure)* make clear that shamanistic rituals have failed to save Aoi. The folded robe signifies the *dead* Aoi's symbolic presence.[78]

Contrary to the *Genji,* where the possessed person is the principal actor in the drama of spirit possession, *Aoi no ue,* as *mugen nō,* reverses the focus from the possessed, who is now beyond help, to the alleged possessor, who is the person considered most in need of healing.[79] In *Aoi no ue,* there is a marginalization of Aoi, accompanied by a centering on Rokujō, that drastically alters the relative importance of the two women in the "Aoi" chapter of the *Genji.* Rokujō's tormented thoughts over rumors that her *living* spirit had invaded the pregnant Aoi—thoughts already present in the *Genji*—continue beyond her death. Rather than having Rokujō reflect upon her dream of violent revenge upon Aoi for the insult at the Kamo lustration, the *nō* provides a stage for reliving the dream long after these events. William H. Matheson asserts that, as a consequence of the genre difference between *monogatari* and *nō,* the "Rokujō lady's dream of

striking Aoi [is] no longer a dream but an enactment, a performance."[80] In Matheson's reading of *Aoi no ue*, Rokujō's posthumous
dream performance eclipses Aoi's actual performance of spirit possession as witnessed by Genji in the *monogatari* and reduces Aoi as a
character to the status paraphernalia of her robe and a mere object of
Rokujō's anger.[81]

That the female medium summoning Rokujō's spirit and the
exorcist expelling her demonic jealousy do not exist in the *Genji's* cli-
mactic moment of Aoi's last, fatal possession are further indications of
the play's shift in emphasis. The medium is called Teruhi, an *azusa
miko* named after the catalpa bow whose twanging calls the spirits of
the living or the dead. Her skills initiate the arduous pacification ritual
for Rokujō's enlightenment. The male exorcist, summoned when
Rokujō's uncontrollable spirit attempts to strike the robe with the fan,
is referred to as Kohijiri, a *yamabushi* from Yokawa on Mount Hiei.
His task is to exorcize Rokujō's jealousy—represented by the white
demonic mask called Shiro Hannya (Plate 1.6)—and bring enlightenment to her tormented soul. He succeeds when the medium, shud-
dering, submits to the tranference of the *mono no ke* and Rokujō
returns peacefully to the realm of the dead. The endlessly turning
wheel of attachment and desire has been arrested and enlightenment
has been achieved.

*Aoi no ue* overcomes the schism between Shinto and Buddhism by
employing the syncretic religious figures of the *miko* and the *yamabushi*; the *Genji* resists the religious transcendence of the conflicts.
The *nō* emphasizes shamanism and the expulsion of the possessing
spirit; the *Genji* stresses the psychological function of spirit possession
as an oblique expression of the possessed person's grievances. In *Aoi
no ue*, the playwright, as Goff correctly remarks, wrests "an unambiguous religious message from a resisting text."[82] If the *Genji* speaks
more directly to the modern reader than *Aoi no ue* does, the reason is
that Murasaki Shikibu, paradoxically, seems closer to us in time than
the author of the *nō*.

In 1951, Mishima Yukio (1925–1970) drew upon classical
sources to create his own modern *nō* play, *Aoi no ue*.[83] Mishima fuses
elements from both his main sources. He translates the shamanistic
figures of the *nō* stage into modern characters. The medium adept at
the catalpa bow—active in the *nō* but absent in the *Genji*—becomes a
hospital nurse whose behavior is guided by doctors with Freudian the-

ories of sexual repression. The *yamabushi* of the classical *Aoi no ue* becomes Mishima's Hikaru Wakabayashi; his name is a clear allusion to the eponym of the *monogatari*.[84]

Translated as *The Lady Aoi,* Mishima's play was "sung in 1956 as a Western-style opera."[85] The influence of Western stage conventions is evident not only in the operatic style and in the stage set, which is reminiscent of the productions of Jean Cocteau, but also in the surrealistic thematic treatment characteristic of the theater of the absurd. What is first presented as a realistic plot—a modern businessman (Hikaru) visits the hospital where his wife (Aoi) suffers from feelings of neglect and periodic abandonment—becomes embedded in so many multiple layers of remembrance of things past that the theatrical present turns unreal. In the end, both dream and reality are cast in doubt. The nurse disappears after telling Hikaru that Yasuko Rokujō's "big silvery car" is approaching the hospital by "viaduct."[86] Mishima has not only skillfully introduced elements of the Heian carriage and the *nō* stage's bridge *(hashigakari)* but converted them into a modern idiom, thereby connecting the dead and the living, dream and reality.

Jealous Rokujō's sickbed visits are ominous. Rokujō tells the astonished Hikaru that, on his behalf, she has been bringing Aoi invisible flowers of pain (suggestive of Baudelaire's *fleurs du mal*).[87] Their loathsome odor is similar to "the scent of the poppy seeds burned at exorcisms" (S:169; 2:36). Rokujō is not, however, merely revenging herself against an incapacitated rival; nor is she there as an exorcist. Her clinical diagnosis of Aoi's fears of a lonely old age and death perfectly mirrors her own state of mind. The two women—one of them in a sleeplike trance, the other a bloodless phantom—share anger at Hikaru's spurning them.

Rokujō reveals to Hikaru that he is the cause of Aoi's illness and the target of both women. To convince the skeptical Hikaru of this, she has "to kill two birds with one stone" by making Aoi suffer and by killing Hikaru. Only then will she be "pitied" by his "dead self."[88] To achieve her goal, she first forces him to travel back in time to the heyday of their affair. By admitting her loss of pride and by arousing his pity, she evokes from him a confession of his strange fascination with her. She was to have been the woman to restrain his youthful passion in her "cage" while simultaneously allowing him his freedom.[89] Mishima thus transposes Heian polygyny into the modern idiom of a double standard allowing male promiscuity.

As if drugged by smoking from the same cigarette, they reexperi-

ence their past, which glides before them in the form of a sailboat.[90]
On stage, the sail itself, symbolic of Time and the Subconscious, separates them from Aoi. Rokujō entrances Hikaru through the power of
her words: she evokes the sight of her house on the lake, the sound of
its foxes and their cries as they kill chickens, the alarming image of
drowning hydrangea. When Rokujō has succeeded in rendering
Hikaru completely spellbound, Aoi's writhing shadow is projected
upon the white sail. Hikaru is so enthralled that he does not recognize
the shadow's meaning. Rokujō distracts him from a rational analysis of
this image by detaining him in their recollected past, insisting that the
cries he hears are a fox's or "the creaking of the mast."[91] Even as
Rokujō's strategy exposes her living spirit's uncontrollable desire to
kill Aoi, he is slow to grasp her meaning. When he finally recognizes
the cries as Aoi's, Rokujō, realizing that she cannot win Hikaru's
heart, disappears behind the sail.

When Hikaru telephones Rokujō at her house from the hospital and
immediately reaches her, he suspects that he has hallucinated her "living
ghost."[92] No sooner has he come to this positivistic conclusion than he
hears a voice from behind the door. Reminiscent of Ueda Akinari's
(1734–1809) ghosts' tendency to leave behind some concrete evidence
of the supernatural, Rokujō's living spirit is requesting the black gloves
she forgot. As he exits, obeying her command and leaving the phone off
the hook, Rokujō's telephone voice increases in volume, causing Aoi to
reach for the receiver. She dies in the effort to make contact.

In the telephone line Mishima has created another modern equivalent of the nō drama's bridge connecting the realm of the living and the
dead, the real and the imagined. Asking which of the two Rokujōs is
"real" is misguided because both are real in their psychological impact
on Hikaru. Jay Rubin has written that "the 'ghost' is but a device for
presenting a universal human emotion on the stage for the audience to
share."[93] True enough. Mishima, however, uses this device to explore
the ontological difference between the stage figure as ghost and as living character. If one can assume that the ghost is behind the hospital
door (in what would be the mirror room, *kagami no ma,* of classical
nō) and the real Rokujō is at the other end of the telephone line, then
Hikaru, despite his rationalizations, ultimately responds to the phantasmal Rokujō. As a result, Aoi, confronted with the voice of her female
rival, dies from a renewed sense of abandonment.

Rather than repeating Murasaki Shikibu's emphasis on Aoi's
mediated message to Genji or the nō's concentration on the ritual pac-

ification of Rokujō's jealous spirit, Mishima has concentrated on
Rokujō's powerful hold on Hikaru. The nurse's lyrical summoning of
Rokujō and Rokujō's extraordinary verbal skills inspire him with
memories of the past and captivate his imagination.[94] Since Aoi's malaise is the consequence of Hikaru's neglect, he has the ability to cure
Aoi of her neurotic fears simply by being at her bedside; but he forsakes this chance when the phantasmal Rokujō seduces him with the
evocative power of her language. Hikaru and Rokujō form a bond of
artistic sensibility that excludes Aoi, who remains trapped in the social
reality symbolized by the hospital. The beauty of art is the proximate
cause of Aoi's death. Lyrical beauty, symbolized by the invisible *fleurs
du mal,* becomes an agent of death. This unorthodox conclusion conforms to Mishima's view of the *nō*: "True beauty is something that
attacks, overpowers, robs, and finally destroys."[95]

If the classical *nō* play *Aoi no ue* shifts the focus from the possessed
person in the *Genji* to the possessing spirit's salvation through shamanism and exorcism, Mishima creates an entirely new dynamic by relocat-
ing the source of conflict in Hikaru's suggestibility. Initially cast in the
role of exorcist, he soon becomes entranced by the nurse's evocation of
Rokujō and becomes possessed himself by Rokujō's poetic remembrance of things past. With artistic passion instead of jealousy as the
driving force for spirit possession in Mishima's modern *nō* play, it is not
surprising that, as Nancy J. Barnes has suggested, neither Buddhist
rites nor Western psychoanalysis can cure Aoi. Indeed, "the notion that
any sort of cure might be desired is rejected."[96] Mishima's redrawing
of the Aoi–Rokujō–Genji triangle appears to reduce Aoi to her role as
victim. Matheson succinctly describes the evolution of Aoi's character
in its three literary versions: "Aoi, once a living character, then a *kosode,*
now is a bed, a dying voice."[97] Mishima does allow her to emerge from
passivity when she reaches for the telephone. Since her pain is literally
inexpressible, the effort to achieve direct communication by means of
an electronic medium is doomed. The effort kills her.

While Hikaru and Rokujō have achieved a fictional suspension of
death through the poetic power of words, Aoi achieves actual death,
which in Mishima's philosophy is "the only thing that belonged eter-
nally to the imagination."[98] Finally, it is only in her first embodiment—in the *Genji*—that Aoi, a willful person rather than a *nō* stage
prop or stylized figure, is granted the theatrical power of impersonation and the ability to enthrall her audience with a magic spell.

PLATE 1.1 The presentation of a white gourd flower on a fan. Tosa school. Pair of sixfold screens. Ink with slight red pigment and gold leaf on mica paper. Detail. Late seventeenth or early eighteenth century. The Museum of Fine Arts, Houston; museum purchase with funds provided by Mr. and Mrs. Harris Masterson III, Mr. and Mrs. John R. Moran, Mr. Carl Detering, Mr. and Mrs. Gary Levering, Mr. and Mrs. M. S. Stude, Continental Oil Company, Mary Alice Wilson, Mr. and Mrs. William Coates, Jr., Texas Pipe and Supply Company, Mrs. Barbara K. Sandy, Mr. and Mrs. Lee B. Stone, Mr. and Mrs. J. R. Thomas.

PLATE 1.2 A female *mono no ke* hovers over Yūgao. Yamamoto Shunshō (1610–1682). *Eiri Genji monogatari* (Illustrated *Tale of Genji*; 1650). Printed book. Ink on paper. Photograph: Sheldan Comfert Collins. The Mary and Jackson Burke Collection.

PLATE 1.3 Ashikaga Mitsuuji, dressed in a kimono with the "Yūgao" *Genji-kō* emblem, holds in his arms Tasogare, who is being threatened by a demon wearing the Hannya mask. (See also Plates 1.6 and 2.4.) Yoshitoshi (1839–1892). Ōban woodblock triptych, 1882. Courtesy of Segi Shin'ichi and Kodansha International.

物の怪に
命をうばばわれ
もはや源氏の
言葉に
答えることの
ない夕顔……

右近の語る
ところによれば
夕顔はやはり
頭中将が見失った
恋人だったのです

PLATE 1.4    The larger-than-life ghost of a woman snatches away
Yūgao's life. The *manga* narrative identifies *mono no ke* as the
cause of Yūgao's death and anticipates Ukon's later revelation that
Yūgao was Tō no Chūjō's lost beloved. *Manga* artist Tsuboi Kou
(b. 1951). Courtesy of Takahashi Chihaya, Shinjinbutsu Ōraisha.

PLATE 1.5   Genji and the possessed pregnant Aoi, a medium and exorcists. Anonymous. *Hakubyō Genji monogatari emaki*. Scroll I. Sixteenth century. Tenri Central Library, Nara Prefecture.

PLATE 1.6   Rokujō's demonic mask in the second half of the *nō* drama *Aoi no ue*. Tatsuemon. Shiro Hannya. Early fifteenth century. Collection of the Kongō School of Nō, Kyoto.

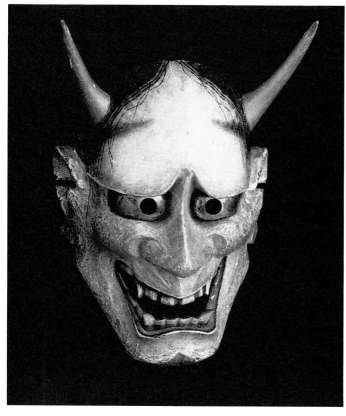

PLATE 1.9 In the absence of Murasaki, Genji faces a medium in trance. Yamamoto Shunshō (1610–1682). *Eiri Genji monogatari* (Illustrated *Tale of Genji*; 1650). Printed book. Ink on paper. Photograph: Sheldan Comfert Collins. The Mary and Jackson Burke Collection.

PLATE 1.8 Genji and exorcists attend to the possessed Murasaki. Anonymous. *Hakubyō Genji monogatari emaki*. Scroll II. Sixteenth century. Tenri Central Library, Nara Prefecture.

PLATE 1.10   Yūgiri plays Kashiwagi's flute, handed down by Ochiba's mother, Ichijō no miyasudokoro. Tosa Mitsunori (1583–1638). *Genji* album: 30 double pages (1 page each of painting and calligraphy) depicting scenes from *The Tale of Genji* (32.27C). Ink, red ink, and gold on paper. Courtesy of the Freer Gallery of Art, Smithsonian Institution, Washington, D.C.

# Murasaki

FAR MORE COMPLICATED than his attempt to substitute his stepmother Fujitsubo for his mother Kiritsubo is Genji's attempt to replace the forbidden and increasingly inaccessible Fujitsubo with the unformed child Murasaki, whom Genji kidnaps, adopts, and then—when she is old enough—marries. In Murasaki, Genji seems, at least initially, to have found what he needed. Despite her youth, Murasaki maintains her composure; there is a dignified air of restraint even in her occasional twinges of jealousy. She seems fully to have overcome the disadvantages of her slightly inferior social position and thus to have proven that a difference in rank between lovers need not end tragically for the woman—as it did in the cases of Kiritsubo and Yūgao.[1] Yet for Murasaki, too, various factors combine to produce an unusually prolonged and dramatic case of spirit possession. To understand fully the motivations and ramifications of Murasaki Shikibu's drama, one must consider the ways in which Murasaki was shaped by her family history and by her marital role in a polygynous society.

## From Motherless Child to Childless Mother

Murasaki's father is Prince Hyōbu, the older brother of Fujitsubo; her mother, Hyōbu's lesser wife, died, shortly after giving birth, from fear of intrigues similar to those encountered by Kiritsubo. Murasaki is, therefore, the niece of Genji's beloved Fujitsubo (fig. 3 in App. B). What constitutes Murasaki's original appeal for Genji is precisely her physical resemblance to her aunt Fujitsubo, the mother of his unacknowledged son and the ideal woman whom Genji loved because of *her* physical resemblance to his real mother. Genji discovers the child Murasaki through his *kaimami* at Kitayama, where she has taken refuge from a cruel stepmother. As an indirect version of the Fujitsubo incident (that is, the tabooed affair for which Genji is seeking a cure in the mountains), the Kitayama *kaimami* succeeds in generating a romantic relationship between Genji and Murasaki that merges idealization and violation.[2]

Another aspect of Murasaki's family history seems to bond her to Genji. Deprived by the very early loss of her mother, she endures a fate similar to Genji's. In other words, Murasaki incorporates Genji's ideal woman because she represents a direct blood link to Fujitsubo (and through her to Genji's mother) and because Genji can identify with her on the basis of their shared family history. Like Genji, Murasaki is of high birth on the paternal side but is reduced in status because she lacks backing from the maternal side; in the wise words of the Akashi nun: "Even when a child has the emperor himself for its father, the mother's station in life makes all the difference" (S:332; 2:419). In addition, Murasaki's father, like Genji's, makes concessions, despite his personal preferences, to the principal wife's demands for her own children. Hyōbu's deference to Murasaki's stepmother leads him to pamper Murasaki's half-sister.

When Murasaki matures, she realizes that she is barren, and she suffers greatly from this inability to fulfill the maternal role prescribed by Heian society.[3] Her childlessness is a grief too intensely sad even for poetry inspired by deep feelings. Murasaki can hardly bear to mention her barrenness to Genji, but others are detached enough to voice an emotional response to this apparent flaw in an otherwise ideal union.[4] Genji's rival Tō no Chūjō expresses both envy and sympathy: "Yes, the great Genji, not a fleck of dust on his name and fame, much too good, everyone says, for our degenerate age. It seems a pity that his favorite lady, a perfect jewel, has no children" (S:446; 3:229). A less ambivalent lament comes from Genji's son Yūgiri, on the occasion of Murasaki's first death anniversary: "The saddest thing is that she had no children" (S:731; 4:526). If Murasaki indirectly symbolizes a mother figure for Genji, it is particularly ironic that she should be deprived of motherhood.

Her pain is intensified by the fact that Genji seems actually to prefer that she remain childless. It is perhaps no coincidence that Genji's courtship of Murasaki began when Aoi, his principal wife, was pregnant. Murasaki's attraction for Genji is based on maternal likeness, yet their romance depends on her remaining childlike. However, she is not altogether deprived of a woman's conventional role. She is granted symbolic motherhood, but her adoption of a child intensifies rather than solves her problem. It sets in motion a fateful sequence that culminates in the most extended case of spirit possession in the *Genji*.

Three facts are crucial. First, although she is sad about not having produced an heir for Genji, the idea of an adoption is not hers: it is his. Second, the child is not just anybody's, but Genji's own daughter by the Akashi lady (Akashi no kimi). Third, the child is adopted just before the death of Fujitsubo (see S:330–337; 2:412–430). In short, Genji asks the substitute for his stepmother to become the stepmother of his daughter. What are the implications of these facts for the drama that ensues? With Fujitsubo's death, Murasaki should have been left as the only candidate to replace Genji's mother, but the adoption complicates their relationship. One might expect that the role of surrogate mother satisfies Murasaki's longing to bestow upon a child some of the love that she herself did not receive from her own stepmother (whose behavior was typical of the stepmothers in folk myths, *monogatari, setsuwa,* and *otogi-zōshi*).[5] One might expect, in other words, that Murasaki's specific history provided her with emotional resources to cope with the difficult situation of her "motherhood." Instead, when the motherless Murasaki loses her status as a childless mother, she becomes more vulnerable rather than less.

To understand just how vulnerable Murasaki becomes in her early thirties, it is necessary to reflect upon the nature of her "maternal" roles and the various phases of her reproductive crises. In polygynous Heian society it was not unusual for a wife to adopt the child of her husband's mistress.[6] There is a literary reflection of this arrangement in the *Kagerō Nikki*, whose author, known as the Mother of Michitsuna, decides of her own accord to adopt her husband's twelve-year-old daughter by a highborn mistress. The birth mother, living in seclusion and thinking of becoming a nun, agrees to the adoption for the sake of her daughter. Having borne Prince Kaneie only one son, the Mother of Michitsuna hopes, with the adopted daughter as her bait, to entice the notoriously neglectful Kaneie to visit her more frequently.[7] This strategy is briefly successful: "It struck me as ironical that our relationship should suddenly have taken this turn after so many years of coolness."[8]

Despite the similarities suggested above, Murasaki's case is very different from that of the Mother of Michitsuna. Murasaki has been able to keep her peace of mind despite her infertility because Genji's other women have produced surprisingly few children. Genji's son by his stepmother Fujitsubo is Reizei, whose identity has been kept secret so that, as far as Murasaki knows, Genji has only one son, by Aoi. And Aoi died when the Genji–Murasaki relationship was still in its infancy. This son, Yūgiri, was raised by his maternal relatives (fig. 2 in App. B). At the time of Aoi's death, Murasaki, thirteen years older than Yūgiri, was not considered for the role of stepmother. (Ironically, the difference in their ages and their separate living quarters combine later to imbue Murasaki with the kind of attraction for Yūgiri that Fujitsubo had for Genji.)[9] The Akashi daughter is the only one of Genji's children to arouse jealousy in Murasaki (a jealousy directed at Akashi, the girl's mother). Despite her socially inferior provincial origins, Akashi is a thorn in Murasaki's side because *her* daughter is, according to prophecy, destined to become empress.

In order for this dream of the Akashi daughter as empress to come true, Genji must go tightroping between Murasaki and Akashi. He moves Akashi from the remote coast where she had been living (and from which her sobriquet derives) to an intermediary station on the way to court. She is settled at the old Akashi family estate near the Ōi River in the western part of Kyoto, where Genji undertakes the painful task of gradually persuading her to part with her child in order for Murasaki to adopt it. Genji's plan crystallizes during his reunion with Akashi at Ōi. He contemplates the future of the child: "The mother *was* of inferior birth, and the disability must not be passed on to the daughter. It could be overcome if he were to take her to Nijō and see to her needs as he wished. Yet there were the feelings of the mother to be considered and of them he was uncertain. Choking with tears, he tried to bring the matter up" (S:326; 2:404). At this time, he manages merely to sound out the mother and prepare her for the ultimate test of parting with her child. He does not want to move ahead with his plan to ask Akashi to give up her daughter until he has secured Murasaki's consent to raise the child at the Nijō-in. Thus his way of asking the permission of both women covers the entire spectrum from humble apologies to cajoling, coaxing, and coercing strategies that, taken together, are tantamount to an elegant form of moral bribery.

When Murasaki first suspects that Genji's excursions to his Katsura chapel are a smokescreen for his reunion with Akashi, she is devastated. Waiting for his return is torture: "Those two or three days were likely to become days enough to rot the handle of the woodcutter's ax" (S:323; 2:399). Extending his absence in order to enjoy a banquet at the Katsura villa, Genji is guiltily aware of Murasaki's suffering: "Today they must definitely go back, said Genji, and soon. No rotting ax handles, please" (S:329; 2:411). He returns to Murasaki with effusive apologies and takes pains to demonstrate how much more important to him she is than the lady at Ōi.

Genji has carefully prepared Murasaki for the adoption of the Akashi daughter by appealing to her sense of compassion: "I don't have children where I really want them, and now there is a child in a very unlikely place. And it is a girl. I could of course simply disown her, but that is the sort of thing I do not seem capable of. I will bring her here one of these days and let you have a look at her. You are not to be jealous now" (S:276; 2:281). Murasaki's immediate response is sharp-tongued and gives evidence of her astute perception of Genji's self-interested argument. She rejects his unwarranted insinuation of jealousy. It is a defining moment in her self-assertiveness when she goes beyond rejecting the idea of jealousy by accusing him of distorting her personality and corrupting her sense of self: "How strange you are. You make me dislike myself, constantly assigning traits which are not mine at all. When and by whom, I wonder, shall I begin to have lessons in jealousy?" (S:276; 2:281). Rather at a loss about her high-strung reaction, which brings tears to his eyes, Genji acknowledges her originality: "Things come into your mind that would not occur to anyone else" (S:276; 2:281–282). Giving her this degree of sophisticated self-analysis, the author has created an exceptional character in Murasaki (whose sobriquet became, oddly enough, a part of Murasaki Shikibu's "name"). In consciously coping with his disparaging male view of female jealousy, Murasaki is unlike other women, who seem to have accepted the male stereotype of female jealousy.

Although Murasaki can dismiss the notion that she is jealous of the mother of Genji's daughter, she nonetheless hesitates to accept his suggestion that she adopt the girl. He then plays upon her sympathy by likening the girl to the pitifully abandoned "leech child" *(hiru no ko)* of Japanese myth. Murasaki can become the girl's savior or, in Genji's more down-to-earth language, one who is not too proud to pin up a child's diapers. The decision, he avers, is all hers. He continues disingenuously. Only she can make the decision because he is too weak to make it himself: "Put yourself in my place, if you will, and make the decision for me. What do you think? Will you perhaps take her in?" (S:330; 2:413). Unlike the Mother of Michitsuna's decision to adopt her husband's daughter by his mistress, Murasaki's "decision" is merely manipulated consent. Although Genji has transformed an awkward situation into what seems to be a triumph of marital diplomacy, he is not so naive as to assume that all will go well. Murasaki is not so immune from jealousy as she claims to be. Silently she recalls the support she provided while Genji was in exile. She realizes that he had amused himself at her expense: "And so while she herself had been lost in infinite sadness, thought Murasaki, he had managed to keep himself entertained. It did not seem right that he should have allowed himself even a playful glance at another woman" (S:276–277; 2:282).

Genji's skill in persuading Akashi to give up her child is equally remarkable. The scene of parting *(ribetsu)* is of such chilling beauty that the reference to Akashi as the "Lady of Winter" *( fuyu no onkata)* seems justified. She too is made to feel that the decision about her daughter is hers alone (see S:333; 2:423). The advice she receives from her mother, the Akashi nun (Akashi no amagimi)—to act in the interest of the child—reinforces her sense that Genji's plan must be right. After all, Akashi will be elevated in status through the eventual rise of her daughter to rank of empress.

In some respects, the Genji–Akashi relationship reflects that of Genji's parents. Both Genji and the Kiritsubo Emperor try to protect their socially disadvantaged women from the intrigues of court while at the same time bearing in mind the welfare of their children. Genji, however, avoids the mistakes of his father by keeping his provincial wife at a safe distance from the Nijō-in, away from those who might envy her not only his love but also her child by him. Genji's prudent behavior and Akashi's patience are rewarded by Murasaki's cooperation, which is the polar opposite to Kokiden's vicious scheming against Kiritsubo. Potential tragedy is reduced to mere anxiety, which is felt to differing degrees by Genji, Akashi, and Murasaki. Although the "uncertainty" (S:332; 2:419) of the situation most deeply affects Akashi, during her lonely days at Ōi, her troubles are not so acute as to extinguish her will to live.[10]

Genji, fearing that he has committed a "crime for which one day he would be summoned to do penance" (S:334; 2:424), justifies to himself the grief the birth mother must endure by congratulating himself on removing Murasaki's "old bitterness" (S:335; 2:427) over her childlessness: "For Murasaki it was as if her last wish had been granted" (S:334; 2:426). Murasaki does seem at first to flourish in her exciting new role. For the twenty-three-year-old Murasaki, the adoption takes the sting out of her infertility, and she becomes a totally devoted surrogate mother (S:337; 2:429–430):

> Murasaki no longer really thought a great deal about her rival. The little girl, scampering and tumbling about, quite filled her thoughts. Yet she did feel for the Akashi lady, knowing how desperate her own loneliness would be in such circumstances. Taking the little girl in her arms, she playfully offered one of her own small breasts. It was a charming scene. What had gone wrong? asked her women. Why was Genji's daughter not hers? But such was the way of the world. [Plate 2.5]

In short, the multiple transactions among Akashi, Genji, and Murasaki appear to go smoothly. Communications between Genji and Akashi, and between Genji and Murasaki, seem to be a model of Heian *mono no aware,* the sensitivity to transient things. Yet one fears that repressed emotions are ready to explode.

Eight years later, after her coming-of-age ceremony at age eleven, the Akashi daughter enters court to be betrothed to the crown prince, the son of Suzaku. Having accomplished the task of raising her adopted daughter in the courtly manner, Murasaki seems willing, of her own accord, to surrender the borrowed girl to her birth mother. Akashi, who has finally been welcomed to live in the northeastern "winter" quarters of the Rokujō-in—Genji's version of the residence of imperial consorts *(kōkyū)*—seems to pose no threat to Murasaki's supreme position there. (The physical proximity to her inaccessible daughter, in Murasaki's custody in the southeastern quarters, may have simultaneously reassured and frustrated Akashi.)

Appearances deceive. Murasaki, now thirty-one, undergoes a painful form of child loss: "Murasaki must now give up the child who had been her whole life" (S:531; 3:442). Her adopted daughter is once again Akashi's daughter, and Murasaki is stricken by the belated realization that she has been no more than a foster mother to the girl. Murasaki cannot but feel diminished as she undergoes a change of identity and, in its transformative wake, a loss of personality.

Most remarkably, it is Murasaki herself who initiates the return of the Akashi daughter to her birth mother. How can one explain this act of generosity? It is possible that Murasaki, subliminally aware of the unspoken condition of the original adoption pact, cleverly anticipates the inevitable call to return the daughter. Vulnerable to this demand, her generosity may—ungenerously—be seen as a form of self-defense. If the necessary surrender is perceived by others as a voluntary move, Murasaki will be admired for her heroic sacrifice. Her reading of the situation is flawless.

A less Machiavellian interpretation of her willingness to give up the child turns on Murasaki's capacity for empathy and compassion. It had taken time for Murasaki to overcome her bad conscience about Akashi's grief over the transfer of the child. Although she had initially repressed her doubts in order to perform her task as an adoptive mother, she comes in time to feel what it must have meant to Akashi to surrender the child. At the proper time, therefore, Murasaki—as the adoptive mother—feels impelled to repeat the sacrifice of the birth mother: Murasaki "thought that the time had come for the girl's real mother to be with her. It was sad for them both, mother and daughter, that they had been kept apart so long. The matter had been on Murasaki's conscience and she suspected that it had been troubling the girl as well" (S:531; 3:440–441).

That the Akashi daughter's identity had not been kept secret even from the girl herself facilitates the return to her birth mother. Murasaki delivers the Akashi daughter to court, where Akashi comes to replace her. To Genji's surprise, the surrender of the adopted child seems to occur with the same compassionate gentleness as the adoption itself. Indeed, Murasaki seems to reach her zenith as she rides home from the Akashi Princess' wedding in a palanquin normally reserved only for a high-ranking consort (*nyōgo*). At the same time, Akashi's cooperation in the difficult transactions proves *her* humble and deferential character, "a model of reserve and diffidence" (S:532; 3:444). The Akashi Princess soon gives birth to her first son, who is later to become crown prince (fig. 3 in App. B). Although she has spent most of her pregnancy in her mother's quarters, Genji has her moved back to Murasaki's more spacious southeastern quarter for the occasion of the birth, at which Murasaki is present as a proud witness: "She had no children of her own, nor had she ever before been present at a childbirth. It was all very new and wonderful" (S:571; 4:101). In her early thirties,[11] Murasaki is celebrated as the prince's "grandmother" (S:571; 4:101). She enjoys a brief respite from her griefs and grievances. "The Akashi princess was fonder of Murasaki than of her real mother" (S:592; 4:159).

## Female Rivals, Female Allies

Her generosity in returning the Akashi daughter to her mother brings Murasaki an unexpected ally. The girl might have been a pawn in the game of love, an occasion for intensified jealousy. Instead, the shared child forms a bond between the two women. Their compliance with the cultural norm for female temperament—elegant restraint—enables them to turn the sort of rivalry between unequals that had plagued Kiritsubo into the polygynous ideal of friendly coexistence. Akashi and Murasaki, two women who recognize their precarious social positions, become a picture-book version of female friendship.[12] The alliance between Akashi and Murasaki goes so far beyond the mutual tolerance expected in a polygynous society that Genji is baffled by it. Although he initially welcomes it, the female pact seems unnatural and even threatening to him. Always warning his women against the other extreme of open hostility, he is uneasy with their female friendship. As if he meant to test the reality of so strange a phenomenon as an alliance between two women, Genji deliberately reminds Murasaki of the ugly carriage quarrel between Aoi and Rokujō; but Murasaki's pacific temperament and Akashi's meekness enable the women to avoid unseemly confrontation.

Is the absence of conflict an illusion? Genji cannot shake off the sense that it must be. The tensions caused by the adoption process and its reversal led him to fear the worst; at most he would have expected neutrality. Therefore, his disbelief over the cooperation among the two mothers and their daughter continues even after the two women have begun jointly to help raise the Akashi daughter's first child. Quite unnecessarily, Genji exhorts the Akashi daughter always to express her gratitude to Murasaki, who is never to be treated as a stereotypically evil stepmother (see S:578–579; 4:121–123).[13] As for Akashi, she points out that Genji need not lecture her about Murasaki's virtues nor her own. Nonetheless Genji, almost paranoid in his suspicion of their female bonding, feels compelled to preach to her, gallantly placing his emphasis on Akashi herself: "You have not chosen to stand on your rights as a mother and that has helped a great deal. I have nothing to complain or worry about. It is amazing the damage that obtuseness and ill temper can do, and I cannot tell you how grateful I am that these lamentable qualities are alien to both of you" (S:579; 4:124).

The first significant female rival to enter Murasaki's life at this point is Genji's first cousin Asagao (fig. 2 in App. B). As if to reassure himself, Genji begins to court her just after his unsuccessful amorous approach to Akikonomu (Rokujō's daughter, now the Reizei Emperor's high consort). Both Murasaki and Asagao are the grand-daughters of emperors, but Asagao has enjoyed significantly more backing in her distinguished career as Kamo Priestess *(saiin)*. Although she resigned from that position after the recent death of her father Prince Momozono (Shikibukyō), she continues to command great respect.

Murasaki muffles her resentment over this new betrayal. Well adjusted to the behavioral norm of her day, she refuses to reveal her anxiety to Genji and instead internalizes the problem: "Though in matters of no importance she could scold him most charmingly, she gave no hint of her concern when she was really upset" (S:352; 2:469). Having just recently managed the potentially explosive Akashi problem, she feels that her disposition toward tacit consent has been taken for granted, and for the first time she becomes seriously disillusioned with her wayward husband. Perhaps irrationally in view of her continued importance to Genji as the substitute for Fujitsubo and as the adoptive mother of the Akashi daughter, she imagines the worst: being discarded. Although he takes note of her depression over his revival of an old infatuation, he treats her distress nonchalantly, down-playing the importance of Asagao in his life. It is difficult for him to admit, even to himself, that his renewed amorous adventurousness may be nothing more than a middle-aged man's testing his virility. Murasaki's crisis—or is it Genji's?—passes relatively quietly when Asa-gao declines Genji's advances.

Genji, who can never learn to leave well enough alone, confronts Murasaki with another kind of rival when he invites Yūgao's daughter Tamakazura (fig. 1 in App. B), of marriageable age and only six years younger than Murasaki, into his Rokujō-in in the guise of a long-lost daughter. When Genji confides Tamakazura's true identity to Mura-saki, he does more harm than good.[14] Murasaki need only recall her own former role as Genji's foster daughter to anticipate his courtship of the new prospect. If Tamakazura resists the pattern of the "daugh-ter" turned bride, it is perhaps because she is more mature than Murasaki was when she came under Genji's tutelage and because Tamakazura was raised in the rough environment of Tsukushi (Kyūshū), more conducive to self-assertive behavior and independent thinking. Nonetheless, Murasaki is right to be apprehensive about Genji's improper infatuation with this "daughter." Since Genji is repeatedly rebuffed by the strong-willed newcomer, a woman past the age of easy malleability, this potentially explosive crisis, like the one over Asagao, is defused.

Murasaki competes not only with living rivals but with dead ones as well. On several occasions, Genji reminisces about his late lovers, implicitly comparing Murasaki to them. When Genji's characterizations of these women are dismissive, Murasaki has little reason to feel threatened. She has no reason to resent Genji's memories of Aoi, whom he characterizes as a "cold intellectual" (S:608; 4:200); nor is Murasaki threatened when she hears of Yūgao, whom Genji describes as "a little too solemn and humorless" (S:426; 3:175). (Ironically, if Genji had not misrepresented Yūgao's character, Murasaki might have learned a lesson from this rival's tragic demise through spirit possession.)

But when Genji idealizes—when he *idolizes* his dead lovers—Murasaki feels utterly vulnerable. Toward the end of the Asagao episode, for instance, Genji and Murasaki contemplate a snowscape eerily illuminated by the moon. Genji enlivens the somber scene by ordering young girls to build snowmen. Thus charmed by evanescent creations, he voices his nostalgia for Fujitsubo. Although Murasaki is aware only of her kinship tie to Fujitsubo and not of Genji's incestuous relationship with her aunt, she senses a dark unknown to which she does not know how to react.

That same night, after reciting to Murasaki an amorous roll call of his women, Genji dreams of a furious Fujitsubo who reprimands him for revealing the secret of their son's birth. Although the accusation has no basis in fact, it reveals Genji's guilt over having concealed from Murasaki the sexual nature of his bond with Fujitsubo. Immediately before falling asleep, Genji had silently and favorably compared Murasaki to Fujitsubo, thereby betraying his ideal and forcing his bad conscience to erupt through the unconscious. Obliquely, the dream signals how close Murasaki has come to replacing Fujitsubo in Genji's heart. The shift occurs, significantly, after Fujitsubo has passed from the realm of the living into that of the dead. (This is confirmed after Murasaki's death when the snow no longer reminds Genji of Fujitsubo but of Murasaki [see S:724; 4:510].) Since Murasaki cannot decipher Genji's nightmare, she is numb with fear.

## The Spirit of the Place: Rokujō and the Rokujō-in

More problematic than Genji's grief for Fujitsubo is his obsession with the memory of Rokujō. Although Murasaki had never come in direct contact with the living Rokujō (see S:608; 4:201), she has nevertheless been well aware of this sophisticated woman's charisma. Almost from the beginning of Murasaki's relationship with Genji, the rumors about Rokujō's role in Aoi's spirit possession must have left a deep mark on young Murasaki's impressionable mind. After Aoi's death, Genji's remarkably conciliatory behavior toward Rokujō and his subsequent willingness to take custody of her orphaned daughter by Zenbō (the younger brother of the Kiritsubo Emperor) must have further convinced Murasaki of this woman's enormous impact on Genji.

The ultimate testimony to her overwhelming importance, however, is Genji's construction at age thirty-four of the Rokujō-in, dedicated to the pacification of Rokujō's restless spirit. The Rokujō-in is much more than a memorial to its eponym. As Hirota Osamu has noted, the Rokujō-in is associated with the historical site of the deposed prince Minamoto Tōru's grand estate, the Kawara-in,[15] and hence with the recalling of imperial spirits and the reclaiming of land.[16] In this architectural expression of his greatest ambitions, Genji compensates for his loss of political power. Indeed, Genji's Rokujō-in is conceived on such a grand scale that it all but eclipses the Imperial Palace itself (to whose inner residential complex for the imperial consorts, the kōkyū, Hirota has compared it).[17]

According to Fujii Sadakazu, the Rokujō-in is a building designed specifically to pacify Rokujō's restless spirit, which is believed to linger near her old estate,[18] but Norma Field is skeptical about the building's pacifying qualities: "And what, after all, are the women's quarters at the Palace and at the Rokujōin if not the breeding ground of the most intense rivalry conceivable among women?"[19] If the Rokujō-in does fulfill its intended function, Field wonders, does it not serve the pacification of Yūgao's spirit as well as Rokujō's? After all, Genji installs both of these women's daughters there. In any event, it seems that Genji's plan is absurdly utopian. Unquestionably, Genji means well, but he walks a fine line when he relies upon archaic folk beliefs in an effort to placate his dead mistress and to enlist her spirit as a house guardian spirit (karyō).[20]

Predictably, Genji succeeds only partially. The splendid edifice accommodates women protected from Genji by taboo (the Akashi daughter), resistant to Genji's wiles due to their ability to assert themselves (Akikonomu and Tamakazura), or compliant enough to live with their rivals under one roof (Akashi and Orange Blossoms [Hanachirusato]). It is difficult to imagine Rokujō dwelling at the Rokujō-in. The women who in fact suffer most in this elegantly disguised female prison are the nonconformists (Murasaki and the Third Princess [Onna san no miya]) who seek to escape with the help of the charisma of others—such as Rokujō.[21] When Murasaki departs to seek refuge elsewhere, her flight reveals the truth about the Rokujō-in and the woman for whom it was named. Rokujō's spirit ought to be most gratified by self-assertive women like Murasaki.

The failure of Genji's pacifying architectural gesture is important. Since *mono no ke* illuminate and literally spell out conflict, as Takahashi Tōru has noted, they gain the power to deconstruct the Rokujō-in by telling *(mono-gatari)* the ineffable *(mono no ke)*.[22] Furthermore, Haruo Shirane has correctly observed that the gradual physical deterioration of the Rokujō-in parallels the spiritual erosion of "Genji's world and the polygamous ideals supporting it."[23] It is in the course of this discussion that Shirane offers his previously quoted insightful remarks about spirit possession as "a dramatic means of expressing a woman's repressed unconscious emotions, particularly jealousy and resentment caused by polygamy."[24] Yet even Shirane, despite his comments about polygyny and resentment, reverts to the conventional Genji-centric tradition. He condemns Rokujō as a negative figure because of her "inability to suppress those forbidden emotions [that turn] her into a symbol of excessive attachment and an emblem of social chaos and destruction. Like the so-called madwoman in the attic, the Rokujō lady is appropriately condemned for her behavior."[25] Norma Field is closer to the mark here when she argues, following Fukazawa Michio, that Rokujō, "in perverse fashion," may be said to be speaking for the women she possesses.[26]

Genji reveals to Murasaki his complex assessment of Rokujō in a remarkably honest reminiscence; by contrast, he had omitted the truth of their forbidden relationship from his earlier description of Fujitsubo (see S:357; 2:481–482). He is truly in awe of Rokujō in the double sense of the word. On the one hand, her artistic subtleties were unsurpassed. On the other hand, her resistance to male dominance clearly was not only outside the range of female behavioral norms but also took unorthodox forms. Although suffering pains similar to those of other Heian aristocratic women, she did not humbly plead with her lover. Nor did she ask for the tonsure until her death was imminent (see S:285; 2:300). And she did not become *subject* to spirit possession. On the contrary, she herself was publicly charged with being the female possessing spirit in Aoi's possession case. During and after Aoi's possession, she herself was surprised at this charge, temporarily susceptible to it, but finally unwilling to be anything other than her own superbly sovereign self.

As the widow of Crown Prince Zenbō, Rokujō no miyasudokoro literally stands alone. She is not only unattached but disconcertingly unaffiliated—indeed of startlingly uncertain lineage (fig. 1 in App. B). All that can be ascertained about her past is that she is the daughter of an ambitious minister and that her husband's premature death made it impossible for her to fulfill her father's political ambitions for her. Some scholars, relying on the traditional understanding of spirit possession as a telepathic phenomenon motivated by the possessing spirit's jealousy, have commented not only on Rokujō's "choice of victims,"[27] but also on her alleged tolerance of rivals like Akashi.

If the most crucial question of motive is shifted from the possessing spirit to the possessed person, as I have argued it should be, then the "choice" is the possessed person's rather than the possessing spirit's. Since active and passive roles appear reversed in the oblique strategy of spirit possession, the possessed person is, in truth, the active agent. Seen in this light, spirit possession dramatizes the possessed person's need to empower herself with the charisma of another, one who emerges as an ally rather than a rival or enemy. By the same token, the possessing spirit constitutes not an initiating force but a reactive presence.

Since Sakamoto Kazuko, Fujii, and Field,[28] among others, have explicitly or implicitly accepted the traditional interpretation of spirit possession, they have found it necessary to explain Akashi's apparent immunity from the attacks of Rokujō's jealous spirit. This they have done by observing that Akashi may be related to the Kiritsubo line (fig. 3 in App. B).[29] Rokujō does not inflict her possessing spirit on Akashi because Akashi can be seen as the successor to Genji's mother (Kiritsubo kōi).[30] H. Richard Okada extends this argument and links Rokujō to this Akashi–Kiritsubo connection on the ground that she too was the daughter of an ambitious minister.[31] This interpretation is unconvincing because it does not explain why a blood relationship to Genji's mother protects Akashi against Rokujō's jealousy when it cannot protect Murasaki and the Third Princess, who are in Genji's mind even more strongly connected to Kiritsubo via Fujitsubo. (Both of these women are seen by these same critics as victims of the dead Rokujō.)

Apart from the issue of Rokujō, about whom Akashi may have heard little, a hitherto overlooked reason for Akashi's immunity to spirit possession lies in the communicability of her problems. Although Akashi's social status is initially presented as a handicap, it stimulates the hero's interest. Akashi's fertility turns out to be a temporary problem, when she must give up the child for adoption, but this problem is openly and extensively discussed with Genji and with her own family. It is not, therefore, internalized or repressed. Her pain is appreciated, rather than ignored or denied, thereby making dramatization through spirit possession superfluous.

Rather than wondering with the critics why Rokujō does not possess Akashi, we would do well to ask why women who have resorted to the oblique aggressive strategy of spirit possession are motivated in times of stress to draw upon Rokujō's charisma. The answer seems to be that women are drawn to Rokujō by an intuitive recognition of the very strength of character that first attracted and then overpowered Genji. Although Rokujō's strength of character does not make her invulnerable, Genji fears her precisely because he does not expect to have a woman as his equal.

Frightfully atypical of the women of her time, Rokujō represents not what women are but rather what they want to be. Rokujō's reputation is painted in such forbidding colors, however, that women tightly controlled by a male-dominated polygynous society cannot openly admit that Rokujō represents an attractive ideal. Nonetheless, to some she is alive as their dream, their fantasy, as a manifestation of their unconscious. A secret feminine role model, Rokujō towers over other female protagonists as the embodiment of female pride and independence.

In recalling Rokujō, Genji admits to Murasaki that, unlike his other women, she did not bow to him. On the contrary, in his commemoration of her, Genji bows symbolically to Rokujō by apologizing, admitting his callous attitude, and asking for retroactive forgiveness: "I could see how the gossip hurt her and how she condemned herself for conduct which she thought unworthy of her position, and I could see that difficult though she might be I was at fault myself. . . . I like to think that [Rokujō], wherever she is, has forgiven me" (S:608; 4:201). It is difficult to know how much of this is formulaic lip service to pacify Rokujō's roaming dead spirit and how much is sincere, but Genji's confession amounts almost to an admission of defeat. Murasaki cannot but come to the unspoken conclusion that Rokujō's power, extending beyond life into death, has a unique hold on Genji. Nevertheless, the context in which Murasaki witnesses Genji's concession to Rokujō's sovereignty is so complicated that we must postpone our discussion of the spirit-possession crisis it precipitates in Murasaki. For the time being, it is important to recognize that Murasaki, under extreme circumstances, might, in an altered state of consciousness, draw upon Rokujō as a feminine ideal and an ally in the rebellion against male dominance.

## In Search of Female Charisma

Apart from her somewhat defective social status and her infertility, Murasaki must confront the inevitable fact that she is growing older. By becoming motherly, Murasaki has disguised the diminution of sexual passion. She and Genji seem to be in midlife harmony, but a real crisis looms when the Retired Suzaku Emperor asks Genji to be the guardian of the Third Princess, Genji's niece (fig. 3 in App. B). The imperial request also implies that she become Genji's bride. It turns out that while Murasaki was able to relinquish the Akashi child and to indulge Genji in his reveries about his past loves, she is not ready, after all, to share her husband with a younger woman of higher status.

The dramatic tension created by the reader's expectation of some kind of psychological explosion is intensified by a ludicrous forerunner to Murasaki's spirit possession. Her extremely complex case is foreshadowed by the incongruent comic seizure of none other than her older half-sister, a woman known only as Higekuro's wife (Higekuro no moto no kita no kata).[32] When seen against the foil of this close relative's handling of strikingly similar difficulties, Murasaki's depth of character and profound understanding of the male/female tensions of her time become especially compelling.

### Higekuro's Wife

The oldest child of Prince Hyōbu, Higekuro's wife is the pampered daughter of Murasaki's cruel stepmother (fig. 3 in App. B). As the *kita no kata* of an important official, Higekuro's wife enjoys a privileged status. More poignant for Murasaki than these factors is her half-sister's enviable fertility: she bears Higekuro a daughter (Maki-bashira) and two sons. Accustomed to having her own way, Higekuro's wife is incensed by the prospect of being ousted from her position of principal wife by Tamakazura. Her complaint is neither unjustified nor unique. It is understandable that she wishes to maintain her position as principal wife, not only for her own sake but for her children's. According to polygynous practice, she was expected to be tolerant of other women joining the household,[33] but she knows deprivation and self-effacement only from hearsay. She is well aware of the behavioral norms; but, unlike Murasaki, she has not been socialized to withstand the onslaught of fierce female competition and to turn female rivals into allies. Rather, she is supported in her impetuousness by her father, who, ironically, had all but abandoned Murasaki to grow up under Genji's guardianship. He fans the dangerous flame of her self-righteous indignation while her husband appeals to Heian female virtues she has never been trained to develop: decorum and self-control, self-effacement and cooperation.

Higekuro, annoyed by Prince Hyōbu's efforts to undermine his marital rights, tries to pacify his wife with flattery of her father. She in turn employs her father and his concern over her reputation as an excuse for her possessiveness. Most important, she argues that her father would not want her to lose in indirect competition with Murasaki: "And you are surely aware . . . that Genji's wife is not exactly a stranger to me. It is true that Father did not have responsibility of her when she was a girl, but it hurts him that she should now have made herself your young lady's sponsor. It is no concern of mine, of course. I but observe" (S:496; 3:353–354). In this studied pose of aloofness, she renounces all responsibility for her shortcomings as a wife by referring to her dutiful filial behavior. Higekuro claims to see through his wife's excuses and vehemently rejects them as "delusions" (S:497; 3:354). In particular, her allegation that Murasaki plotted Tamakazura's match to hurt her strikes him as unfounded. After all, he should know best who assisted him in winning Tamakazura's hand.[34]

By warning his wife not to let rumors of their strife reach Genji, Higekuro temporarily quells her fits of jealousy. Indeed she appears "calmly lucid" (S:497; 3:354–355), but it is a calm before the storm. For a while, each of them humors the other. She even succumbs to conventional etiquette and directs the perfuming of his robes in preparation of his visit to Tamakazura. Such humble deference to him, such generosity to her rival, cannot but arouse his suspicions, and he tries hard to pretend that it is difficult to leave her for another woman.

Higekuro's instincts are correct. His wife's altruistic action backfires. Her mood shifts from apparently serene composure to open violence. If he wants to visit Tamakazura, she cannot prevent him. What she can do is to embarrass him by delaying his departure. As if by sudden reflex, she grabs the censer used just a moment before to make her husband more attractive for the other woman and dumps its ashes on Higekuro's head (Plate 1.7).[35] The aggrieved woman's aggressive violence has an almost poetic logic: the instrument of her self-torture becomes her weapon of self-defense.

How do others view this unusually violent incident? While Higekuro has for some time been aware of his wife's emotional instability, he is taken by surprise. Awareness of her prolonged and mounting stress, evident from her peculiar symptom of massive hair loss (see S:495; 3:352), neither prevents her dramatic crisis nor lessens his shock when she, instead of punishing herself, attacks him. In her fit of hysteria she fails to impress him, much less bring him down to his knees, as is normally the case in spirit possession. He merely proclaims her "ill" (S:498; 3:358) and orders exorcist rituals. Moku, Higekuro's attendant and intimate *(meshūdo)*, fully understands his wife's sense of frustration and impotence while perfuming her husband's robes; she composes an apt *waka* (3:360; S:499):

> *hitori ite    kogaruru mune no    kurushiki ni*
> *omoi amareru    honoo to zo mishi*

> Alone with thoughts which are too much for her,
> She has let unquenchable embers do their work.

Her women express to one another their sympathy for the trials their mistress must endure as Higekuro's wife. They understand gender inequality and the sexual double standard. But they find her sadly lacking in face-saving skills and politic restraint. In short, they see her indignant and undignified behavior as that of a madwoman, and they diagnose her bewildering state as an abnormal form of spirit possession: "If she had not had the excuse of her *derangement* he would have marched from her presence and vowed never to return. It was a *very perverse sort of spirit* that possessed her" (S:498, my italics; 3:357).

In a cultural milieu intensely devoted to elegant indirections and subtleties, the unabashed directness of the woman's physical attack on her husband gives her incongruous action a slightly comic touch. Precisely because her motivation is undisguised, the infuriated woman's action appears to be inexplicable except as an instant of "derangement." In Heian eyes, only a "very perverse" possessing spirit could account for what seems to the modern reader a thoroughly understandable response to severely injured pride. Norma Field has speculated that the "attack on Higekuro is possibly the most secularized, psychological manifestation of the possessing spirit in the work."[36] It is precisely because the religious aura of ritual behavior is missing and the psychological motivation so overtly manifested that the possessed woman fails to elicit respect and the possessing spirits fail to strike terror in the hearts of the audience. Compared to the major cases of spirit possession in the *Genji*, this one is a fiasco.

Higekuro's wife's uncontrolled seizure illustrates that spirit possession takes specific, culturally defined forms that must be meticulously adhered to in order to succeed. Her case is significant precisely because it demonstrates complete failure. Doomed because it is direct and not oblique, this seizure fails to impress through the mystique associated with possession. Instead of letting a medium do all the ranting and screaming, Higekuro's wife does it herself.[37] Her unmediated spectacle contrasts sharply with Aoi's languid movements, coaxing words, and enticing *waka*. Her seizure is so perfectly obvious to the audience in terms of both motivation and target that there is no need to speculate about the identity of the possessing spirits. Yet the fundamental basis for this bungled occurrence is the same as in the most solemn and dignified cases of spirit possession: the sufferings inflicted on women by a polygynous marital system. Higekuro's wife realizes in her more lucid moments that her violent outburst won her some sympathy and cost her a great deal of respect. The afflicted woman understands that she can salvage a little self-esteem only by returning to her father's residence, thereby abandoning her identity as Higekuros's wife for the safe but regressive identity as Hyōbu's daughter.

Little suspecting that she would some day find herself in a situation similar to that of her inept half-sister, Murasaki is surprised to discover that she has become a scapegoat for her half-sister's resentment (see S:503; 3:372). Prince Hyōbu and his wife share their oldest daughter's anger and conclude that her bright future had been threatened ever since Genji took Murasaki under his wing. They suspect that their favored daughter has been totally eclipsed, through Murasaki's scheming, by Tamakazura. For them, the defeat is all the more humiliating because Tamakazura grew up, like Murasaki, as a motherless child later cared for by Genji. Higekuro's in-laws are not entirely wrong in their analysis of the complex of grievances. Murasaki harbored no animus against her spoiled half-sister, but one might, nonetheless, think of Tamakazura as having sought retributive justice on Murasaki's behalf.

### The Third Princess

Two years after her half-sister's recourse to embarrassing direct physical violence, Murasaki encounters her most serious living rival: the Third Princess. Unlike her privileged half-sister, Murasaki has no home to go back to and no parental backing to rely on. Since she has no children of her own and has already returned the Akashi daughter to her birth mother, she cannot use children as leverage against her husband. Yet she struggles in more culturally respectful ways than her half-sister to emerge as her own self. It is a struggle that consumes the last decade of Murasaki's life and involves her in the longest and most frequent bouts with spirit possession—alternating with requests for the tonsure—in the entire *Genji*.

The Third Princess' background has a great deal to do with Murasaki's innermost fears. The new arrival in the Rokujō-in is the favorite daughter of the Retired Suzaku Emperor by Fujitsubo nyōgo, the half-sister of Fujitsubo and Hyōbu (fig. 3 in App. B). Genji is attracted to the idea of becoming her guardian because of her blood relationship to Fujitsubo. If Murasaki had earlier been in spatially and temporally remote competition with her aunt Fujitsubo, she must now compete under the same roof with her first cousin. All her life Murasaki has dealt successfully with rivals of one sort or another, but this time the odds are against her.

In addition to the Third Princess' unimpeachable rank, Murasaki must also fear her rival's youth—she is only fourteen.[38] Murasaki is more than twice her age, old enough to be her mother. Furthermore, Murasaki recalls that the beginning of her own relationship with Genji was defined not only by her connection *(yukari)* to Fujitsubo but also by her status as a child abandoned by her father. Therefore, she refuses to be soothed by Genji's reassurances of loyalty and by his claim that he is disinterested in this bride with a childish disposition.

Suzaku himself considers Genji's original guardian relationship with Murasaki as a model for his daughter's future marital prospects. Foremost on his mind is his favorite daughter's "education" (S:541; 4:21), a duty he himself has neglected and now hopes an appropriate suitor will fulfill: "It would be quite the best thing if someone could be persuaded to do for her what Genji did for Prince Hyōbu's daughter" (S:541; 4:21). With this thought in mind, Suzaku suggests to Genji that he once again combine the roles of guardian and husband. Genji, concerned about his age, at first declines to be a husband as well as guardian (see S:545; 4:33). But, just as Suzaku is proposing to divide the duties of guardian and husband between Genji and his son Yūgiri, Genji changes his mind and agrees to marry the Third Princess.

While Genji is still summoning the courage to tell Murasaki in person, she is shocked to hear the news in the form of a rumor. He uses his advanced age of forty to downplay the importance of the match and to reassure Murasaki of her uncontestable place in his affections. When he appeals to her to cooperate as she did when she took in Akashi's daughter, Murasaki responds with an apparently effortless affability and show of concern that carries an almost imperceptible note of sarcasm: "The only thing that worries me is the possibility that she might feel less than completely at home. I shall be very happy if our being so closely related persuades her that I am no stranger" (S:550; 4:46). Genji is made uneasy by her excessive sweetness: "How silly that this very willingness to accept things should bother me. But it does" (S:550; 4:46). He closes his intimate conversation with the formulaic admonition against jealousy: "Do not start imagining things, and do not torture yourself with empty jealousies" (S:550; 4:47).

Genji's platitudes expose his reluctance to cross the threshold of knowledge about the female psyche. And so, although Murasaki's life as a woman seems to have been fulfilled, she now stands alone at a crossroads, not knowing which way to turn. Her future seems increasingly uncertain. She worries about her stepmother's renewed tendency "to blame and to gloat" (S:550; 4:47) because of Tamakazura's invasion of the Higekuro household. She knows that Genji's marriage to the Third Princess is inevitable and that she can only disgrace herself by confessing her fears of replacement by the younger, higher-ranking bride. Despite her skillfully controlled facade, her self-confidence plummets: "She did not want the world to think that she had been crushed by what had to come" (S:550; 4:47).

When Genji compares Murasaki to his new wife, the former has the advantage in everything but age and rank. Murasaki nearly breaks Genji's heart when she helps with the arrangements for the three nuptial nights. Although a wife was conventionally expected to scent her husband's robes even when he was to spend the night with another woman, Murasaki's dutiful performance has undertones from her incensed half-sister's symbolic incineration of Higekuro. Both women try extremely hard to submit to the unwritten rules of etiquette, but Murasaki appears to be in complete control (as Higekuro's wife was not). Is Murasaki better off for enduring the pain and preserving her good reputation? Or does she, in the long run, inflict far greater damage upon herself by suppressing her true feelings? Outwardly she conforms to custom even as she seeks spiritual and emotional reparations. Through the symbolism of the censer, which is turned upside down, Higekuro's wife subverts Heian mores at the price of her reputation; Murasaki acts more slowly and subtly to create a mirror in which others might read—if willing and able—not only her suffering self but the Heian female condition.

Genji has mixed emotions when he observes Murasaki's attentiveness to his robes. Impressed by this demonstration of her selflessness, he stands in such awe of her that he no longer understands why he acceded to Suzaku's request (see S:554; 4:57). Underneath the pretty picture, however, lies Murasaki's unseen fear: "For the first time in years she felt genuinely threatened" (S:554; 4:56). Although he is celebrated for his exquisite sensitivity, Genji remains unwilling to act upon his flickering awareness of Murasaki's pain. He implores her indulgence for the three nuptial nights with the Third Princess (S:554; 4:57–58):

> Genji was near tears. "Please excuse me just this one more night. I have no alternative. If after this I neglect you, then you may be sure that I will be angrier with myself than you can ever be with me. We do have to consider her father's feelings."
>
> "Do not ask us bystanders," she said, a faint smile on her lips, "to tell you how to behave."
>
> He turned away, chin in hand, to hide his confusion.

The sharpness of Murasaki's reply might make even a modern feminist shiver. Her poems, too, are full of dark premonitions of change for the worse.

Murasaki has never been so lonely. Since a Heian noblewoman

could not confide in other noblewomen, who were by definition her rivals, she is isolated from those who might best understand, commiserate, and console her. A second invisible fence separates Murasaki from the lower-ranking women physically closest to her. Although her ladies-in-waiting may be silently sympathetic, they cannot afford to encourage their mistress's self-assertiveness, much less the self-defeating rebelliousness of Higekuro's foolish wife. Overt protest might lead to marital rupture and the dispersal of the entire household. While female attendants were inhibited by the threat of losing their status and security, Heian nurses—like the nannies of English and American folklore—were more devoted and provided significant emotional comfort. But there is no old nurse to whom Murasaki can open her heart. Denial seems to be the best strategy. When her attendants and her female rivals and allies in the other quarters of the Rokujō-in express their guarded sympathy, which may or may not be sincere, Murasaki acts lightheartedly, as if to chat away the ugly gossip. She minimizes the importance of the Third Princess by highlighting her rival's childishness.

Talking deep into the night fails to alleviate her loneliness: "She was lonely, and the presence of all these women did little to disguise the fact" (S:556; 4:61). Pretending to be asleep, she lies awake all night. As she recalls how faithfully she waited for Genji when he was in exile at Suma, she is tempted to imagine that he might have died then and spared her her present agony. This cruel but understandable thought sends vibrations through the night air. The ripple effect is felt by Genji in his dreams that night. We are not told what Genji dreams, but it is apparent that he is jolted from his complacency about how much Murasaki can endure. In a panic, he interrupts his third nuptial night and rushes back to her.

Norma Field has argued that this dream visitation is "the closest [Murasaki] comes to being a possessing spirit."[39] Haruo Shirane, too, sees a similarity: "Heian aristocrats believed that one's spirit traveled to and appeared in the dreams of a person one was obsessed with, thus revealing, in a manner reminiscent of an evil spirit, one's deeper emotions."[40] In other words, the dreamer's mind is invaded the way possessing spirits invade a possessed person. Whether or not spirit possession can occur in a dream has also been hotly debated by Japanese scholars. Unfortunately, they tend to conflate spirit possession and dreams.[41] Although there are indeed resemblances between dreams and spirit possessions, there are also crucial differences. Above all, dreams occur to individuals in private whereas spirit possession must be recognized as a public event. Furthermore, the dreamer does not confuse his own identity with that of the person who appears in his or her dream. In spirit possession, however, the possessed person, temporarily at least, becomes other by assuming the charismatic persona of the possessing spirit.

Genji's dream is not, like spirit possession, a psychological weapon—an unconscious form of aggression that empowers the possessed and relieves the suffering caused by repression. The supreme authority of his gender exempts Genji from the necessity of drastic action. The dream serves merely to alleviate Genji's twinges of conscience. It propels him to make gestures of atonement and respect. In short, he acts as he would if Murasaki had become subject to spirit possession. In a very different sense from that meant by Field and others, the dream may be seen to signal the graver incidents to come—Murasaki's multiple spirit possessions—but one must bear in mind the epistemological distinction between dreams and spirit possession and the psychological differences between the simpler and the more complex phenomena.[42]

Genji and Murasaki experience his three nuptial nights with his new bride as a disruption of their relationship, but they paper over their differences. Murasaki resembles neither an angry possessing spirit nor an entranced possessed woman. Keeping him at arm's length, she appears firmly in control. For the moment, simply being her formal, properly socialized self suffices to reclaim Genji. Nonetheless, while this particular rift between them is gradually mended, new rifts threaten to emerge elsewhere in the tightly interwoven threads of their lives. Like the patches of snow Genji observes all around him, his life has become fragmented (see S:556–557; 4:62–64). One sign of disarray is that Genji fails to conform to protocol in his obligations to the Third Princess and fears that he has insulted Suzaku.

Murasaki shares this fear. Suzaku begs her to be "tolerant" of his "artless" daughter. In response, Murasaki sends him an inscrutable "impromptu" (S:559; 4:69) poem that disturbs him further because he cannot fathom it. Meanwhile, Genji, as if to restore Murasaki to her supreme and uncontested position, exposes his new bride's incompetence by letting Murasaki see a badly written childish note from her. Murasaki is encouraged to think she may be winning the battle despite her rival's rank and youth when she hears Genji speak of the immature princess as if she were merely the hollow shell of her robes; yet, at the same time, it bothers Murasaki all the more that he continues to pay homage to such a nullity.

### Oborozukiyo

Genji's sudden resumption of his old affair with Oborozukiyo (fig. 3 in App. B), Suzaku's "sacred property,"[43] his *naishi no kami*,[44] provides an odd kind of relief to the pressure on Murasaki. Genji's first affair with his half-brother's wife had led to his self-imposed exile at Suma. At that time Genji had sought to distract gossipers from his secret passion for Fujitsubo by enduring the disgraceful exposure of the lesser scandal. Like almost everyone else, Murasaki has known only half the story behind Genji's exile (see S:358; 2:483).

It appears that Genji is now trying to deflect Murasaki's attention from the formal liaison with the Third Princess and from the princess' blood tie to Fujitsubo by reviving this old affair with a woman who may, in political terms, be "antithetical to Fujitsubo."[45] Another complication is that Oborozukiyo was formerly the triumphant rival of the Third Princess' mother (see S:537; 4:12), but it is unlikely that Genji actually intends to humiliate the Third Princess (who appears oblivious to such matters). Genji's diversionary maneuver fails, not because Murasaki flies into a jealous rage, but because she does not. If he intended to distract her from the threat of the Third Princess by reviving this old affair, he has miscalculated. Murasaki reacts in such an unfamiliar manner that he is baffled. When upon his return from Oborozukiyo Murasaki greets him with dead silence, he is disconcerted: "Her silence was more effective than the most violent tantrum, and made Genji feel a little sorry for himself. Did she no longer care what he did?" (S:562; 4:78). It is unlikely that this question had ever occurred to him before. It signals an important shift in the psychological balance of power.

Murasaki astonishes him further with an unexpected combination of understated sarcasm and clinical description: "A suggestion of a smile came to her lips. 'Such a marvel of rejuvenation.' But her voice trembled as she went on: 'An ancient affair is superimposed on a new one, and I am caught beneath' " (S:562; 4:78: *nakazora naru mi*). Unwilling implicitly to admit his guilt by defending himself, Genji takes issue with the unpleasant form rather than with the painful content of the complaint. And so he sees fit to scold her: "Sulking is the one thing I cannot bear. Pinch me and beat me and pour out all your anger, but do not sulk. It is not what I trained you for" (S:562; 4:78).

His words increase rather than diminish the emotional distance between them.

Murasaki remains so much in control of her outward behavior that Genji soon forgets the rebuke he received when returning from Oborozukiyo. He continues to idealize Murasaki's "noble sort of dignity" and "her power of constant renewal" (S:564; 4:82). Limited by his male perspective, he ignores the new signals of her despair. Genji is not the only one concerned but unaware of the chaos in her heart: "How, everyone asked, was Murasaki responding to it all?" (S:565; 4:85). No one knows. Murasaki's facade is perfect serenity, solemnly displayed in her religious offerings for Genji at a Saga temple, followed by her banquet in his honor at the Nijō-in, Genji's mother's old residence, rather than at the Rokujō-in.

### Murasaki's Ominous Perfection

When Genji asks Murasaki to educate the immature Third Princess, she complies for unstated reasons, turning the challenge of mentorship into a strategy for transforming the Third Princess' advantage into her own. Initially, she had to fear not only her rival's superior rank (about which she could do nothing) but also the ingenuous charm of her youth. Now, middle-aged and fearing permanent replacement by the younger woman, Murasaki schemes to turn her attractively childish rival into an unattractive adult or, in the imagery befitting the Third Princess, a mere heap of clothes. From her own experience with Genji—roles reversed—she intuitively understands that to educate the princess is to deprive her of the charming naïveté that is her most attractive feature. The training in gender relations that Genji seems to envision for the Third Princess would enable her to distinguish between her role as princess and her role as principal wife. Her carefree spirit would be transformed into female compliance. Although Murasaki first seeks to gain control over the Third Princess by teaching her to become mature—hence less attractive for Genji— she soon gives up in the face of the Third Princess' apparently invincible childishness. Murasaki realizes that the Third Princess remains unresponsive to her teaching: the princess prefers dolls to *monogatari*.

Six years pass by. Murasaki returns the task of mentorship to Genji. When the Third Princess' resistance to development is finally broken, Genji is giddy with pride. He claims credit for her greatly improved musical ability at a concert rehearsal for the Retired Suzaku Emperor's fiftieth birthday. When asked for her opinion, Murasaki compliments Genji, but she adds a remark of delphic ambiguity: "Now she is very good indeed [as a musician], so good that I can scarcely believe it is the same person" (S:606; 4:195). Having witnessed the Third Princess' belated progress,[46] she can now anticipate her rival's fall as she loses the charm of childhood innocence.

Blinded by flattery of his mentorship, unable to perceive the troubles ahead, Genji praises Murasaki for *her* performance at the women's concert rehearsal. Murasaki's "perfection," however, is referred to as "ominous" (S:607; 4:196), and Genji feels uneasy when Murasaki refuses to give him much credit for educating and training her to his ideal conception of a woman. In a bluntly aggressive remark that seems to come out of nowhere—indeed, it has been interpreted as ironic (see S:607, n. †)—she claims that only her prayers have kept her from succumbing to her unhappiness (see S:607; 4:198–199). Genji abruptly changes the subject to sidestep having to see things from her point of view.

To win the contest between them, Genji must now convince Murasaki of her true worth and what Genji believes, despite her protestations, to be her privileged position. Since his praise of the Third Princess has already been put into perspective by his even greater praise of Murasaki, he proceeds to denigrate his other women. He begins with his first principal wife, Aoi, whom he criticizes for her aloofness. Rokujō was jealous beyond any man's endurance. None of this is new, except the context. Genji is once again appealing to Murasaki to imagine herself above these other women and to appreciate her better lot. She refuses, once again, to dissemble her feeling of profound unhappiness or to pretend that Genji's manipulative view of her situation is correct. While her first refusal to be indirectly flattered was so abrupt as to cause Genji's instinctive change of subject, her second refusal is subtle and indirect. Above all, she declines to comment on Aoi and Rokujō, averring that she never knew them personally and hence cannot pass judgment on them. About Akashi, with whom Genji had sympathized, she can be positive with the reservation appropriate to a rival turned ally. Genji hears in her comments an agreeable note, and he concludes his critique of his women with Murasaki herself. His comments are, as usual, delivered in a bantering tone, suggesting Murasaki's unseemly proclivity toward critical outspokenness.

This most significant conversation between Genji and Murasaki ends, as it began, with praise of the Third Princess. Genji lets

Murasaki know that he must reassure his newly accomplished pupil that she has "quite satisfied [her] teacher" (S:609; 4:203). His reassurance takes the form of spending the night with her, leaving Murasaki alone to sink slowly into an abyss of despair and depression. Murasaki seeks diversion and comfort in *monogatari*, but this time she finds no solace in tales of tumultuous romances ending in happy monogamous marriages. Murasaki rejects these *monogatari* as she rejects Genji's picture-book portrait of her existence: "But were the ache and the scarcely endurable sense of deprivation to be with her to the end?" (S:609; 4:203).

Murasaki's flash of anger and insight into her own dilemma may well be inspired by the figure of Rokujō, whom Genji had just described so vividly, unsparingly, truthfully. Before the grieving Murasaki is the verbal portrait of a proud, dissatisfied, and demanding woman who knew how to gain control over a man and leave a lasting impression on him. Momentum is gathering for Murasaki to want to be that kind of woman. From there it is only one additional step for her to desire Rokujō's charisma and acquire it through spirit possession. Yet the moment for spirit possession has not yet come. Murasaki is in the depths of her crisis of deprivation, but, before resorting to the dramatic and eerily transformative strategy of spirit possession, she must feel there is no alternative. In anticipation of her worst fears of total displacement, she had asked Genji repeatedly to allow her to take the tonsure. Leaving this world in order to take Buddhist vows would not only assure her the respect of both genders but would also exempt her from the humiliating role of unwanted sexual object.

It is important to understand the significance of the female tonsure for Heian court life. As Norma Field has pointed out, women who became nuns were more often elderly than still in the prime of their womanhood.[47] For older women contemplating death and the afterlife, vows were motivated by the hope of salvation. For sexually attractive young women, taking the tonsure need not have been religiously motivated. It may have been a denial of their sexuality and a renunciation of the world of men. European and Heian women shared the benefits of this escapist route, namely, an "honorable alternative to forced marriages and . . . an effective escape from the very real fears and dangers of childbirth,"[48] but Heian aristocratic culture was far less dogmatic about the religious life than European culture was. Neither young women nor old were necessarily caught up in the "obsession with the perfect life" that characterized the ideal European nun.[49] Taking the tonsure in Japan was not a radical shaving but an inch-by-inch trimming, done tentatively. It was, moreover, a reversible process, not marred by loss of honor.

Because they understood how rejection and subversiveness could be wrapped in a religious cloak, Heian aristocrats were reluctant to permit their young wives to take the tonsure. With a flattering statement of his admiration and devotion—by claiming emotional dependence—the courtier would frequently try to dissuade a woman from religious withdrawal. Genji and Murasaki perfectly illustrate this paradigm.

Murasaki's first request for the tonsure came at a time of political upheaval and generational turnover, just after the Reizei Emperor had abdicated and been succeeded by the crown prince (the Akashi daughter's husband [see S:592; 4:158–159]). Genji astutely sensed that Murasaki's motivation was not wholly religious.[50] Defending himself from the criticism implied by her desire for withdrawal, he denied her wish. His refusal was so forbidding that Murasaki did not dare ask again when the thought next crossed her mind, which it did when Genji's attentions turned to the Third Princess. Then, however, Murasaki's pride and sense of propriety prevented her from fulfilling her innermost wish: "She wanted to anticipate the inevitable by leaving the world. She kept these thoughts to herself, not wanting to nag or seem insistent" (S:597; 4:169). Murasaki's second request for the tonsure came immediately after Genji's lecture on her privileged position, but Genji blunted this sharp thrust at his self-esteem by praising Murasaki's perfection and defaming his other women, especially Rokujō. Knowing him well, Murasaki was not surprised by Genji's denial of her wish: "It was the usual thing, all over again" (S:608; 4:199). The third request follows their intense conversation about their relationship—within the context of polygyny. It comes when Murasaki falls ill, suffering acutely from chest pains and a fever.[51] As Field has noted, her illness is motivated by "the sheer need to announce a departure from the world of men."[52] Genji comes rushing to her side, then moves her from the Rokujō-in (the symbolic site of polygyny) to the Nijō-in (the symbolic site of maternity). There he stays with her for several weeks of her fluctuating illness. Although the threat of death seems to give her request a religious motive and thus to clear him of any implied criticism, Genji once again denies her wish. As before, his reason is totally self-centered: "Can you now think of deserting me?" (S:610; 4:206). Attempting weakly to guard himself against the appearance of selfishness, he claims to have wanted more than once to take religious vows himself but was too closely tied to this world by his responsibilities to his loved ones—including, of course, Murasaki.

Once again denied the wish to be released from human attachment, Murasaki has dark thoughts of death and prepares for it by saying good-bye to those around her. Shocked by the thought of losing her, Genji resorts first to denial and then to the power of positive thinking: "Everything will be all right if only we manage to think so" (S:610; 4:207). Continuing to blindfold himself to Murasaki's most desperate needs, Genji proves himself impervious to subtle hints, rational argument, emotional pleas, and the imminent dangers of mortal illness. Short of death itself, where can Murasaki turn? What powers can she appeal to?

### The Self Becomes Other

Murasaki's old self, the self formed and adored by Genji, dies when Murasaki becomes possessed. She temporarily becomes other— Rokujō—to allow a new self to rise from the ashes of the old. Genji's resistance to this transformative process is immense. As Murasaki slips away into an undefinable illness, Genji prays to "all the native and foreign gods" (S:610; 4:207) and summons ascetics and miracle workers. He recognizes that Murasaki has been seized by a "malign force" (S:611; 4:208: *onmono no ke*). It is important to recognize, however, that Murasaki provided this diagnosis herself and thereby accelerated the forming of ritual machinery to treat her case of possession. She revealed this insight into her liminal condition in order to protect the pregnant Akashi Princess, who was then visiting at her sickbed, from becoming susceptible to the *mono no ke* driving her (see S:610; 4:206).

Almost by design, the worst news possible reaches Genji during the Kamo (or Aoi) Festival, when he is still lingering at the Rokujō-in, preoccupied with the complaints of the Third Princess. Murasaki has died. Genji is totally beside himself and rushes to her "deathbed." When he discovers that she is alive but possessed, he summons ascetics, clinging to the belief that she will return to him if the *mono no ke* can be expelled (Plate 1.8). As Fujimoto Katsuyoshi has pointed out, Genji is violating religious custom by ordering Buddhist rites during the Kamo Festival when they were forbidden. By doing so, Genji further provokes the spirits believed to be rampant at this time.[53]

When the medium falls into a trance and speaks with the voice of

Rokujō, Genji is horrified rather than encouraged by this sign of successful mediumship because Murasaki has suddenly become wholly other (Plate 1.9). In fact, Murasaki's indirect assumption of Rokujō's voice upsets Genji much more than Aoi's unmediated impersonation of Rokujō had done. Although Murasaki, unlike Aoi, never confronted Rokujō, she knows her from Genji's descriptions and she recognizes her female genius, which is why she intuitively chooses proud Rokujō as the possessing spirit in her oblique aggressive strategy. Since Genji had not permitted Murasaki the tonsure, a symbolic sexual death, she has put on the mask of a woman so frightening that Genji wishes he had indeed let Murasaki take religious vows. In fact, after the ritual performance of Murasaki's spirit possession, Genji has a token tonsure administered for her. By that time, however, Murasaki has forever changed and is untouched by Genji's compromise.

The critics' emphasis in explaining Murasaki's possession has been on the dead Rokujō's hurt pride over Genji's defamation of her to Murasaki.[54] This interpretation, based on the widespread belief that the aggrieved dead haunt the living, is insufficient because it fails to consider that the living have a stake in acquiring the charisma of the dead and in fulfilling their legacy. Not only does Rokujō come alive through the possessed women; women like Aoi and Murasaki also speak, unmediated or mediated, on behalf of Rokujō.

Apart from adopting the defamation theory, critics have cited the ailing Murasaki's weakened condition to explain her susceptibility to the invasion of Rokujō's spirit. Since Murasaki's contemporaries certainly believed that the spirits of the dead were capable of such acts of revenge, there is reason to consider this interpretation. But it has one great disadvantage: it reduces the *monogatari*'s most complex female character to the role of a passive victim. The intricate weave of events leading to Murasaki's crisis is then quite pointless. The argument that Murasaki's possession is simply the result of Rokujō's spirit's anger at Genji's one careless remark attributes to the dead Rokujō an independent power that is in fact dependent on the living who are obsessed with her memory. It seems much more plausible to imagine that the author has cast Murasaki as an active and not merely a passive performer in the carefully staged drama. What then is it in Murasaki's psyche that has never been revealed before, and what triggers its release?

In her crucial conversation with Genji—who better than anyone else represents the mores of Heian society—Murasaki had been told to consider her social situation a very lucky one. At first, she could not but agree that it was—compared to the lot of most aristocratic women—but the passage of time and the evolution of their relationship made her increasingly aware of her social disadvantages and her vulnerability to Genji's whims. Her discontent intensified in accord with her superb ability to imagine a different and better world—the more nearly egalitarian monogamous world of the old *monogatari* (see S:609; 4:203). That this world was far from realistic she would have been the first to admit, but her utopia nonetheless incorporated a deep-rooted conviction about how women should be treated by men. Since Genji seemed unable to understand her dissatisfaction or respond to her grievances when she tried to express them, she gradually withdrew from her attempts to communicate with him.

Haruo Shirane, among others, has pointed out that "an irreparable gap opens up between her outward demeanor and her inner emotions" and argues that "the contrast between the calm surface and the darkness within" can be explained by "her emotional inability to accept the new course of events" that began with the arrival of the Third Princess.[55] Her behavior not only allows no clues to her true beliefs; it is totally contrary to them. What hurts is not so much that she presents a false portrait of herself to the world—for the world adores that portrait—but that she has been untrue to herself. The more Genji's formidable mentorship shaped her to his true and her pretended ideal, the more she despised herself for the false image of docile conformity that belied her true feelings.

What exactly disturbed Murasaki when Genji praised her (and Akashi) and defamed Aoi and Rokujō? Is it not the sharpness of the contrast between women she secretly admires—Aoi and Rokujō—and the "ideal" women admired by her society—herself and Akashi? If Rokujō, who wanted Genji all to herself, is Murasaki's unacknowledged ideal (in modern terms: her feminine role model), it is not surprising that Murasaki now seeks to become possessed by that charismatic woman. Murasaki had been extremely skillful in turning female rivals into allies, but since those allies were women like herself (Akashi, for instance), their alliance never really empowered her. By becoming possessed, Murasaki destroys the "ideal" self she has come to loathe. In the throes of possession, Genji may find her hideous, but she becomes her dream ego: the self-assertive Rokujō who is perceived as exceptionally free to protest her mistreatment by Genji and to insist on rights undreamed of by "sane" women.

PLATE 2.1 A *monogatari* reading. Anonymous artists. *Genji monogatari emaki*. "Azumaya I" scene. Twelfth century. Tokugawa Reimeikai Foundation.

PLATE 2.2    The vine-wrapped Yūgao in the light of
the harvest moon. Yoshitoshi (1839–1892). Ōban
woodblock print, "*Genji*—Yūgao no maki," from the
series *Tsuki hyakushi* (One Hundred Aspects of the
Moon). 1886. Collection Robert B. Kleyn, The
Netherlands.

PLATE 2.3 *The Tale of Genji:* Battle of the Carriages. Matabei school. Sixfold screen. Color with gold ground on paper. Detail. Seventeenth century. Etsuko and Joe Price Collection. Los Angeles County Museum of Art. L.83.45.64.

PLATE 2.4 Miniature ivory carving *(netsuke)* of the Hannya mask, attached by a drawstring fastener *(ojime)* with ivory heartvine emblem to a lacquer box *(inrō)* featuring a carriage. The artistic ensemble refers to the *nō* drama *Nonomiya*, although the Hannya mask is not worn in this play. Kōami Nagayoshi, lacquer artist. Late eighteenth century. Courtesy of the Inrō Museum, Takayama.

PLATE 2.5  Murasaki offers the Akashi daughter
her breast. Anonymous. Tokugawa *Genji* album.
Ink, color, and gold on paper. Seventeenth century. Tokugawa Reimeikai Foundation.

PLATE 2.6 Her cat running wild, the Third Princess, standing, watches court football *(kemari)*. Tosa Mitsuyoshi (1539–1613). *Genji* album. Kyoto National Museum.

PLATE 2.7 Kashiwagi with his cat fetish. Tosa Mitsuyoshi (1539–1613). *Genji* album. Kyoto National Museum.

PLATE 2.8 The Retired Suzaku Emperor and Genji deliberate over the Third Princess' request for religious vows. Anonymous artists. *Genji monogatari emaki*. "Kashiwagi I" scene. Twelfth century. Tokugawa Reimeikai Foundation.

PLATE 2.9  Tō no Chūjō consults with the ascetic from Mount Katsuragi about exorcizing his son Kashiwagi's possessing spirit (left; front cover). Kashiwagi, near death from self-starvation, reads the Third Princess' poem-letter, illuminated by Kojijū's lighted taper (right; back cover). Attributed to the circle of Chōjirō. Early seventeenth century. Painted book covers for "Kashiwagi" (S: "The Oak Tree"), chapter 36 of the *Genji monogatari*. Ink, color, and gold on paper. Spencer Collection. The New York Public Library. Astor, Lenox, and Tilden Foundations.

PLATE 2.10 Kashiwagi's apparition appears to Yūgiri in a dream. Tosa Mitsuyoshi (1539–1613). *Genji monogatari tekagami*. Kubosō Memorial Museum of Art, Izumi.

PLATE 2.11   With the Uji Bridge in the background,
the Eighth Prince is performing his prayers. In the
foreground, Bennokimi, like a medium in trance,
transmits to Kaoru the secret of his birth, contained
in the red pouch  with his parents' love letters. Tosa
Mitsuyoshi (1539–1613). *Genji monogatari tekagami*. Kubosō Memorial Museum of Art, Izumi.

PLATE 2.12 The Bishop of Yokawa and his entourage find Ukifune in the back of the deserted Uji villa of the late Suzaku Emperor. Attributed to Kaihō Yūsetsu (1598–1677). *Genji monogatari emaki.* Scene from two handscrolls. Ink and color on paper. Photograph: Sheldan Comfort Collins. The Mary and Jackson Burke Foundation.

PLATE 2.13 The Bishop of Yokawa supervises Ukifune's tonsure at the Ono nunnery. Attributed to Tawaraya Sōtatsu (d. 1643?). Fragment from a pair of sixfold screens (seal: Inen); mounted as a handscroll. Colors on paper. MOA Museum of Art, Atami.

PLATE 2.14  *The Tale of Genji:* Ukifune at *Tenarai*
("Writing Practice"). Anonymous. Late seventeenth to
early eighteenth century. Ink and color on gold paper.
Etsuko and Joe Price Collection. Los Angeles County
Museum of Art. L.83.50.119.

The spirit's first words, uttered through the medium, could very well be Murasaki's if Genji, the exclusive audience, could imagine her capable of direct accusation. But Genji, who was unable to comprehend Murasaki's frank statement about her intense unhappiness, now lets himself believe, through the distancing institution of the medium, that it must be someone other than Murasaki herself who is accusing him with such unprecedented aggression: "I have wanted you to suffer," says the spirit, "as I have suffered" (S:617; 4:226). There is nothing mysterious about the message but a great deal of confusion about the identity of the messenger. Genji's conventional preconceptions make it impossible for him to recognize the meaning of the unambiguous message or to take into account the obliqueness of its delivery in the transformative process of spirit possession.

Genji's difficulty lies in his inability to decode the complex interplay between message and messenger. He attributes the medium's words to the possessing spirit, who consequently becomes responsible for Murasaki's illness, which, in truth, has its origins in Murasaki's discontent over Genji's treatment of her. Thus Genji's twisted perception pinpoints precisely where the strategy of spirit possession can miss its mark. By interpreting the possessing spirit as one woman's malignant influence on another, Genji can ignore the message composed of collective female grievances. Appalled by the unsightly spectacle of the medium's accusatory ranting and raving, he cannot imagine that he is culpable of anything. In his view, Murasaki is the victim of Rokujō's aggression and he himself merely an authoritative presence on the witness stand.[56]

Genji feels authorized to judge the case because he has had repeated traumatic experiences with spirit possession. The pattern seems so uncannily familiar to him that he has to wonder, even before he begins to probe into the identity of the spirit, if it is Rokujō. Still, despite his prior experience with Aoi's possession by the *living* spirit of Rokujō, he initially resists the temptation to conclude that in Murasaki's case the dead Rokujō is the possessing spirit.[57] After all, twenty-five years have passed since Aoi's affliction by Rokujō's living spirit. He tries to reassure himself with the folk belief that "foxes and other evil creatures" (S:618; 4:226) can play tricks on us.

As in ordinary cases of possession treated by professional exorcists, Genji asks the spirit to identify herself so that she can be expelled by the magic of that identification. The spirit evades his request with an assertion that questions his sincerity: "You pretend not to know me."

Announcing mysteriously that "you are the same" (S:618; 4:227), the spirit seems to imply both Genji's inability to change and her own metamorphosis into the other: "I am horribly changed" (S:618; 4:227). The spirit not only calls attention to the fact of her transformation; she also provides a clue to her identity: "I am dead" (S:618; 4:227). Genji reluctantly concludes that the possessing spirit is indeed Rokujō, but he cannot see that Murasaki is speaking her own mind by adopting Rokujō's, just as Aoi once spoke hers, disguised as Rokujō's.

It must be underscored that the medium has the almost impossible task of communicating the ineffable. She must mediate between parties that have never been able to communicate. The impetus in this case comes from Murasaki, and the female medium begins with thinly coded abstract representations of Murasaki's emotional state. As Genji, deeply puzzled, begins to interfere by questioning the spirit's identity, the medium adapts her message, translating it into terms insinuated by Genji himself. Once the powerful figure of Rokujō rules the scene, Genji's fear of her closes his mind completely to the positive aspects of the mediated message.

Halfway through the performance, the spirit is moved to compose a *waka*. At this point, Genji's much admired sensibility betrays him and he misses the clue to achieving a harmonious coexistence between the dead and the living, men and women. The *waka* contains a sad complaint of dynamic female transformation eclipsed by static male sameness (4:227; my translation):

| | |
|---|---|
| *waga mi koso* | My body |
| *aranu sama nare* | transformed |
| *sore nagara* | ignoring |
| *sora obore suru* | this form |
| *kimi wa kimi nari* | you are you |

Interestingly, Seidensticker here follows Waley's example of translating *waka* as prose: "I am horribly changed, and you pretend not to know me. You are the same" (S:618; 4:227). The topic of the transformative power of death may seem gruesome and unsuitable as poetry, yet categorical change contains the promise of revelation and the possibility of reconciliation. The skilled male translators duplicate Genji's act of closure and obscure the spirit's plea for reciprocal change.

Although Genji "wanted to hear no more" (S:618; 4:227), the spirit continues, criticizing his tendency to slander, to sow discord among women, and to undermine their self-esteem. The spirit's bio-graphical references gradually become more specific as Murasaki's grievance is assimilated to Rokujō's. In other words, it is possible to read the overt references to Rokujō's troubled history as Murasaki's covert anticipation of her own defamation after death. In the double entendre of spirit possession, Rokujō's "daughter" (Akikonomu) becomes Murasaki's Akashi "daughter" and Rokujō, whom Genji defames before a "lady" (Murasaki), becomes Murasaki, who might very well fear a similarly scathing posthumous evaluation in front of the Third Princess. To both Rokujō and Murasaki, the thought of open and direct criticism is less upsetting than Genji's didactic expo-sure of their flaws to other women who are unable to hear their defense. It is—in modern terms—female solidarity that is expressed when the spirit announces in unambiguous terms: "I do not hate her" (S:619; 4:228).

Remarkably, the spirit's speech ends with an apology. Even more remarkably, this is where Genji terminates the spirit's performance. He can see only vindictive accusations where there are also pleas for help and understanding. The female spirit has revealed her otherness and her anxiety, but Genji has withdrawn completely into a defensive position. He has no antenna for otherness. He is blind to Murasaki lurking behind the mask of Rokujō and cannot (or will not) hear the quite literally interchangeable grievances of the living and the dead. Absurdly fearful of their transformative power, Genji cannot imagine granting them the peace they are asking for. A specific instance of his insensitivity occurs when the spirit requests that he warn her daughter against jealousy. Genji registers the words but overlooks the fact that it takes courage for a woman to refer to jealousy and to share with a man her insight into the consequences of this self-destructive emotion.

Genji's inability to understand the medium's words is related to his inability to imagine what Rokujō means to Murasaki—and that, in turn, is related to his self-centered concern with his own relationship to his dead mistress. Troubled by a bad conscience, he has done his best to safeguard against Rokujō's posthumous revenge. If he has never been threatened by her *dead* spirit (*shiryō*), the reason is that he has prudently taken precautions: he has provided splendidly for Rokujō's daughter and he has built the Rokujō-in on territory for-merly owned by Rokujō (see S:383; 3:70).

If, however, we examine Murasaki's possession case from a per-spective wider than Genji's field of vision, we see that Rokujō's appearance is more than a sign of Genji's bad conscience or the dead Rokujō's hurt pride.[58] It is also an oblique aggressive expression of Murasaki's troubled self, which is hurt in its self-esteem and strangled in its self-expression by Genji's insistence on her impossible perfection. Paradoxically, Murasaki must first "die" before she can assume the persona of a dead woman more powerful than she. She must cast away the mask she was made to wear before she can show her true face. Since scholars have shifted indiscriminately between the male and female perspectives of Murasaki Shikibu's protagonists in analyzing the *mono no ke* phenomenon, they have missed the crucial function of the possessed person's mediated role in the drama.

From the beginning of her marital crisis with Genji, Murasaki's wishes have been no secret to her women; indeed, they have been of deep concern to them. Murasaki's attempts to downplay, disguise, and repress her untold sorrows were sensed by these women who care most about her and best understand how her position is threatened by Genji's new, youthful, and royal principal wife. It is therefore plausible that one of them—a sensitive girl medium—should respond to Genji's insinuations and seize (or, in the more familiar passive voice, be seized by) the powerful female spirit hovering over the Rokujō-in.

In this literary conceptualization of Heian male/female conflicts acted out through the drama of spirit possession, Rokujō serves Murasaki and other women as a spiritual repository—a kind of blood bank—that women can draw on. The startling metaphor is not mine. The contemporary woman writer Enchi Fumiko (1905–1986), a translator of the *Genji monogatari* and rare defender of Rokujō,[59] has used it in the course of characterizing a female protagonist modeled on Rokujō. In Enchi's novel *Onnamen* (Masks; 1958), the character Mieko, composing an essay about the *Genji*, conceives of other women as allies through the metaphor of blood:

> A woman's being . . . is a stream of blood flowing on and on, unbroken, from generation to generation.
>
> Just as there is an archetype of woman as the object of man's eternal love, so there must be an archetype of her as the object of his eternal fear, representing, perhaps, the shadow of his own evil actions. The Rokujō lady is an embodiment of this archetype.[60]

In the case of Murasaki's spirit possession, Genji, despite his ability to identify the spirit's mask as Rokujō, whom he intuitively perceives as the epitome of female power, cannot go beyond that perception to ask himself what it means that his fairly outspoken wife suddenly speaks with the voice of the only woman he ever imagined to be his equal. Unable to lift the mask, he cannot understand that the performance is ultimately inspired by none other than Murasaki. In theatrical terms it is she, represented on stage by the female medium, who is wearing Rokujō's powerfully expressive mask. As the main actor, she is thus fully disguised as other.[61]

Three women—Rokujō, the medium, and Murasaki—voice one message: women need at the very least to participate in the formation and the evaluation of their selves. Otherwise, they cannot develop autonomy and self-esteem. When this need is denied, women must have recourse to some means by which they can demonstrate that they are other than what men wish them to be. Suicide is the most drastic of means; the most dramatic is the performative spectacle of spirit possession. Women require tremendous courage and honesty in order to deconstruct their conventional selves because they must confront men's anger if they do. The great advantage of spirit possession as a woman's weapon is that its obliqueness permits the "victim" to attack without the fear of reprisal. Women have also been conditioned to fear jealousy as a destructive factor, not only because men despise the monster they themselves have created, but because jealousy separates women from each other and drives them into complete isolation. It is only in spirit possession that this dividing barrier can be temporarily overcome.

In this psychological struggle, Genji has not scored a complete victory, nor does Murasaki suffer a total defeat. At a complete loss as to the spirit's uncharacteristic offer of apologies and pleas of forgiveness, Genji attempts to terminate the spirit possession by force: "It was not a dialogue which he wished to pursue. He had the little medium taken away and Murasaki quietly moved to another room" (S:619; 4:228). His impulsive action precludes a proper ritual end to spirit possession through exorcism. Thus Murasaki remains unexorcized, and her bonding with the kindred female *mono no ke* continues to cast a permanent veil over her character. Immediately after silencing the medium, Genji remembers Murasaki's earlier requests for the tonsure. Unwilling to forgive the spirit, he is nonetheless eager to pacify Murasaki, if only by granting her a "token tonsure" (S:620; 4:232). Despite the concession, the possessing spirit lingers on as if Murasaki had not quite said her piece. After all, Genji's tardy concession has purely symbolic value, for Murasaki still cannot remove herself from a society that requires her to endure jealousy in silence. Precisely because she is not allowed to express herself fully through spirit possession or a religious life, the *mono no ke* stays and is, significantly, never exorcized. Instead, in the course of several months, the allied spirit is absorbed into Murasaki's altered self through internalization, or adorcism,[62] unique in the *Genji*.

### In the Aftermath of Fictional Death

When the crisis ends, Murasaki no longer quarrels, quibbles, or sulks. Genji should be pleased, but at the same time he cannot fail to notice, at least vaguely, that she is no longer quite the same. After all, she has overcome a grave psychosomatic illness through the threat of real death that is avoided by means of spirit possession. She has shed her old skin, but her new self is not what she ultimately desired. It is a mere shadow of what she wished to become. Genji continues to be devoted to her, but, no more insightful than before the traumatic episode, he cannot see the darkness of this shadow.

Predictably, others are even less perceptive. Murasaki Shikibu gives us an interesting cross section of the immediate perceptions of Murasaki's unusual sequence of putative death and actual spirit possession. Although the cathartic scene was mainly acted out through a female medium, with Murasaki as the seemingly passive and Genji as the active participant, there was no other eyewitness. Even the ubiquitous women were banned from the room and the notoriously ineffectual but obligatory male exorcists kept at a distance (upon the request of the medium). An artist's rendering throws interesting light on this scene. In Yamamoto Shunshō's 1650 woodblock print, a priest is present, but he has discreetly turned away from Genji and the disheveled medium. The artist spares Murasaki altogether from association with the unsightly confrontation between Genji and the medium: Murasaki is not shown (Plate 1.9). Of course, the aesthetic discretion in Murasaki's extraction from the scene underlines Genji's notion of her passive "victimhood" rather than her own role as initiating agent.

The crowd's first reaction is to rumors of Murasaki's death. Then Genji informs them that the sad news was but a false alarm. Interestingly, he withholds the fact that her dramatic revival occurred through spirit possession—perhaps because such news would have given rise to speculations about the spirit's identity and motivations, rumors that might have slowed Murasaki's recovery from her long illness. Public reactions to Murasaki's "death" derive their peculiar poignancy from the Kamo (or Aoi) Festival and the associations provoked by the complications in Genji's life. This festival took place in the Fourth Month along with other Shinto festivals. During this time, those susceptible to *mono no ke* were in special danger because Buddhist rituals were suspended.[63] For Genji and his coevals, the festival brings memories of the pregnant Aoi's fateful quarrel with Rokujō, followed, some months later, by Aoi's possession and her subsequent death. Twenty-five years before, Genji had been the cause of the quarrel on the Day of Lustration and then had aroused much admiration on the festival day proper as he rode with young Murasaki in a palanquin. Now it is not his attendance at the festival that seems worthy of narration but his rushing from the indisposed Third Princess at the Rokujō-in to Murasaki at the Nijō-in. Hearing that Murasaki has died, the crowd's responses range from heartfelt grief to mean-spirited gloating. There is even a sense of satisfaction as some assert that now Genji need no longer neglect the Third Princess. In other words, some perceive Murasaki's "death" as punishment for the superiority that impelled Genji to prefer her to his new principal wife (who both replaces Aoi and displaces Murasaki as Genji's de facto *kita no kata*).

The public does not witness Murasaki's spirit possession. It derives its information from clues provided by the intimate group of three participants: Genji, Murasaki, and the medium. Although a few men in Genji's innermost circle are initiated into this knowledge, they are not told of the possessing spirit's identity. It is not until much later that the rumor of Rokujō's possessing spirit reaches Rokujō's daughter Akikonomu through the gossip of the female entourage, perhaps with the medium as the source (see S:675; 4:376).

What the crowd thinks is less important than what Murasaki feels. When the Third Princess appears "unwell" (S:621; 4:234) and her troubled condition is diagnosed as pregnancy, Murasaki's condition gradually improves. She finds some relief from her frustrating standoff with Genji because she senses that her privileged rival is now vulnerable to the vicissitudes of womanhood. This counterpoint moment has failed adequately to startle readers. Murasaki's eerie calm is incomprehensible without the transformative experience of spirit possession. Her composed self-confidence is a sign that she has overcome both her sorrow about her own barrenness and her envy of other women's fertility. She has become immune to conflict with Genji and indifferent to her rivals. Yet in terms of her interest as a fictional character she has, paradoxically, all but died.

After her spirit possession, Murasaki never again reverts to her old self. Until her death four years later, Murasaki's existence in the novel is a mystifying blank. This blank becomes painfully evident in Murasaki's philosophy of silence (see S:699; 4:442).[64] Upon the occasion of her stepson Yūgiri's marital problems, which lead to further female unhappiness and jealousy, Murasaki resigns herself to obeying the Heian imperative for women to endure their emotional constraints in silence. Significantly, this philosophy is not communicated orally but, true to its content, is expressed in the form of an interior monologue. She deeply regrets the fate of Heian women, who keep the domestic peace at the cost of their self-fulfillment (S:699; 4:442):

> Such a difficult, constricted life as a woman was required to live! Moving things, amusing things, she must pretend to be unaffected by them. With whom was she to share the pleasure and beguile the tedium of this fleeting world? . . . Like the mute prince who was always appearing in sad parables, a woman should be sensitive but silent. The balance was certainly very difficult to maintain. . . .

Murasaki likens a woman's lot to that of male enlightened beings like the Mute Prince (Mugon Taishi) who met the sorrows of this world with thirteen years of silence. While the bold comparison may be intended desperately to uplift women in their capacity for discipline, it may also imply a sad, if not chilling, comment on male ascetics.

Murasaki's silence after the exhausting protest of her spirit possession appears like the calm after a storm. Just as the Mute Prince abandoned all hope of healing the woes of the world with words, so she has abandoned her countless attempts to communicate with a resistant Genji in the hope of being recognized as her true self. Murasaki's silence is a symptom of the breakdown of her will to fight the gender inequalities inherent in Heian society. The effect of this silence on Murasaki's character is twofold: while endowing her with serenity, it also undoes much of the power attained through spirit possession. Murasaki's last appearance is as the epitome of conformity to Heian ideals of femininity rather than as advocate of transforming those patriarchal ideals to suit the needs of women. As Susan R. Bordo has remarked: "The pathologies of female protest function, paradoxically, as if in collusion with the cultural conditions that produce them, reproducing rather than transforming precisely that which is being protested."[65]

Having obtained a religiously detached vision of herself through the strategy of spirit possession, Murasaki is nonetheless restrained by a frightfully stoic formality. Betraying no emotion, she prepares nun's garments for former rivals entering the religious life (see S:628; 4:256)—for Asagao, Oborozukiyo, and the Third Princess. Without protest she parts with her "children." Her earlier, lively beauty has changed to a "delicate serenity" (S:717; 4:490), standing perhaps for the religious vows that Genji allows others but continues to refuse her. When she vanishes like the dew (see S:717; 4:492), Genji wishes it were another spirit possession (see S:718; 4:492); but there is no need for another (and no reason to believe that Genji would learn more from it than he had from previous possessions). Murasaki finally achieves what she so profoundly desired, stripped of obliqueness and equivalents: her death.

# The Third Princess

CLEARLY, a turning point in the *Genji* has been reached with the arrival of the Third Princess in the Rokujō-in. Murasaki had feared replacement by the Third Princess, who posed a threat because of her superior rank, her blood link to Fujitsubo, her youth, and her child-bearing capacity. Anxious over the way the Third Princess might affect his relationship with Murasaki, Genji became increasingly deaf to her plaintive confessions while she in turn became increasingly aware of spending all her energy on displaying her discontent rather than discussing its content. Her worries about the state of her marriage aggravated Murasaki's fundamental problem with her identity, a problem that reached its climax at the Kamo Festival. On the Day of Lustration preceding the festival, the Third Princess' illicit impregnation marked the turning point in Murasaki's crisis. When Genji left the seriously ill Murasaki to attend to the Third Princess because of her "indisposition," Murasaki intuited the true cause, "died," and reclaimed Genji by adopting the strategy of spirit possession.

From the perspective of the Third Princess, however, these inter-related events look quite different. Female rivals are no concern of hers. Instead, the Third Princess' case of spirit possession occurs when she is caught in the nets cast by the three men in her life: her father, her husband, and her lover. It is not surprising that she has been characterized almost exclusively from the dominant male viewpoint. Although it is imperative to understand how father, husband, and—most important—lover see her, the female perspective is equally essential if we are to gain an adequate picture of her character.

The shift in perspective is facilitated by the fact that Genji is no longer the only important male actor on stage. What happens when Genji's male dominance is challenged—when another male from the next generation crosses the path of the prototypical hero? What happens when jealousy seizes not the woman but the man? Murasaki Shikibu invites her audience to examine the meaning of these fundamental changes. With the shift in the figural constellation from one man and several women to one woman and several men also comes a fresh approach to *kaimami,* the act that traditionally has excited the man to peek through the fence and whose forbidden aspect had been assimilated into male courtly etiquette.[1] Can *monogatari* convention accomplish the same assimilation for a woman engaged in *kaimami?*

## The Third Princess: Childhood and Marriage

The Third Princess' genealogy (fig. 4 in App. B) combines elements from the families of Genji and Murasaki, Rokujō and Akashi. She is the daughter of Suzaku (Genji's half-brother) and Fujitsubo nyōgo, Suzaku's high-ranking consort (who should not be confused with Genji's stepmother). The Third Princess' paternal grandmother is Kokiden, Genji's mother's fateful rival and the head of the faction opposing Genji's claim to power. Her maternal grandfather is the emperor preceding Genji's father. This means that the Third Princess' mother is the half-sister of both Fujitsubo and Hyōbu, Murasaki's father (fig. 3 in App. B). Like Genji, the Third Princess' mother was removed from the imperial succession and granted high court rank. Despite this demotion, she, like Rokujō, hoped to become empress by marrying a crown prince.[2] These hopes, however, did not materialize because of *her* mother's undistinguished career as an imperial consort.[3] She herself fared poorly as the wife of Suzaku, who preferred Oborozukiyo, the younger sister of Kokiden. In short, the Third Princess, like Genji and Murasaki, grew up with the anxieties stemming from having a mother displaced by female rivals.

When Genji first glimpsed the ten-year-old Murasaki through the eroticized gap in the fence, she was shown in a moment of childish abandon made poignant because of her precarious position as a motherless child neglected by her father and threatened by her stepmother. Genji was charmed by her immaturity; he cherished and preserved Murasaki's fragile childhood innocence until he took her for his wife at the age of fourteen. The Third Princess is exactly that age when she too is wedded to Genji, without the *kaimami* prelude of romantic courtship. The marriage is arranged as was Genji's marriage to his first principal wife Aoi.

Unlike Aoi, who carried all the responsibility for a good marriage, the Third Princess can be carefree because she is her permissive father's pampered daughter. When the time comes to make marital plans, Suzaku's careful screening of suitors recalls similar scrutiny by the ambitious Akashi Priest (Akashi no nyūdō). In the end, both doting fathers, the former in preparation for taking religious vows and the latter after taking them, entrust Genji with their daughters. Unlike the Akashi Priest, however, Suzaku neglected to give his daughter the meticulous education crucial to making a superior match. His excuse for his neglect is her precarious situation as a princess of the blood (naishinnō) who was likely to remain single in the period of Fujiwara rule (sekkan) or to marry beneath her status.[4] Whether Suzaku intended it or not, the Third Princess is never motivated to be anything other than her father's little girl. She retains her childish nature far beyond childhood.

When the Third Princess approaches an age suitable for marriage, she must face separation from her father. The difficulty of severing a tight father-daughter bond becomes evident when a father wishes to take religious vows and retire from the world or, as in the case of the Akashi Priest, pursue a more rigorous path to salvation. This religious step necessitates the search for a husband or guardian to replace the father in providing for and loving the daughter. It is no accident that the Akashi Priest selects Genji, a distant relative through his maternal Kiritsubo lineage. The blood link (ketsuen) between father and husband-guardian is even more direct between Genji and his half-brother Suzaku.[5] In addition, there is the Third Princess' kinship tie to Fujitsubo and Murasaki, who are erotically linked (murasaki no yukari) in Genji's mind.[6] Thanks in part to these family connections, the Genji–Third Princess match provides each partner with a parental substitute: for Genji, the new wife substitutes for his beloved (step) mother; for the Third Princess, her husband substitutes for her father.

Told to accept her uncle Genji as guardian and husband, she obeys her father; but she does not conceal her indifference to Genji, and she continues to enjoy children's games. For her, the ritual of the three nuptial nights is meaningless. Genji is too embarrassed to show Murasaki his immature wife's morning-after letter (kinuginu no fumi). Genji has the impression that the Third Princess is hidden inside her clothes. As Murasaki Shikibu puts it in an unusual expression, the Third Princess tends to be all clothes (see S:558; 4:66: ito onzogachi ni).[7] Although startled by this, Genji does not feel compelled to dis-cover her. He is baffled but rather pleased by another trait. The Third Princess does not conform to the Heian code that requires an aristocratic woman to be shy or reserved: "She did not seem shy before him, and if it could have been said that her openness and free-dom from mannerism were for purposes of putting him at his ease, then it could also have been said that they succeeded very well" (S:558; 4:66).

On the whole, Genji is puzzled by Suzaku's failure to have edu-cated his favorite daughter: "The mystery was that he had done so lit-tle by way of training her" (S:558; 4:67). At the same time, Genji regards her as already too old, despite her inappropriate childishness, to be shaped into his conception of the ideal. He delegates this peda-gogical task to Murasaki, who is, as we have seen, soon frustrated by this peculiarly resistant pupil who is bored by illustrated *monogatari* and in love with her dolls. The Third Princess remains innocently childlike until Genji deems it necessary to "improve" her image as a present to her father on the occasion of his fiftieth-birthday jubilee.

At this point in her life, the Third Princess seems to have no sub-stance. Norma Field has flatly stated that she is "literarily uninterest-ing."[8] She suffers by comparison to her cousin Murasaki and, like Aoi, fails to awaken Genji's romantic interest. Because Genji's obsession with Fujitsubo and Murasaki has made him critical of new substitutes, readers who have adopted his viewpoint have failed to assess the char-acter of the Third Princess on its own terms. There is more to her than meets Genji's jaundiced eye. Certainly the hero's blind spot con-cerning women should not be mistaken for the author's or that of her largely female audience. As John J. Winkler has noted about the diffi-culty of fathoming the texts of Greek antiquity, "we ought on the one hand to be cautious not to fill those deliberate gaps with fantasies of our own making (a well-worn warning) and on the other we must be alert to the possible significance of the almost-said, the discretely understated, the meaningful gestures left incomplete."[9] There is much that is puzzling in this sense about the thin outline of the Third Prin-cess' initial portrait.

## Kashiwagi's Traumas

The Third Princess emerges from near nonentity and comes to life, as Norma Field says, "through Kashiwagi's illicit attachment."[10] In order fully to appreciate Kashiwagi's impact on the Third Princess, it is necessary to fathom the mystery of her cat, who first appears at the climax of a game of *kemari*. This cat later inspires Kashiwagi, one of the *kemari* players, to have an affair with the Third Princess that is almost synchronous with Murasaki's "death" and spirit possession.

### The Courtship of Tamakazura

But who is Kashiwagi? As so often in the *Genji*, the relationships among the characters are complicated (fig. 4 in App. B). Tō no Chūjō's son Kashiwagi is the best friend of Yūgiri, Genji's son. The fathers of the two youths continue their rivalry and interfere as each man's son courts the other's daughter. Genji schemes to block Tō no Chūjō's ambitions for his daughter Kumoinokari and to punish him for his contemptuous treatment of Yūgiri, whose courtship of Kumoinokari Tō no Chūjō resists until he must give up his hope of his daughter becoming an imperial consort. Genji plays even more devious marriage politics with Kashiwagi. Falsely presenting Tamakazura to the world as his own daughter (although she is actually Tō no Chūjō's long-lost daughter by Yūgao), Genji encourages many of her close relatives, foremost among them Kashiwagi, to commit unwitting acts of incest.

Kashiwagi is indeed attracted to Tamakazura, but he discovers the truth about her paternity in time to retreat. Still, his shock upon discovering that the woman who aroused his passion is his half-sister becomes his primal trauma. Having just barely escaped the trap of sibling incest laid by Genji, Kashiwagi feels humiliated. Impelled now by the social rules imposed by the incest taboo—which in the *Genji* are for all intents and purposes extended to half-sibling- and step-relationships—Kashiwagi must change his behavior radically from impassioned amorous advances to utmost brotherly propriety. Naturally, this sudden reversal appears ludicrous to Tamakazura's women: "The change in Kashiwagi, until but yesterday the picture of desolate yearning, amused her women" (S:487; 3:331). A poetry exchange with Tamakazura on the topic of forbidden sibling attraction (see S:488; 3:333) dampens the erotic fire and somewhat eases the pain of disappointment and humiliation; but Kashiwagi remains obsessed with "unbrotherly feelings" (S:510; 3:389) for Tamakazura even after she has become a mother. In "Fuji no uraba" (S: "Wisteria Leaves"), Tō no Chūjō seeks reconciliation with Yūgiri by permitting his marriage to Kumoinokari; Genji, by contrast, does nothing to assuage Kashiwagi's hurt feelings over the aborted courtship of Tamakazura.

### The Courtship of the Third Princess

When Suzaku begins to search for a husband-guardian for the Third Princess, he considers Yūgiri, but Yūgiri's marriage to Kumoi-nokari makes him unsuitable. Suzaku then considers Kashiwagi because he is unusually ambitious and reportedly "determined to marry a princess and no one else" (S:544; 4:30).[11] In the end, however, Suzaku chooses Genji over the other suitors, which causes one critic to recall Genji's betrayal of Suzaku with Oborozukiyo (Suzaku's *naishi no kami*) and to wonder whether "there [is] an unconscious element of revenge in [Suzaku's] insistence many years [after the Oborozukiyo scandal] that Genji marry his immature daughter, the Third Princess."[12] Deeply enamoured of Murasaki, Genji is at first reluctant to become the princess' guardian and accept the obligation to find a husband for her. It is only when Suzaku suggests Yūgiri for this task that Genji hastens to comply and become both guardian and husband to the Third Princess.

Yūgiri and Kashiwagi are both disappointed to see the Third Princess fall into the hands of another man, but Yūgiri quickly adjusts when he realizes how little she seems to mean to his father. He concludes that Genji respects this new wife for her rank rather than for her person. In Yūgiri's estimation, the Third Princess, whose immaturity seems more obvious with every passing month, falls far short of the ideal woman he sees in Murasaki. Kashiwagi, however, unaware of Genji's indifference to the Third Princess, remains resentful, indulging himself in the irrational hope that he might take over as the Third Princess' husband when Genji leaves this world, either literally or in a metaphoric religious sense.

## A Game of *Kemari*

In "Wakana jō" (S: "New Herbs: Part One"), Genji soars to political success on the wings of his marriage to the Third Princess and the nearly simultaneous birth of his daughter's, the Akashi Princess', first child, later to become crown prince (fig. 3 in App. B). At the same time, Genji has to pay the high price of Murasaki's alienation over the matter of the Third Princess. His own son begins to lose respect for his father for having raised the childish Third Princess above the more deserving Murasaki. Thus Genji's steady acquisition of official status stands in inverse relationship to the gradual erosion of his domestic situation. Tamakazura's sudden and unexpected marriage to Hige-kuro, partly mediated by none other than Kashiwagi, had been the first severe blow to Genji's control of his women. At the end of "Wakana jō," Kashiwagi prepares to deliver a second blow.

In fact, Genji invites his own unmaking as uncontested hero when he summons Kashiwagi, Yūgiri, and others to a game of *kemari* near the Rokujō-in's southeastern quarters.[13] The scene, which the anthropologist Victor Turner has singled out as a prime example of liminality, is full of contrasts.[14] Genji, now middle-aged, watches from the sidelines and makes disparaging remarks while the young men eagerly play. Their bold movements contrast with the drifting clouds of delicate cherry blossoms that enfold them. Moreover, the game particularizes the players: while Yūgiri moves gracefully, always in perfect control, Kashiwagi excels in sporty abandon (Plate 2.6).

When Yūgiri and Kashiwagi pause to catch their breaths, something extraordinary occurs. While Genji has enjoyed an unobstructed view of the youths at play, the women of the Rokujō-in have been straining to watch without being seen. After all, Heian discourse, in both words and gestures, is defined by indirection and restraint. Then, in utter disregard for courtly feminine etiquette, the women themselves push aside the blinds that function much like the fence in a traditionally male *kaimami*. A woman in informal dress steps into view, intent on retrieving her escaped cat. Almost worse than the conspicuous display is the fact that she is observed standing. It is the Third Princess. The enormity of her breach of etiquette can be understood only in the hyperbolic terms of the peculiarly restrictive behavioral convention propagated through Heian fiction—namely, that women at the Heian court were expected to shield themselves from the male gaze by remaining in the darkened recesses of their rooms, reclining behind the protective curtains of state *(kichō)*, revealing at best a glimpse of colorful robes. The courtier, by contrast, was challenged by the male prerogative of *kaimami* to penetrate women's mysteries through an opening in the proverbial fence. That a woman has recklessly exposed herself, making a spectacle of her spectatorship, raises the possibility that women may not always have subscribed to the behavioral norm prescribing feminine reclusive immobility. The painter Tosa Mitsuyoshi (1539–1613) reproduces Murasaki Shikibu's gender twist on *kaimami* by showing the *kemari* scene, one of the most famous scenes in *Genji-e*, from behind the Third Princess' revealing blinds (Plate 2.6). Unlike other painters, he thus urges the viewer to take the woman's perspective rather than judge her from the male playing field or the viewpoint of an unrepresented arbiter—such as Genji—situated on the sidelines.[15]

The princess' dash for her cat excites Kashiwagi and appalls Yūgiri, in whose eyes the scene is a repulsive form of immodest behavior. In any event, it should be emphasized that neither Yūgiri nor Kashiwagi actively seeks the forbidden moment through the traditionally male prerogative of visual penetration in *kaimami*. On the contrary, the Third Princess is herself responsible for her scandalous exposure. She had been playing in her rooms with a pretty Chinese cat on a long cord. When she is distracted by her glimpse of the attractive young men at play, the cat, trying to escape from a larger cat, becomes entangled in the blinds. The Third Princess emerges from the safety of her rooms in order to rescue her pet.[16] By disobeying the imperative of female reclusiveness the princess subverts the male topos of *kaimami*.

The freak accident exposes for the first time her unbridled sexual anima, made visible in an erect body and associated with the animality of the cat.[17] Like the cat breaking loose with the leash in tow, the Third Princess pulls away from her year-old marriage ties. Both temperamental creatures break through the blinds that symbolize civilized behavior and rules of etiquette. Yet both are recaptured, one soon, one later, by those who literally or metaphorically own them. Under Heian behavioral norms, the Third Princess, once she has been glimpsed through an accident that achieves the effect of a *kaimami* without conforming to its structure, has become fair game for Yūgiri and Kashiwagi.

Yūgiri is constrained by the incest taboo. Insofar as he has forbidden thoughts about stepmothers, they are focused exclusively on Murasaki, whom Yūgiri cannot imagine capable of violating decorum as boldly as the Third Princess has. He thinks to himself: "Murasaki would never have been so careless" (S:584; 4:135). Yūgiri is also perceptive enough, and familiar enough with improper urges, to analyze Kashiwagi's response as an amorous one. He sees that Kashiwagi is not at all repelled by the Third Princess' scandalously overexposed physicality. In fact, her guileless posture impresses Kashiwagi—perhaps *because* it violates men's, especially her domineering husband's, behavioral rules. After all, Kashiwagi has been so restricted in his actions by Genji, especially in his aborted courtships of Tamakazura and the Third Princess, that he may long in his own moments of frustration to break the rules himself. He is spellbound by this woman who obeys instincts as fresh and vivacious as those of her cat. Unlike the more conventional Yūgiri, Kashiwagi is not compulsively proper and is therefore able to appreciate both the Third Princess' usual "abundance of quiet, unpretending, young charm" (S:584; 4:133) and her surprising boldness.

Kashiwagi is, however, constrained in his immediate advances toward the Third Princess by the prohibition of adultery. Genji, who obeyed neither that prohibition nor the stronger one against incest, involves the love-stricken Kashiwagi in a conversation that further provokes the young man's resentment and ambition. Genji thinks of *kemari* as a rough game at which only ruffians excel. He sarcastically compliments Kashiwagi on his play: "It may seem flippant to speak of a football heritage, but I really believe there must be such a thing, unusual talent handed down in a family. . . . This would be a most interesting and edifying item for a family chronicle" (S:584; 4:136).[18] Kashiwagi does not fail to detect the irony in Genji's words.

Whether or not Kashiwagi has decided to violate the prohibition against adultery, he feels propelled to initiate a poetry exchange, choosing as his intermediary Kojijū, the daughter of the Third Princess' nurse and the niece of Kashiwagi's own nurse. Through this wet-nurse *(menoto)* connection Kashiwagi can claim a certain familiarity with the Third Princess.[19] When Kashiwagi dashes off a love poem full of unambiguous allusions, it elicits the "civilized" response of acute embarrassment in the princess. What does this new facet of the Third Princess' temperament mean? It is clearly the result of Genji's "training" (S:580; 4:126), by which he has forced her into the patriarchal value system just as he earlier compelled the incomparably more malleable Murasaki. While Murasaki unconsciously suffered from the split between her female impulses and her completely internalized social self, the previously uninhibited Third Princess now flushes "scarlet" (S:586; 4:141) at the prodding of a newly discovered bad conscience.

She has complicated reasons to feel guilty as she recalls Genji's most important lesson—not to let herself be seen by another man, especially not by her stepson Yūgiri. Since she understands that Genji had merely done his guardian's duty in marrying her, her first reaction might be described as a daughter's guilt. While she fears that Yūgiri may report her transgression, she knows from Kashiwagi's poem that her appearance has reignited the flames of passion in this former suitor. In emotional disarray, the Third Princess does nothing to encourage or discourage Kashiwagi, leaving it to Kojijū to send an emphatic poem-letter rejecting the infatuated Kashiwagi (see S:586; 4:140). So forbidding is this mediated reply that Kashiwagi reverts to thoughts of the princess' cat.

## Cat and *Kin*

For six years Kashiwagi must pine for the Third Princess before he can consummate his illicit love. It seems that second-generation characters like Kashiwagi and Yūgiri are placed in unendurable situations resembling noblewomen's proverbial waiting for their lovers or husbands. During his extremely long waiting period Kashiwagi resorts to one unfamiliar and one familiar strategy for overcoming the painful absence of the beloved. With great enthusiasm he keeps a fetish; with much reluctance he accepts a human substitute for the Third Princess. Meanwhile, the princess, forced to replace her cat with the musical instrument of the *kin*, becomes temporarily alienated from the woman with whom Kashiwagi had fallen in love.

### Kashiwagi's Surrogates

Since the Third Princess made *kaimami* unnecessary, Kashiwagi must find an equivalent to the conventional hole in the fence. The Chinese cat, whose exotic beauty and untamed foreign nature represent the princess' anima, becomes the focus of Kashiwagi's displaced erotic interest (Plate 2.7). Acting through the Third Princess' half-brother, the crown prince, Kashiwagi borrows the cat and never returns it. His sudden obsession strikes others as bizarre, but for Kashiwagi the cat has become a surrogate for the Third Princess. In a *waka* with a charm of its own (rendered as prose in English translation; see S:589), Kashiwagi addresses the animal as the image of his beloved (4:150; my translation):

| | |
|---|---|
| *koiwaburu* | you I tamed |
| *hito no katami to* | my love's |
| *tenaraseba* | memento |
| *nare yo nani tote* | why cry |
| *naku ne naruramu* | what purring purpose |

The cat's behavior, "sporting with the hem of his robe" (S:589; 4:150), suggests, according to ancient lore, that the cat embodies the vagrant spirit of a lover.[20] During the six years that elapse before

Kashiwagi's secret affair with the Third Princess finally comes to fruition on the eve of the lustration for the Kamo Festival, the fateful cat serves as a lively reminder of the forbidden woman.

So infatuated is Kashiwagi with his cat that he refuses Prince Hyōbu's offer to marry his granddaughter Makibashira (fig. 3 in App. B). Instead, in unconscious imitation of Genji's kinship linkage between Fujitsubo, Murasaki, and the Third Princess, Kashiwagi marries the coveted Third Princess' half-sister, the Second Princess (Ochiba), Suzaku's daughter by a lesser consort (Ichijō no miyasudokoro) (fig. 4 in App. B). The attempt at substitution fails, and Kashiwagi soon regrets this bond to a woman he disparagingly likens to a "Fallen Leaf" (hence her sobriquet "Ochiba"). This sadly nondescript woman cannot distract him from his obsession for her forbidden half-sister.

### The Third Princess' Musical Instrument

In "Wakana ge" (S: "New Herbs: Part Two") the crown prince elevates the Third Princess, his half-sister, in rank, but the promotion seems to retard rather than further her progress toward adulthood. The slowness of her development exasperates Genji. While he is pleased to see his daughter, the Akashi Princess, rapidly becoming a competent woman, he finds his principal wife still fixed in the role of "daughter" (S:597; 4:170). Since neither Murasaki's nor Genji's attempts at educating the Third Princess have been successful in transforming her into a reliable, responsible adult, Genji seizes an opportunity to resume his efforts when the Retired Suzaku Emperor expresses his wish to see his beloved daughter once more. Genji believes he can exploit the strong father-daughter bond to awaken his child-wife's dormant qualities. Perhaps it is not too late for her to blossom into a more substantial woman. In the hope that she will excel at a women's concert planned for Suzaku's fiftieth jubilee he cleverly resumes the music lessons where her father had left off. Between rehearsals and the jubilee concert itself, however, there occurs a series of postponements symbolic of the Third Princess' obstructive character.

The Third Princess does improve enough for Genji to praise her musical abilities. To boost her self-confidence, Genji appoints her to be hostess of the grand concert rehearsal. She is assigned the seven-stringed Chinese koto *(kin)* while Akashi plays the lute *(biwa)*, Murasaki the six-stringed Japanese koto *(wagon)*, and the Akashi daughter the thirteen-stringed Chinese koto *(sō)*.[21] The exotic instrument Genji chooses for the Third Princess fits her foreign character as did the Chinese cat. Although Yūgiri has an incurable preference for Murasaki, even he must acknowledge the Third Princess' new accomplishment on an unusually difficult instrument. Genji too is touched by her improvement on the "unmanageable" koto (S:604; 4:189). For the first time, the Third Princess seems to be an adult: "One looked in vain for signs of immaturity" (S:605; 4:193).

Congratulating himself on his expert mentorship in regard to all four of his women, Genji magnifies the Third Princess' talent by contemplating the power of her instrument: "We are told that in ancient times there were many who mastered the whole tradition of the instrument, and made heaven and earth their own, and softened the hearts of demons and gods" (S:604; 4:189). At the same time, Genji warns that anything less than complete control will precipitate disaster: "The seven-stringed koto was the instrument that moved demons and gods, and inadequate mastery had correspondingly unhappy results" (S:605; 4:190). While rejoicing at his young wife's progress, he imagines it as fragile as the first shoots of a willow, disturbed by the faintest flutter of a warbler's wing (see S:602; 4:183).

Genji's concern is justified. He observes the Third Princess flagrantly violating etiquette by presenting gifts to Yūgiri, the forbidden stepson. Clearly his hope that the development of her musical talents has changed her personality seems misguided. Although rather an improvement over the previous addiction to dolls, the musical performance signals no fundamental personality change. Nonetheless, it remains to be seen whether Genji's mentorship puts the Third Princess—who is less malleable and more resistant to Genji's ambitions than Murasaki was—at risk for spirit possession.

## The Kamo Complex

In order to arrange a secret meeting with the Third Princess, Kashiwagi needs an intermediary. His choice is, once again, Kojijū. Kashiwagi must employ all his diplomatic skills to persuade the reluctant Kojijū to act for him. (The scene is reminiscent of Genji's arrangement of a secret meeting with Fujitsubo through Ōmyōbu.) He presents himself as a man eager to compensate for Genji's neglect and to allay Suzaku's worries about his daughter. He blames the Third Princess' troubles on Murasaki, whom he faults for having monopolized Genji's affection. All these reasons, he argues, impel him to rescue the unhappy princess from the sadness of her marriage. Every time Kojijū counters an argument, Kashiwagi invents another. In the end, Kojijū complies.

Kashiwagi's plan is to try for another glimpse of the Third Princess, this time by *kaimami* rather than by the fortuitous conjunction of *kemari* and a cat. He does not linger in the preliminary moment of *kaimami*. On the eve of the lustration for the Kamo Festival, Kashiwagi forces himself physically upon the speechless Third Princess, assuring her that this is what her father really wants. He pleads precedents as well, alluding to Genji's own transgressions. He consummates his love. In a state of shock, the Third Princess can hardly be faulted for being "speechless" (S:613; 4:216). Not having learned the reflexes expected of women in such situations, she is "unresisting" (S:614; 4:216), which leads one to wonder if she has in fact unwittingly encouraged Kashiwagi as she had done at the time of the *kemari* incident. If she is in a state of shock, he seems to be in trance-like ecstasy, and the two of them are barely conscious of having sexual intercourse. Kashiwagi has a postcoital dream in which he returns the fateful cat to the princess. Now that Kashiwagi has bridged the six-year interval of yearning between the first sight of the Third Princess and the consummation of his love, the feline fetish is no longer needed. Kashiwagi intends to explain the meaning of his dream—said in folklore to signal conception—but he fails to mention it amidst his nostalgic outpourings about the game of *kemari* and his first sight of his beloved.

Kashiwagi interprets the Third Princess' initial "muteness" (S:615; 4:218) as a rejection, but in fact it expresses her terror of Genji. She finds Kashiwagi's conduct "outrageous" (S:615; 4:219) and fears that she may have conceived and that Genji will be furious to discover her pregnant with Kashiwagi's child. In defense of his violent action, Kashiwagi reminds her of her provocative posture during the *kemari* incident. Kashiwagi's judgment of her complicity in the adultery is finally confirmed. Since she has never resisted Kashiwagi from the time she was first amused by his illicit correspondence, it does not occur to her now to accuse him of violating her and thereby exonerate herself from adult(erous) guilt and responsibility. The remarkable fact that she composes an impromptu poem to send him on his way suggests her inability, if not her unwillingness, to remain indifferent. At the same time, her *waka* about vanishing into the dawning sky like a dream reveals the hopelessness of this liaison and the despair that will eventuate in spirit possession. When her lover is gone, she falls into a moral pit of silent brooding. When Murasaki enters the final phase of her extended crisis at the Nijō-in, the Third Princess' psychic burden is compounded rather than lightened. How can she not contrast Murasaki's faithfulness to her own transgression?

The princess' fear that she is pregnant by Kashiwagi is justified. Can the child born of this transgression be seen as karmic retribution for Genji's incestuous affair with Fujitsubo, which resulted in the birth of Reizei, and for the trauma inflicted on Kashiwagi by Genji's incestuous game with Tamakazura? If Kashiwagi's violation of the Third Princess is indeed a form of revenge, it is certainly one with great risks for him. As Haruo Shirane puts it: "Kashiwagi betrays not only his superior, a personal patron and supporter, but the *jun daijō tennō,* a man equal in status to a retired emperor."[22] Norma Field goes one step further by portraying Kashiwagi as "violating the pseudo-empress-wife of his pseudo-emperor-father."[23] Moreover, by seducing the Third Princess as Genji had seduced Yūgao, Kashiwagi avenges his father Tō no Chūjō for Genji's appropriation of *his* mistress and daughter (Yūgao and Tamakazura).

## Kashiwagi's Pseudo-Possession

There is no explicit indication of guilt due to incest in the episode surrounding Kashiwagi's relationships with Ochiba and the Third Princess.[24] The circumstances of Kashiwagi's fate, however, suggest that more than one serious transgression occurred. Kashiwagi's love-less marriage to Ochiba provides some clues. It makes a travesty of the hitherto meaningful, though dangerous, strategy of substitution pursued by the Kiritsubo Emperor and Genji. For Kashiwagi, the substitute has become an empty cipher. Moreover, Kashiwagi's sexual violation of Ochiba's half-sister, the Third Princess, adds an incestuous element to mere adultery. Kashiwagi and the Third Princess are safe from serious repercussions only so long as they can keep their transgression secret. Since they have committed their doubly forbidden act to paper, their secret comes to Genji's attention in the form of a love letter. It later manifests itself in the confused lives of Ochiba and her mother in the devious form of Kashiwagi's flute and handwriting. In short, Kashiwagi's handling of his transgressions and his secret profoundly unsettles his parents, his wife, and his mother-in-law. The less understood the transgressions produced by Kashiwagi and the Third

Princess, the more damaging the impact on others seems to be. *Mono no ke* represent these mysterious threats. The same was true for Genji and Fujitsubo.

Unquestionably, Kashiwagi's aggressive behavior has psychic costs. Although his first reaction is merely to feel pity for Ochiba, the unsuspecting "fallen leaf" (S:616; 4:224), a sprig of *aoi* (heartvine; also lovers' "meeting") alerts him to having polluted the Kamo festivities. More important, as a poetic emblem the *aoi* spurs awareness of the link between Kashiwagi's adultery against Genji and his incestuous offense against his wife. When Genji and Fujitsubo committed adultery and incest, they violated a single person: the Kiritsubo Emperor. The Kashiwagi–Third Princess affair splits the injury between Genji, the victim of adultery, and Ochiba, the victim of incestuous transgression. Kashiwagi and the Third Princess focus their attention on Genji, the more powerful of the two victims. (It is not until Kashiwagi's death that the consequences of the offense against Ochiba surface.) When Genji visits the pregnant Third Princess, Kashiwagi begins to experience the consequences of his transgression. His symptoms are not what one might expect: he is consumed by "female" jealousy. With the provocative behavior displayed by the Third Princess and Kashiwagi, the author ceases to depict gender relations in terms of male *kaimami* and female jealousy.

The Third Princess and Kashiwagi not only act contrary to gendered role expectations, they must also endure the unendurable as the first taboo violators in the *Genji* who are directly confronted by their victim about their secret. When Genji discovers a love letter through the carelessness of the Third Princess, Kashiwagi realizes that Genji knows about the adulterous affair. Worrying about what this might mean and searching to explain to himself the sequence of events, Kashiwagi traces his loss of self-control to the excitement of the game of *kemari* and to the Third Princess' sudden unethical appearance. He attempts to alleviate his sense of guilt and to stifle his sexual desire by blaming the Third Princess: "It may be that he was now trying to see the worst in the princess and so shake off his longing" (S:626; 4:249).

While the Third Princess is undergoing her difficult pregnancy, Kashiwagi suffers mortification at the hands of Genji. Subjected to Genji's subtle verbal torture, he is reduced by anxiety to a shadow of his former athletic self. Once able to kick the *kemari* ball better than anyone else, he now complains to Genji about having "such trouble with my legs" (S:632; 4:266). When he is forced to participate in the final rehearsal for Suzaku's jubilee, he agonizes over Genji's insincerely gentle words. He falls into despair. As his crisis approaches a climax (parallel to the Third Princess' coming to term), he loses all desire to live. Realizing that Kashiwagi is dying, his mother (Shi no kimi) and mother-in-law (Ichijō no miyasudokoro) compete for his loyalty and legacy. Torn between them, Kashiwagi flees. He abandons his wife and his mother-in-law and returns home to his parents. Suzaku's jubilee is celebrated without Kashiwagi.

Kashiwagi initiates one last poetry exchange with the Third Princess in which the two avow their love for each other, a love striving to transcend death. While waiting in great suspense for the Third Princess' reply, Kashiwagi is overcome by what is diagnosed as a case of spirit possession. As in Fujitsubo's pregnancy, here too the uninformed public seeks an explanation for life-threatening symptoms by looking for *mono no ke*. Kashiwagi's parents, the robust Tō no Chūjō and the strong-willed Shi no kimi, cannot otherwise comprehend their son's sudden and precipitous decline in health. They reluctantly conclude that he is possessed by the jealous spirit of a woman (4:284: *onna no ryō*) and must therefore undergo the rituals of exorcism, but they cannot be confident of their diagnosis.[25] Neither they nor anyone else can convincingly speculate on the identity of the female spirit. If Kashiwagi, a man who married late and appears indifferent to his wife Ochiba, has fallen into the clutches of a jealous woman, they cannot imagine who that woman might be. After all, Kashiwagi is not known to have affairs. If he were in fact secretly obsessed with another woman, should it not be Ochiba, rather than Kashiwagi, who becomes possessed? By placing their son in the unlikely role of possessed male, his parents seem to imply that he is the blameless victim of a jealous wife whose mother, acting on behalf of her neglected daughter, has displayed an immodest possessiveness of her stricken son-in-law.

Kashiwagi does indeed exhibit symptoms associated with the possessed as well as those associated with possessing spirits. As if inspired by his parents' misdiagnosis, Kashiwagi develops the charisma to "speak" to Genji through another, just as Aoi and Murasaki spoke to Genji through Rokujō. As Aoi and Murasaki allied themselves with Rokujō to humble and impress Genji, Kashiwagi allies himself with the Third Princess. After he has considered the belief that he has been possessed, and forcefully rejected it, he reads the Third Princess' reply to his last letter. He anticipates her request for the tonsure and wishes for a safe delivery of the child he is now certain was conceived through his magic dream about the cat. Not unlike a *mono no ke*, this mysteriously charismatic feline has passed back and forth between them. Its aura seems to have penetrated the Third Princess—almost as if it, rather than Kashiwagi, were responsible for the Third Princess' pregnancy.

In his psychic turmoil Kashiwagi also displays traits associated with possessing spirits. In some intriguing ways, he appears to resemble Rokujō. Like her, he must respond to the charge of involvement in spirit possession and admit the possibility that his soul (4:285: *tamashii*) is "wandering loose" (S:638; 4:285). As in the possessed Aoi's *waka*, Kashiwagi is following folk belief in asking that his errant soul be caught. In intimate conversation with Kojijū, he acknowledges a state of dissociation similar to Rokujō's when she was rumored to have possessed the pregnant Aoi. While he is treated by others as if he were possessed, he struggles, in the manner of Rokujō, to maintain a clear head. Just as Rokujō felt trapped in an incriminating wisp of poppy-seed incense used in exorcist ritual, so Kashiwagi feels caught by the mystic chants that are unable to bring out the truth of his transgression but nonetheless remind him of his lost secret.

Public perception fails to note the signs that Kashiwagi remains in command of his destiny, indeed, of his dying. Even the ascetic summoned from Mount Katsuragi—not to mention all the other ascetics, diviners, and soothsayers—is helpless in identifying and expelling *mono no ke* from the troubled man. Norma Field has astutely noted that the "best exorcists in the world cannot stop his dying, since he has not been possessed."[26] In short, their efforts are futile because Kashiwagi is not in a trance suspending his rational faculties and enabling him to assume the persona of another (as is commonly the case in authentic spirit possession). Unlike the women trapped in total silence by patriarchal rules of behavior, Kashiwagi is far less restricted in his options: he communicates freely with the person who matters most to him, the Third Princess. He demonstrates that he has a full intellectual grasp of his situation. While nearby his father is entreating the ascetic from Mount Katsuragi to expel his *mono no ke*, Kashiwagi can analyze his emotional state and communicate its complexity to his confidante and intermediary, Kojijū (Plate 2.9). Those capable of dissecting their state of mind, no matter how disturbed, are not prone to spirit possession. Kashiwagi suffers from a guilty conscience battered by the repeated traumas inflicted by Genji, but he does not suffer from the unspeakable as a permanent condition, as do the women who resort to spirit possession. In short, although he pays a fearful price for it, he is the only male character to have succeeded in besting Genji at his own game—not *kemari,* but taboo violations. Now, neither truly possessed nor wishing to possess another, Kashiwagi lingers guiltily in a liminal situation between life and death.

In an uncharacteristic burst of self-determination, the Third Princess expresses her love of Kashiwagi and her wish to die with him. Fulfilled by her promise, Kashiwagi embarks on his final journey toward death. His last *waka* to her, "the words . . . fragmentary and disconnected and the hand like the tracks of a strange bird," speaks of a more intense phase in his state of dissociation (4:286; S:639):

> *yukue naki    sora no keburi to    narinu tomo*
> *omou atari o    tachi wa hanareji*

> As smoke I shall rise uncertainly to the heavens,
> And yet remain where my thoughts will yet remain.

Kashiwagi no longer views his imminent death as unfortunate. His complete resignation greatly shocks his parents. Having taken care of matters of the heart, the dying man can put his affairs in order. As a failed husband, he is acutely aware of Ochiba's unspoken resentment. After hinting at his double transgression (against Genji and Ochiba) to an uncomprehending Yūgiri, Kashiwagi entrusts Ochiba to him and then he vanishes like foam on water (see S:647; 4:308). As Kashiwagi lies dying, the Third Princess gives birth to their son (Kaoru), receives the tonsure from her father, and becomes possessed.

## The Third Princess' Possession

As the visible signs of her pregnancy become more pronounced, the Third Princess finds herself in a position that is alien to her true self. Whereas Murasaki had been shaped by Genji into his ideal of a civilized woman, neither Genji nor Murasaki has been able to bring the Third Princess into conformity with Heian culture. The child growing within her makes the Third Princess aware of the discrepancy between her impulsive nature and the sober responsibilities of married womanhood. As in the case of Aoi, the physical consequences of pregnancy literally and symbolically outline an altered self. Yet the circumstances and the sequence of events in the two cases are quite different. In the case of the Third Princess, a safe delivery precedes spirit possession. As a new element, the tonsure intercedes between childbirth and spirit possession.

### Pregnancy and Childbirth

As the Third Princess undergoes the physical transformation of pregnancy, she experiences psychic trauma. When Genji discovers Kashiwagi's love letter—and with it the truth about the Third Princess' pregnancy—she faces a dilemma. She is torn between her husband, whose efforts to shape her have had at least some effect, and her lover, who has restored her lost anima (symbolized by the mysterious cat that he returns at the time of their dreamlike sexual intercourse). Should she turn to Genji, who formed her social self but is otherwise indifferent to her, or to Kashiwagi, who passionately adores her untamed personality? Should she commit herself to the man who not only inseminated her but aroused her sexually as her husband never did? Her dilemma is worsened by the fact that Genji, who is now well aware of her infidelity, demands that she not confide in her still doting father. Her anxiety is compounded by fears that her father might discover the truth in the distorted form of rumors.

When Kashiwagi attends to the Third Princess during her pregnancy in "visits as fleeting as dreams" (S:621; 4:234), her mind is completely dominated by Genji's legal claims on her. She is so awed by his acclaimed political stature that she fails to register the intensity of Kashiwagi's risky devotion. Yet she and Genji become increasingly alienated from one another. The more the unforgiving Genji scolds her for her childishness, heedlessness, and infidelity, the more she withdraws into herself. Even when he says nothing, she feels that he is reproving her in silence (see S:627; 4:250). Stifled by guilt, she shows symptoms of depression.

Publicly, she carries Kashiwagi's child as if it were Genji's. There is no doubt that all this feigning and prevarication, worsened by seclusion, causes the pregnancy to be very difficult. Her father expresses concern over her precarious physical and emotional state, which he attributes to Genji's neglect. Suzaku is the one person to whom she might speak of her despair, but Genji censors her every move with the argument that he must protect the reputations of all affected by the adulterous affair as well as preserve Suzaku's religious peace of mind and trust in Genji. He dictates her reply to Suzaku.

Thus the Third Princess' once carefree self has been reduced, in Emily Dickinson's haunting phrase, to "zero at the bone." Genji not only ties her hand in correspondence now but also gags her when he threateningly reminds her of the frequently postponed Suzaku jubilee festivities for which she had trained so hard and enthusiastically on her *kin*. This "unmanageable" musical instrument, a symbolic representation of the Third Princess' character as controlled by her husband-mentor, had temporarily replaced the cat—until Kashiwagi returned the exotic animal. Circumstances are such that the *kin*'s potential of moving demons and gods has been perverted and threatens now to produce "unhappy results" (S:605; 4:190).

There are few clues to the Third Princess' innermost thoughts in response to Genji's threats, now insinuated, now crassly direct. What is missing in overt self-analysis is expressed in unmistakable psychosomatic symptoms. When Genji dictates a letter of equivocations in reply to Suzaku's inquiry about his daughter's physical health and state of mind, her trembling hand indicates more forcefully than words her revulsion from Genji and her sense of impotence. Rather than analyzing her emotional state, she acts on impulse—as she did in the *kemari* incident. In her reckless spontaneity she resembles Yūgao. Upset by mistreatment and frustration in her attempts at verbal communication, Yūgao fled from Tō no Chūjō only to be carried off to Genji's villa, where she dramatically expired in her abductor's arms.

Genji's unrelenting pressure makes the Third Princess believe that she is the sole malefactor rather than one of several guilty persons. Unaware that Genji also blames Kashiwagi (see S:631; 4:265), she intuitively resists what seems to her her husband's unfair accusations. What once seemed unthinkable now becomes a viable option: her forbidden and doomed bond with Kashiwagi. To claim, as one critic has, that "the Third Princess bears only contempt for Kashiwagi" overlooks her dying lover's vital importance in her emotional life.[27] When, at the height of her difficult pregnancy, Kashiwagi sends his last letter, she adds her death wish to his and challenges him to a contest of hopeless love (4:286; S:639):

> *tachisoite   kie ya shinamashi   uki koto o*
> *omoimidaruru   keburi kurabe ni*

> I wish to go with you, that we may see
> Whose smoldering thoughts last longer, yours or mine.

The strength drawn from this new commitment to the man who is sac-
rificing his life for love sustains her through the ordeal of childbirth.
Their son Kaoru represents a forbidden liaison belatedly confirmed.
He also stands for further resistance to Genji's efforts at control.
Unwittingly, the woman who gives birth to this child is a character
extension of the more self-conscious female resisters to Genji's will:
Akikonomu, Tamakazura, and—most important—Rokujō.

### The Tonsure and Spirit Possession

The Third Princess' death wish intensifies as she observes the
signs of Genji's revulsion from her newborn son. Since it was considered a grave sin to die in childbirth or its aftermath, she resorts to the
only respectable alternative: the tonsure. She informs Genji that she
wishes to take religious vows. Although his initial reflex is to deny her
desire as he had denied Murasaki's repeated requests, he is inclined to
accede because he realizes that the Third Princess' religious seclusion
can serve his own purposes. While outwardly he can protest and
lament her decision, inwardly he is tempted by the thought of not
having to keep up a false front and pretending to love her. If Genji is
not more vengeful, it may be that he recalls and regrets his own far
more serious taboo violation against his father.

When Genji finally allows the Third Princess to communicate with
her father, Suzaku violates his monastic vows and leaves his holy mountain retreat in order to assist his daughter in extremis. For Genji,
Suzaku's unexpected visit lightens the burden of responsibility in the
final decision about the tonsure. The two men discuss the Third Princess' precarious situation and her fervent wish (Plate 2.8). Genji argues
that "an outside force" (S:642; 4:295: *zake*) has inspired the request.[28]
It is in Genji's interest to do so because he fears that his half-brother
will comply with his daughter's request, thereby removing her from his
control and endangering the secret of her child's parentage. Suzaku
counters with the argument that *mono no ke* (4:296) tend to shrink
from persons with holy intentions, preferring instead to draw the
already afflicted into a still darker world. Suzaku also ponders the case
in his own mind and considers partially granting his daughter's wish by
installing her at his nearby Sanjō mansion, where she can live like a nun
while remaining under Genji's protection. Neither of the estranged
marital partners likes this proposed compromise: Genji resists Suzaku's
offer to administer preliminary vows; the Third Princess vehemently
rejects the suggestion that she remain under Genji's "protection."

Is her resistance a sign that she now is possessed? Hirota Osamu has attributed the Third Princess' gesture of shaking her head in protest over Genji's denial of the tonsure as a manifestation of the *mono no ke* already possessing her.[29] Fujii Sadakazu points to the transformation of the Third Princess' character from naive childishness to rebellious maturity, and he too attributes the change to the emboldening force of *mono no ke*. Her resolute insistence on the tonsure is a sign of initiation sickness *(fubyō)* that, Fujii argues, leads to a "black [demonic] tonsure" *(kuroi shukke)* deriving its energy from *mono no ke*.[30] Fujimoto Katsuyoshi, by contrast, argues that Suzaku fully realizes that his daughter is neither possessed nor religiously inspired when she asks him to administer vows; instead, Suzaku has severe misgivings about his daughter's pregnancy because of Genji's cold treatment of her. If the Third Princess had been possessed by *mono no ke* when she took vows, argues Fujimoto, she would have been vexed instead of feeling refreshed in embracing the Buddha's way.[31]

If we are to interpret the gesture of her shaking head with any degree of accuracy, we must make clear the viewpoint from which we observe it. Since Murasaki Shikibu's complex narrative technique involves the distribution of knowledge among several fictional characters, none of whom is aware of the whole truth, she requires us as readers to piece together fragments of information in order to arrive at a more complete picture of "reality" than that available to any single character in the narrative. To examine the gesture of the Third Princess' shaking head from the point of view of those who witness it, Genji and Suzaku, produces contradictory and limited results. Interestingly, Genji—despite his knowledge of the situation underlying the Third Princess' plight, namely, her adulterous affair—refuses to apply this knowledge honestly in interpreting his wife's intentions. For Genji, suspended between knowledge and denial, *mono no ke* is the only feasible explanation for his wife's recalcitrance. Suzaku does not know the facts. Although he is able to intuit his daughter's distress, he believes a practical solution can be found and has no reason to suspect the presence of *mono no ke*. What might the Third Princess herself have intended with this unexpectedly defiant gesture? In my view, the Third Princess' pact with Kashiwagi, sealed by their final *waka* exchange, constitutes the crucial act that endows her with the strength to shake off Genji's claims on her. When this expression of her wish for the tonsure is reduced to preliminary injunctions *(jukai)*—which do not ensure her freedom from Genji—her use of spirit possession as a woman's weapon becomes inevitable.

Having administered an abbreviated form of the tonsure that

allows his daughter to renounce sexuality and become childlike again, Suzaku leaves before the crisis can be resolved. He repeats his request that his daughter, should she survive her crisis, live neither in a mountain nunnery nor the Rokujō-in, but in a quiet place like his Sanjō mansion where Genji can continue to look after her. While religious vows may serve the Third Princess as a sign to her father of her unhappiness and as a spiritual bond with him, they do not achieve her liberation from Genji. When her father returns to his mountain retreat, the Third Princess can expect nothing better than imprisonment. So long as the cuckolded Genji is alive, she will remain under his firm supervision in the Rokujō-in so that the secret of her child's identity can be kept.

If the token tonsure satisfied neither the Third Princess' desire to confess her true condition to her father nor her need to demonstrate to her husband her deep commitment to Kashiwagi, spirit possession can at least provide a mechanism for oblique expression of her needs and desires. In unbearable distress, she enters an altered state of consciousness during Buddhist services at the break of dawn. Although Takahashi Tōru has asserted that a *mono no ke* causes the Third Princess to become a nun,[32] his argument seems inconsistent with Heian beliefs, according to which the *mono no ke* should have fled from her before rather than after she submitted to Buddhist injunctions. In other words, Suzaku was right to assume that, distressed as she may have been, she was lucid and not possessed when she asked for the tonsure. The possession is triggered by her sudden realization that she has been abandoned by her father and entrapped by her husband. Since it is considered an anomaly to be stricken by *mono no ke* after taking religious vows, the Third Princess' sudden seizure comes as a total surprise.

Genji cannot understand why the Third Princess' solemn Buddhist vows have not protected her. No longer in control of events at this turning point in his life, Genji has lost the ability to probe for the identity of the spirit. It is too taxing to imagine a replacement for the formidable Rokujō, who has all these years served Genji well as the embodiment (or en-spirit-ment) of female jealousy. In truth, she threatened him as his only equal. It is too difficult to imagine a similar figure to emerge in the form of a male rival. By vaguely veering toward Rokujō but remaining in a daze about the possibility of a raucous male spirit, Genji neither fails nor succeeds in identifying the Third Princess' *mono no ke*.

Despite the male diction of the spirit's speech, critics have been more decisive than Genji and have unanimously identified it as Rokujō's (S:644; 4:300):[33]

> Well, here I am. You see what I have done. I was not at all happy, let me tell you, to see how happy you were with the lady you thought you had taken from me. So I stayed around the house for a while to see what I could do. I have done it and I will go.

In accordance with the Rokujō theory, Edward G. Seidensticker chooses a female pronoun in translating Genji's immediate reaction to the spirit's speech: "So *she* still had not left them!" (S:644, my italics; 4:300). Hirota Osamu has observed that, consistent with their mysterious identity, *shiryō* are generally not referred to by personal pronoun (*ninshō*) unless they clearly belong to identifiable historical figures.[34] Accordingly, the original gives *mono no ke,* which can refer to either a male or female, a living or a dead, a human or a nonhuman spirit.

Although Genji holds back from naming Rokujō as the possessing spirit, the Rokujō theory does seem to make some sense if one adopts Genji's perspective. Read in this way, the spirit's speech implies that Murasaki's possessing spirit, unambiguously identified as Rokujō, was never exorcized. But convenient as it may be for Genji to think that Rokujō's angry spirit simply moved from Murasaki to his principal wife, such a move makes little sense even on its own terms. Within the logic of a Genji-centric interpretation, the *mono no ke* should have seized Murasaki again, not the Third Princess. Whether the spirit's aim was to destroy the couple's happiness after Murasaki's brush with death or merely to let Genji know that it remained in control of Murasaki and that he had rejoiced too soon about winning back his favorite wife, the seizure of the Third Princess is an excessively convoluted way to communicate the message.[35] If this "transfer theory" is true, then obliqueness has become so extreme that a glancing blow is none at all. It is more plausible that Genji's instant reaction to the spirit's speech is misguided. It betrays how Genji's thinking continues to revolve around Murasaki and how little the Third Princess means to him by contrast.

There are further difficulties with the Rokujō theory. The raucous laughter accompanying the spirit's words has greatly puzzled the critics. The signals given by this laughter should not be ignored. Mae Michiko proposes the unusual view that the outburst signifies Rokujō's liberation from women's constraints at her last appearance, long after her death.[36] Saigō Nobutsuna attributes the gleeful and triumphant laughter to Rokujō's achievement of making the Third Princess a nun (and he chides her for such an undignified prank).[37] Agreeing with the Rokujō theory, Field perceives a reversal in narrative technique: "Whereas the Rokujō Lady's earlier appearances as a possessing spirit had offered flashes of psychological revelation when the surrounding tale was largely innocent of introspection, here her spirit turns demonlike and unrecuperably otherworldly."[38] There are reasons to agree with Field. The suggestion that here *mono no ke,* the subtle manifestation of the Heian psyche, turn into *oni,* which are essentially monsters of the medieval popular imagination, is borne out by *Shikimi tengu,* a *nō* play "too unorthodox" to have remained in the current repertoire.[39] Although the play has no direct reference to the Third Princess' possession, the chief mountain goblin *(tengu)* transports Rokujō's restless ghost to the Rokujō-in, which becomes a veritable hell for her.[40] All that is left of Rokujō at the end of the *nō* is "a roar of laughter."[41]

Rokujō's enigmatic laughter contrasts sharply with the poetic sensibilities that characterized her earlier appearances as *mono no ke* and has led some critics to question Murasaki Shikibu's literary judgment in depicting such a breach of behavior. Haraoka Fumiko concludes that Rokujō becomes a contradictory character (but one without an apparent split, *"bunretsu,"* in her personality).[42] Taya Raishun has dealt with the problem of Rokujō's inexplicable behavior by defining her appearances in the form of a living or dead spirit as a literary manifestation of the transcendental in Genji's life.[43]

Yet there is good reason to think that the spirit Genji never names is not the woman whom the critics assume he must be thinking of. Since Murasaki Shikibu has by now thoroughly proved the main witness to be an unreliable source for interpreting the dynamics of spirit possession, it becomes necessary to shift to the motivations of the possessed woman and her use of the possessing spirit if we are to avoid reducing the phenomenon to nothing more than an act of vengeance on the part of the *mono no ke.* The Rokujō theory fails this test. It is important to see why. If female jealousy were indeed the sole motivating factor for a possessing spirit, then, in respect to the Third Princess, the woman most prone to such emotions would be Murasaki, especially because of her rival's childbirth.[44] Since the spirit asserts that the Third Princess is "a lady you thought you had taken from me," it might be argued that Genji is being blamed for snatching the Third Princess from Murasaki, who was acting as her teacher, but it is difficult to imagine that Murasaki felt deprived of her insipid pupil. There is no indication that Murasaki did not gladly resign from the hopeless enterprise of luring her childish rival out of a state resembling autism.

Another suspect fitting the conventional role of the jealous female is Kashiwagi's Ochiba. While it is true that Kashiwagi took this princess as a substitute for her half-sister, Ochiba, who is unaware of her husband's liaison with the Third Princess, has no reason to accuse him of anything worse than indifference. Not even her alert mother, who opposed the match from the beginning, introduces the notion of jealousy into the mind of her timid daughter. Furthermore, the spirit's accusation that Genji took someone away disqualifies Ochiba as possessing spirit.

If no jealous and resentful female candidate emerges plausibly to account for the possession of the Third Princess, then two related questions arise: Is the spirit, for the first time in the *Genji*, male? Does this putative male spirit direct his jealousy and resentment at Genji rather than at the possessed person? If one answers both questions positively, then one sees—in a flash—that Genji simply cannot conceive of himself as the target of the spirit's aggression. The mechanism of denial explains his—and the critics'—interpreting the male tone of the speech as if it were female. His cultural reflexes allow him to cling to the belief in female jealousy that had always exempted him from feeling himself under attack. But who might Genji's male challenger and nemesis be?

Responding to the Third Princess' discontent, difficult childbirth, and request for the tonsure, Suzaku had earlier concluded that Genji must have neglected his principal wife. The royal father's unconfirmed speculations are so deeply worrisome that he abandons his priestly seclusion and rushes to his daughter's side. He rejects Genji's suggestion that some evil influence is inciting her to ask for religious vows. When Suzaku leaves, having finally administered an abbreviated form of the tonsure, he repeats his trust in Genji, but this trust has clearly been shaken. Shortly thereafter, the possessing spirit speaks, presumably through a medium, in male diction. Is the voice that of Suzaku himself—expressing his anger and resentment at Genji more forcefully than before, reclaiming his daughter by allowing her to join him in the Buddha's path? Suzaku does have motives sufficient to explain the spirit's uninhibited outburst. The half-brothers have a long history of political tensions alternating with periodic gestures of reconciliation. Genji's earlier betrayal of Suzaku with Oborozukiyo—for which Genji went into exile—seems to pale in comparison with Genji's neglect of Suzaku's most beloved daughter.

The Suzaku hypothesis also satisfies my contention about the dynamics and motivations of spirit possession—namely, that the possessed person's innermost anxieties and desires find expression in the complex phenomenon of oblique aggression. There is no doubt that the Third Princess remains more deeply attached to her father than to Genji. In effect, even her impulsive affair with Kashiwagi can be attributed to her forced separation from her father and her indifference to Genji. Her unabated longing for her father, her repressed anger at Genji for torturing and despising her as an adulteress—these factors combined may be seen to compel her to form an alliance with Suzaku as her protective paternal spirit. Standing as Genji does in awe of his successful half-brother, he might well be impressed by such an alliance if his mind were not fixed on—in the film *Casablanca*'s immortal phrase—"the usual suspects."

The author's complex weave of characters and events, however, allows for another hypothesis that is even more plausible. The unidentified *mono no ke* admits to having "done" something—whether impregnating or tonsuring or both—out of resentment for Genji's rapprochement with his errant wife. The person most likely to feel such resentment, and the person most likely to support the Third Princess in her oblique attack on Genji, is Kashiwagi. If we begin as in the traditional approach, by first identifying the spirit and determining its motivations, then the spirit's words fit perfectly Kashiwagi's "jealousy" (S:622–623; 4:238) of Genji and his anger over his humiliation by Genji. But so long as Genji considers the possessed as the victim of the *mono no ke*, he cannot conceive of himself as the target. He blocks out this conclusion because his self-esteem and self-confidence have plummeted since his realization that he has been cuckolded. He shrinks from further devastating knowledge of the sort taught him by his discovery of Kashiwagi's telling letter.

Since the possessed and the spirit are of different sexes, the rationale of female bonding does not hold for this cross-gender variant of spirit possession. The possessed person's empowerment through a charismatic male spirit humiliates the targeted male witness even more pointedly than through the traditionally jealous female spirit.[45] As a charismatic spirit, Kashiwagi has become Rokujō's successor. Thus the Third Princess' possession demonstrates nothing less than a serious symptom of Genji's decline.

   In view of the Third Princess' self-satisfied character and her apparent indifference to female rivals, especially Murasaki, it is logical that she feels no need to form a surreptitious female bond. Her need to express herself through the oblique aggressive strategy of spirit possession develops in dramatic stages, beginning with the *kemari* incident and culminating in her taking vows. After the scandal of her exposure to Yūgiri and Kashiwagi, the Third Princess realizes that her husband is undertaking the task of educating her, changing her, endangering her untamed nature. It is her secret lover Kashiwagi who safeguards and preserves intact this nature in the form of her cat. When he returns the cat to her in the Kamo incident, she has already been sufficiently transformed by Genji's mentorship to grasp instantly the meaning of this "return gift." But as the child starts to grow within her, as she begins to regain her old self, Genji learns the truth about her adulterous conception, and she must face his anger. This alone might not have been enough to precipitate a crisis, but Genji commands the Third Princess to live a lie and deny her nature altogether. Although she may be more careless than Fujitsubo about keeping her illicit affair secret, she cannot, unlike Fujitsubo, live a lie.

   Kashiwagi, the Third Princess knows, is one who does not want to change her, who accepts and loves her to the point of risking his reputation and throwing his life away. She has no secrets to keep from Kashiwagi. Their last *waka* exchange testifies to their commitment to each other through the trials of life and beyond death. The Third Princess is further emboldened to assume Kashiwagi's persona in the form of *mono no ke* because she knows that Genji, her tormentor, has been defeated by Kashiwagi and is fearful of his presence. Through the theatrical performance of spirit possession, the Third Princess, empowered by the charisma of Kashiwagi, is parading before Genji's eyes the secret that plagues him. His angry knowledge of their affair provokes the confessional outburst. Her rebellious spirit, long held in check by Kashiwagi, is now released in the form of his spirit's raucous laughter.[46] If spirit possession subverts the Heian ideal of restraint in verbal and nonverbal discourse in order to challenge those in control, the raucous laughter expresses the ephemeral triumph of the oppressed. It takes a man like Kashiwagi to break through the limitations of male consciousness and reach an understanding of women's double consciousness. For a woman to ally herself with his spirit against the prototypically dominant male (Genji), Kashiwagi must, ironically, cease to be a man—literally, by dying; metaphorically, by appearing to Genji's hesitating mind as a somewhat suspect female spirit.

Finally, in a strictly psychological reading of spirit possession, the encoded speech can be interpreted in terms of the Third Princess' divided self. Left in her natural state of childhood innocence by Suzaku, she entered marriage unprepared for the role her husband expected her to play and resistant to all efforts to socialize her. The "accident" of her exposure to Kashiwagi made visible the self she sought to preserve. In this sense, the *mono no ke*'s words—"the lady you thought you had taken from me"—might refer to the Third Princess' untutored, untamed self. Appreciated and appropriated by Kashiwagi, threatened and reclaimed by Genji, this self is finally secured by Kashiwagi's act of spiritual intervention. United in the figure of *mono no ke,* the lovers—she with her reconstituted psyche and he in his limbo between life and death—speak as one, in opposition to Genji. If Genji fails to recognize the possibility of a new dynamic, it is perhaps because he can more easily deal with old fears (Rokujō) than confront new ones (Kashiwagi). Genji misinterprets the Third Princess' possession, but he is affected by it (as he was affected by the previous possessions without ever completely understanding them). Although he seems to be at the peak of flowering fame and fortune, he is in fact past his prime. His discovery of his principal wife's poorly kept lovers' secret causes him to change from a man of action to a man of reflection, "sicklied o'er with the pale cast of thought" (*Hamlet*, III.i.85). For the first time in the long narrative, Genji is absorbed in a sustained interior monologue, contemplating the ethics of his own behavior.

### The Nun as Mother

In the aftermath of her spirit possession and in the wake of Kashiwagi's death, the Third Princess must endure Genji's continued subtle stabbing at her conscience. Although she resumes intimate communications with her father and begins to recover from her trauma, Genji is still able to intercept her pleas to join Suzaku in his mountain retreat (see S:658; 4:336). She is not allowed to escape from Genji's constant censorious frown by moving into Suzaku's Sanjō mansion. Instead Genji remodels her quarters in the Rokujō-in so that they resemble a nunnery; the garden is landscaped into a moor. Even in these solemn surroundings she feels herself to be the prey of Genji's amorous glances and insinuations. Only now does she fully realize what motivated her crisis and its resolution: "He managed to make it clear to her that she found his attentions so distasteful that she had become a nun. She had hoped that she might now find peace. . . . She longed to withdraw to a retreat of her very own, but she was not one to say so." In her eyes, Genji seems burdened "with endless regrets" (S:671; 4:368).

To the Third Princess, Genji behaves as if he had forgiven her infidelity. Although he can now admit to himself that he "never found [the Third Princess] very interesting or exciting" (S:727; 4:517), he admires her religious devotions, noting the irony in her preceding him on the path to enlightenment. In what appears to be an unusually sensitive gesture intended to draw the Third Princess out of her pious melancholy and reserve, Genji plays for her on her instrument, the *kin* (4:370 and n. 4), and thus reminds her of the glorious concert rehearsal for her father's jubilee. He also contrives to let her overhear his eulogy on the late Kashiwagi (see S:672; 4:371).

Genji's behavior with others, however, demonstrates that he is unreconciled to his role as cuckold and still angry at his wife's physical and emotional withdrawal. Realizing the Third Princess' true motivation for taking the tonsure, he lectures Rokujō's daughter Akikonomu about the vice of an easy flight into religion. (This is in the autumn following the Third Princess' spirit possession.) Aggrieved by his principal wife's religious inaccessibility, Genji warns Akikonomu against taking religious vows prematurely. According to Seidensticker's rendering of that conversation, Genji attributes Akikonomu's desire for the tonsure to her deep concerns about her mother's wandering spirit, concerns raised by rumors that Genji has identified the Third Princess' *mono no ke* as "the vengeful spirit of the Rokujō lady" (S:675; 4:376: *Miyasudokoro*). Genji, however, emphatically denies that he ever told anyone of this identification; in other words, the Rokujō theory did not emanate from him. The childless Akikonomu's resurgent piety is more likely to stem from the public event of Murasaki's spirit possession than from the brief, private, unexpected eruption of the Third Princess' spirit. Moreover, the latter case necessitates discretion because of the appearance of *mono no ke* after the administration of religious vows. Since Akikonomu is unaware of the affair between Kashiwagi and the Third Princess, she cannot know that the Rokujō rumors, whether spread by Genji or not, in fact protect him from speculations that might expose him as a cuckold. It is natural for those ignorant of the affair between Kashiwagi and the Third Princess to infer that the notorious Rokujō had moved from Murasaki to haunt yet another of Genji's women, especially this high-ranking one, and it is equally natural to assume that Genji would not have wanted to contradict them.

It is not until after Genji's death that the Third Princess moves into Suzaku's Sanjō mansion (see S:736; 5:13–14). Yet the personal integrity achieved through the tonsure and spirit possession is threatened when her child grows up to question his origins. Thus, painfully for her, religious goals become incompatible with maternal responsibilities. Her tranquility is severely troubled by her son Kaoru's gnawing questions about his paternity and about the rumors concerning his mother's rather oddly timed tonsure immediately following his birth.[47] Like Genji's son Reizei, Kaoru is unable to learn the truth about his birth from his biological parents; he too must seek on his own to solve the mystery of his existence. But there is a subtle difference. While Reizei never suspected any secret surrounding his identity until he was confronted with irrefutable facts, Kaoru grew up sensing an element of uneasy reserve between his parents and in their attitude toward him. His mother, frozen in the mute state dictated by Genji's categorical imperative for secrecy about the adulterous affair, is incapable of revealing the truth (see S:737; 5:17). Ultimately she has not succeeded in preserving, much less in extending, the moment of rebellion represented by her affair and her spirit possession.

## The Ochiba Complex

For every forbidden affair in the *Genji* there is an even more serious transgression that cannot be narrated because it is taboo. Murasaki Shikibu directs us through her narrative technique to look behind the screen of the first affair in order to penetrate to the hidden secret of the second. This requires us to read one plot line in terms of another. The author's technique of substitute narratives is analogous to her substitute characters. The Genji–Yūgao affair is the substitute narrative for the Genji–Fujitsubo affair, just as Yūgao is a substitute figure for Fujitsubo. In the second generation of characters, the Kamo complex involving the Kashiwagi–Third Princess affair is screened by the Ochiba complex involving the Yūgiri–Ochiba affair. The two complexes of events are inextricably intertwined and both culminate in the mystery of spirit possession.

After his haunting death, Kashiwagi is eulogized most fervently by Yūgiri, his closest friend and rival. Beginning in "Kashiwagi" (S: "The Oak Tree") and culminating in "Yūgiri" (S: "Evening Mist"),

Yūgiri endeavors to fathom the secret Kashiwagi hinted at on his deathbed and to obey to the letter his friend's last will by taking care of his widow, Ochiba. Her mother, Ichijō no miyasudokoro, becomes afflicted with *mono no ke*. Ichijō seizes upon the spirit of Kashiwagi for reasons so obvious that they fail to provoke the beholders of the phenomenon into speculation about the nature of this new possession.

Beyond what is usual in a society apprehensive about marriages between princesses and commoners, Ochiba's mother is determined single-handedly to control her daughter's fate. She originally disapproved of the match between her beloved daughter and Kashiwagi, the rejected suitor of the Third Princess. As a status-conscious low-ranking consort *(kōi)* of the Suzaku Emperor, Ichijō objected to the marriage because it left her daughter close to the position of "one of the old women who are cast out on mountainsides to die" (S:611; 4:208). After the marriage, Ichijō vaguely suspects that Kashiwagi prefers some woman other than her daughter, and she knows that the dying Kashiwagi chooses to be with his mother rather than with her. After Kashiwagi's death, she muses sadly and somewhat self-righteously that her political instincts about this match between a princess and a commoner had been all too correct (see S:647, 652; 4:309, 319–321). Meanwhile Ochiba, suffering from a maternally induced inferiority complex (see S:691, 697, 701–702; 4:423, 436, 449–450), shuts herself in a closet in the mountain village of Ono.

Ichijō continues to exhibit a sensitivity to hierarchy and pedigree in her dealings with Yūgiri, who now shows an interest in his deceased rival's young widow. Expressing her lingering resentment at her daughter's disastrous match with Kashiwagi, Ichijō elicits Yūgiri's sympathy, but she has no desire to lose her beloved daughter to a second marriage. Why Ichijō gives Kashiwagi's flute to Yūgiri is unclear. Perhaps she wishes to discard this memento of an unwise marriage. Perhaps all she wants is to secure Yūgiri's sympathy. He, however, receives the flute as if Ichijō were handing him a phallic icon of matrimony (Plate 1.10). The symbolic importance of the flute is clear to Yūgiri, who knows that Kashiwagi wanted his descendants to inherit it (see S:663; 4:348).[48] Yūgiri, whose awareness of sacrilege is revealed in a dream of Kashiwagi, is an uneasy recipient of this instrument suggestive of sexual power and musical enchantment. The flute signifies for him what the cat signified for Kashiwagi. And just as Genji was unable to control the feline character of his principal wife, so his son now feels "wholly inadequate" (S:662; 4:345) to master the musical instrument. Yet he is more aware of his shortcomings than his father was.

Foreshadowing in semicomic shades the dark gloom generated by the deathbed promises and last wills of the Uji chapters, Yūgiri light-heartedly abuses Kashiwagi's legacy of the flute by playing it for his own wife, Kumoinokari. At the same time, he is accurate in his assessment of Kashiwagi's "strangely hollow" (S:663; 4:347) relationship with Ochiba. So long as Yūgiri shies from guessing the secret Kashiwagi hinted at on his deathbed—namely, that he cuckolded Yūgiri's father—Yūgiri cannot play the flute for the proper audience.

As a result of Ichijō's misdirected gift of the flute, Yūgiri has a nightmare in which an angry Kashiwagi claims the instrument for his descendants (see S:663; 4:348). The painter Tosa Mitsuyoshi (1539– 1613) succeeded in depicting both the elusive subject of the dream itself and Yūgiri's realistic pose of dozing off, having rested his head on a pillow with his court hat still on. In an almost precise reversal of these two actors' roles, the scene recalls Kashiwagi's dying and Yūgiri's presence at his deathbed. Thus the painter captured in microscopic detail what is invisible except in his artistic imagination and in the dreamer's dream. The late Kashiwagi appears to Yūgiri in an ethereal, almost transparent gossamer robe (Plate 2.10). Although dream apparitions are often mistaken for *mono no ke,* this one echoes Kashiwagi's death rather than the Third Princess' spirit possession. There is, after all, nothing in the *Genji* text to suggest that the dream has a functional similarity beyond a structural analogy to spirit possession. Moreover, the dream/spirit possession analogy is incomplete because the witness crucial to possessions is absent from dreams.

Contemplating Kashiwagi's restless spirit, as revealed in the dream, Yūgiri detects a strong physical resemblance between Kaoru and Kashiwagi. With all these clues in mind, he questions Genji about the mystery surrounding Kashiwagi's death and the legacy of the flute. It is fully apparent that Genji knows more than he wants to admit to the inquisitive Yūgiri, but he keeps the secret of Kaoru's birth, as he did the secret of Reizei's. Correctly interpreting Yūgiri's dream, Genji reclaims the flute in the name of Kashiwagi's descendants, which means that he cannot give it to Kaoru without revealing the truth about who fathered him.

Yūgiri's loss of control by Genji's appropriation of the flute is hardly what Ichijō intended. Sensing that she has been undermined and thwarted, she allows herself to fall into the clutches of a *mono no ke* (see S:676; 4:384). As her crisis intensifies, a learned priest *(risshi)* from Mount Hiei rushes to her side. Although the *mono no ke* is not formally exorcized, it can be identified by its peculiar features, such as the fragmented handwriting, "like the strange tracks of a bird" (S:687; 4:412), traceable to Kashiwagi. The priest advises Ichijō in one of her more lucid moments to guard her daughter against Yūgiri's advances and the humiliating prospect of becoming second to Yūgiri's principal wife, Kumoinokari. (That the priest speaks Ichijō's mind becomes evident when, just before falling into a lethal coma, Ichijō exhorts her widowed daughter not to remarry, for it would be especially disreputable for a princess to do so [see S:690; 4:421–423].) As for the spirit troubling Ichijō, the priest claims to be in control of it, hinting, in terms involuntarily echoing Kashiwagi's description of his distressed soul (see S:638; 4:285), that evil spirits (4:403: *akuryō*) are "lost souls, no more, doing penance for sins in other lives" (S:684; 4:403). The priestly advice is already too late. Ichijō's misappropriation of Kashiwagi's flute has inadvertently encouraged Yūgiri's courtship of Ochiba. By giving the flute to Yūgiri, Ichijō may have wanted to rid herself of the last trace of Kashiwagi rather than incite Yūgiri to take amorous steps toward her daughter. If so, she has miscalculated.

Ichijō is far from healed when she realizes this. Doubts about the progress of Yūgiri's advances disappear when a morning-after letter written by Yūgiri provides her with evidence of her daughter's seduction. The motif of the revealing love letter underscores the similarity of the affairs of Ochiba and her half-sister. The Third Princess failed to hide Kashiwagi's letter from Genji, and Ochiba fails to hide Yūgiri's from her mother. (Significantly, the preeminent secret of the first generation, represented by Genji and Fujitsubo, was kept so well so long because it involved a literally unspeakable taboo that could hardly be put into spoken or written words.) Another letter plays an equally fateful role. Ichijō's miscalculation in the matter of the flute is aggravated by a letter that encourages Yūgiri in his courtship. She seems to demand on behalf of her daughter that the affair of a single night become a great deal more (4:412; S:687):

> *ominaeshi   shioruru nobe no   izuko tote*
> *hito yo bakari no   yado o karikemu*

> You stay a single night. It means no more,
> This field of sadly fading maiden flowers?

This letter, written in a confused hand resembling Kashiwagi's (see S:687–688; 4:412–413), causes Kumoinokari's second outburst of jealousy.[49] (Her first tantrum was inspired by Yūgiri's new flute.) Kumoinokari makes a scene, snatching the incriminating letter away from her husband (see S:688; 4:413–414).[50] Ironically, the impulsive wife almost instantly forgets all about the letter, Ichijō dies of spirit possession, and Yūgiri abducts the orphaned Ochiba to the Ichijō mansion and makes her his wife.

If Ichijō's possessing spirit suggests Kashiwagi, because its handwriting so precisely matches his, then what oblique aggressive strategy is expressed here? The spirit does not emerge in the traditional way, through the mouth of the possessed woman or a medium, but expresses itself in writing. The form of the letter, with indecipherable handwriting, becomes the telltale sign of all the broken taboos and unguarded secrets haunting the second generation. But if the message is unreadable, who can be the spirit's target? The key to these questions lies in a pathologically close mother-daughter relationship. Ichijō's hold on her daughter was not seriously loosened by Ochiba's marriage to Kashiwagi, an indifferent son-in-law who can hardly be said to have taken daughter away from her. All that Ichijō had to worry about was her daughter's reputation as Kashiwagi's wife. So long as Ochiba was treated respectfully, Ichijō was able to overlook Kashiwagi's neglect. Of his affair with the Third Princess, she knew nothing. After his death, the mother-daughter bond tightened once again, only to be threatened when Yūgiri began to follow in his late friend's footsteps.

Yūgiri's pursuit of Ochiba confronts Ichijō with a dilemma. On the one hand, she realizes that her careless daughter has been seduced by Yūgiri and that he was encouraged in this by her own unfortunate gift of Kashiwagi's flute and by her own regrettable reproach ("You stay a single night"). On the other hand, she clings to the vain hope that she can still prevent the marriage to Yūgiri and keep her daughter for herself. The haunting presence of Kashiwagi's dead spirit reinforces her ambivalence: Kashiwagi wanted Yūgiri to protect Ochiba but not necessarily to marry her. Thus possessor and possessed share a single anxiety. In this sense, Ichijō can be said to enter into an alliance with Kashiwagi, the *mono no ke* representing the peculiar charisma of the second generation.

In the case of the Third Princess, Kashiwagi's living spirit empowered her to target Genji; in Ichijō's case, Kashiwagi's dead spirit empowers his mother-in-law to target Genji's son Yūgiri. Thus Kashi-wagi's spirit is employed to strike in both directions: by the Third Princess to target Genji, the male representative of the first genera-tion, and by Ichijō to target Yūgiri, of Kashiwagi's own generation. Neither Genji nor Yūgiri realizes fully that he is the target of female aggression, but they nonetheless suffer as a result of the spirit posses-sions that disturb their marital lives. The Third Princess dies a sym-bolic death when she makes her religious vows; Ichijō's possession is instantly followed by her actual death. By contrast, Ochiba does not become possessed but is extremely mortified by the sudden loss of her mother's protection.

The immediate effect of Ichijō's death on Yūgiri is Ochiba's with-drawal. If this is the result Ichijō subconsciously desired through spirit possession, it is temporary and therefore ultimately ineffective. This is no surprise, however, for the ultimate goal of the transformative power inherent in spirit possession and its crushing effect on the oppressor is seldom fully realized or permanently sustained but approximated to varying degrees. Mercifully for Ichijō, she does not live to experience the outcome of her trance. With her death, the mother-daughter bond is finally severed and Ochiba cannot protect herself from Yūgiri's advances. Koshōshō, Ochiba's *menotogo*, explains to Yūgiri exactly what has happened in terms suggesting a regular pat-tern. The *mono no ke* seized Ichijō whenever her daughter's honor was at stake or the mother-daughter bond was threatened. As a conse-quence of Ichijō's seizures, however, Ochiba became so unhappy that her mother would always recover in order to comfort her (see S:696–697; 4:436). It was only when Ochiba betrayed her mother's confi-dence by allowing Yūgiri to catch a glimpse of her that Ichijō's posses-sion strategy failed.[51]

Spirit possession involving second-generation characters comes to an end with the farcical version staged by Yūgiri's notoriously shrew-ish wife, Kumoinokari. Jealousy, or fear of status loss to a princess, seems to be the main factor in Kumoinokari's flagrantly self-assertive behavior. This demanding wife, otherwise known to scold her hus-band openly and eloquently, responds to stress with a peculiarly devi-ant form of emotional expression. She seizes the occasion of her child's sudden illness to diagnose the tantrum he has fallen into as spirit possession brought on by Yūgiri's neglect of his family.[52] Seeing the child as an extension of herself, the mother uses it as a medium for her own grievances. She complains to Yūgiri that his exuberant play-

ing of Kashiwagi's flute and his thoughtless opening of moongazing
shutters invited a case of evil spirits (see S:664; 4:349: *rei no mono no
ke no irikitaru*).

By labeling the child as the victim of Yūgiri's paternal neglect,
Kumoinokari assumes she can conceal her jealousy over her husband's
new amorous interest. Yūgiri pretends to be a good sport, admitting
his insensitivity in the matter, but he does so with a condescending
smile that causes further annoyance. Although he is impressed by
Kumoinokari's cunning in displacing marital conflict onto the child,
he cannot help hinting that he sees through her tactic. Neither
Kumoinokari nor Yūgiri realizes what the author chose to share only
with her readers: the child's clamoring for attention represents the
unspoken complaints of the legitimate owner of the flute, Kashiwagi's
heir Kaoru.

Kumoinokari's second outburst is triggered by Ichijō's letter to
Yūgiri. Kumoinokari seizes the letter that she assumes proves her husband's involvement with another woman, but she displays no interest
in the letter's authorship and content. She wisely waits for the outcome of Yūgiri's difficult courtship of Ochiba. It is only when he is
about to break through to the closeted princess that Kumoinokari
faces him as a self-declared "devil": "You have always known that I am
a devil" (S:705; 4:458: *oni*). It is important to note that she uses the
folkloristic term *"oni,"* suggesting sprightly goblins, rather than the
more awesome term *"mono no ke."* Yūgiri exasperates his outspoken
wife further by demanding to be scared by a more impressively frightful monster. This provokes her to reject him in disgust and wish him
dead. Despite the earnestness of her wish, its form and style render it
ridiculous: "I do not like the sight of you and I do not like the sound
of you. My only worry is that I may die first and leave you happily
behind" (S:705; 4:459). To the reader, this domestic scene appears as
a parody of spirit possession.

In character and temperament, Kumoinokari is totally unsuscepti-
ble to spirit possession. When forceful emotions such as hers are communicated without reservation, complexity, or subtlety, there is little
need for oblique aggression. She is unwilling and unable to repress
her anger for even a brief moment of deliberation. She is given neither
to brooding nor to melancholy. Yet the very characteristics that make
her a relatively healthy woman in twentieth-century eyes deprive her
of the most cherished qualities of Heian femininity. Why did the
author of the *Genji* deliberately construct Kumoinokari's image to

appear undignified and her actions violent? Throughout her narrative spanning three generations, Murasaki Shikibu gives a whole spectrum of women responding to the female condition in Heian society. Kumoinokari stands at the extreme end of this spectrum. More effectively than Higekuro's wife, she represents the possibility of open rebellion against Heian customs.

The seriousness of the conflict expressed by Kumoinokari's outbursts was understood by the *nō* playwright who cast her in the role of principal actor *(shite)* in *Darani Ochiba*. Janet Goff is puzzled by the discrepancy between the expectations raised by the title of the play and the startling revelation that the *shite* is Kumoinokari rather than Ochiba.[53] But there is a close thematic connection in that both of these women consciously or unconsciously undergo the trauma of betrayal by their spouses. The play becomes especially meaningful if seen as a dramatic supplement to the play *Ochiba*, which focuses narrowly on Ochiba's attachment to Yūgiri.[54] *Darani Ochiba* suggests that the ultimate victim of Kashiwagi's affair with the Third Princess was not Ochiba (for she was lovingly pursued by Yūgiri after Kashiwagi's death) but Kumoinokari, whom no suitor comforted because she belonged to Yūgiri. At the same time, the *nō* depicts Kumoinokari's capacity to identify with her rival Ochiba, who is apparently the *shite* of the second half of *Darani Ochiba*. After all, Ochiba too suffered from neglect, even though she remained unaware that the true cause was Kashiwagi's infatuation with the Third Princess. Thus *Darani Ochiba* modifies the unfavorable image of the aggressive Kumoinokari by assimilating it to the more conventionally sympathetic image of the passive Ochiba.

The affair at the mountain village of Ono, with its marginal characters and liminal setting, is pivotal in linking the capital world of Genji and the Uji wilderness.[55] What characterizes all the figures involved in the misty Ono episode involving Yūgiri, Ichijō, Ochiba, and Kumoinokari is their inability to fathom the mystery underlying their attractions and antagonisms. If Genji's affair with Fujitsubo provided the secret driving the first generation of characters, Kashiwagi's secret affair with the Third Princess determines the lives of the second generation. In the Uji chapters that follow Yūgiri's Ono affair, both secrets are powerfully combined and linked with the further secret affair of the Eighth Prince. The anguish that results sends the third generation of characters into a maze of existential wandering.

# Ukifune

THE UJI CHAPTERS, more forcefully than any others, reveal the darker aspect of the *Genji*—the aspect often overlooked in the dazzling procession of the Heian elite with their fabulous robes, seductive perfumes, poetry exchanges, and painting contests, their dances, glamorous excursions, pilgrimages, and festivals. This darker side can be detected even in Genji's world if one is willing to look beneath the shimmering surface. In the darkened world of Uji, the proportions of light and shadow are reversed. To leave the capital on horseback and cut through the mists and snowdrifts of a forbidding wilderness to Uji, a proverbially gloomy place,[1] requires a new kind of hero. His search for sexual adventure is also a quest for identity. His repeated journeys, made necessary by the mysterious heroine's various displacements, take on the aura of an existential quest that tests the psychic as well as the spatial boundaries of the Heian court. In the end, the profoundly disturbing wandering appears to subside in the mountain village of Ono at the foot of Mount Hiei, nearer the capital than Uji and therefore more familiar, though no less mystifying as a religious site.

Although the dramatic climax of Ukifune's story lies in her spirit possession, its mysteries cannot be understood unless one unearths the secret buried in the Uji chapters. This fatal secret is intricately linked to the earlier secrets that shrouded Genji's love of his stepmother Fujitsubo and Kashiwagi's affair with the Third Princess. While both of these earlier secrets involved Genji and affected him deeply, the third secret seems to have nothing to do with the eponymous hero and has, therefore, been subjected to less critical scrutiny.

188

## The Uji Secret

Haruo Shirane, who begins his chapter on Ukifune by listing three betrayals dominating the three parts of the *Genji,* discusses the first two betrayals in terms of the first two secrets and identifies the third betrayal as "Niou's liaison with Ukifune."[2] If, however, the world at Uji is governed by a secret on the order of the first two, following their pattern of taboo violation and illegitimate birth (Reizei and Kaoru), then Niou's clandestine liaison with Ukifune fits the pattern only in that it is a taboo violation. Another male figure, less obviously ominous than Niou, is responsible for another and more fateful secret: that of Ukifune's birth. The ramifications of this last secret include Ukifune's anguish, her attempted suicide, and—ultimately— her possession crisis. The figure behind this secret and Ukifune's plight is none other than her father, the Eighth Prince (Hachi no miya), Genji's younger half-brother, a man whom most critics have seen as a paragon (fig. 5 in App. B). Norma Field, attributing the Eighth Prince's political troubles and personal misfortunes to Genji's efforts to restore his own lost power, describes him as Genji's "innocuous victim."[3] Field is by no means extreme. Many critics have considered the Eighth Prince saintly by virtue of his religious aspirations.

But there is a dark side to Murasaki Shikibu's portrayal of this intriguing (in both senses) character. The Eighth Prince's secret and his darker side are initially screened from the reader's gaze by the author's narrative technique. At the beginning of the Uji chapters a whole new set of characters is introduced (fig. 5 in App. B). Genji has been dead for two decades and his younger half-brother, the Eighth Prince, "an old man" (S:775; 5:109) at the time, is deeply concerned about the fate of his two grown daughters, on whom he dotes. The Eighth Prince seems at first encounter an extreme version of his (and Genji's) older half-brother Suzaku, who, in order to take religious vows, reluctantly parted with his favorite third daughter as soon as she came of marriageable age. Although as eager as Suzaku to take the tonsure, the Eighth Prince has clung to his two daughters and postponed the ultimate religious step.

The Eighth Prince's excessive attachment is understandable, if not forgivable, in light of the traumatic loss of his beloved wife. Himself orphaned at an early age, the "womanish" (S:779; 5:116) Eighth Prince was married to the daughter of a former minister (fig. 6 in App. B), a woman who resembled Rokujō in her ambition to become empress. His love for her seems to have been intensified rather than threatened by their long period of childlessness. When their first daughter, Ōigimi, was born, the prince's joy had been immense, but it was shattered not long thereafter when his wife died after giving birth to their second daughter, Nakanokimi. The reader is led to believe that the Eighth Prince's response to his loss was to be "an uncommonly good father" (S:781; 5:121), too devoted to his daughters to leave this world behind but religiously determined to keep pure the memory of their mother. His adoration for his wife seems to echo his imperial father's love of Kiritsubo (Genji's mother but not the Eighth Prince's) and his prolonged mourning for her death. The bereaved emperor was able to replace the lost beloved with Fujitsubo, thus giving Genji a surrogate mother, but the Eighth Prince refused a similar consolation through the process of substitution.

This impression of a noble private life is sentimentalized by a pathetic public career. Political success seemed possible when the Eighth Prince became Kokiden's pawn in a scheme to replace Reizei as crown prince *(tōgū)*, but this scheme failed and the prince became dismally depressed. In short, a combination of personal and political misfortunes gradually drove the Eighth Prince toward asceticism. To describe his often puzzling behavior, Murasaki Shikibu coined the unusual term of lay ascetic or "'the saint who is still one of us'" (S:780; 5:120: *zoku hijiri to ka*), an "oxymoronic sobriquet" that seems specifically designed to fit the Eighth Prince's liminal position between the sacred and profane.[4] It suggests the possibility of a dark tension in the prince's psyche. The final inspiration to take the Buddhist path came to him through the Lotus Sutra's parable of the burning house.[5] When the Eighth Prince's last mansion in the capital burned to the ground, his mountain villa at Uji became his last resort, or, rather, his final retreat. The troubled prince's struggle to realize his religious aspirations further contributes to his positive reception among literary critics.

When Kaoru first overhears a conversation in the capital between his guardian Reizei and the Uji abbot *(azari)* about the prince's divided character, he is fascinated, for the Eighth Prince mirrors his own troubled self torn between secular security and religious enlightenment. As the secret of his own birth is revealed piecemeal to Kaoru, the narrative interest focuses on him rather than the Eighth Prince. When, long after the Eighth Prince's death, Kaoru confesses to Nakanokimi his religious need to idolize her deceased sister Ōigimi,

Nakanokimi responds to his declaration with what should be a truly startling revelation: her father had a third, unacknowledged, daughter. The Eighth Prince did, after all, betray the memory of his idolized wife. Moreover, the betrayal occurred with a blood relative of his *kita no kata,* one Chūjō no kimi (hereafter Chūjō), a high-ranking *nyōbō* in attendance to the Eighth Prince (fig. 6 in App. B). Acting upon his feelings of remorse and self-loathing, the Eighth Prince soon rejected Chūjō, his late wife's niece, and Ukifune, the daughter she bore him. Subsequently, the Eighth Prince made every effort to conceal the affair and its consequences. He "had to the end denied recognition" (S:945; 6:34). The revelation of the secret has no immediate effect on Kaoru because he is obsessed at that moment by his need to replace the lost Ōigimi. The important point is not that Kaoru is too distracted to appreciate the gravity of the revelation. It is rather that the Uji story unfolds almost as if it were a mystery tale; the reader wanders blindly through the maze, as lost as the heroes from the capital and the heroines in their hinterland.

## Kaoru's Quest

When the Uji chapters begin, Kaoru is living under the guardianship of Reizei because Genji's brilliant design has brought together, perhaps for mutual comfort, these two "sons" born of dark romantic secrets and troubled by the mystery of their identity. When Reizei is entrusted with the secret of his birth by a cleric, it comes as a complete surprise. His identity changes in an instant but for himself alone; he feels he must protect his parents' legacy by keeping their secret. Kaoru, on the other hand, grows up sensing an element of uneasy reserve in his mother's and his putative father's responses to him and to each other. For years, Kaoru has been sadly aware of his mother's insufficiency. He senses that he has been orphaned into a premature adulthood: "Sometimes he almost seemed more like a father than a son" (S:737; 5:17). He confesses to Bennokimi (fig. 7 in App. B), the woman who holds the key to his birth secret, that he grew up virtually without parents.

Kaoru teeters on the brink of guessing the truth about his mother and Kashiwagi. Her tonsure and Kashiwagi's premature death are linked through insinuating gossip. Kaoru shares Yūgiri's intuitive reluctance to imagine Genji as cuckold and Kashiwagi and the Third Princess as adulterers—a reluctance that prevents them both from drawing the obvious conclusion of a love triangle. Of the two, it is Kaoru who is naturally more deeply motivated to pursue the mystery, as it amounts to nothing less than a question about his true origins, his legitimacy within a hierarchical social structure determined more by birth than by merit.

The arduous quest for the secret of his birth shapes Kaoru's character. Driven to understand the Third Princess' maternal remoteness and Genji's paternal ambivalence, Kaoru finds himself powerfully drawn to the uncanny (defined as that which provokes intellectual hesitation because of an uncertainty about the boundaries between the real and the imaginary, the familiar and the unfamiliar). As a small child, Kaoru was uneasy in Genji's embrace. As he approaches manhood, he develops an inexplicable fear pointing to a castration complex.[6] As explained in my previous chapter, Genji had unlawfully taken possession of Kashiwagi's flute, an heirloom instrument with undeniable phallic overtones, after it had passed mistakenly—and ironically—to his son Yūgiri instead of its rightful heir Kaoru. Thus deceived and deprived of the sign of his male identity, Kaoru shows symptoms of sexual inhibition. At court, his quiet reserve contrasts with the conventional courtier's amorous ways. His avoidance of dalliances, let alone marriage, is attributed to his supposed religious bent. But the truth is rather that he becomes so obsessed with solving the riddle of his parents' unparental behavior toward him that he fails to engage in ordinary social commitments. Not until the Eighth Prince—who represents in one figure the return of the father as double (Genji and Kashiwagi)—enters the cast of characters does Kaoru find a first clue to the mystery of his identity. And it is not until he has undergone repeated exposure to the uncanny that he may, at long last, begin to free himself of his deep-rooted anxieties. (Kaoru's liberation from these anxieties must remain hypothetical because the inconclusive "end" of Murasaki Shikibu's narrative invites the reader merely to speculate beyond the boundary of the text.)

At age twenty, Kaoru sees a chance to fill the blank spot in his genealogy. He not only becomes the devoted disciple of the Eighth Prince, whom he believes to be his uncle; he soon idolizes him as a paternal figure.[7] Having fallen irrevocably under the spell of the Eighth Prince as a consequence of lingering unease about Genji as his putative biological father, Kaoru is attracted rather than disturbed by the Eighth Prince's pronounced sexual androgyny. Elsewhere I have analyzed in detail the Eighth Prince's homoerotic appeal for Kaoru.[8]

The impact of the prince's "womanish" traits on Kaoru is attributable not only to Kaoru's need for a father figure; it also points to his longing for a mother figure stronger than his biological mother, the incurably childish Third Princess.[9]

When Bennokimi finally initiates Kaoru into the secret of his birth, the manner in which she transmits the secret of Kaoru's existence is reminiscent of spirit possession. As Bennokimi solemnly evokes the untold past, her narration strikes Kaoru as "a story in a dream, like the unprompted recital of a medium in a trance" (S:789; 5:139: *ayashiku, yumegatari, kamunagi [miko] yō no mono no towazugatari*).[10] During his next meeting with Bennokimi, when she presents him with a uterine "pouch" (S:797; 5:154: *fukuro*) of love letters containing the secret of his birth, Kaoru senses an ominous mystery suggestive of *mono no ke* (see S:797; 5:155: *ayashiki koto*) lurking behind his informant's unspeakable tale *(towazugatari)*. As in spirit possession, a secret is divulged. Bennokimi's revelation of Kaoru's birth secret replays a scene from the past and evokes the psychodynamics of spirit possession. In the actual possession scene, the Third Princess spoke Kashiwagi's words through an unnamed medium and confessed their adulterous love to a bewildered Genji. In this symbolic reenactment, Bennokimi's evocation of a past *mono no ke* through narration *(mono-gatari)* is a re-presentation of the broken taboo in the form of the emblematic uterine pouch (Plate 2.11).

Although the revelation of Kaoru's birth secret leaves him no less troubled than he had been, he respects his mother's continued resistance to divulging the past; he does not reveal to her what he has learned. He is drawn to his mother by the desire to tell her that he now knows the secret of his true paternity; but he hesitates, apparently for fear of seeming to question the sincerity of her religious devotions.[11] His inability to communicate the knowledge of his birth secret repeats his parents' trait of concealment. Reizei, by contrast, could more easily accept his parents' secret, transmitted orally as an act of complete trust. Kaoru must continually confront the uncanny as that which "ought to have remained . . . secret and hidden but has come to light."[12]

At the time of Bennokimi's revelation, Kaoru had been visiting the Eighth Prince for nearly three years without paying so much as a courtier's conventional respects to the prince's daughters. The composition of Tosa Mitsuyoshi's painting reflects Kaoru's painfully divided hopes of following the religious example of his idolized

Eighth Prince and solving the mystery of his identity (Plate 2.11).
Ironically, Kaoru, just before he learns the secretive circumstances of
his birth and realizes that he cannot publicly fulfill his filial duties, is
asked by his chosen "father" to be a father figure to Ōigimi and
Nakanokimi. Not surprisingly, he is both intrigued by and apprehensive of the challenge to become a guardian for the two Uji sisters.

When the Eighth Prince dies, without having taken the tonsure,
Kaoru is deprived of the only "father" he has ever known. The birth
secret and its shameful implications of adultery and incest continue to
bother Kaoru to the point of wondering whether Ōigimi and
Nakanokimi have learned about his true identity from Bennokimi.
The possibility of the sisters' initiation into his birth secret motivates
Kaoru to continue acting as their guardian and thereby to exercise
control over them. At the same time that Kaoru feels compelled to
preserve the secret of his birth, he longs for someone to whom he can
safely communicate it. While Reizei could share his knowledge in solemn silence with Genji, Kaoru cannot do the same with his surviving
parent, the Third Princess. Thus Kaoru develops a strong desire,
shared with both Ōigimi and Nakanokimi, to communicate,[13] not so
much through the elegant but detached literary media of poems or
letters as through direct, unmediated dialogue. What distinguishes
Kaoru is not only this extreme desire for intimate conversations but
also his ability to articulate the need to communicate.

## Ōigimi's Choice

It is not only Kaoru who must struggle with the secret of his birth
and his true paternity. Despite her certainty about her parentage,
Ōigimi too is mystified by her father, the Eighth Prince. Although she
never learns about the secret that came to govern her father's life, she
is affected by it to such an extraordinary degree that others suspect
spirit possession. Ironically, it is the Eighth Prince who brings Kaoru
and Ōigimi together and keeps them apart.

### The Testament

Although the Eighth Prince's last will casts Kaoru in the role of
guardian if not husband, Ōigimi and Nakanokimi believe that their
father meant them to live out their lives at Uji and not succumb to
men's enticements. Their *nyōbō* were instructed not to let them make
unsuitable marriages. This contradictory testament, which replaces

through the terror of words the resentful spirits ruling Genji's world,[14] perfectly reflects the Eighth Prince's ambivalence about male-female relations. Ōigimi, who resembles her father more than Nakanokimi does, is loyal to his memory. Her eloquence and willingness to articulate her feelings enhance her attractiveness to Kaoru, but she is determined to remain true to what she believes to have been her father's will and, consequently, never to marry. When Niou, Genji's grandson, begins to court the Uji sisters with clear romantic intent, she sends polite replies expressing her reserve.

She feels a stronger affinity to Kaoru—her guardian and her father's religious disciple—and prefers chastely to communicate with him. But as the sisters tie ritual trefoil knots *(agemaki)* in preparation for the first anniversary of the Eighth Prince's death, Ōigimi realizes that Kaoru is neither a pious protector nor an ordinary suitor. Although he feels a great deal of affection for his ward, his obsessive need for parental love and recognition excludes the customary romantic dalliance leading to marriage and reproduction. In a state of confusion, Kaoru deviates from conventional courtship patterns and urges his friend Niou upon Ōigimi. She, citing her father's last will as legitimization for intending to remain alone, rejects the suggested match and points out to Kaoru that her closeness to *him* has had unfortunate consequences in that people expect the two of them to marry: "It was exactly because I did *not* want to make things difficult for you that I let you come so near—so near that people must think it very odd" (S:823; 5:216). In a state of considerable confusion, admitting candidly that he is "an odd person . . . not much interested in the sort of things that seem to interest everyone else," Kaoru tells Bennokimi that he will marry the resistant Ōigimi because her sophisticated conversation makes her a perfect match and because "the prince wished us to" (S:824; 5:217).

Kaoru's ambivalent behavior vis-à-vis Ōigimi is in stark contrast to the romantic passions of his actual, putative, and chosen father figures: Kashiwagi, Genji, and the Eighth Prince. Similarly, Ōigimi's reluctance to engage in a conventional love affair deviates from the pattern expected of highborn women. Her case, like those of the Third Princess and Ochiba, raises once again the dilemma of "fallen princesses": should they marry commoners or remain single? Between loss of status and loneliness, Ōigimi chooses the latter. Having been raised to symbolize her father's fulfillment of his love for his wife, she can remain unconditionally his favorite daughter only by not marrying.

Ōigimi's intimate ties with her father recall the Third Princess' longing for *her* father after her arranged marriage to Genji. A further touch
of morbidity is added in Ōigimi's case because her longing for the
Eighth Prince continues after his death and beyond the mourning
period. She is totally committed to memorializing her father and
keeping his will, which, in her understanding, dictates a solitary life. It
is precisely Ōigimi's morbidity that attracts Kaoru, for it is the counterpart of his own struggle to come to terms with himself. Their com-
patibility is established in the memorable chapel scene.

### The Chapel Scene

Although Ōigimi is Kaoru's preferred substitute for the Eighth
Prince, his spiritual attraction to her is complicated by conventional
courtship expectations produced by a cross-sexual substitution unprecedented in the *Genji*. Their first close encounter occurs when the two
of them spend the night together observing rituals in honor of her
father. Throughout the encounter, Kaoru tries to communicate his
chaste disposition without making Ōigimi feel sexually unattractive,
but formal compliance with the code of gallantry mars his sense of personal sincerity and integrity: "His own want of decision suddenly
revolted him" (S:827; 5:225). It is at this crucial moment that Ōigimi
demonstrates her understanding of the incongruity between appearance and reality. She articulates her complicity in allowing a situation
to develop that signals romance when neither of them is sexually
inclined: "I am at fault too. I am not up to what has to be done, and I
am sorry for us both" (S:827; 5:225).

Kaoru remains highly ambivalent about stepping into the role of
lover when both of them recognize that their love is quite the opposite of physical. Although he continues for a while to scold her for
wearing "robes of mourning" (S:827; 5:225), her attachment to the
memory of her father is what most attracts him. His own confessional
needs make him receptive to the symbolic presence of the Eighth
Prince in the memorial ritual of "anise" (S:828; 5:226: *shikimi*)
incense burning. The smell of incense creates an atmosphere of chas-
tity and shared spiritual intimacy, and it functions like an invisible
screen between them. Indeed, Ōigimi requests a literal screen, arguing
that, paradoxically, "a screen might bring us closer" (S:828; 5:228).
In the fragrant smoke symbolic of the Eighth Prince's wandering
spirit, appearances are at odds with reality.

At the end of their first sexually uneventful night together, Kaoru resigns himself to the fact that all the external signs of the romantic scene are delusory. Just as the outwardly romantic setting deceptively suggests the couple's conventional bliss, knowledge of the true state of affairs falsely insinuates frustration. In fact, Kaoru and Ōigimi are neither happy in the conventional way of the world nor frustrated by their asexual relationship. To ease Ōigimi's fears of aggressive masculinity, Kaoru formulates an unorthodox vision of their relationship (S:828; 5:227–228):

> Do you know what I would like? To be as we are now. To look out at the flowers and the moon, and be with you. To spend our days together, talking of things that do not matter.

Locked into the rhetoric of Heian courtship ritual, they have managed nonetheless to communicate their mutual sexual indifference.[15] In learning to accept Ōigimi's wishes—so similar to his own—Kaoru distances himself from the male imperative to initiate a physical relationship; but it is not until the two agree to be "curiosities" (S:828; 5:228) that Kaoru ceases to find excuses for not making the usual overtures. For her part, Ōigimi formulates the principle of spiritual union that eventually inspires her to anorexic starvation for the sake of mystic union with her father.

### To Wed or Not to Wed

When he finds himself despite all his precautions attracted to Ōigimi, Kaoru startles her by suggesting that she accept his friend Niou as her lover. Ōigimi now returns the "favor" and suggests that Kaoru marry Nakanokimi. When Kaoru realizes that Ōigimi wishes this, his astonishment reflects his failure to recognize his own behavior in hers: "What, he asked himself, could have turned a young girl so resolutely away from the world?" (S:833; 5:241). The unconventionality of his courtship is even more striking when Bennokimi leads him to the room where the sisters sleep together. Ōigimi, still awake, slips away like a cricket into a wall, and Kaoru spends an uneventful night with the startled Nakanokimi. Blaming herself for being unable to interfere on behalf of her utterly helpless sister, Ōigimi is "huddled in the cramped space between a screen and a shabby wall" (S:834; 5:242). She regresses to a state of childish dependence on her father: "Her sorrow and longing for her father were so intense that it was as if he were here beside her now" (S:834; 5:243).

In this scene of mistaken identities,[16] Ōigimi and Nakanokimi represent the split personality of the Eighth Prince.[17] Ōigimi remains as pure as her father had been when he venerated the memory of his beloved wife, while Nakanokimi represents him as he had been when he betrayed her through the affair with Ukifune's mother. The scene causes discord among the sisters who had previously been "two ladies with but a single heart" (S:837; 5:248). Kaoru seeks to restore harmony by encouraging Niou, who has never ceased to be enamoured of the sisters, to focus now upon Nakanokimi. At the very moment that Ōigimi requests of Kaoru that he "be to her sister as he had thought of being to herself" (S:839; 5:254), she is "duped" (S:840; 5:254) by Niou's physical consummation of his love for Nakanokimi, whom he is ready to marry.

The prospects are not encouraging. The Uji household has all but ceased to exist after the death of the Eighth Prince. Since Niou, an imperial prince, cannot maintain the customary duolocal marriage with a fallen princess as far away as Uji, he will have to neglect Nakanokimi or move her to the capital, where she will be separated from the older sister upon whom she has always relied. Disaster is not certain, however. Despite Nakanokimi's engagement to Niou and Ōigimi's unorthodox arrangement with Kaoru, relationships are still in a state of flux. The men's next visit to Uji is postponed until an autumn-foliage boat party on the Uji River, a celebration carefully planned by Kaoru to legitimize Niou's wedding. The Uji sisters observe the arriving courtiers splendidly decked out in gorgeous fall colors. While the men revel in fond remembrances of the Eighth Prince, the sisters suffer pangs of remorse at what they feel is their betrayal of their father's desire that they remain unattached.

The tantalizing display of male beauty provoking a female version of *kaimami* resembles the *kemari* episode—except that at Uji the men on the river must pretend not to see and the women on the far shore not to care. In a gender reversal, the charge of indecent exposure is no longer restricted to the woman (the Third Princess) but can now be directed at the wantonly reveling men. Gloomy depression falls over the women's hopes and the men's revelry when Niou is called back to the capital before a meeting can take place. The Akashi Empress disapproves of outings that might jeopardize her son's chances for the imperial succession.

Of the four, the person most deeply affected is Ōigimi. Whereas each of the other ill-starred lovers is aware of having disobeyed parental advice, Ōigimi emotionally participates in the consequences of the disobedience of all four. She considers herself responsible for her sister's behavior as well as her own. The realization that she has broken her father's last will fills her with such remorse that she becomes "physically ill" (S:854; 5:288). Brooding over her complicity, she conceives a death wish and begins to starve herself: "The prisoner of these anguished thoughts, she quite refused to eat" (S:855; 5:290).

### Female Asceticism

As the cultural historian Caroline Walker Bynum has remarked about the extreme fasting practices of religious women in medieval Europe, food in all its various aspects is indispensable to an understanding of female asceticism.[18] Bynum has shown that medieval women's refusal to eat can be seen as a version of anorexia nervosa, the eating disorder that has achieved such notoriety in recent years. What the medieval and the modern types of anorexia nervosa frequently share, despite the radically different cultural context, is young women's desire to deny their female sexuality and reproductivity by extreme fasting—which halts menstruation—and to reject marriage. By inedia medieval women sought utterly to eliminate ordinary physical functions and thereby to spiritualize the body. Reacting to a social environment hostile to women, they punished themselves. Their female eucharistic devotion—abstaining from ordinary foods and feeding instead on the sacramental wafer and wine—aimed at an *imitatio Christi.*

Ōigimi's refusal to eat combines elements of both medieval and modern motivations. To begin with, Ōigimi's rejection of marriage, much debated by the critics, has its roots in her father's last injunction, which corresponds to the signals of the overcontrolling parents of modern anorectics. After Nakanokimi's marriage to the unreliable Niou, however, Ōigimi's determination not to marry takes on the aura of religious atonement and mystic union with her idolized father, which corresponds to the eucharistic devotion of medieval European women.

Within Heian culture, the religious component of Ōigimi's asceticism was more familiar than the secular. Beginning in the Heian period, food abstention in its most extreme form was inspired by Kūkai (Kōbō Daishi, 774–835), the founder of Shingon Buddhism. At "death," Kūkai attained Buddhahood in this very body *(sokushin jōbutsu)* through a state of suspended animation *(nyūjō).* This state was achieved by the esoteric food practice of dessiccating the body

with a diet composed mainly of pine needles.[19] It was inconceivable
for women to aspire to such unpalatable asceticism because, according to Buddhist doctrine, they had to become men first to overcome
the Five Obstructions *(goshō)* that kept them from achieving full
enlightenment.

Murasaki Shikibu refers explicitly to these notions about different
gender-related capacities for spirituality and religiosity versus carnality
and corruptibility. When Kaoru first sounds out Bennokimi about the
Uji sisters' disposition toward sexuality and marriage, the experienced
family intimate expresses her dismay about the sisters' zealous asceticism. In her understanding of female religious propriety, Ōigimi and
Nakanokimi have lost all reasonable perspective and are engaged in
self-denial even more severe than that of the sometimes lax mountain
priests *(yamabushi)*: "Even the monks who wander around gnawing
pine needles—even they have their different ways of doing things,
without forgetting the Good Law. They cannot deny life itself, after
all" (S:825; 5:219). Ōigimi pays no heed to such counsel.

If Ōigimi had merely wanted to die, she could have ended her
misery more swiftly by means other than fasting. Why does she turn
against her body by abstaining from food? It cannot be said that food
has been especially thematized in earlier chapters of the *Genji*. The
aristocratic female protagonists are rarely shown in women's traditional role of preparing food, and the primeval act of breastfeeding
was commonly performed not by high-ranking mothers but by professional wet nurses.[20] At festivals, the characters enjoy a great deal of
merrymaking, including drinking, singing, dancing, music, and poetry
contests. The consumption of food appears less important than its
presentation, often in a ritual context, as is the case with the rice cakes
prepared to commemorate the third nuptial night *(mika no yo no
mochii)*. Eaten by the newly married couple, they "incorporated [the
bridegroom] into the household."[21] As the senior surviving member
of her family, Ōigimi awkwardly but dutifully accepts the unaccus-
tomed labor of preparing the rice cakes for her sister's third night with
Niou (see S:843; 5:264). Ironically, these rice cakes signify the opposite of their ordinarily joyful symbolic content. Ōigimi soon realizes
that she has prepared not a wedding banquet *(tokoroarawashi)* but a
last supper, foreshadowing betrayal by the men and the separation of
the sisters. Through the rice cakes, Ōigimi has begun metaphorically
to feed her own body to Nakanokimi.

Ōigimi becomes increasingly morbid. Realizing that she is growing older, she broods on the ephemerality of a woman's beauty. She anticipates her own decay, foreshadowed in the image of the grotesquely made-up older women around her: "Observing . . . how there was not one among them who could escape charges of decking herself out in grotesque brilliance, Ōigimi feared that she too was passing her prime. Each day she saw a more emaciated face in her mirror" (S:846; 5:270). In scrutinizing herself for symptoms of old age, she is overcome by melancholy sadness *(aware)* and begins to mourn her flesh. Although she continues to receive Kaoru for conversations and they spend another night, chastely, "as do the pheasants" (S:850; 5:279), Niou's neglect of her sister hardens Ōigimi's determination to remain unmarried. In a typical prefigurative symptom of anorexia nervosa, Ōigimi's perception of her own body becomes warped. Although she is as morbidly attractive as ever in the eyes of the devoted Kaoru, who repeats his proposal of ceremonial marriage, she has become obsessed with the belief that she is physically repulsive: "I am afraid that my mirror offers me 'an uglier visage' each morning. I would not, after all, like to see disgust written large on your own visage. And do you know, I cannot think why that should be" (S:850; 5:279). In fact, by Heian standards (eerily like those of the English Pre-Raphaelites), she becomes even more beautiful: "Her hair had long gone untended, and yet not a strand was in disarray as it flowed down over a white robe. The pallor from days of illness gave to her features a certain cast of depth and mystery. The eyes and forehead as she sat gazing out into the dusk—one would have longed to show them to the world of high taste, to connoisseurs of the beautiful" (S:859; 5:301). As Esperanza Ramirez-Christensen has pointed out, Ōigimi is "the embodiment of ascetic passion" through which "her corporeal frame literally dissolves into a pure, unearthly beauty."[22]

As she becomes fully resigned to the decay of the body, the emaciated Ōigimi begins to focus her thoughts on religious atonement. For the shocked Kaoru, she characterizes the breaking of the Eighth Prince's will as a fateful transgression. Convinced that her father's spirit is suffering in "hell" (S:859; 5:301) because of her disobedience, Ōigimi longs to be united with him through dreams, but this solace, which comforts Nakanokimi, is denied her.[23] Ōigimi interprets this failure as additional proof of her unworthiness. She attributes the Eighth Prince's restless "wandering in some limbo" (S:860; 5:302) to her obsessed attachment to him, which obstructs the prince's release from suffering.

Disillusionment with Niou's behavior deepens her despair. She expected Niou to bring Nakanokimi to the capital, just as Kaoru had offered—in vain—to move her to his Sanjō residence. But Niou, who is the third son of the Akashi Empress and the Kinjō Emperor, procrastinates because his prospects for imperial succession are still under consideration (see S:850; 5:280).[24] He is under pressure to make a match acceptable to his family before indulging himself with a fallen princess. In Ōigimi's eyes, her sister's marriage becomes a "cruel joke" (S:856; 5:291) when she hears rumors that Niou may wed Yūgiri's daughter Rokunokimi.

When Kaoru learns from Bennokimi that Ōigimi has starved herself almost to death, he summons priests to perform more elaborate rites, including an uninterrupted reading of the Lotus Sutra (hokkekyō), the only Buddhist scripture that does not categorically deny salvation to women.[25] But it is too late for Ōigimi to conceive of any way to be united with her father other than through death. Like a woman possessed, she wants to become other, and her chosen strategy of anorexia nervosa permits her to deny her womanhood. Her death as a woman opens her way to the male path of Buddhist enlightenment. Rejecting Kaoru's medicines, she has a last audience with the Uji abbot (the preceptor and intimate of the late prince), which intensifies her wish to sit on the same lotus with her father. Instead of comforting Ōigimi, the abbot adds to her distress by relating an unsettling dream about the prince's relapse into spiritual darkness. The abbot seems positively sadistic in his insinuation that Ōigimi is the cause of her father's straying from the path to enlightenment.

That the dream is the abbot's, and not Ōigimi's, is important. Since he acted as the Eighth Prince's confidant, he may well have been privy to the dark secret of Ukifune's existence. Even if the prince said nothing of his unrecognized daughter, the Uji abbot (azari) might have learned of Ukifune from his sister—Ukifune's nurse (see S:1016; 6:201) (fig. 7 in App. B).[26] Is the abbot's pessimistic dream an expression of his own frustrated efforts to reform the prince and an attempt to justify his failure as preceptor by indirectly reprimanding the prince's disobedient daughters? After all, the prince had died without allowing the eager abbot to "sever the last ties with this world" (S:808; 5:179). At that time, the abbot's adamant refusal to allow the Uji sisters a last glimpse of their father had seemed "somewhat distasteful" (S:808; 5:181) to them. If the abbot is not motivated by piety in telling his devastating dream to Ōigimi at her deathbed, might he also have contributed, consciously or not, to the misogynist force behind the prince's love-hate relationship with women?

This insoluble question aside, the message for Ōigimi is clear: "Oigimi wanted only to die, at the thought of the burden of sin she must bear for her father's troubles. She longed to be with him wherever he was, to join him before his soul had come to its final rest" (S:863; 5:311). Ignorant of their father's dark secret, which her sister discovers only after her death, she feels compelled to emulate what she believes to have been his pure religious aspirations. It seems cruelly ironic that Ōigimi should be so totally devoted to a man whose secret transgression and contradictory will blighted her life and the lives of both her sisters. She was certainly truer to him than he to his unfortunate daughters, but she is unaware of her delusion.

Impressed by the abbot's dream, Kaoru—like Ōigimi—imagines the Eighth Prince's restless spirit wandering the skies (see S:864; 5:312: *amakakerite*).[27] At this point, the attentive reader of the *Genji* expects another episode of spirit possession. But Kaoru, who has ordered both Buddhist and Shinto rites, observes that there were "no signs . . . that the sick lady was the victim of a possession" (S:864; 5:313).[28] Why then does Ōigimi not become possessed? Fujimoto Katsuyoshi considers hurt family pride, the denial of marriage, and the obstruction of her father's religious salvation as sufficient to motivate a death wish; *mono no ke* are superfluous.[29] But similarly severe stress led other women to seize the weapon of spirit possession. Why does Ōigimi not feel this need?

Ōigimi longs for mystic union with her father, whose spirit is presumably available to her as an ally in an act of oblique aggression against a third party, but there is no one, other than herself, against whom Ōigimi can direct her aggression. Like Kashiwagi, Ōigimi blames herself and articulates an ascetic strategy to overcome her sense of guilt. Neither Kashiwagi nor Ōigimi needs to resort to the phenomenon of spirit possession to express what words cannot or must not convey. It is true that both have reason to be resentful—Kashiwagi of Genji, and Ōigimi of Kaoru and Niou—but they feel their own guilt to be incomparably greater than their hurt. Ōigimi blames herself for her sister's disastrous unrecognized marriage more than she blames Niou. And she never confronts Kaoru with the aggression, no matter how well concealed, that is characteristic of spirit possession. Ōigimi and Kashiwagi share a desire to exonerate themselves from the disgrace they believe they have brought on those they love most. Unlike spirit possession, their strategy involves self-sacrifice rather than self-assertion.

In her last encounter with Kaoru, Ōigimi does not hide what remains of her physical self. On her deathbed, wrapped in "soft white robes," she has become ethereal and pure. She is likened to the dolls *(hina)* that are sometimes floated down a river *(katashiro, nademono)* in Shinto purification rites and sometimes elaborately dressed and put on display. The doll analogy suggests purification and sacrifice, for "her voluminous clothes hid the absence of a body" (S:865; 5:316). Ōigimi complies with the Heian ideal of an ethereal body as expressed in the emphasis on splendid robes and hair. But as Ōigimi pursues this ideal to excess, her body literally disappears into her robes.[30] On the liminal threshold, she is a living doll, dead while still alive.

Once again confronted with an instance of the uncanny, Kaoru remains profoundly uncertain whether or not the woman's aestheti-cized ascetic death "signifies the 'death of the other,' both totally appropriated by [his] fantasies and totally inaccessible."[31] Thus Ōigimi has succeeded in crafting an ambiguous existence in response to the complex social construct of Heian women's lives.[32] If women like Yūgao, Aoi, Murasaki, and the Third Princess demonstrate the "death" of their male-constructed selves by temporarily becoming other in spirit possession, Ōigimi, deprived (like Kaoru) by her omi-nously duplicitous father of a sexual identity, can realize her self only by literally dying, a permanent and irreversible act. To Kaoru she has become a beautiful feminine corpse, a transformation that, in Elisa-beth Bronfen's view, "functions like a screen memory and . . . simul-taneously represses and represents . . . the 'castrative threat of death.'"[33]

It is not too much to say that Ōigimi's death is an indirect result of her father's sins. Although she dies literally unaware of his adultery and the existence of her younger half-sister Ukifune, she suffers from the confused directives of her father's last will, a confusion that stems from his transgression and its consequence, the obstruction to his reli-gious fulfillment. She dies in the mistaken belief that her father's post-humous path to enlightenment is darkened solely because of her disobedience to his will.

After Ōigimi's death, the nature of the bond between her and Kaoru is clarified. He is so much Ōigimi's kindred spirit that he mourns her as she mourned her father. He tries to resist the Kinjō Emperor's marriage offer of the Second Princess (Onna ni no miya),

the only child by his consort Reikeiden (fig. 5 in App. B).[34] Like
Ōigimi, Kaoru also indulges in fantasies of bringing back the beloved
dead through the magic of incense (see S:890; 5:372). Above all,
Kaoru shares Ōigimi's anxiety about appeasing the dead. As he felt
before about the Eighth Prince's restless spirit, so he thinks now—in
the same ominous term *"amakakerite"* or "roaming the skies"—about
the deceased Ōigimi, who "would be looking down from the heavens
in anger" (S:892; 5:378; see also S:864; 5:312). In a mournful *waka*
that expresses his longing for Ōigimi, he alludes revealingly to the legend of the Boy of the Himalayas (Sessen Dōji; see 5:323, n. 18) who
sacrifices himself to obtain the second half of a stanza of which he had
learned only the first half (see S:869; 5:323). Eventually, Ōigimi's sacrificial death not only brings Kaoru closer to understanding the
Eighth Prince's character and his reasons for not taking the tonsure
before his death; it also makes way for the revelation of the Uji secret:
the existence of Ukifune.

## Nakanokimi's Influence

In the wake of Ōigimi's death, Kaoru hopes to comfort himself
with the friendship of Nakanokimi, now residing as Niou's favorite
wife at the Nijō-in. Although Nakanokimi is very much her mother's
child in physical appearance, Kaoru is driven by his longing for Ōigimi
and the Eighth Prince to reconstruct Nakanokimi's features. With the
passage of time, he imagines a resemblance in the sisters' voices where
none seemed to have existed before. Thus Kaoru's melancholic bond
with Ōigimi is retied with Nakanokimi, in less somber colors, as if to
create a brighter variation of the trefoil knots *(agemaki)* theme. If one
can speak of comic relief amid the gloom of the Uji chapters, it occurs
during Kaoru's pursuit of Nakanokimi.[35]

Kaoru's relationship with Nakanokimi is facilitated by her marriage to Niou. Because she is forbidden to him, Kaoru need not pretend to have sexual interests that he does not possess. Inextricably
bound to Heian courtship conventions and consistently ambivalent
about his sexual inhibitions, Kaoru nonetheless must make his passes.
It is possible, after all, to feel erotic attraction without seeking sexual
intercourse. This pattern confused Kaoru's relations with the eligible
Ōigimi, but it is entirely appropriate with Nakanokimi. Another feature of this pattern lics in Kaoru's bifurcated approach: each new
human focus of his interest is overshadowed by an older one—the

Eighth Prince by his biological father, Ōigimi by the Eighth Prince, and Nakanokimi by Ōigimi. What distinguishes Kaoru's chain of substitution from Genji's, however, is Kaoru's conviction of inevitable betrayal built into the process of substitution. His sexual inhibition derives from this consciousness. In the eyes of numerous scholars, Kaoru's indecisiveness is a deplorable degeneration from Genji's brilliant heroic stature, but this reading neither explains Kaoru's problems nor does justice to his struggle truly to understand women, a struggle unprecedented in this *monogatari*. The price Kaoru willingly pays for his astute perceptiveness of female consciousness is his masculinity.

When Kaoru turns his attention to Nakanokimi, he finds her in a conflicted state. Although she has been able to make the traumatic psychic transition from Ōigimi to Niou, symbolized by her move from Uji to the capital, she is now torn between mourning for her sister and savoring the joys of marriage. By the time that Nakanokimi realizes she is pregnant, Niou has agreed to an arranged marriage to Rokunokimi, threatening Nakanokimi's position as favorite wife. While Niou and Rokunokimi are preoccupied with their nuptial-night ceremonies, the memory of the ceremonial rice cakes that had planted the seed for Ōigimi's anorexia nervosa triggers Nakanokimi's refusal to eat. Nakanokimi's crisis, however, takes a milder form. Her depression is caused by her husband's legitimized disloyalty rather than, as was the case with Ōigimi, by the guilt occasioned by sororal betrayal and filial disobedience. Furthermore, since it was considered a grave sin to die in childbirth, Nakanokimi must live for the sake of the child within her.

To Kaoru, Nakanokimi's inaccessibility as a substitute becomes fully evident when he notes that she is pregnant with Niou's child. He abruptly consents to a perfunctory marriage to the Second Princess. In his disturbed mind he entertains the far-fetched hope that she might "just possibly resemble Oigimi" (S:904; 5:406), who is her first cousin once removed (fig. 5 in App. B). He postpones his wedding, however, until Nakanokimi has successfully given birth to a prince.

In the critical period before Kaoru's marriage and Nakanokimi's childbirth, the two lay plans to commemorate the Eighth Prince and Ōigimi at Uji. It is at the dramatic height of this transitional period that Kaoru reveals to Nakanokimi his desire to make sacred the prince's Uji villa by incorporating it into the abbot's mountain monastery and to enshrine Ōigimi's image in a new house at the Uji River. Kaoru's discussion with Nakanokimi concerning the "image" of

Ōigimi to be venerated in the rebuilt Uji villa introduces a mode of communication that differs fundamentally from what has gone before. Extraordinarily long and excruciatingly probing dialogues become the norm, replacing the elusive lyrical style that used language sparingly.

Nakanokimi is confused over the precise nature of Kaoru's plan to immortalize Ōigimi. Does he want to transform her into a religious idol or a secular art object? Kaoru explains that he has in mind a "statue" (S:915; 5:437: *hitogata*) or a "picture" (S:915; 5:437: *e*) to represent the dead Ōigimi, but he concedes that no sculptor and no painter could produce an adequate likeness.[36] In Kaoru's mind she has become, posthumously, an ideal that others can only aspire to but never reach. Kaoru's aestheticization of the beloved dead marks a categorical change in coping with loss. Unlike the Kiritsubo Emperor and Genji, who had sought human substitutes that closely resembled their lost loves, Kaoru aestheticizes the dead and attempts to turn them into art objects that may also serve as religious icons. At first Kaoru had followed the conventional path of substitution, replacing his biological and putative fathers (Kashiwagi and Genji) with a chosen father figure (the Eighth Prince). When the Eighth Prince died, Kaoru entered into an asexual relationship with Ōigimi, the daughter who most resembled the prince. Whereas in previous generations the technique of substitution laid persistent longing to rest, Kaoru was unable to find fulfillment in Ōigimi, partly because she, unlike the substitutes of previous generations, shared his interminable mourning—for the same person (the Eighth Prince).

Ōigimi had solved the amorous impasse with Kaoru by staging a female ascetic death in the hope of joining her father on the same lotus. The fearful intensity of her death wish and the beauty of her death leave Kaoru with an uncanny ambivalence that lends itself to articulation in religious art rather than life.[37] However, he desires the artistic double to represent the dead Ōigimi while at the same time reanimating her. Thus his provocation of the uncanny is similar to the kind of doubling that had occurred to Genji in the form of *mono no ke* possessing four of his women. Whereas in Genji's time, women had doubled their selves to confront the male with the uncanny, now it is Kaoru who is searching for ways to produce the uncanny by doubling Ōigimi. While their unstable, insecure hold on Genji motivated his women to become possessed by *mono no ke* in order to empower themselves, Kaoru feels compelled to duplicate the woman whose body eluded him.

Nakanokimi objects to this process—in particular, to the association of her sister with *hitogata,* the word Kaoru uses for "statue." Like the *hina* to whom Kaoru had likened the dying Ōigimi, *hitogata* are paper dolls used in Shinto ceremonies to wash away impurities, especially forbidden attachments, down a river of lustration generically known as Mitarashigawa (see S:916; 5:437). While Nakanokimi approves of religious services to pacify her sister's spirit, she feels uneasy about a ritual that turns Ōigimi into a paper-doll medium bearing away Kaoru's sin *(tsumi)* of attachment. It seems to Nakanokimi that this rite might diminish, even soil, her sister's memory.

Kaoru must agree that neither religion nor art offers a way to re-create Ōigimi's image. As a measure of his despair, he is hoping for a "miracle" (S:916; 5:437: *henge no hito*)—that is, an apparition, incarnation, or embodiment *(gonge).*[38] (The dark connotations of the term *"henge"* recall Yūgao's ambivalent longing for Tō no Chūjō and her perception of Genji as an "apparition" [S:65; 1:227].) Nakanokimi, realizing that Kaoru's devotion to her family amounts almost to idolatry, decides at this point to share her recent discovery of the Eighth Prince's dark secret. She reveals the existence of a *henge* that might satisfy Kaoru's secular and religious needs. This mysterious *henge,* a creature located in an uncertain twilight zone between dream and reality, is her half-sister Ukifune. Having been spared confrontation with *mono no ke* during Ōigimi's crisis, Kaoru is now presented with the embodiment of the uncanny in Ukifune.

Nakanokimi finds it difficult to acknowledge her half-sister. Rather than sympathizing with Ukifune's painful existential state, which is causally related to her own, Nakanokimi has continued the Eighth Prince's treatment of Ukifune as a shameful inferior. Significantly, Ukifune is introduced to Kaoru as a *hitogata,* a purification sacrifice, just as, in Genji's eyes, Yūgao became a sacrificial figure for Fujitsubo. By referring to her sister as a *hitogata,* Nakanokimi implies that, while the memory of Ōigimi is too precious for the Mitarashi River and too challenging for even the most talented artists, Ukifune may nonetheless serve Kaoru as a substitute. In other words, Kaoru can keep Ōigimi's memory pure and at the same time console himself with Ukifune—until it is time, metaphorically, to discard her down the river. Yet at the same time that Nakanokimi herself has initiated the ritual process of creating a new identity for her deceased sister, she is shocked by Kaoru's eager acceptance of Ukifune as the embodiment of Ōigimi.

## Ukifune's Way

Between the startling announcement of Ukifune's existence and her actual appearance at the end of "Yadorigi" (S: "The Ivy"), major events occur in the capital (Nakanokimi's birth of a son to Niou and Kaoru's marriage to the Second Princess) and in Uji (Kaoru's plans to remodel the Eighth Prince's mansion [*shinden*]). As Nakanokimi becomes established as Niou's first childbearing wife (see S:944; 6:33: *kita no kata*),[39] Kaoru's unhappy, forced marriage to the Second Princess makes him an ever more restless wanderer between the capital and the mountain village.

In seeking the abbot's approval for converting the Uji villa into a "memorial hall" (S:918; 5:443) for the monastery complex, Kaoru was rewarded with an "edifying tale" (S:919, n.). The abbot, who apparently considers the relocation of the villa from the river to the mountains as an aid for the Eighth Prince's spirit, tells a parable about a father's excessive attachment to his deceased children. This man was so devoted to them that he carried their bones around his neck until he received a sign (see S:919; 5:444: *hōben*) from the Buddha to throw these mementos away and be enlightened at last. Although the abbot seems to have intended this parable in support of Kaoru's plan to remodel the villa, the tale can be read as covert criticism of the Eighth Prince, whose excessive devotion to his older daughters is the major obstacle to his enlightenment.

In addition to the abbot's puzzling parable about a grief-stricken father's attachment, Kaoru learns from Bennokimi that his own biological father, Kashiwagi, longed for him: "He did so want to see the child" (S:919; 5:446). Kashiwagi's longing stands in sharp contrast to the Eighth Prince's willful denial of Ukifune. Whatever new information Kaoru may receive concerning moral behavior in father-child relationships he cannot but read against his own and Ukifune's background. At this point in the narrative, readers too are invited to join Kaoru in pondering the juxtaposed paternal treatment of children born from secret affairs.[40]

Not only paternal obligation but also filial respect comes under indirect scrutiny. When Bennokimi tells Kaoru of Ukifune's desire "to pay respects at her father's grave" (S:921; 5:449), Kaoru may well read this bit of harmless information as a rebuke. Because he has imposed upon himself severe constraints about sharing his birth secret (for the sake of his mother's reputation), he has been unable to fulfill his filial duties to his own father. It appears that, with the revelation of the Eighth Prince's secret, unambiguously informative words now assume mystifying double meanings.

Kaoru's visit to Uji ends with an image drawn from a poetry exchange between him and Bennokimi, his valuable informant both about his birth secret and about Ukifune's problematic father-daughter relationship. In a *waka*, Kaoru implicitly likens the Uji sisters and their suitors to aimlessly wandering ivy. In her reply *waka*, Bennokimi depicts the ivy as covering a rotting tree (see S:921; 5:450: *kuchiki*), which on one level simply repeats the harshness of her earlier self-characterizations (see S:797; 5:154). In the logic of poetic imagery, the tree has secret roots in progenitors pursued by inquisitive offspring in search of parental recognition and love. On a deeper level, however, the decayed tree may also evoke memories of the Eighth Prince and the inadequate support he provided for his daughters.

### Enter Ukifune

When Kaoru returns to Uji to inspect his architectural projects, he thinks first of visiting the "rotting, ivy-covered tree" (S:931; 5:474), but his visit is intercepted by Ukifune's procession across the Uji Bridge. The moment is of liminal significance, for it suspends Ukifune in an unforgettable religious tableau between two pilgrimage sites: Hatsuse (Hasedera), the Buddhist temple renowned for its efficacy in reuniting the bereaved with their lost loved ones, and Uji, the site of her father's grave.

On this pilgrimage, undertaken without her mother, Ukifune's religious tribute to her father is ironically jeopardized by someone whose quest for a father has paralleled her own. Their paths cross, and romantic love will deflect them both from their devotional purposes. As Ukifune emerges from her carriage to enter the unfinished *shinden*, her first words betray fears that strike her women as unfounded: "I have a feeling I am being watched" (S:932; 5:476). Although the customary barriers for *kaimami* are literally absent, they are metaphorically present in the form of the unfinished building. Thus Ukifune's intuition is correct. Her fears stem from *kaimami* as a peculiar form of Heian courtship defined by the social necessity of men's spying and women's concealment. While men pretended that women were unaware of their secretive activity, women knew that fences and walls, screens and curtains had eyes.

Although Kaoru is informed about the identity of the person he sees, he has only begun to fathom the significance she will have for him. The situation anticipates a fundamental principle of *nō* drama in which the priest *(waki)* first encounters a person *(shite)* whose true identity emerges only from an agonizing confrontation that reveals as much about the *waki* as about the *shite*. Ukifune has finally appeared on the Uji Bridge,[41] but in Kaoru's mind she assumes significance primarily as a reincarnation of Ōigimi and the Eighth Prince: "The girl before him, though unrecognized, was without doubt the Eighth Prince's own daughter. He wanted to go in immediately and say to her: 'So you were deceiving us. You are still alive' " (S:934; 5:481). Ukifune becomes for Kaoru the person she herself is looking for— namely, the Eighth Prince. She is the return of the dead. In terms of the uncanny, Ukifune is and is not Ukifune; she is Ukifune to the extent that she represents Ōigimi and the Eighth Prince. She is other.

### Three Traumatic Incidents

The chapter entitled "Azumaya" (S: "The Eastern Cottage") elaborates on Ukifune's existential dilemma from three different angles. The disadvantages of her provincial upbringing at the foot of Mount Tsukuba as the stepdaughter of the boorish Vice-Governor of Hitachi are evident in the failure of her mother's marriage arrangement with a lieutenant in the imperial guards (Sakon no shōshō). When the materialistic lieutenant discovers that Ukifune is not really the child of the Vice-Governor (hereafter: Hitachi), he transfers his suit to Hitachi's favorite daughter Himegimi (fig. 6 in App. B).[42] Since nuptial-night preparations for Ukifune were already under way when the lieutenant abruptly changed his mind, she is understandably mortified.

The essence of this traumatic experience, however, is not in the broken marriage arrangement per se but rather in Hitachi's indecent failure to back his stepdaughter—an act that repeats her biological father's refusal to recognize her as his daughter.[43] For Ukifune it is as if she had once again become an outcast. Although she is informed about the trauma caused by her birth, her response is diametrically opposite to that of her mother, who vividly recalls the Eighth Prince's cruelty to her upon the birth of their daughter. For Chūjō, the initial expulsion from the Eighth Prince's house was even less forgivable than Hitachi's subsequent selfishness. But for Ukifune, the villain—in a gender reversal of the traditional stepmother tale—is her stepfather. Furthermore, since Chūjō's direct criticisms of the Eighth Prince are not intended for Ukifune's delicate ears, her real father can assume an idealized ancestral aura. Indeed, her stepfather's callousness only intensifies Ukifune's longing for her true father.

The second traumatic incident in "Azumaya" involves Ukifune in a repetition of the failed engagement. Made homeless by that humiliating incident, Ukifune gratefully accepts shelter arranged by her mother and provided by her half-sister, but her presence in Nakanokimi's household creates yet another problem.[44] To promote Kaoru's project, which is now to use Ukifune as a *hitogata* for Ōigimi, Nakanokimi keeps from Niou her knowledge of Ukifune's identity. He stumbles upon the forbidden situation unwittingly. In a classic *kaimami* scene, he is aroused by a glimpse of the unknown woman's beauty. Although circumstances prevent him from acting immediately, his interest in Ukifune forces a wedge between the half-sisters. Nakanokimi's attendant Ukon conveys the horror appropriate to incest when she informs her mistress Nakanokimi of Niou's desire to begin an affair with her half-sister.

Given time for reflection, Nakanokimi realizes that Ukifune is innocent of any desire to entice Niou. Nakanokimi grows even closer to Ukifune, for whom she has shown compassion despite considerable apprehension about her sororal loyalties. The emotional state of the half-sisters is poignantly suggested in the "Azumaya I" scene of the *Genji monogatari emaki* (Tokugawa Reimeikai Foundation).[45] Their collaborative participation in *monogatari* reading is an emblem of their tense sisterhood (Plate 2.1).

Thus Ukifune's second problem with a suitor, like the first, recedes into the background in the face of a more profound problem. In this second traumatic incident, Ukifune's pain is transposed from Niou to Nakanokimi, just as in the first incident it was transposed from the guards lieutenant to her stepfather Hitachi. Yet in both incidents Ukifune's precarious position can be traced back to the Eighth Prince's secret and its disastrous impact upon her life. Although Ukifune is able to penetrate the surface layer of these traumatic experiences with her suitors, so much pain is generated in the process that she is unable to discover the ultimate cause of her existential wandering *(sasurai)*.

When Chūjō hears of Ukifune's newest trouble, she rushes to remove her offensive daughter from Nakanokimi's sight. Sequestered in a rustic, eastern-style cottage *(azumaya)* in the vicinity of Sanjō, Ukifune becomes prey to yet another suitor, who precipitates a third traumatic experience. Although things are rapidly going from bad to worse, Ukifune finds temporary comfort in poetry exchanges *(zōtōka)* with her distressed mother, who is grievously impotent concerning her fate. This crisis marks the beginning of the vital role of poetry in Ukifune's increasingly troubled life.

After Sakon no shōshō and Niou, the third man attempting to enter Ukifune's life is Kaoru. While on an inspection visit to the new Uji hall (S:963; 6:77: *Uji no midō*), he is sunk deep in melancholy thoughts of the Uji dead and hoping vainly to see their reflection in the Uji waters. Consumed by this longing, he is inspired to ask Bennokimi about Ukifune's whereabouts. The fact that Ukifune is now sequestered near his own and his mother's Sanjō residence should ordinarily have been an advantage. In this case, however, Ukifune's proximity makes Kaoru uneasy. It might cause further discord with the Kinjō Emperor whose daughter, the Second Princess, Kaoru established at his mother's Sanjō residence, a marital arrangement that already horrified her father because it undermines the custom of matrilocality.[46] Hoping to keep his wife in the dark about his new interest and susceptible to the romantic appeal of Uji as a memorial site, Kaoru decides to abduct Ukifune to his new Uji villa (as Genji had taken Yūgao by force to a deserted villa of frightful historic associations).

Kaoru's accomplice for arranging the abduction is Bennokimi. She easily gains access into Ukifune's circle because she is no stranger, having provided a resting place at Uji during Ukifune's Hatsuse pilgrimages. Ukifune trusts the nun precisely because she "had served her father" (S:965; 6:82). It appears that Ukifune's existential state as an outcast—in her own imagery, a boat upon the waters *(ukifune)*— predisposes her once again to be subliminally guided by her father's shadow and to rest her hopes for anchorage in him.

Backed by his accomplice Bennokimi, Kaoru plays upon his Uji ties in order to connive his way into Ukifune's cottage. It has frequently been noted that the consummation of Kaoru's love amidst the noisy bustle of plebeian life and the subsequent abduction to remote Uji resemble Genji's treatment of Yūgao. It has not been observed that the overt theme of male rivalry (Kaoru is to Niou as Genji was to Tō no Chūjō) runs parallel to the covert theme of the protagonists' longing for a lost parent and their search for a substitute. Genji had courted Yūgao at the time when he yearned for Fujitsubo as a forbidden substitute for his mother. Similarly, Kaoru abducts Ukifune because she promises to serve as a *hitogata* not only for Ōigimi but also for the Eighth Prince (who is himself a substitute for Kaoru's real father). While Ukifune may fail in Kaoru's mind to be Ōigimi's equal, she is unquestionably the Eighth Prince's daughter, whether her father recognized her or not.

The Uji sequence is complicated by the fact that the female protagonist is pursuing her own dream of parent-child reunion, a dream that coincides in its objective (the Eighth Prince) with that of her lover (Kaoru). Although Kaoru initially compares Ukifune to his lost Ōigimi, the image of the Eighth Prince resurfaces from the depths of his memory. Upon his arrival in Uji, Kaoru's superimposed memories of Ōigimi and the Eighth Prince threaten to overwhelm him.

When Kaoru, in Ukifune's presence, plays the prince's koto, the experience is almost too much for him: "Sadness for the past flooded over him as he began to play. He had not touched a koto in the Uji house since the prince's death, he did not himself know why" (S:970; 6:92). When he concludes his playing, Kaoru asks Ukifune about *her* musical skills and, by clever double entendre, hints at his interest in her as a substitute for her sister and her father. (The *azuma koto* to which Kaoru refers can mean both "east country" and "wife's koto.") Ukifune matches Kaoru's pun with one of her own. Adding the syllable *ba* to *yamato koto*, she asks him how he can expect her to play a capital koto (*yamato koto*) when she cannot even speak the language of the capital (*yamato kotoba*). Her witty reply indicates an acute awareness of the insufficiency that is attributable to the social gap—created by the Eighth Prince—between her ascribed and her true identity. In this brief conversation about the koto she has translated Kaoru's double entendre on sexual experience and musical ability into a question of linguistic ability and social acceptability. Her rejoinder leaves him pondering some questions: Can she learn to play the koto and be both her father's daughter and his wife? What happens when Ukifune tautologically becomes the Eighth Prince's daughter?

### The Eighth Prince Revisited

In sharp contrast to the critical portrayal of the Eighth Prince by her mother, her half-sister, and her lady-in-waiting, Ukifune clings to an idealized portrayal of her father. Scholars have usually dismissed criticism of the prince as petty if not preposterous. They have been content not only to explain but also to justify the prince's refusal to acknowledge Ukifune as his daughter. After all, her mother's position in his household was that of a *meshūdo*, a woman whose attendance on her master frequently included sexual service.

The scholarly dismissal of criticism of the prince has been too hasty. Immediately after Ukifune's failed engagement to the guards lieutenant, her mother complains to Ukifune's nurse about her own treatment by the Eighth Prince: "The only man you can trust is the man who is willing to make do with one wife. I know that well enough from my own experience. The prince at Uji was a fine, sensitive gentleman, but he treated me as if I were less than human" (S:943; 6:30). For Chūjō, this treatment remains her "old sorrow" (S:949; 6:43). Her complaints are petty only if seen from the polygynous viewpoint of the dominant male aristocracy. Other women are sympathetic. When Chūjō requests that Nakanokimi provide shelter for Ukifune, she forces her to reflect upon her father's behavior. Are Nakanokimi's loyalties exclusively to his memory, or should she show compassion for Chūjō and for Ukifune? Nakanokimi is assisted in coming to grips with her moral dilemma by Tayū, a woman in her service, who endorses Chūjō's point by emphasizing the Eighth Prince's emotional rigidity: "Your good father was altogether too inflexible" (S:945; 6:34).[47]

Chūjō has difficulty articulating her most forceful argument against the Eighth Prince's treatment of her because of her shame. She was not a mere *meshūdo* but also a niece of the prince's *kita no kata*. If she had been treated according to her kinship rather than her occupational status, she would now be in the relatively powerful position of stepmother to Nakanokimi. Instead she is forced to beg Nakanokimi's favor on behalf of the homeless Ukifune: "Was she herself so utterly inferior to the wife of the Eighth Prince? No, he had refused to accept her only because she had been in domestic service. There could be no other reason for such scorn. Forcing her daughter upon the princess had not been easy for her" (S:946; 6:36). Chūjō's position is humiliating. Small wonder that, in a discussion with Nakanokimi about women's vulnerability and Ukifune's uncertain future, Chūjō can no longer restrain herself from direct accusation: "'Your esteemed father was not kind to her, I have always thought, and that is why the world has chosen to treat her as if she were less than human'" (S:949; 6:43).

Of the Uji sisters, only Nakanokimi is directly exposed to such sharp criticism of the Eighth Prince. The lesson she learns from realizing the bitter truth about her father is that she must not idealize men. She resolves to indulge them in their foibles yet keep her emotional distance from them. Thus Nakanokimi is fully prepared to deal with

Niou's pursuit of Ukifune in a diplomatic way. While keeping Niou at arm's length during the triangular crisis, she actively promotes Kaoru's cause by removing Ukifune from Niou's reach.

### Incestuous Tangles

Nakanokimi, having been forced to face the truth about her father, learns to guard herself against men's mistreatment of her. Ukifune, however, represses the truth about the Eighth Prince's character. It cannot have escaped her altogether, but she cherishes her imaginary construct of a benevolent father, an illusion that dooms her to further victimization by other men. In either case, the impact of the Eighth Prince's failed succession struggle and the conflict between his amorous and religious life can be felt in the confused lives of the Uji characters.

The chapter "Ukifune" (S: "A Boat Upon the Waters") bears the name by which the last female protagonist of the Uji chapters is traditionally known, appropriately so because it is the focal point of her existential crisis. One strand of the chapter follows Niou in his amorous pursuit of Ukifune. Since Kaoru is one step ahead of Niou, Kaoru's efforts to consolidate or domesticate his affair with Ukifune form the subplot to Niou's romantic adventure. The men's erotic rivalry over Ukifune gradually turns into a political competition between themselves: which of them will bear her away to the capital? Another strand of this closely woven chapter dramatizes Ukifune's dilemma between Niou, for whom she feels dark romantic love, and Kaoru, who offers her a safe haven. When her women begin to debate these affairs in front of her, she realizes that neither suitor will do. Ukon, her *meno-togo*,[48] will be loyal to her even if she takes the forbidden path with Niou while the frivolous Jijū makes a shrill pitch for Niou's romantic appeal as a lover. Both women argue self-interestedly, hoping to return to the capital; they warn Ukifune that indecision is the worst choice of all. To illustrate the point, Ukon tells her sister's tragic story of a love triangle that mirrors Ukifune's own tale of hopeless love. The chapter ends with Ukifune's resolve to sacrifice her own life in order to prevent "rough business" (S:1005; 6:173) between the men.

Despite the intensity of Ukifune's volatile affairs, she has not forgotten her filial obligations to her mother, nor has she shed her guilt toward Nakanokimi about her unintended exposure to Niou's eyes. If the blows to her self-esteem that Ukifune received in "Azumaya" came primarily from men, beginning with her stepfather, in "Ukifune" they come from women—foremost among them her own mother, who is never there when most needed and who turns against the daughter she has long ceased to understand. Isolated and with no one to confide in, Ukifune is, like Ōigimi before her, drawn to the call of the monastery bell that had summoned her father's spirit. Like Ōigimi, too, Ukifune becomes suicidal, attracted to the river whose waters are associated with her father. The chapter ends with her disappearance and apparent suicide in the river. Ukifune remains absent throughout "Kagerō" (S: "The Drake Fly"), a chapter aptly entitled after an ephemeral insect that epitomizes the fragility of human attachment as much as its tenacity. She does not reappear until "Tenarai" (S: "At Writing Practice"), the chapter that centers on her spirit possession.

When Niou first journeys to Uji in search of Ukifune, whom he had encountered at his own Nijō residence, he is still unaware of her blood relationship to his wife Nakanokimi. Arriving at Uji he comes upon Ukifune and her women. Niou's *kaimami*, which is visually immortalized in the thirteenth-century *Genji* ink-line illustrations (*Hakubyō e-iri Genji monogatari*), second "Ukifune" scene, Tokugawa Reimeikai Foundation,[49] as well as many other art works, presents him with a powerful image of an archetypal female activity. Ukifune's women are engrossed in sewing, as Amaterasu's maidens were engaged in weaving when Susanoo frightened the heavenly weaving maiden to death with a piebald colt (see *Kojiki;* 712).[50] Yet the "Ukifune" sewing scene, like its predecessor in "Sawarabi" (S: "Early Ferns"), is not the picture-book image of female patience and industry it seems to be. Unknown to Ukifune, her women are attempting to shape their own destiny by plotting their mistress' future. While the *nyōbō* are absorbed in self-confidently planning the future, they have taken no precautions against men's *kaimami*. Ukifune's experiences, however, caution her to be more wary.

Ukifune does not join the women's excited discussion of her mother's plan to visit the Buddhist temple of Ishiyama (Ishiyamadera) with her. Her mind is occupied with thoughts of Kaoru's impending visit. That she is not totally lost in revery becomes obvious when her *nyōbō* envision their lady in as grand a position as Nakanokimi. Her sudden protest at that comparison reveals her revulsion at having come perilously close to an incestuous affair with Niou. As her nurse remarked at the time of that incident, "'Your own brother-in-law—why the shame of it had me glowering at him like a proper devil'" (S:956; 6:60).[51] After her humiliating removal from the Nijō-in, Ukifune had refused to visit Nakanokimi on account of "that awful thing" (S:974; 6:103: *tsutsumashiku osoroshiki mono*). In other words, Ukifune has been sufferering greatly from the knowledge of Niou's identity from the moment of their very first encounter. His situation, by contrast, resembles Genji's with Yūgao in that Niou shields himself from full realization of Ukifune's identity even as he engages in an act of *kaimami* at Uji that should have eliminated all doubts of who she is. But this is not an ordinary situation: it is one involving a forbidden relationship. Niou, like Genji in the Yūgao affair, blinds himself until he can no longer afford to ignore the facts.

What hidden political agenda determines Niou's "agony of impatience" (S:979; 6:114) to make Ukifune his? Under Heian rules, his undefined position as an imperial prince third in line of succession throws his identity in limbo, making his actions and affairs as a potential crown prince impossible to judge with certainty. It is for this reason that his encounter with Ukifune cannot be easily assessed. After all, the nature of the transgression with his wife's half-sister depends on his status. Niou lives in a political subjunctive and is driven to the edge in his amorous liaison with Ukifune. Whereas Genji recognized his demotion and violated the rules in order to regain his position, Niou, who never experienced demotion, is encouraged by his mother, the Akashi Empress, to play by the rules in order to gain imperial heights. Fettered by his high rank, Niou seems reluctant to respond to the call of emperorhood, the ultimate constraint. Instead, he seeks out the darkest of romantic love with Ukifune.

In the Uji chapters, uncertainty is the rule. While Niou suffers from uncertain rank, Kaoru suffers from uncertain paternity, and Ukifune suffers from both. Kaoru's self-deception complements that of Ukifune, who represses any inkling of Kaoru's former bond with her half-sister Ōigimi. This repression on her part plays into Niou's hands when he seeks to gain access to her by impersonating Kaoru. His ruse succeeds, and Ukifune's first response is to relish at last the bittersweet joys of romantic love. Although she is troubled by a sense of guilt for betraying Nakanokimi, she nonetheless feels herself privileged by a man for the first time (see S:982; 6:121). Niou erases the pain of humiliation Ukifune has had to endure with other men. Like Genji with Fujitsubo and Kashiwagi with the Third Princess, Niou risks his reputation, perhaps emperorhood, for his love of Ukifune, whose sense of self is accordingly elevated. Ironically, her *nyōbō* now invent a monthly defilement and even hint at "some evil spirit" (S:982; 6:123:

*mono*) to prevent the planned Ishiyama-dera pilgrimage with Ukifune's mother. Thus Ukifune's moment of happiness is overshadowed
by her women's lies and her own helplessness.

Niou cannot tarry in Uji. But before returning to the capital, he
leaves Ukifune a drawing as a pleasant memento. The sketch of two
lovers lying charmingly together brings about a turning point in their
relationship because Niou coaxes Ukifune into revealing her identity
in return for this extraordinary *hitogata*-style present. The twofold
impact of this new knowledge begins to show almost immediately.
Although Niou's awareness of his complicity in a forbidden liaison
with his sister-in-law is of prime importance, he is concerned at first
about his more conventional male rivalry with Kaoru who, Niou now
realizes, has a prior claim on Ukifune. In the immediacy of this rivalry,
Niou's consciousness of the more serious violation against Nakanokimi and against his mother's imperial ambitions for him is veiled by
the poetic imagery of his parting poem to Ukifune, in which Niou
sees his path back to the Nijō-in as "a road [of] utter darkness"
(S:985; 6:127). It appears that the Uji geography plays a significant
role in Ukifune's and Niou's emotional distancing from the moot area
of "affinal" or "secondary" incest and their increased anxieties over
the more conventional betrayal of Kaoru.[52]

Upon his return to the capital, Niou attempts to shift the blame
for his new entanglement onto his wife by accusing her of having kept
"secrets" (S:986; 6:130) from him—namely, the secret of Ukifune's
existence. With Nakanokimi as with Ukifune, he seeks to repress his
guilty sense of forbidden love by using Kaoru as a scapegoat. Niou
insinuates that his wife prefers Kaoru to him, an obvious effort to
deflect her attention, and his own, from the graver offense (affinal
incest) to the milder one (male rivalry for a woman).

Niou's visit to Uji is followed by Kaoru's. Predictably, Ukifune in
Uji is tormented to an even greater degree than Niou at the Nijō-in.
She understands that the double standard of her culture requires her,
as a woman, to have known not only how to protect herself against
her brother-in-law but also how to have refused any man other than
the one who had already made her his, namely Kaoru. Like Niou, she
too attempts to repress thoughts of incest by concentrating her attention on the more immediate love triangle. In a poignant poetry
exchange, Kaoru uses the Uji Bridge as a symbol of his firm commitment while Ukifune warns of its gaps and imminent decay (see S:989–
990; 6:137). Kaoru is too self-absorbed to interpret Ukifune's bleak

words as a sign of distrust in him, and he is unaware that Niou too has plans to move Ukifune to the capital. He fails to attribute her despair to anything more serious than the Uji air.

In the midst of all these manifold cross-purposes, the weather too plays a role. The earlier Uji mists have condensed into snow and now threaten the protagonists not with impaired vision but with total blindness. At a poetry contest in the capital, Niou's jealousy of Kaoru and his sense of urgency in their male competition for Ukifune mount with the falling snow. He sets out for Uji, where the snowdrifts are nearly insurmountable, and abducts Ukifune to the other shore of the Uji River.

Ukifune's dilemma has been attributed to her inability to choose between two men. The men's inability to make decisive moves to claim her has been attributed to their ineffective characters. These attributions make sense, but the effort to understand motivation should go beyond the identification of a conventional love triangle and a pair of weakened male psyches. Poetry exchanges characterize Ukifune as a "boat upon the waters" (S:991; 6:142) and as a woman "caught, dissolv[ing] in midair" (S:993; 6:146). Both images signal her social marginality and existential liminality. The events adumbrated in the text's increasingly dark poetic imagery have taken Ukifune to the point where she is gradually but inevitably developing a death wish. In this way, she is unconsciously reacting to the pressures of repeatedly representing the uncanny for others. No sooner has she begun to realize that she is a forbidden woman to her brother-in-law Niou than she senses that she serves Kaoru as a *hitogata* for her other half-sister, once Kaoru's intended, the late Ōigimi.[53]

Like Ukifune, the male rivals hover in an indeterminate state of knowledge and represssion. Throughout "Ukifune," they act as though in competition with each other for bringing Ukifune to the capital. It is as if at Uji—the misty territory beyond the scope of the law of the capital—Ukifune might belong to either. But each man in his own way procrastinates. Neither can admit, even to himself, why he has not reclaimed Ukifune from the other. The true reason is that she is a forbidden woman. Because the taboo is much less clearly definable than in the cases of Genji (incest with his stepmother) or Kashiwagi (adultery with Genji's principal wife), it is also more easily repressed and couched in the conventional terms of male rivalry for a particularly inaccessible woman.

But their rivalry is less conventional and more complex than it appears to be. Their interest in Ukifune is not entirely for her own sake. Niou is interested in her because Kaoru is—just as Kaoru is interested in the First Princess (Onna ichi no miya) precisely because she is Niou's sister.[54] Like the heroines scrutinized in Eve Kosofsky Sedgwick's *Between Men,* Ukifune is less a bone of contention than a bond that unites Niou and Kaoru in homoerotic attraction. This unacknowledged attraction explains why Niou can be jealous of Kaoru even though he knows that Kaoru lacks carnal desire for women. When Niou, at the height of his romance with Ukifune on the far bank of the Uji River, tests her out for possible service in the retinue of the First Princess, is he not asking for Kaoru to discover her there? Is Kaoru not ready to fall in with Niou's plan? None of these motivational undercurrents is visible if we observe merely the surface of heterosexual love.

### Between Parents

It is not enough to say that Ukifune simply cannot decide between two suitors, one of whom she prefers as a lover (Niou) and the other as a guardian (Kaoru). The obvious love triangle (Ukifune–Niou–Kaoru) can be envisioned as supplemented by three additional triangles to form a pyramid. Aside from Ukifune and her two male lovers, there are the two triangles relating Kaoru and Niou with Ukifune's half-sisters Ōigimi and Nakanokimi, for both of whom Ukifune is a surrogate. The crucial foundation of this pyramid, however, is composed of the Eighth Prince, his principal wife, and Chūjō.

While Ukifune relies primarily on her mother, the only surviving member of the pyramid's basic triangle, she also reaches out to her father's literal and spiritual offspring: Nakanokimi and Kaoru. After Ukifune has become convinced that Niou and Kaoru as well as Nakanokimi know of her involvement with both men, she appeals once again to her mother. Although Chūjō has been extremely critical of the Eighth Prince because of his humiliating treatment of her and their daughter, her relentless matchmaking makes her a negative rather than a positive influence on the desperate Ukifune. When Ukifune asks for a last refuge at her stepfather's mansion in the capital, her mother rejects the plea with no better excuse than the danger of upsetting the pregnant Himegimi. Nonetheless, Chūjō is worried enough to suspect, for the first time, that *mono no ke* (see S:997; 6:156) may have seized her troubled daughter.

Chūjō does more than simply reject Ukifune's request to come home. In a conversation with Bennokimi, in the presence of Ukifune, she discusses Ukifune's missed opportunities to be supported by her half-sisters. Ukifune is made to feel that her relationship with Kaoru and Niou soiled the memory of Ōigimi and betrayed Nakanokimi far beyond "that unfortunate incident" (S:998; 6:158), a reference to the dangerous encounter between Ukifune and Niou under Nakanokimi's own roof. When Chūjō threatens to disavow Ukifune as her daughter if Niou consummates his forbidden desire, Ukifune faces a dilemma: she must either confess the fait accompli and lose her mother or keep silent and live with a tormenting conscience. Because she can endure neither option she feels "as if she were being cut to shreds" (S:999; 6:159). For the first time she conceives of death as the only solution to her dilemma.

Ukifune's silent thoughts of death are facilitated by her mother's gloomy comments on the roaring Uji River and by her women's reports of the victims it has claimed.[55] In addition, her mother's plan for purification rites suggests to Ukifune that the waters of the Mita-rashi River might "wash away" the "stain" of her sins (S:999; 6:160). Using the excuse of Himegimi's pregnancy, Chūjō abandons Ukifune to her sense of defilement, doing to her desperate daughter on the brink of death what her father did to her at her birth. As Chūjō does this, she has a guilty nightmare that anticipates Ukifune's disappear-ance much as the abbot's dream of his intimate, the Eighth Prince, foreshadowed Ōigimi's death. Ukifune does then in fact disappear, accompanied by the tolling of the monastery bell that is, for her and for us, intimately associated with the Eighth Prince. In her ominous last poem to Chūjō, Ukifune links the tolling of the bell with the sound of her sob as she departs from this world (see S:1011; 6:187). She decides to kill herself by throwing herself into the Uji River.

### Ukifune's Disappearance

Just as Murasaki's reported death traumatized Genji, Ukifune's two lovers are stunned by her disappearance. If Kaoru's reaction is more extreme than Niou's, it is because Kaoru's interaction with Uki-fune falls outside the pattern of transgression established by Genji and followed by Niou. Kaoru has created a radically new way to overcome loss by replacing human substitutes with human icons. Seeking to immortalize or enshrine the dead Eighth Prince and Ōigimi in the "image" *(hitogata)* of Ukifune, he has been denying the death of the Uji prince and his oldest daughter while denying life to Ukifune. In her analysis of Dante Gabriel Rossetti's poem "The Portrait" (1870), Elisabeth Bronfen refers to such a pattern as "a metaphorical 'killing' of the woman on two scores—the image, by replacing body with sign, negates her presence, while in a more specific way it addresses her death semantically by representing her as a saint or relic, invoking her death before its actual occurrence."[56] Ukifune escapes those who would "kill" her in this way. She simply disappears. Kaoru is most deeply affected, but Nakanokimi, Niou, and Chūjō are also implicated to various degrees.

In mourning for Ukifune, Kaoru now puts into words her bewitching power over her lovers: "In death she seemed to have a stronger hold on him than in life" (S:1020; 6:212). In other words, Kaoru's reflection upon Ukifune's "death" confirms that she has para-doxically created an existence by means of a disappearance. In their different ways, both Niou and Kaoru recognize Ukifune's presence in her absence. They now erase the mark of parental disavowal that has underlined her existential state of nonexistence. In "Kagerō" (S: "The Drake Fly"), Ukifune's uncanny identity fixes itself in the minds of the male protagonists.

After the initial shock of Ukifune's disappearance, both men con-clude that she committed suicide by throwing herself into the Uji River; but their doubts are subsequently aroused by reports of a hasty and quite unconventional funeral. They do not realize that the cere-mony took place without a body. The empty ritual was, moreover, directed by none other than the Eighth Prince's shady intimate, the abbot *(azari)*, whose knowledge of Ukifune's disappearance came from his sister, Ukifune's nurse (fig. 7 in App. B). Not long after the funeral, the Uji *azari* is promoted to archdeacon *(risshi)*. He is called upon to administer Ukifune's forty-ninth-day Buddhist memorial ser-vices, which are made farcical by the noisy presence of Hitachi, her stepfather. In terms of the poetic image that had so powerfully upset Niou, Ukifune remains suspended in "midair" (S:993; 6:146: *naka-zora*). For everyone involved—for those who sincerely mourn and even for those who may secretly rejoice—it is difficult to deal with the fact that Ukifune may have committed suicide. Like soldiers "missing in action," she is neither dead nor alive.

Among those aware of the absence of Ukifune's dead body, specu-lations abound as to whether or not she actually drowned in the river. Her bereaved mother in particular seeks an alternative explanation in supernatural events such as abduction by a "fiend" or "fox spirit"

(S:1015; 6:198: *oni; kitsune*). Casting wildly about in search of an explanation, Chūjō also considers placing the blame for Ukifune's disappearance on a jealous woman. According to the commentaries (see S:1015, n. †; 6:199, n. 19), her suspicions are directed at Kaoru's wife, the Second Princess. The critics' assumption that the Second Princess is resentful of Ukifune does not, however, fit the serenely conformist character of the Second Princess, who had assured Kaoru that she would not be jealous if he were to bring Ukifune to Sanjō (see S:996; 6:153). It should have been more likely, especially from Chūjō's informed perspective, to suspect Nakanokimi, who, after the brink-of-incest incident at the Nijō-in and its serious aftermath at Uji, has reason to consider Ukifune a threat to her domestic peace.

Niou and Kaoru too immerse themselves in dark speculations about the cause of Ukifune's presumed self-destruction. Although they are still gathering evidence to prove to themselves what they already know—namely, that they were both involved with the same woman—they also search for the deeper reasons of her despair. Niou falls mysteriously ill from overwhelming feelings of incestuous guilt, and there are rumors that he has been afflicted by *mono no ke*, much as Genji had been rumored to be possessed after Yūgao's death. When Niou tries to release some of his anxiety in conversation with Kaoru, he fails because he cannot bring himself to be candid. In fact, Niou's halfhearted effort to confess aggravates his malaise because Kaoru cruelly stabs at his friend's conscience (see S:1019; 6:211). Kaoru parades his knowledge of Niou's taboo violation against Nakanokimi by sending to the Nijō-in a provocative poem evoking the "dead" Ukifune (see S:1021; 6:213). Frustrated by Kaoru's action, Niou confides to his wife a partial truth about having sought out her half-sister.

Less plagued by feelings of guilt and less hampered by court obligations than Niou, Kaoru can afford to investigate Ukifune's disappearance with greater vigor. He finds the roots of her despair in the Uji house—"an abode of devils, perhaps" (S:1017; 6:205)—and he blames himself for having kept her in this wilderness. Moreover, he wonders now what "strange legacy" (S:1023; 6:219) tied him to the Eighth Prince. Although Kaoru is unable to acknowledge to himself that he was initially drawn to the Eighth Prince because the prince promised to fill the paralyzing blank in his life left by Genji's false fatherhood, Kaoru does realize that Ukifune constitutes his last connection (S:1023; 6:219: *yukari*) to this quondam father figure. While Niou's "indisposition" (S:1018; 6:207) can be attributed to his guilt over affinal incest with Ukifune, Kaoru's anxieties are the result of symbolically incestuous behavior that can be traced to his pursuit of Ukifune as a *hitogata* for her half-sisters (especially Ōigimi), her father, and, ultimately, his own father, Kashiwagi.

Kaoru's curiosity about the forbidden love between Niou and Ukifune is motivated by his need to find accomplices to share in the burden of guilt. He thinks also of Nakanokimi, recalling that she was neither an innocent victim of her husband's betrayal nor an innocent bystander to his own abuse of Ukifune as an "image" (S:1026; 6:225: *hitogata*). There can be no doubt that Nakanokimi had served both men as an intermediary in their encounters with Ukifune.

The quest for the unresolved mysteries beneath the waters of the Uji River continues after Ukifune's forty-ninth-day memorial services. The quest takes one of two now familiar forms: either finding a surrogate who resembles the lost love, ideally through a kinship connection, or searching for the lost love in the territory of a male rival who may have hidden her away. The first object of the men's attention is one Kosaishō, who is in the service of the First Princess, much as Ukifune might have been had she not disappeared. In a spectacularly voluptuous *kaimami* in which the observed women, clad in thin gossamer robes, are observed charmingly chipping ice to survive the heat of summer, Kaoru's admiring gaze alternates between Kosaishō and the First Princess, Niou's coveted sister. He becomes fixed on the latter because she poses the greater challenge in the male contest and, more important, because his sister-in-law presents the alluring possibility of a forbidden liaison. After this *kaimami*, Kaoru hastens to turn his own Second Princess into a replica of her half-sister by making her wear a gossamer robe and chip ice. In this masquerade Kaoru is mimicking, without consummating, Niou's affinal incest with Ukifune (his wife's half-sister).[57]

In "Kagerō" (S: "The Drake Fly"), taboo violations are very nearly exposed as such. The Akashi Empress, Genji's daughter, has been extremely wary of her son's amorous escapades and now hears through the *nyōbō* grapevine that Niou had been involved with Nakanokimi's younger half-sister, who is rumored to have died an unnatural death, presumably as a result of this forbidden affair. The critical commentaries attribute the empress' horror (see S:1034; 6:247, nn. 18–19) to the fact that suicide was not an acceptable way for an aristocratic woman to escape from an unwanted courtship; but the empress, who is scandalized far beyond her previous outburst of

anger over Niou's improprieties,[58] makes no effort to scotch the
rumors about what Ukifune may or may not have done. Instead, she
orders the concealment of her son's role in his wife's half-sister's
affairs. In other words, the thought of her son's taboo violation upsets
her more than the thought of Ukifune's suicide.[59]

The thought of having lost Ukifune in a violent act of self-
destruction has left the male protagonists in a virtual state of impotence. Having realized the nature of his transgression, Niou never
recovers his dashing manhood. When he attempted a last visit to Ukifune, he was ignominiously repelled by barking dogs. His advances to
Kosaishō are so ineffective that he is ignored. He becomes interested
in Miyanokimi, the daughter of the late Prince Kagerō (Shikibukyō no
miya) and a niece of the Eighth Prince, in the conventional hope that
she might resemble her cousin Ukifune, but nothing comes of this
interest. With both Kosaishō and Miyanokimi, Kaoru has some success. Less marked than Niou by the stigma of an actual taboo violation, he feels freer to return to Uji, the scene of the unconscious
expression of his innermost fears and desires. He fully understands
that his desire to support Miyanokimi in her plight as a fatherless
fallen princess has its origins in the Uji family. In the fragile, short-
lived insect of the *kagerō,* a symbol of the uncertain boundaries
between the dream world of the unconscious and the tangible, verifi-
able world of reality, he captures the meaning of Uji. More at home in
this shimmering twilight zone than any other male protagonist in the
*Genji,* Kaoru seems prepared to decode the uncanny mystery of Ukifune when he composes this solitary *waka* at the end of "Kagerō"
(6:264; S:1042):

> *ari to mite   te ni wa torarezu   mireba mata*
> *yukue mo shirazu   kieshi kagerō*

> I see the drake fly, take it up in my hand.
> Ah, here it is, I say—and it is gone.

In its evanescence the *kagerō* is symbolic of Ukifune. Contemplating
its elusive character, Kaoru realizes the meaning of Ukifune as *hitogata.*[60] When he first contemplated having an artist produce a perfect
replica of his lost Ōigimi, Nakanokimi had directed him instead to the
dream of Ōigimi's reincarnation in Ukifune. The result for Ukifune
was tragic because her ascribed role as *hitogata* made her a vehicle

(*nademono,* a "thing to be rubbed") for the inauthenticity inherent in the process of substitution. (The dangers of the role in which her lovers have cast her is suggested by Chikamatsu's view of verisimilitude in the puppet theater [ *jōruri* or *bunraku*]: "If one makes an exact copy of a living being . . . , one will become disgusted with it.")[61]

### The Abduction

But Ukifune does not die. Like the *kagerō,* Ukifune has merely given an illusory impression of her "death." Although out of reach, she is still alive. Her resolve to die has hardly been converted into a vigorous will to live, but live she does. Months later, after she has recovered from a period of amnesia, she remembers that something interfered with her resolve to throw herself into the Uji River. She recognizes that her own fear of death had made her waver and that she had appealed to "evil spirits" (S:1050; 6:284: *oni mo nani mo*) to "devour" her. She had experienced an abduction fantasy, which, like a dream, is a phenomenon similar to but distinct from spirit possession: "As she sat hunched against the veranda, her mind in a turmoil, a very handsome man [ *ito kiyoge naru otoko*] came up and announced that she was to go with him, and (she seemed to remember) took her in his arms" (S:1050; 6:284–285).[62] It is yet another indication of Ukifune's extreme emotional fluctuations, her liminal state between life and death, that she can think of the demonic and the "very handsome man" in one breath.

Who is the handsome abductor? Whether or not Ukifune is able after her spirit possession two months later to recognize her father's fateful role in her traumatized existence is a question whose answer depends on our interpretation of Ukifune's own tentative identification of her abductor. Following the traditional commentaries, Edward G. Seidensticker assumes in his translation that the handsome man of the abduction fantasy must be Niou: "It would be Prince Niou, she said to herself" (S:1050; 6:285; see also 6:284, n. 14). But the original identifies the abductor merely by his rank; he is referred to as *miya.* Which prince is meant must remain a matter of speculation. Field sees in the description of the abductor a "linguistic conflation of Kaoru and Niou." She bases this identification on the mistaken claim that the adjective *"kiyoge,"* modifying the abductor, is "reserved for Kaoru," who is "Niou's double." Kaoru, accordingly, bears the "responsibility for Ukifune's 'death'."[63] In fact, Murasaki Shikibu also uses *"kiyoge"* in introducing the Eighth Prince, whom she describes as "an extremely handsome man" (S:777; 5:114: *yōbō ito kiyoge ni owashimasu miya nari*). She portrays him as such even in his last moments (see S:807; 5:177). Although the text does not allow interpretive certainty, I believe that the contradictory figure of the abductor is best understood as a projection of Ukifune's increasingly ambivalent conception of her father.

Ukifune's response to her imagined abduction is as ambivalent as her response to experienced reality. The handsome prince satisfies her innermost wish to escape the world, and he physically assists her by taking her in his arms and carrying her away. The prince is a projection of Ukifune's desire for a father rather than for a more conventional lover. This interpretation seems plausible because the fantasy abductor abandons Ukifune in extremis as her father did in actuality.[64] There is no doubt about the pain of this imagined abandonment: "He carried her to a very strange place and disappeared. She remembered weeping bitterly at her failure to keep her resolve [to kill herself], and she could remember nothing more" (S:1050; 6:285). In this traumatic state she is discovered by yet another father figure.

Much is made in the critical literature of the fact that she is found weeping under a gnarled old tree. As we have seen in the case of Yūgao's demise at an abandoned villa, certain trees were believed to attract wood spirits *(kodama)* who could seize passersby at will. But it is just as important to note that her desperate state of mind drove her to perish or seek shelter—it is not clear which—just outside the Uji villa of the late Suzaku Emperor *(ko* Suzaku-in).[65] According to Ukifune's recollections after the exorcism of her possessing spirit two months later, she was abducted from her veranda and abandoned at the neglected Uji villa of the late Suzaku Emperor. Ikeda Kazuomi notes that Yūgao's and Ukifune's incidents of spirit possession both occur after abductions by handsome men to ruined villas.[66] While Yūgao was indeed forced by Genji to go to his deserted villa, the experience of the amnesiac Ukifune can more properly be described as an abduction fantasy. Her later memory to the contrary, the suicidal Ukifune seems to have wandered to the villa instead of the river in a liminal state between life and death. There is, incidentally, no indication in the text that she ever threw herself into the Uji River, as is so often asserted.

In this highly symbolic landscape, it is no accident that Ukifune is drawn to her uncle's villa; after all, Suzaku successfully combined religious devotion with his duties as an exceptionally loving father. As such, he stands limned in sharp contrast to the harsh portrait painted of his half-brother, the Eighth Prince, who failed in the struggle to succeed him. After having been driven from her father's house at birth and reinstalled in its replica by her father's disciple Kaoru, Ukifune now exiles herself to a place symbolically comparable to her father's home. Instead of choosing suicide, Ukifune hopes to be saved by an avuncular figure.

Such a savior seems to appear in the form of the "bishop of Yokawa" (S:1043; 6:267), but the Yokawa no Sōzu (fig. 8 in App. B) proves himself to be no less shady a character than the other clerics in the *Genji*. In their zeal to find historic models for fictional characters, scholars have, since Yotsutsuji Yoshinari's *Kakaishō* (1364) commentary, identified this Sōzu with the historic priest Genshin (942–1017), author of the popular *Ōjōyōshū* (Essentials for Rebirth in the Pure Land; 985). Recently, Edward Kamens has critically examined this illustrious but unfortunate identification, which has prevented the exposure of the negative character traits of the fictional Sōzu.[67]

Our first impression of the Sōzu is indeed positive. He interrupts his religious austerities on Mount Hiei and hurries to Uji in order to attend to his ailing mother. The aged nun and her middle-aged daughter, "the widow of a high-ranking courtier" (S:1052; 6:288: *kandachime no kita no kata*), were on their return journey from a pilgrimage to Hatsuse when the former's illness forced them to stop at the house of an acquaintance who had just left for *his* pilgrimage to Hatsuse. In order to be near his mother, the Sōzu, apparently no stranger to Uji and its people, moves into the late Suzaku Emperor's Uji villa. Hatsuse pilgrimages and the possibility of impending death are the focus of everyone's attention when, by accident, the priests accompanying the Sōzu find Ukifune under an old tree in the back of the villa (Plate 2.12). Failing at first to recognize her as human, they frighten themselves with folk beliefs about foxes *(kitsune)* and demons *(oni)*, but the Sōzu is able to identify Ukifune as a young woman rather than a "ghost" (S:1045; 6:271). He speculates that she may be someone who revived after her supposed corpse had been discarded (as was the custom for ordinary people). She must be moved inside the building. So far the Sōzu can indeed be said to conform to the historic Genshin's high ethical standards of compassion for all human beings.

Yet the Sōzu seems anything but a benevolent humanitarian when he becomes an accomplice to his sister's unlawful appropriation of the helpless creature. This sister had lost her own daughter and is pleased that her "dream at Hatsuse" (S:1049, see 1047; 6:280: *yumegatari;* see 6:274) has been fulfilled by the unknown beauty whom she now embraces as a substitute (see S:1047; 6:276: *hito no kawari*). When she and her clerical brother attempt to revive Ukifune, they are thwarted by a certain *azari,* the Sōzu's most skilled exorcist. (This *azari* is not to be confused with the Uji *azari,* or the Eighth Prince's preceptor, even though a parallel between the two men gradually suggests itself.) The Sōzu's *azari* argues that, should they fail to revive the stranger, the pollution from her death (see S:1047; 6:275) would inevitably delay the recovery of the Sōzu's ailing mother. Thus, if the Sōzu and his sister, who are instrumental in Ukifune's rebirth, can be seen as avatars of Ukifune's parents, then the figure of the *azari* appears, like his zealous Uji predecessor, intent on averting pollution *(kegare)* from the Sōzu and his family by persuading the Sōzu to deny Ukifune's existence.

For Ukifune, who lingers on the liminal threshold between death and life, the traumatic events of her life repeat themselves in condensed form and consequently reinforce her death wish. She articulates her conflict with remarkable clarity: "'I have been thrown out. I have nowhere to go.' The girl barely managed a whisper. 'Don't let anyone see me. Take me out when it gets dark and throw me . . . in the river'" (S:1047; 6:276).[68] Whereas she initially had decided to die in solitude, with the burden of suicide resting on herself alone, she now seeks not only witnesses but assistants. Not surprisingly, she is denied this wish by the Sōzu's sister, who has—not unlike Ukifune's real mother—marriage plans for this "daughter."

In the midst of these attempts to revive Ukifune, the Sōzu receives reports about the funeral the night before of the Eighth Prince's daughter. Since the Sōzu, who is familiar with Uji, knows that Ōigimi is dead and Nakanokimi is residing safely in the capital, he infers correctly that the Eighth Prince had a third daughter. He instantly realizes the connection between that daughter and his highborn foundling (S:1048; 6:277):

> So that was it. Some demon had abducted the Eighth Prince's daughter. It scarcely seemed to the bishop that he had been looking at a live human being. There was something sinister about the girl, as if she might at any moment dissolve into thin air.

Nonetheless, like the Eighth Prince before him, the Sōzu refuses to acknowledge Ukifune's identity. Instead he retreats from his realization of the truth and wonders, "But who might it [the dead woman] be?" (S:1048; 6:278). He now declines to make the connection he had already made between the Eighth Prince's "deceased" daughter and the high-ranking young woman discovered near the brink of death. Something other than mere obtuseness must have caused the Sōzu to repress his correct initial conclusion that the woman in his custody is an unrecognized daughter who is wrongly assumed to be dead. Why does he shuffle back and forth across the threshold of awareness?

One reason may be concern for his sister's grief for the daughter lost five or six years before (see S:1055; 6:298) and her hopes for a replacement. Yet fraternal charity is not the only emotion aroused in his breast by the beautiful foundling. Not only did the Sōzu have rather a good look at her when he pronounced her human (see S:1046; 6:273); he also arranges for other chances to look in on his sister's new charge. When the whole party returns to the Ono nunnery, the Sōzu stays with the women for some time. His overt reason is that he must supervise his mother's recovery. But there is also a covert reason for his lingering at the Ono nunnery: his interest in Ukifune, whose existence he keeps secret, imposing silence on his sister and her women. As for Ukifune, by not confessing her identity she chooses the relative security of the Ono nunnery over a return to the secular world she wants so desperately to escape.

## Spirit Possession

Ukifune's conflict shares elements with the conflicts other female protagonists endured before they seized upon spirit possession as a woman's weapon. Not surprisingly, her unprecedentedly powerful death wish is now transformed into spirit possession. The Sōzu, who has in the meantime returned to his austerities at the Yokawa retreat, hears from his sister that Ukifune has become possessed. In order to exorcize the demons, he hurries down the mountain to the Ono nunnery. This crucial episode in the *Genji* has not received the attention it deserves;[69] in fact, many critics ignore Ukifune's possession scene altogether. Haruo Shirane, for example, deals extensively with Genshin as the model for the Sōzu and his role as savior but does not mention the Sōzu's role as exorcist.[70] The identification between the fictional Sōzu and the historic Genshin is especially unfortunate because the association seems to have inhibited critics—who have been eager to identify all other major possessing spirits in the *monogatari*—from identifying

Ukifune's.[71] Careful scrutiny of the possession scene and its meaning for Ukifune is long overdue.[72]

When the Sōzu sees the afflicted Ukifune, he is confirmed in his earlier view of her unusual, attractive appearance: "She is very pretty indeed. I did think all along that there was something unusual about her" (S:1049; 6:281). The impression that he himself has taken a fancy to Ukifune can no longer be denied. As he prepares for the rites of exorcism, he remains "deeply perplexed" (S:1049; 6:281–282). That the presence of this woman has had an improper effect on the Sōzu has apparently not escaped the notice of his clerical entourage. In an effort to justify his having interrupted his strict religious practice for the sake of saving an attractive young woman, he involuntarily reveals his carnal thoughts about Ukifune (S:1049; 6:282):

> You must say nothing to anyone. I am a dissolute monk who has broken his vows over and over again, but not once have I sullied myself with woman. Ah, well. Some people reveal their predilections when they are past sixty, and if I prove to be one of them, I shall call it fate.

In exchange for this confession he imposes the utmost secrecy on his fellow clerics. Norma Field has commented astutely on the way that the scenes of the abduction and spirit possession are connected through "the economy of the possessing spirit taking the form of a defrocked priest."[73] She has critically reviewed the readers' reception of the Sōzu as a fictional incarnation of the historic Genshin by questioning the Sōzu's alleged saintliness: "Many readers, in their haste to applaud the Bishop's generosity of spirit over the narrow-mindedness of the lesser clerics, neglect to attend to this disclaimer [of his carnal interest in women]. Doesn't he protest too much? Is it really safe for him to save Ukifune?"[74] Although Field does not answer these questions, she is right to raise them. He does protest too much; and Ukifune is indeed not safe in his hands. He is an apparently pious father figure whose amorous feelings for Ukifune set the stage for Ukifune's expression—through spirit possession—of her angst, at the core of which is a riddled father-daughter relationship.

When Ukifune was first found bedraggled and weeping under a tree at the Uji villa of the late Suzaku Emperor, she was not immediately diagnosed as possessed. Quite the contrary: initial speculation pointed in another direction. Ukifune was thought to be a *henge,* an animal disguised as a human being. Once her human nature was established by the Sōzu's penetrating eye, she was nursed back to physical health. It is important to note that more than two months pass before Ukifune develops distinct symptoms of spirit possession that require an exorcism. In these two months Ukifune is repeatedly exposed to the gaze of the Sōzu and subjected to his sister's coercive attempts to remodel her as her "daughter." Her rebirth from symbolic death, from her failed attempt at suicide, confronts her with an ironic replay of the troubled life from which she had taken flight. In response, she becomes possessed.[75]

If Ukifune's death wish is replaced by the oblique aggressive strategy of spirit possession, at whom is her protest directed? Hers is the first major case in the *Genji* in which the eponymous hero is not the prime target of the woman's weapon. The established pattern of Genji witnessing a female trance and perceiving female jealousy as the cause of spirit possession cannot apply to Ukifune's case. The relatively few scholars who attend to Ukifune's possession and exorcism cannot adopt the familiar perspective of an authoritative figure like Genji but are forced instead to focus on the possessed person herself for clues about the identity of the possessing spirit. As Field has correctly observed, "our interest was directed to the possessor and not the possessed victim. The scene of possession is different in Uji."[76]

The person found weeping under an old tree is a human nonentity without a past. As this existential void gradually fills—with the fantasies of others rather than the few clues provided by Ukifune—her passive resistance to forced socialization is perceived by those around her as an intolerable obstruction. The Sōzu and his sister revived Ukifune, but they missed their chance, indeed refused, to recognize her as the Eighth Prince's daughter. Her obstinate silence and lack of cooperation constitute her response to their virtually having taken her prisoner. Through the strategy of spirit possession she protests the paternal denial and maternal distortion of her existence. Her immediate targets now are the Sōzu and his sister, symbolic parental figures, the former a perversion of Ukifune's longed-for father, the latter a perpetuator of her mother's ruthless ambitions.

What makes this case of spirit possession especially difficult to decode is the symbolic nature of Ukifune's targets. Obliqueness is an inextricable feature of spirit possession—necessary to protect the possessed person from the retribution that always threatens those who articulate the forbidden. Spirit possession combines the aggressive and the erotic, disguising the alliance between the possessed and the possessing spirit as antagonism. What, then, are the contradictory emotions Ukifune voices through the female medium? (See S:1050; 6:282: *hito;* n. 13: *yorimashi.*) And what is the significance of the maleness of the possessing spirit?[77]

Ukifune's possession constitutes an incestuous fantasy, a mysterious text that can be read from the related perspectives of the possessed person, the possessing spirit, and the exorcist. The speech of Ukifune's *mono no ke* provides significant clues to the mystery (S:1050; 6:283):

> "You think it is this I have come for?" [the spirit] shouted. "No, no. I was once a monk myself, and I obeyed all the rules; but I took away a grudge that kept me tied to the world, and I wandered here and wandered there, and found a house full of beautiful girls. One of them died, and this one wanted to die too. She said so, every day and every night. I saw my chance and took hold of her one dark night when she was alone. But Our Lady of Hatsuse was on her side through it all, and now I have lost out to His Reverence. I shall leave you."

The spirit clearly belongs to a deceased male cleric whose dissolute behavior, like that of the Sōzu, poses an obstacle to enlightenment. Mitani Kuniaki's recognition of the dubious nature of the Bishop of Yokawa and his entourage of self-centered relatives leads him to the ingenious conclusion that the *mono no ke* (revealed to be an apostate) is a projection of the Sōzu as exorcist.[78] That dissolute priests of the highest order were known to afflict high-ranking women is demonstrated by the frequently cited case of Bishop Shinsai possessing the Somedono Empress (r. 864–900).[79] The *Kojidan* (Stories of Ancient Matters; 1212–1215), an early Kamakura *setsuwa* collection, features Shinsai as a long-nosed goblin *(tengu)* and the exorcist-ascetic as a blue demon.[80]

Closer to hand, however, is the Uji *azari's* dream just prior to Ōigimi's death.[81] In this dream, the wandering spirit of a deceased monk held an unspecified grudge. That monk was unambiguously the Eighth Prince. Through Ukifune's possession, another "grudge" is revealed, and the cause of this priest's grudge lies in the "house full of beautiful girls."[82] Although the *mono no ke* hints quite bluntly at the Eighth Prince's daughters Ōigimi and Ukifune ("One of them died, and this one wanted to die too"), the Sōzu continues to repress awareness of this figural constellation in order not to learn of Ukifune's identity as her father's unrecognized daughter.

If the speech refers to both the Eighth Prince and his living avatar, the Sōzu, what is its meaning from the perspective of the major actor in the drama, Ukifune herself? The answer depends on her present feelings about her father. The immediate crisis that caused her disappearance was motivated by her multiple failures to achieve happiness by marrying, but her resultant death wish can be traced back to her longing for an idealized protective and loving father figure. This longing had been evident in her pilgrimages to Hatsuse (Hasedera), the Buddhist temple associated with reunions (by cultural tradition and by Tamakazura's intertextual example). Ukifune's entanglement in secular love affairs in which others abused her as a *hitogata* led to her tragic resolve to be united in death with her archetypal father figure. What, if not the suspicion that this father figure might be less than pure, held her back from the final step of suicide? Unlike Ōigimi, who knew nothing of her father's secret, Ukifune knew, no matter how hard she may have tried to repress the knowledge, of her father's cruelty.

It is precisely this ambivalence toward an archetypal father figure that is the crux of her dilemma. When another unworthy priest, the Sōzu, aided by his selfish sister, forces her to be reborn into yet another existence that is not her own, she goes into a trance that frightens her parental avatars into confronting the riddle of the existence they have unethically appropriated. Her possession occurs when the saviors of her body attempt to become the captors of her psyche. In a curiously paradoxical way, Ukifune might be seen as now forming an alliance with her father's spirit in opposition to the forbidden fantasies of the Sōzu. In other words, Ukifune may have succeeded in her trance in splitting into two the ambiguous image of her father: the *mono no ke* on the one hand and the clerical exorcist on the other. Clearly these two forces stand in an antagonistic relationship because the spirit symbolizes Ukifune's last hope of paternal recognition while the exorcist represents the continuation of her father's denial.

Ukifune's encounter with the Sōzu sharpens the conflict between the images of paternal piety and carnality. Her spirit possession is a woman's weapon against the Sōzu's illicit, unwanted fatherly claims on her and, at the same time, an instrument of alliance with her father in the guise of *mono no ke,* come at last to claim her as his daughter. In the possession scene, Ukifune's father appears not in the idealized form of a handsome abductor but rather as a former monk who admits to a grudge. This paternal manifestation no longer dominates and controls others at will but seeks to absolve himself from the guilt

incurred by either mistreating his daughters or by being overly posses-
sive of them. The *mono no ke* is converted by the exorcist's mirror
image of himself; rather than abandoning Ukifune, the Eighth Prince
can now leave her under the protection of the Hatsuse Kannon.[83]

It is ironic that the proximate consequence of Ukifune's deeply
troubling experience with her suitors was her inconclusive abduction
fantasy while the seemingly positive rescue by the Sōzu precipitated
her ultimate dramatic confrontation with her father in the form of a
*mono no ke*. Through the obliqueness of spirit possession, Ukifune is
finally able to face her father-daughter conflict. She is free now to seek
enlightenment through religious vows, but she continues to be trem-
ulously uncertain: "It had been cruel of them to save her. The future
filled her with dread" (S:1053; 6:290). Despite her dread, Ukifune is
determined to struggle like no other female protagonist before her to
forge an identity of her own. Although in the tentative manner of
someone fearfully unsure of success, she has already begun to recon-
stitute the fragmented pieces of her self through literary creativity disguised as mere writing practice.[84] Her art must, like her identity, be
kept secret from the world. To ensure success, Ukifune must, like
Fujitsubo, hide her self—get herself to a nunnery.

### Religious Vows

It is yet another irony that Ukifune asks the wanton Sōzu to
administer these vows (see S:1051; 6:286). The Sōzu reluctantly
agrees to administer a token tonsure. Soon thereafter the Sōzu's inter-
fering sister renews the pressure on Ukifune to reveal her background,
but she must be satisfied with Ukifune's vague remembrance of the
abduction scene (see S:1051; 6:287–288). Ukifune emphatically
repeats her earlier request that the secret of her past remain a secret so
that she can lead the peaceful life of a nun, the only form of existence
that ensures her safety from those who desire her as their *hitogata*.

Successfully resisting this relatively mild pressure, Ukifune begins
to recuperate at the Ono nunnery, a setting recalling Ichijō's flight
from the capital in the hope of curing herself from repeated bouts of
spirit possession (see S:1053; 6:289–290). As Ukifune recovers her
physical and psychic health, she realizes the precariousness of a religious life in the face of the encroaching secular interests of the capital.
Against this threat to her fragile serenity she employs the resources of
art. But even as she takes up her brush to practice her woman's hand
*(onna-de)* with poetry, she realizes that its conventional purpose is to

delight others by means of a particularly elegant form of communication (Plate 2.14).[85] *Her* poems are for none to see.[86] They translate Ukifune's ascribed *hitogata* self into her own self as religiously enlightened textuality.

Events do not favor Ukifune's wishes for a secluded life. She is besieged even in the nunnery, where religious vows seem only to add to her mystique.[87] The Sōzu's sister begins to scheme for a spirit marriage *(meikon)* between Ukifune, representing her dead daughter reborn, and her son-in-law, a captain of the guards, with whom she exchanges poems about Ukifune (fig. 8 in App. B). For her part Ukifune wants only to be left alone: "She had no wish to return to the past, and the attentions of a man, any man, would inevitably pull her towards it. She had been there, and she would have no more of it" (S:1054–1055; 6:295). Her wishes are ignored by the nuns, who agree that Ukifune and the captain would make "a handsome couple" (S:1054; 6:295). After catching a glimpse of the anonymous beauty, the captain joins the plot to make her his wife. His efforts reach a crescendo when his mother-in-law absents herself on a pilgrimage. Although aware of the dangers of remaining at the nunnery virtually unprotected but no longer wishing for a reunion with lost loved ones, Ukifune refuses to accompany the Sōzu's sister to Hatsuse.

When the captain makes his move, Ukifune flees at night to the quarters of the Sōzu's aged mother. Awakened by her own cough, the old nun, still half asleep, addresses Ukifune as if she were still under the tree at Uji. The frightened Ukifune recalls the abduction scene yet again, this time by envisioning a "malign being" (S:1065; 6:318: *oni*) who had abducted her in female guise. The string of associations leads Ukifune to Nakanokimi and thus to Ukifune's betrayal of her half-sister with Niou. Ukifune recalls in anguish "that untoward incident" at the Nijō-in and "that hideous blunder" (S:1065; 6:319) at Uji. As symptoms of her affection for Nakanokimi and her resurgent guilt about the incestuous offense, Ukifune now makes a Freudian slip in thinking of Nakanokimi as a sister of the same womb (6:319: *harakara*). In horror at herself, she succumbs briefly to longing for Kaoru and the less threatening of her two affairs. At the end of this painful remembrance of things past, Ukifune emerges even more strongly resolved to renounce the world.

It is in this memory-laden volatile situation that the Sōzu announces himself for a brief visit on his way to court for the exorcism of the spirits troubling Niou's sister, the First Princess (fig. 5 in App.

B). Ukifune appeals to him to administer final vows to her.[88] Why
does he agree? He knows as well as Ukifune that these vows will frus-
trate his sister's wish to have Ukifune marry the captain. What compels the Sōzu to conspire with Ukifune against his absent sister? He
had administered a token tonsure earlier in order to sequester Ukifune
in the Ono nunnery under his sister's care. Now, after the disturbing
appearance of the captain, the Sōzu realizes that he had miscalculated.
Only complete vows will assure his own complete appropriation of
this beauty. In response to Ukifune's pleas the Sōzu recalls the
"malign spirit" (S:1067; 6:324: *mono no ke*) he had exorcized earlier
and that might threaten her again. Since his newest mission is to perform an exorcism for the First Princess, his mind fills with an unspeakable apprehension. He recognizes Ukifune's crisis as real. Together
with his sister's maidservant Komoki, the Sōzu watches his disciple
raise scissors to the abundant hair that Ukifune has tossed over the
protective curtains to renounce her female sexuality (Plate 2.13).
Once again the Sōzu's possessiveness evokes that of the Eighth Prince.
Like the Eighth Prince in his *mono no ke* manifestation, the Sōzu is
attempting simultaneously to claim Ukifune and to deny her.

This unpriestly interest must be disguised. The Sōzu must protect
his reputation as a cleric in the increasingly likely event that news of
Ukifune's existence reaches the outside world. Therefore, before anyone can ask unwelcome questions about his motivation for installing
this unknown woman in the Ono nunnery, he presents his version of
the story to the Akashi Empress, Genji's daughter and Kaoru's putative half-sister. Having just saved the daughter of the empress from
possessing spirits,[89] the Sōzu is in an excellent position for claiming
credibility and inspiring trust. He tells the empress of having rescued a
beautiful woman possessed by the unspecified evil spirits hovering
about the neglected Uji villa of the late Suzaku Emperor. Fearing that
he might now be suspected of an unseemly desire to keep Ukifune as
his own, the Sōzu emphasizes her otherworldly dedication and his
altruistic compliance with her sincere wish to take religious vows. He
evades the question of Ukifune's identity even at the risk of being
charged with having exceeded his religious authority by administering
the tonsure to an unidentified woman.

The Sōzu's evasiveness about Ukifune's identity, intended to
underline his innocence, arouses doubts in Kosaishō, the woman in
attendance to the First Princess and an informant to the Akashi
Empress. She immediately questions the thoroughness of the Sōzu's

investigation: "Surely you have found out who she is?" (S:1071; 6:334). He insists that he has not, but he admits knowing that she appears to be of high rank. Although the empress lets the matter drop, she wonders if there is a connection between this mysterious foundling and the equally mysterious Uji funeral of a hitherto unknown daughter of the Eighth Prince.

The suspicions of the empress pose no immediate threat, but the Sōzu's hold on Ukifune is endangered by the nuns on whom he has relied to safeguard his prize. No different from scheming *nyōbō*, the nuns aid the guards captain in his pursuit of Ukifune and even arrange perfect conditions for a *kaimami* (see S:1073; 6:339). The captain, deceitfully posing as a "brother" to win her confidence and affection, only confirms Ukifune in her resolve to cut even the last of her human ties: "Those disastrous events had so turned her against men, it seemed, that she meant to end her days as little a part of the world as a decaying stump" (S:1074; 6:342: *kuchiki*). The imagery of Ukifune as a decaying stump extends the imagery used to symbolize the Eighth Prince and his offspring as a rotting tree wrapped in ivy. Yet even a decaying stump has roots, and Ukifune's agony of remembering continues.

On the anniversary of her "death," she learns through the old nun's grandson, the Governor of Kii (Ki no kami), (fig. 8 in App. B),[90] that Kaoru has attended memorial services on her behalf at Uji, services that fill her with both terror and joy. When asked to join in preparing votive robes for further memorial services, she declines. She is fully aware that her "death" is a fabrication, yet it is a fiction that she will not undo. If others discover the truth of her survival, she will nonetheless maintain the metaphysical truth of her fiction, which is all that remains of her. The collective memory of the woman she had been before her disappearance lingers like the nun's vague recollections of "the gentleman they used to call 'the Shining Genji' or something of the sort" (S:1077; 6:347).

At court, in the aftermath of Ukifune's incestuous affair and her dubious "death," the Akashi Empress and Kaoru become secret allies against Niou. In an echo of Nakanokimi's telling Kaoru about her newly discovered half-sister, the empress commissions Kosaishō to provide Kaoru with tantalizing clues about the foundling whom the empress has now identified as Ukifune. In scheming to tie Ukifune to Kaoru (in order to exclude Niou from improper amorous pursuit), the Akashi Empress may eventually fail just as Nakanokimi had failed with a similar strategy, but Murasaki Shikibu leaves this question open.

As soon as Kaoru learns what the Sōzu has done, he realizes that the beautiful foundling is "someone I had been wondering about" (S:1079; 6:353). He anticipates another competitive round of Niou's rivalry (see S:1079–1080; 6:354–355) and suspects his friend of having conspired with the empress in keeping secret the truth about Ukifune's resurrection. Recalling the traumatic struggle over Ukifune, Kaoru decides to give up all thought of "making her his own" (S:1080; 6:354). He resigns himself to a temperate inquiry. He queries the empress and is reassured when he senses that her primary goal is not to see him married to Ukifune but rather to prevent Niou from renewed involvement and further transgression.

In the Uji chapters, the need for secrecy about broken taboos and violated trust has gradually turned conversations into skilled exercises in double talk. Kaoru is well aware that he has been less than forthcoming in his conversation with the empress and that she has her own politics to pursue, especially safeguarding Niou's reputation and the possibility of his imperial succession. Under the cloud of suspicion that hovers over everyone who attempts to discuss Ukifune, Kaoru sets out to consult with the Sōzu about the hidden Ono nun. His encounter with the Sōzu brings the art of double entendre to its culmination in "Yume no ukihashi" (S: "The Floating Bridge of Dreams"), the last chapter of the *Genji*.

The two are no strangers, for the Sōzu had occasionally given Kaoru religious advice. This hitherto unrevealed connection between the two men is additional evidence that the Sōzu's mute response to the news of the Eighth Prince's daughter's funeral had been dishonest, a flagrant violation of his responsibilities. If he had wanted to inquire into the identity of the woman found under the Uji tree, he need only have contacted Kaoru, whom he must have known was well informed about events at Uji. Put on the spot now by Kaoru's probing questions about "a person I once knew" (S:1081; 6:360), the Sōzu tells the story, manipulating the facts to show himself and his sister in the most charitable light. Minimizing his own role in the episode, he pretends not to have known that Kaoru had a claim on Ukifune: "How could I have dreamed, sir, that she was somehow of importance to you?" (S:1082; 6:363). He also pretends complete ignorance, even at this late date, of Ukifune's identity. Not surprisingly, "the bishop was feeling guilty" (S:1083; 6:364).

Kaoru is as devious as the Sōzu. Instead of revealing his liaison, he gives a curiously distorted—though not wholly inaccurate—account of Ukifune, identifying her not as the unrecognized daughter of the Eighth Prince but rather as "an obscure cousin of the emperor himself" (S:1083; 6:364). Claiming that he wants merely to reestablish ties between Ukifune and her mother, Kaoru appeals to the Sōzu to arrange a meeting with Ukifune. But, like the legendary bamboo cutter who clung to the unearthly Kaguyahime,[91] the Sōzu is extremely reluctant to comply. His dilemma is that he must now acknowledge the rightful claims of the secular world, which means relinquishing Ukifune, or insist on his religious authority in order to keep her at Ono, which means risking accusations of unclerical self-interest.

The Sōzu's actions escaped scrutiny so long as nobody suspected that his administering the tonsure to Ukifune involved a transgression. Once the secret of Ukifune's identity is revealed, he is forced to salvage as much of his clerical reputation as he can, even if it should become necessary to sacrifice Ukifune. In a much debated, controversial letter to Ukifune that demonstrates the Sōzu's diplomatic skills, he offers her the chance to relinquish her vows. If she confirms her resolve to quit the world, she will remain a nun and no one can charge the Sōzu with improper use of his authority.

In an earlier crisis, the Eighth Prince, in the guise of *mono no ke,* had set Ukifune free to pursue a religious life under the protection of the Hatsuse Kannon. But Ukifune's liberation through spirit possession occurred at the price of an unforeseen enthrallment to the Sōzu and his sister. Influenced by them, Ukifune allowed the Sōzu to administer final religious vows, a step that the Sōzu now fears "might call down the wrath of the holy powers" (S:1086; 6:373). To avert the danger and avoid further critical scrutiny of his behavior, he admits his "sense of remorse and guilt" (S:1086; 6:371). He releases Ukifune from her vows and leaves her truly free at last to shape her own destiny—to pursue or not to pursue the religious path. No longer fearful of the gaps in the Uji Bridge, Ukifune is now entranced by another bridge: the floating bridge of dreams *(yume no ukihashi).*

## Ukifune in the *Nō*

There are two *nō* plays dramatizing Ukifune's release from despair. In the early fifteenth century the warrior-poet and amateur playwright Yokoo Motohisa wrote *Ukifune,* a play to which Zeami contributed a musical score.[92] *Ukifune* is performed by the Kanze, Komparu, Kongō, and Kita schools. The other play, *Kodama Ukifune,* is of uncertain origin. It appears neither in the *Kanzeryū Yōkyoku Hyakuban* (101 Plays of the Kanze School) nor in the *Yōkyoku Nihyakugojūban-shū* (Collection of 253 Plays). According to Janet Goff, this play, attributed to Naitō Tōzaemon in a 1524 catalog, has no performance record.[93]

In *Ukifune,* the *waki,* on his return to the capital from a pilgrimage to Hatsuse, stops at Uji, where he meets the female *shite.* Upon his request, the woman tells the priest the sad local story of Ukifune who, torn between two lovers, vanished. Herself a visitor from Ono, the woman invites the priest to visit her there. As the woman disappears, the chorus reveals that her body is inhabited by a *mono no ke* ("nao mono no ke no mi ni soite").[94] After the interlude *(ai),* the *waki* arrives at Ono and offers prayers for the woman he met at Uji. The *shite* reappears in her true form of Ukifune. In response to the priest's compassion, the *shite* tells how the importunings of Niou and Kaoru resulted in an abduction fantasy. She can recall no more than that an unknown man approached her to entice her to go with him ("shiranu otoko no yorikitsutsu izanai yuku").[95] By ruling out Niou and Kaoru as her abductors, she herself raises the unstated possibility that the unknown man is the father she had never known.[96] Furthermore, it is important to recognize that the abductor not only prevented Ukifune from committing suicide but also caused the spirit possession that ultimately led to religious salvation. In her anguish dance *(kakeri),* Ukifune expresses her continuing sense of a suspended existence but places her trust in the Hatsuse Kannon. She is grateful to the Sōzu for having expelled the *mono no ke,* thereby allowing her a chance to find enlightenment in the heavenly realm of Maitreya, the Buddha of the Future (J. Miroku Bosatsu).

The two parts of the *nō* drama *Ukifune* seem to succeed all too well in bridging the gulf between Uji and Ono. As a consequence of the *nō*'s strategy of concealment and disclosure, whereby the *maeshite* and the *nochi-shite* are revealed as one, the abduction and the possession become conflated incidents that lead to Ukifune's enlightenment. Whether the abductor and the *mono no ke* are also meant to be identical remains unclear. It is, however, possible that the *waki* himself appears to the *shite* as a reincarnation of the Sōzu who carried Ukifune to Ono, there to reenact the exorcism of the *mono no ke* and to effect her spiritual release from worldly attachment.

*Kodama Ukifune* places the emphasis not on the abduction but on the possession. This preference on the part of the playwright may have doomed the play's performance chances. As Goff has pointed out, except for the *Hikaru Genji ichibu uta* (1453), "*Genji* handbooks generally ignore [Ukifune's] possession or present a simple, one-sided account."[97] The sixteenth-century Osaka manuscript of the *Genji monogatari ekotoba,* for example—a copy of earlier manuals for painters and calligraphers of illustrated *Genji monogatari*—deals with the discovery of Ukifune under a tree at the Uji villa of the late Suzaku Emperor while completely ignoring the possession and exorcism scene at Ono. The playwright of *Kodama Ukifune* may have been Naitō Tōzaemon, the presumed author of *Hajitomi,* a *nō* play about Yūgao. If Naitō was indeed the author of *Kodama Ukifune,* his knowledge of spirit possession in the *Genji* was probably more profound than that purveyed by the handbooks.[98]

*Kodama Ukifune* features a *waki* in retreat at Ono. He builds a simple grass hut and is determined to find out the identity of the woman who daily brings him brushwood. The female *shite* reveals in her dialogue with her female companion *(tsure)* Shōshō that the rice fields at Ono remind her of Hitachi, where she was raised. At first her answers to the *waki*'s questions about her Uji connections are reluctant and evasive. But in response to the *waki*'s comment on the colors of her brushwood—echoing Kaoru's question about which sister (Ōigimi or Nakanokimi) has the deeper hue (that is, passion)—she reveals her identity as Ukifune. She reveals also that, although she received religious vows from the Sōzu, she remains in limbo and must receive new vows to sever her ties to the world. In words spoken in part by the chorus, which is the convention in *nō*, Ukifune relates the sad story of the Eighth Prince whose "secret seed" she is.[99] In remarkably seamless diction, the Eighth Prince is replaced by Kaoru, who seeks in Ukifune a *hitogata* for Ōigimi. The whirl of disguised identity then continues with Niou's impersonation of Kaoru. Ukifune, caught between two men, feels suicidal despair. The first part of the *nō* ends with the classic image of Ukifune at writing practice *(tenarai)* in the Ono nunnery. In an unusual departure from convention, the *shite* and chorus announce that the *shite* will reappear in a "yet more loathsome form."[100]

This warning is not the play's only unusual feature. According to *nō* convention, the disguised *shite*'s identity is revealed at the end of the first part; in the second part the *shite* reappears to express—usually in a cathartic dance—the grievance that kept the *shite* in an unenlightened state of wandering. In other words, *mae-shite* and *nochi-shite* are ordinarily the same person. *Kodama Ukifune* calls into question this

implication of the fundamental coherence of self. In a manner reminiscent of spirit possession, *Kodama Ukifune* demonstrates the
entranced self's capacity for becoming other. The playwright first signals this departure from convention by having the *shite* disclose her
identity as Ukifune much earlier than is usual.

After the scarcely endurable suspense of the interlude *(ai)*, a *shite*
appears who is not Ukifune. Goff is disturbed by what seems to be a
"failure to identify the main character."[101] Her discomfort stems from
the play's deviation from the customary pattern of transformation
from an unknown to an identified person. Who, then, is the *shite* in
the second part of *Kodama Ukifune?* The *shite*, not bound by human
limitations, has switched gender.[102] He informs us first who he is not
and then explains the nature and purpose of his appearance: "I am
neither a wood spirit nor a spirit from a mountain forest but have simply come in the form of an apparition to confess my sins."[103]

The emphasis shifts to Ukifune's possession scene, with the *shite*
speaking in the words of the *mono no ke*. Revealing himself to be a
man of religious ambitions who had sought professional instruction
about the path to enlightenment,[104] the *shite* confesses that "a slight
grudge" caused him to fail to renounce the world.[105] Although Goff
conjectures that the *shite* in *Kodama Ukifune* combines "the roles of
Ukifune, the possessing priest, and the medium,"[106] she is reluctant to
identify the possessing priest whose confession bears an uncanny
resemblance to the words of Ukifune's *mono no ke* in the *Genji*. We
see, in other words, that the *nō* play dramatizes Ukifune's existential
crisis from her perspective as the Eighth Prince's unrecognized daughter and then, after the interlude, shifts to her father's complaints that
Ukifune is a hindrance to his final enlightenment. Paradoxically, it is
Ukifune's death wish that overcomes her father's grudge. It compels
him—whether as *mono no ke* in the *Genji* or *nochi-shite* in *Kodama
Ukifune*—to possess her and by this extreme act to bring about a
mutual recognition of their father-daughter bond. In the sense that
possessor and possessed merge identities in trance, Ukifune, the *shite*
in the first part, and the Eighth Prince, the *shite* in the second part,
become one. Once he has been expelled as a *mono no ke* by the Sōzu's
exorcism and by Ukifune's commitment to the religious path, the
Eighth Prince too can "end this punishment as a demon."[107] He and
Ukifune, having become one in spirit possession, free one another
from grudging and longing. They can set out together on the single
path to enlightenment.

# Exit *mono no ke:*
## Spirit Possession in *The Tale of Genji*

MODERN ANTHROPOLOGISTS have studied the phenomenon of spirit possession as it has persisted relatively unchanged through time. To accomplish this, they have embarked on field trips to remote islands and to isolated pockets of culture once marked by mysterious white spots on ethnographers' maps. There is also increasing interest in studying spirit possession when it appears in modern industrialized societies—which it does. Despite the social and religious transformations of the last millennium, spirit possession continues to flourish in the interstices of Japanese life. In the last century and a half, as charismatic religious figures have created an entirely new cultural framework for the phenomenon, manifestations of spirit possession have become especially common in the New Religions *(shin shūkyō)*. Nevertheless, Murasaki Shikibu's dramatization of life at the Heian court and in the hills beyond does more than give us access to a vanished world of elegance and refinement. *The Tale of Genji* also provides insights into the social problems and psychic dilemmas of modern men and women.

At the end of this detailed study of five women's experience of spirit possession in the *Genji,* an assessment of the effective use of this "woman's weapon" seems in order. The danger, of course, is that any endeavor to judge spirit possession in terms of success and failure will obscure the subtleties of motivation and simplify the complexities of the outcomes of spirit possession's oblique aggressive strategy. Still, bearing in mind the reductionist danger, one can draw some cautious conclusions.

Within the broad social framework of Heian polygyny depicted in the *Genji,* it can be said with certainty that the resort to spirit possession does not change the status quo for women as a social class. Nor is there any suggestion of spirit possession as family tradition. The apparently spontaneous outbreak of spirit possession can be traced to a specific syndrome of social tensions, but there is in the *Genji* no pattern of transmission of *mono no ke* from mother to daughter. Women who resort to spirit possession do not inherit the strategy from close kin. Nor do the descendants of possessing spirits become spirits themselves.[1] If anything, the daughters of the possessed and those of the possessing spirits develop alternate routes to self-assertion in order to avoid resorting to spirit possession. This lack of a pattern of transmission underscores Murasaki Shikibu's apparent conviction that spirit possession is an individual woman's response to pervasive discontent rather than the inherited affliction of a single person, family, or clan.

The question, then, is whether individual women succeed or fail in using the weapon of spirit possession to articulate their grievances and overcome their psychic traumas. Of five major spirit possessions, two result in death, one in virtual silence foreshadowing death, one in the tonsure, and the last in a combination of religious withdrawal and poetic creativity. Is it a foregone conclusion that death is proof of total failure, or is there triumph in these particular deaths? Is there an admission of failure in silence or in withdrawal from the world of men by taking religious vows? Is a combination of religion and art the key to self-fulfillment? These questions remain a challenge even after extensive analysis of each woman's affliction and resolution.

It is impossible to dissociate the problem of the efficacy of a woman's resort to spirit possession from its impact on others. In the *Genji*, the effects of women's strategy on the men they target (as well as on Rokujō, the one living person implicated as *mono no ke* in the "Aoi" chapter) are relatively easy to observe but not so easy to evaluate. If a man like Genji undergoes change after exposure to his wife's dramatic affliction, is this change solely attributable to spirit possession or is the change the product of other factors as well? If men seem largely unaffected, what does their apparent indifference say about the significance of the elaborate ritual surrounding trance behavior? Does its meaning lie merely in maintaining the status quo of male hegemony or in offering women a way of surviving in a social world that severely disadvantaged them?

Spirit possession is the most graphic form of the "double consciousness" characteristic of Murasaki Shikibu's work. In the *Genji*, the afflicted are invariably women, and as women they share a social status inferior to that of men, but they vary among themselves as to psychic disposition and physical condition. Although the specific nature of their discontent varies, its underlying source is social and political. Their anxiety and unease derive from their unspoken sense that they live in a world constructed by men. They must be constantly on their guard against *kaimami* and sexual taboo violations. When they become possessed by *mono no ke,* they present to men the frightful possibility that the social order may not be uncontested. During the brief spectacle of spirit possession they in fact seem to transcend the limitations assigned their female gender, especially when the possessing spirit is of the opposite sex.

Compared to men, Murasaki Shikibu's women are severely restricted not only in their emotional freedom but in their physical movements. This is what makes disappearances, like Yūgao's and Ukifune's, so extraordinary. Scholars have glossed over this apparent departure from the norm presented in women's prose fiction and private diaries; according to this gendered construct, women are immobile and strictly safeguarded by their families. They are shielded from the male gaze and boxed in by numerous enclosures—by fences and screens and their many-layered robes *(jū-ni hitoe)*.[2] Like the Third Princess, they are constrained to observe men's more active lives by peeking through screens and blinds. When they venture out in the open air, as Aoi and Rokujō do for a spectacular procession of courtiers on the Day of Lustration preceding the Kamo Festival, they are hidden inside stationary carriages. Only their colorful dangling sleeves hint at their actual presence. As forcefully stated in women's fiction and private diaries, physical segregation inscribes interiority onto the female psyche. It is for the man—for Genji, Kashiwagi, Yūgiri, Kaoru, and Niou—to break through the multiple enclosures to reach the woman. For the woman to reach out to the man is a serious breach of etiquette.

In the world of the "Shining Prince," polygyny is the single most important factor motivating spirit possession. Although Murasaki Shikibu's women are members of a privileged upper class, they have little choice but to consent to the marital decisions of others. When Heian court marriages are not simply arranged by fathers and mothers, it is sons who embark upon an ever more popular romantic search of spouses whose social position has become uncertain. Beyond accepting the status quo and tolerating other wives and mistresses, Heian women were expected to bear children and compete with female rivals for their children's benefit. As in other cultures, fertility was women's most valuable asset; but as it "is neither predictable nor always controllable, it is in essence a wild card, and may be of no help at all."[3] Not surprisingly, then, maternal crises are at the core of all but the last of the *Genji*'s major possession cases. The case of Yūgao may seem remote from a reproductive crisis because Yūgao successfully bears Tō no Chūjō's daughter, but this birth enrages Tō no Chūjō's principal wife, who has been childless, and Yūgao flees the household with her infant daughter. The flight exposes her to abduction by Genji, which leads to her lethal possession crisis. Childbirth precipitates other crises. Aoi invites her spirits immediately before her delivery. The Third Princess seizes the woman's weapon immediately after hers. Murasaki's possession occurs in the context of her infertility and her temporary adoption of Genji's Akashi daughter. In the Uji chapters, only one of the Eighth Prince's three daughters, Nakanokimi, becomes a mother. Ōigimi, the oldest daughter, denies marriage and motherhood altogether, thereby circumventing any need for spirit possession. Ukifune calls into question the very idea of reproduction because of her precarious existence. For the last of the Uji heroines, spirit possession serves as a religious catalyst for converting the repressed energy of sexual reproduction into literary productivity.

In short, Murasaki Shikibu repeatedly portrays women who encounter such severe problems during courtship and marriage that they are driven to extreme responses. Suicide is unthinkable for young women of the high nobility—not so much because of any Shinto or Buddhist prohibitions but because those who take their own lives upset the ancestral order by preceding their parents in death. As they attempt desperately to escape from a host of social and psychic constraints, women have recourse to other strategies. Some—like Murasaki—seek comfort in the abnegations of religious life; others—like Ōigimi—seek an extreme of religious asceticism that leads to death. But the religious path was often denied women because of their inferior status or men's sexual claims on them. Men realized all too well that women's religious aspirations can conceal a latent struggle to approximate male power and prestige. When Genji and other men cite the Five Obstructions (*goshō*) to women's enlightenment and bar the religious path to spiritual self-realization, Murasaki, the Third Princess, and Ukifune all resort to spirit possession as a means to an end.[4] Spirit possession offers these desperate women a momentary reprieve, a compromise presided over by Buddhist authorities employing Shinto mediums, a way to wrest from men the permission to take the religious vows that will finally release them from their conjugal obligations. Spirit possession in this sense is not merely a woman's weapon to fight repression in the domestic realm. It is also a means to regain through trance the spiritual power—though no more, perhaps, than a distant echo of archaic shamanism—suppressed by the introduction of male-dominated Buddhism in the sixth century.

Apart from access to religious life, what do Heian women, as portrayed in the *Genji,* gain through the oblique aggressive strategy of spirit possession? They can open "new channels of communication" to express indirectly what their culture prevents them from saying in any other way.[5] Their message is mediated and symbolic—and often misunderstood. The spirit's voice constitutes an exteriorization of a narrative technique resembling the modern stream-of-consciousness or interior-monologue style known in *Genji* parlance as *shinnaigo.* This mysteriously indirect form of communication demands decoding by both the active and passive participants, but the public ritual of exorcism seems designed to obfuscate the message and deflect the protest. Noisy concentration on the task of identifying and expelling the possessing spirit muffles the voice of the possessed. The exorcist, the medium, and the audience all encourage the possessed woman to return to an ordinary state of consciousness. In the *Genji,* spirit possession as a symptom of male-female conflict points to a fundamental tension in Heian culture that seemed to defy understanding—and thus resolution—even after it was articulated. Society settles back into its routines, triumphant over its defeat of evil. The possessed remember nothing or very little of their state of dissociation,[6] and the memory of the terrified targeted person is short-lived and gradually repressed. And yet each case of spirit possession leaves its mark on both the individual psyche and the social fabric. Unlike a real weapon, spirit possession acts as an instrument to reduce rather than eliminate gender conflict. In most cases it is ameliorative rather than salvific.

In the *Genji,* the effect of spirit possession on the main male protagonists is difficult to assess because it is unacknowledged or denied. It may be no coincidence, however, that Genji's heroic stature gradually declines after repeated and direct exposure to his possessed women. Similarly, in the course of the Uji chapters, Niou's dashing manhood plummets to ineffective philandering and Kaoru's sexual inhibitions finally evolve into a rejection of the conventional male role. Genji's decline as hero coincides with the emergence of Kashiwagi as a new kind of hero, or antihero. Paradoxically, as male characters become more aware of the difficult position of women and empathetic toward their needs, male *mono no ke* emerge as empowering figures for possessed women (the Third Princess and Ukifune). In contrast to Genji, neither Niou nor Kaoru is an immediate witness to spirit possession, but both are inclined to ponder its causes and effects precisely because of their greater distance from the spectacle. Of the three men, Kaoru alone comes close to understanding the woman's weapon of spirit possession. Troubled by his uncertain identity, he is motivated to embark on a search for self that has uncanny affinities to a woman's search. In the process, Kaoru approximates women's double consciousness in his growing awareness of both male and female roles.

In every case, the paradoxical process of women becoming other in order more fully to realize themselves takes an enormous toll. In Yūgao's case, spirit possession is synonymous with death; Aoi's death occurs in lieu of another possession. Yet Murasaki Shikibu's collective portrait of Heian womanhood is not completely dark. The women who survive the liminal experience of spirit possession are far from defeated. Although Yūgao and Aoi pay the ultimate price, they live on for Genji through their children (Tamakazura and Yūgiri). As a mirror reflection of Rokujō, erroneously perceived to be the *mono no ke* par excellence, they acquire a posthumous charisma that redeems their shortened lives. The Third Princess and Ukifune forestall a repetition of their possession experiences by religious withdrawal from the world. Murasaki, the Third Princess, and Ukifune arrive at their radically different postpossession states with considerable pain, but they are no longer bitterly resentful. Although the "cost of conformity" is great,[7] all three extricate themselves from crises that seemed both unbearable and irresolvable. Murasaki achieves a stoic silence; the Third Princess abjures secular court language in order to intone the sacred sutras; and Ukifune finally succeeds in constructing her own existence, no matter how precarious, by immersing herself in the language of poetry. The recourse to spirit possession has given all three of them the strength to insist on their own modus vivendi. By voicing the unspeakable they have made their silence significant. In the end, their distinctly feminine strategy has achieved a poetic silence, a religious serenity, an entrancing text.

# Appendix A
## *Genji* Chronology

GENJI AND KAORU are the two male protagonists whose biographies traditionally serve as the chronometer to measure *Genji* time.[1] Their ages follow the Oriental count, which gives the number of years in which one has lived rather than the full years. The Occidental age count lies either one or two years below the Oriental count.

### *Genji* Chapters

| Chapter | Genji's Age |
|---|---|
| 1. The Paulownia Court (Kiritsubo; 桐壺) | 1; 3; 4; 6–8; 11–12 |
| 2. The Broom Tree (Hahakigi; ははき木) | 17 |
| 3. The Shell of the Locust (Utsusemi; 空蝉) | 17 |
| 4. Evening Faces (Yūgao; 夕顔) | 17 |
| 5. Lavender (Wakamurasaki; 若紫) | 18 |
| 6. The Safflower (Suetsumuhana; 末摘花) | 18 |
| 7. An Autumn Excursion (Momiji no ga; 紅葉賀) | 18–20 |
| 8. The Festival of the Cherry Blossoms (Hana no en; 花宴) | 20 |
| 9. Heartvine (Aoi; 葵) | 22–23 |
| 10. The Sacred Tree (Sakaki; 賢木) | 23–25 |
| 11. The Orange Blossoms (Hanachirusato; 花散里) | 25–26 |
| 12. Suma (Suma; 須磨) | 26–27 |
| 13. Akashi (Akashi; 明石) | 27–28 |
| 14. Channel Buoys (Miotsukushi; 澪標) | 28–29 |
| 15. The Wormwood Patch (Yomogiu; 蓬生) | 28–29 |

251

## *Mono no ke* Chronology

| Chapter | Genji's Age | Age of the Possessed |
|---|---|---|
| 4. Yūgao | 17 | 19 (Yūgao) |
| 7. Momiji no ga | 18 | 23 [Fujitsubo] |
| 9. Aoi | 22 | 26 (Aoi) |
| 31. Makibashira | 37 | ? (Higekuro's Wife) |
| 35. Wakana ge | 47 | 40 (Murasaki; age 37 in text) |
| 36. Kashiwagi | 48 | 32 [Kashiwagi] |
| 36. Kashiwagi | 48 | 22 (Third Princess) |
| 39. Yūgiri | 50 | ? (Ichijō) |

| Chapter | Kaoru's Age | Age of the Possessed |
|---|---|---|
| 47. Agemaki | 24 | 27 [Ōigimi] |
| 53. Tenarai | 27 | 23 (Ukifune) |
| 53. Tenarai | 27 | ? (First Princess) |

## Important Events

| Genji's Age | Events and Time (lunar month and day) |
|---|---|
| 3 | Death of Kiritsubo kōi (Genji's mother). |
| 4 | Suzaku (age 7) becomes crown prince. |
| 6 | Death of Genji's grandmother. |
| 11 | Fujitsubo (age 16) becomes Genji's stepmother. |
| 12 | Genji's arranged marriage to Aoi (principal wife). |
| 17 | The Rainy Night Discussion of Women's Ranks (V). |
| | Utsusemi rejects Genji (V). |
| | Genji overcomes Rokujō's resistance. |
| | Genji's affair with Yūgao begins at Gojō. |

**Yūgao's spirit possession and death (age 19) at the villa (VIII.16).**

18    Genji's first secret meeting with Fujitsubo (III).

Genji's *kaimami* of Murasaki (about age 10) at Kitayama (end of III).

Genji's second meeting with Fujitsubo; conception of Reizei (end of IV).

Fujitsubo announces she is three months pregnant (VI).

**Fujitsubo is erroneously thought to be afflicted by *mono no ke*.**

19    Birth of Reizei (middle of II); Fujitsubo (age 24) becomes empress (VII).

20    Genji's first encounter with Oborozukiyo (II.20).

21    The Kiritsubo Emperor abdicates.

22    Suzaku (age 24) becomes emperor; Reizei becomes crown prince.

Aoi humiliates Rokujō in the carriage quarrel on the Day of Lustration before the Kamo Festival (middle of IV).

**Aoi's spirit possession and birth of Yūgiri; Aoi's death (VIII.20).**

Genji's marriage to Murasaki (X).

23    Genji visits Rokujō (age 30) at Nonomiya (IX.7).

Death of Genji's father, the Kiritsubo Emperor (XI.1).

24    Fujitsubo (age 29) becomes a nun (XII.10).

25    Genji's scandal with Oborozukiyo.

26–28   Genji's self-imposed exile at Suma.

Genji makes Akashi pregnant (VI).

29    Reizei (age 11) succeeds the Suzaku Emperor (II.20).

Birth of the Akashi daughter (III.16).

Death of Rokujō (age 36).

31    Akashi moves to the capital.

Murasaki (age 23) adopts the Akashi daughter (XII).

| | |
|---|---|
| 32 | Death of Fujitsubo (age 37) (III). |
| | The Reizei Emperor learns the secret of his birth 49 days later. |
| | Genji has a nightmare of an angry Fujitsubo. |
| 33 | Rokujō's daughter Akikonomu becomes empress. |
| 34 | Genji builds the Rokujō-in. |
| 35 | Tamakazura leaves the provinces for the capital (IV). |
| | Genji completes the Rokujō-in (VIII). |
| | Genji installs Tamakazura (age 21) at the Rokujō-in (X). |
| 36 | Genji's fireflies prank (V); the courtship of Tamakazura. |
| | Yūgiri's *kaimami* of Murasaki during a typhoon (VIII). |
| 37 | **Higekuro's principal wife becomes possessed.** |
| 38 | Tamakazura becomes Higekuro's favorite wife. |
| 39 | Betrothal of the Akashi daughter to the crown prince. |
| | Murasaki accompanies the Akashi daughter to the palace (IV.20). |
| | Preparations for Genji's fortieth birthday; Genji becomes *jun daijō tennō*. |
| | Suzaku takes the tonsure (age 42); Kokiden dies. |
| 40 | Genji's marriage to the Third Princess (age 14 or 15) (middle of II). |
| | Genji resumes his contact with Oborozukiyo. |
| | The pregnant Akashi Princess returns to the Rokujō-in. |
| 41 | The Akashi Princess gives birth to the future crown prince (middle of III). |
| | *Kemari* scene: the Third Princess exposes herself to Kashiwagi (III). |
| 46 | Kinjō (age 20) succeeds the Reizei Emperor (age 28). |
| | Murasaki's first request for the tonsure. |

| 47 | The women's concert rehearsal (I.19) for Suzaku's fiftieth birthday. |
|----|----|
| | Murasaki falls ill and moves to the Nijō-in (III). |
| | Kashiwagi marries Ochiba. |
| | Kashiwagi impregnates the Third Princess on the eve of the lustration for the Kamo Festival (middle of IV). |
| | **Murasaki's "death," spirit possession, and token tonsure (Kamo Festival).** |
| | The Akashi Princess gives birth to Niou. |
| 48 | The Third Princess gives birth to Kaoru. |
| | **Kashiwagi is misdiagnosed as possessed.** |
| | **The Third Princess takes religious vows and becomes possessed.** |
| | Death of Kashiwagi (age 32 or 33). |
| 49 | Yūgiri receives Kashiwagi's flute from Ichijō. |
| 50 | Akikonomu prays for the salvation of her mother Rokujō's restless spirit. |
| | **Ichijō retires to Ono, becomes possessed, and dies.** |
| 51 | The Akashi Princess (age 23) becomes empress. |
| | Death of Murasaki at age 44 (VIII.14). |
| 52 | Birth of Ukifune. |
| | Genji burns Murasaki's letters and contemplates leaving the world. |
| ? | Genji dies sometime during the next 8 years, a blank in the narrative. |

| *Kaoru's Age* | *Events and Time (lunar month and day)* |
|----|----|
| 20 | Kaoru first learns of the Eighth Prince. |
| 22 | Kaoru's *kaimami* of Ōigimi (age 24) and Nakanokimi (age 22) at Uji. |
| | Bennokimi tells Kaoru the secret of his birth. |
| | Kaoru tells Niou about the Uji princesses. |
| | Kaoru promises the Eighth Prince to be his daughters' guardian (X.5, 6). |

| 23 | On his return from Hatsuse to the capital, Niou stops at Uji (II.20). |
| | Kaoru and Niou court the Uji princesses. |
| | Death of the Eighth Prince (about age 60) (VIII.20). |
| 24 | Kaoru and Ōigimi in the Eighth Prince's chapel. |
| | Nakanokimi becomes Niou's wife. |
| | Ōigimi begins to starve herself. |
| | **Ōigimi's lethal crisis (age 26) does not involve spirit possession.** |
| 25 | Nakanokimi moves to Niou's Nijō-in (II.7). |
| | Nakanokimi tells Kaoru about the existence of Ukifune (about age 20). |
| 26 | Nakanokimi gives birth to Niou's son (II). |
| | Kaoru marries the Second Princess (age 16) (II). |
| | Kaoru obtains possession of Kashiwagi's flute. |
| | Kaoru's *kaimami* of Ukifune on the Uji Bridge (end of IV). |
| | Niou's forbidden encounter with Ukifune at the Nijō-in. |
| | Kaoru abducts Ukifune from the Eastern Cottage to Uji (IX.13). |
| 27 | Niou and Kaoru compete over bringing Ukifune to the capital. |
| | Ukifune despairs over her involvement with two men. |
| | Ukifune resolves to throw herself into the Uji River. |
| | Yokawa no Sōzu (over age 60) discovers Ukifune under a tree. |
| | The Sōzu and his sister (about age 50) install Ukifune at the Ono nunnery. |
| | **The Sōzu exorcizes Ukifune's possessing spirit.** |
| | Ukifune avoids a spirit marriage with the Sōzu's sister's son-in-law. |

Ukifune persuades the Sōzu to administer the tonsure (IX).

**The Sōzu cures the possessed First Princess.**

28 Ukifune at writing practice.

Kaoru consults with the Sōzu about Ukifune and vainly tries to reach Ukifune.

## Age Relationships

*Approximate Years Older than Genji*

| | | | |
|---|---|---|---|
| Aoi | 4 | Suzaku | 3 |
| Fujitsubo | 5 | Yūgao | 2 |
| Rokujō | 8 | | |

*Approximate Years Younger than Genji*

| | | | |
|---|---|---|---|
| Akashi | 9 | Ōigimi | 45 |
| Akashi daughter | 28 | Reizei | 18 |
| Akikonomu | 10 | Tamakazura | 14 |
| Kaoru | 48 | Third Princess | 26 |
| Kashiwagi | 16 | Ukifune | 52 |
| Murasaki | 8 | Yūgiri | 21 |
| Niou | 46 | | |

## Note

1. This *Genji* chronology *(toshidate)* follows Suzuki Kazuo, "*Genji monogatari* nenpu/keizu," in Akiyama Ken, ed., *Genji monogatari jiten* (Gakutōsha, 1989), pp. 376–394. For some variations, see Suzuki Hideo, "*Genji monogatari* toshidate," in Akiyama Ken, ed., *Genji monogatari hikkei I* (Gakutōsha, 1978), pp. 127–137; Takahashi Kazuo, *Genji monogatari no shudai to kōsō* (Ōfūsha, 1971), pp. 154–186. For a discussion of problems in *toshidate* scholarship, see Aileen Gatten, "Three Problems in the Text of 'Ukifune'," in Andrew Pekarik, ed., *Ukifune: Love in The Tale of Genji* (New York: Columbia University Press, 1982), pp. 94–102.

# Appendix B
## Genealogical Charts

### Key to the Figures

| | | | | |
|---|---|---|---|---|
| ═══════ | marriage | – – – – | illicit; unrecognized offspring |
| = = = = | affair | ▬.▬.▬ | putative |
| ◆◆◆◆◆ | adultery | +++++ | foster; adopted |
| ◇◇◇◇◇ | (affinal) incest | ~~~~~ | male rivalry |
| < > | intended (adultery, incest, etc.) | ••••• | substitutes |

| | | | | |
|---|---|---|---|---|
| △ ○ | male, female | ❖ | tonsure |
| ▲ ● | deceased | ✳ | spirit possession |
| KK | principal wife (*kita no kata*) | ✝ | suicide |
| MR; ML | Minister of the Right / Left | (✝) | thwarted suicide |
| CP | Crown Prince | ? / ( ) | unverifiable |
| E / -In | Emperor/Retired Emperor | | |

*Note:* The genealogical charts in this appendix are selective and cover only the characters and relationships most relevant to each case of possession. Superscript numbers refer to *Genji* chapters in which crucial events are recorded.

Characters are boxed to highlight their significance or to enhance clarity in graphic design.

# Figure 1: Yūgao

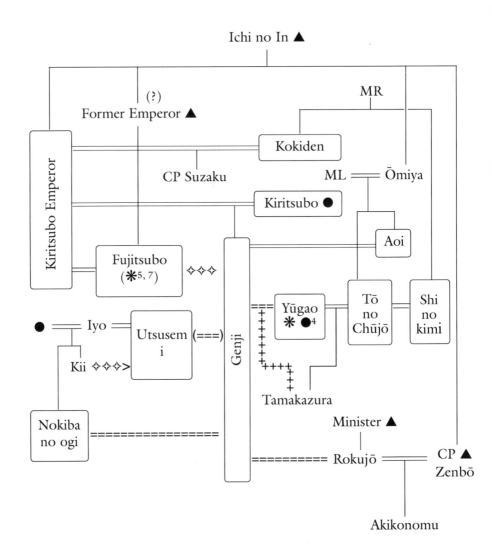

# Figure 2: Aoi

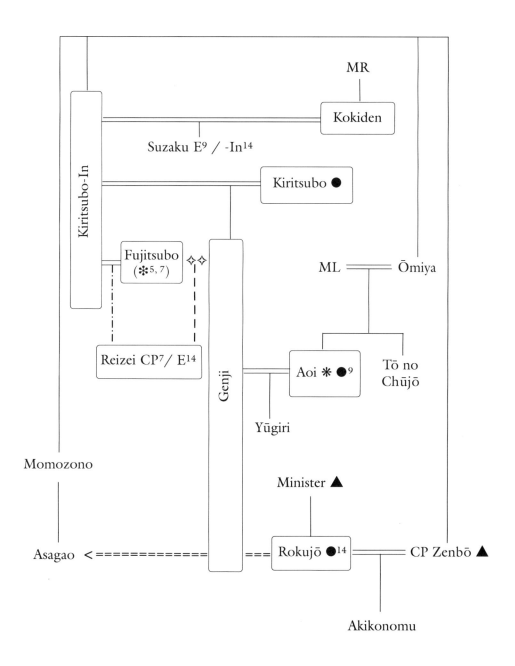

# Figure 3: Murasaki

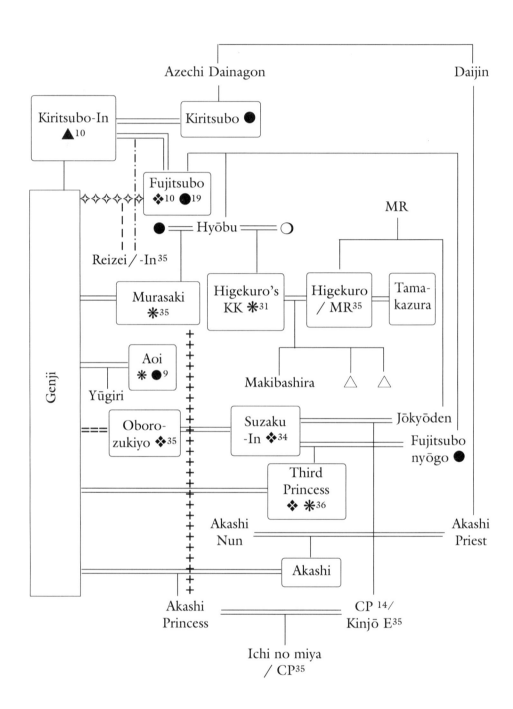

# Figure 4: The Third Princess

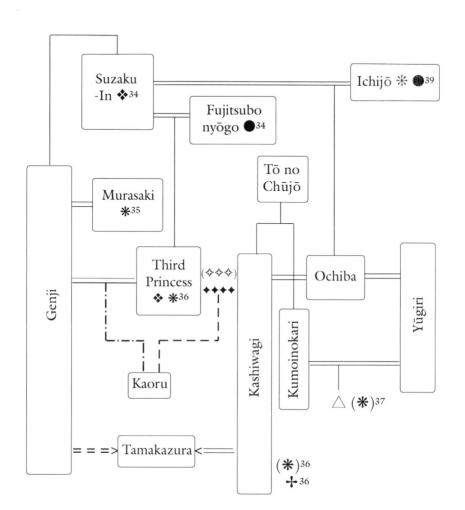

# Figure 5: Ukifune

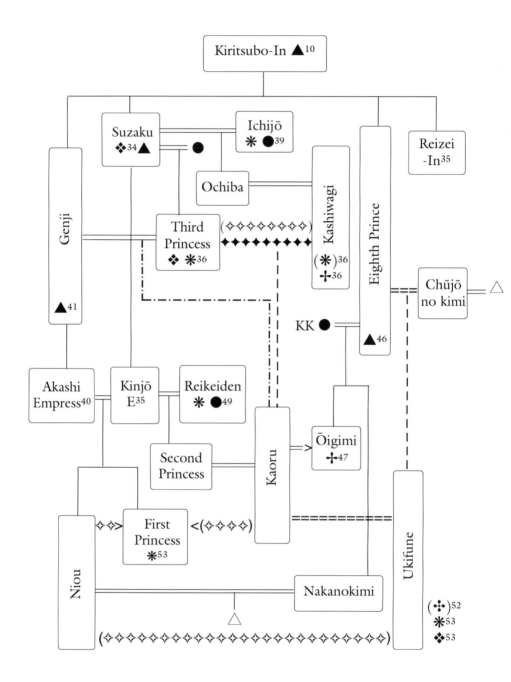

# Figure 6: Chūjō no kimi
## (Ukifune's Mother)

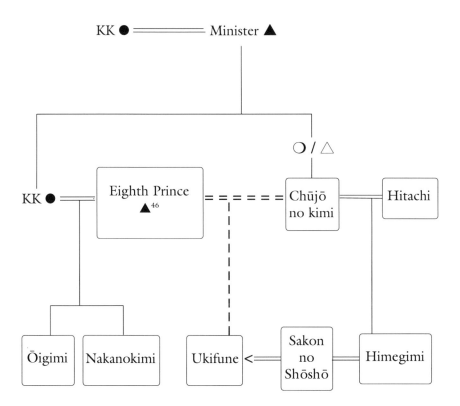

# Figure 7: Bennokimi/Uji *azari*

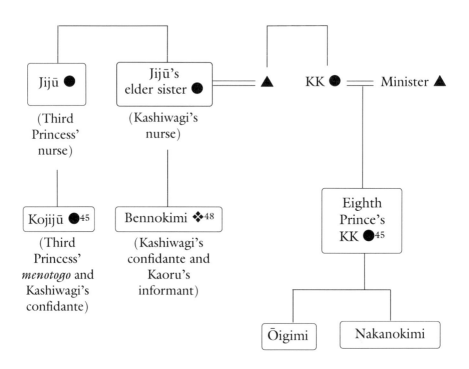

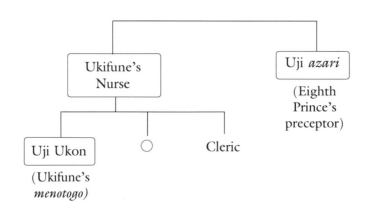

# Figure 8: Yokawa no sōzu
## (Bishop of Yokawa)

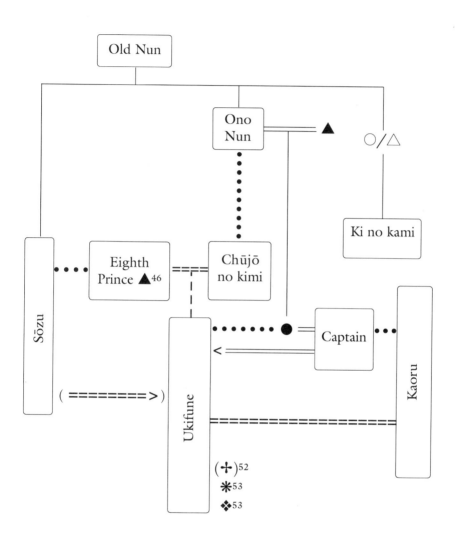

# Abbreviations

The following abbreviations are used in the notes and bibliography:

*GMH*    *Genji monogatari hyōshaku*. Edited and annotated by Tamagami Takuya. Kadokawa shoten, 1964–1968. 12 vols.

*KGMS*    *Kōza Genji monogatari no sekai*. Edited by Akiyama Ken, Kimura Masanori, and Shimizu Yoshiko. Yūhikaku, 1980–1984. 9 vols.

NKBT    Nihon koten bungaku taikei. Iwanami shoten. 1957–1968. 102 vols.

NKBZ    Nihon koten bungaku zenshū. Shōgakukan. 1971–1976. 51 vols.

SNKBT    Shin Nihon koten bungaku taikei. Iwanami shoten. 1989–.

# Notes

For complete bibliographical information, see the bibliography. Citations from the *Genji monogatari,* in both text and notes, give the page number of the Seidensticker translation ("S") and then the Japanese volume and page number from the six-volume edition of Abe Akio, Akiyama Ken, and Imai Gen'e (vols. 12–17 in NKBZ).

## Introduction

1. *Mono no ke* are possessing evil spirits. A detailed explanation of the term and its meaning will be given in "Enter *mono no ke*," after a brief genealogy of the spirits, foreign and indigenous, from whom *mono no ke* may have descended. Since Japanese nouns like *"mono no ke"* do not distinguish between singular and plural, one must rely on the context.

2. For the complexities of the Chinese views of fiction and the equally complex Japanese assimilation of these views, see J. Thomas Harper, "Motoori Norinaga's Criticism of the *Genji monogatari:* A Study of the Background and Critical Content of His *Genji Monogatari Tama no Ogushi*" (Ph. D. diss., University of Michigan, 1971), pp. 6–28.

3. The T'ang poet Po Chü-i (J. Haku Rakuten, 772–846) became famous in Japan for his defense of poetry against the Buddhist rejection of literature as a form of worldly attachment. While condemning his "wild words and fancy phrases" *(kyōgen kigo)*, he hoped that poetry could be transformed into a means of praising the Buddha and attaining enlightenment.

4. For the implications of a male diarist's adoption of a female narrative persona on conceptions of gender, see Lynne K. Miyake, "*The Tosa Diary:* In the Interstices of Gender and Criticism," in Paul G. Schalow and Janet A. Walker, eds., *The Woman's Hand: Gender and Theory in Japanese Women's Writing* (Stanford: Stanford University Press, 1996).

5. Among the female authors assumed for the *Eiga monogatari* are Akazome Emon (fl. 976–1041), Idewa no Ben, and an unknown court lady.

6. John J. Winkler, *The Constraints of Desire: The Anthropology of Sex and Gender in Ancient Greece* (New York: Routledge, 1990), p. 12; for an extensive discussion, see chap. 6, "Double Consciousness in Sappho's Lyrics," pp. 162–187.

7. The author of the *Genji* was a Fujiwara but her given name is not known. Her sobriquet mingles fiction and fact: it is composed of an outstanding female character (Murasaki) from the *Genji* and the office her father held (Shikibu). For details on the author and *Genji* texts, see Haruo Shirane, *The Bridge of Dreams: A Poetics of "The Tale of Genji"* (Stanford: Stanford University Press, 1987), app. B, pp. 215–226.

8. Michele Marra, *The Aesthetics of Discontent: Politics and Reclusion in Medieval Japanese Literature* (Honolulu: University of Hawai'i Press, 1991), p. 176, n. 1.

9. Peter Nickerson, "The Meaning of Matrilocality: Kinship, Property, and Politics in Mid-Heian," *Monumenta Nipponica* 48(4) (Winter 1993):460.

10. See Mimi Hall Yiengpruksawan, "What's in a Name? Fujiwara Fixation in Japanese Cultural History," *Monumenta Nipponica* 49(4) (Winter 1994):423–429, 448–453.

11. See William H. McCullough and Helen Craig McCullough, trans., *A Tale of Flowering Fortunes: Annals of Japanese Aristocratic Life in the Heian Period* (Stanford: Stanford University Press, 1980), pp. 5–6.

12. Ibid., p. 7. Suzanne Gay discusses the issue of using literary texts to supplement historical source materials in her "Introduction" to Wakita Haruko, "Marriage and Property in Premodern Japan: From the Perspective of Women's History," *Journal of Japanese Studies* 10(1) (Winter 1984):73–76.

13. Claude Lévi-Strauss, *The View from Afar,* trans. Joachim Neugroschel and Phoebe Hoss (New York: Basic Books, 1985), p. 73.

14. The subtitle to Fujimoto Katsuyoshi's *Genji monogatari no "mono no ke"* (Kasama shoin, 1994) is *Bungaku to kiroku no hazama,* which translates as "the gap between literature and factual accounts."

15. Winkler, *The Constraints of Desire,* p. 98. See also Walter Burkert's enormously influential *Homo Necans: The Anthropology of Ancient Greek Sacrificial Ritual and Myth,* trans. Peter Bing (Berkeley: University of California Press, 1983). Originally published in 1972.

16. For an overview of *Genji* scholarship, see Norma Field, *The Splendor of Longing in The Tale of Genji* (Princeton: Princeton University Press, 1987), pp. 3–17; and Shirane, *The Bridge of Dreams,* pp. xv–xxiii.

17. Burkert has defined the two basic characteristics of ritual behavior as "repetition and theatrical exaggeration"; *Homo Necans,* p. 23.

18. My analysis builds upon and complements Janet Goff's *Noh Drama and The Tale of Genji: The Art of Allusion in Fifteen Classical Plays* (Princeton: Princeton University Press, 1991).

19. In Western scholarship, prefatory lists of principal characters describing just a few kinship relations have been more common than the elaborate genealogical charts indispensable to Japanese scholarly editions, modern translations, and critical studies of the *Genji*. In my study, diagrams of the complex pattern of kinship in the *Genji* are essential to elucidating the characters' subversion of their society's sophisticated rules governing love, marriage, and power.

## Enter *mono no ke*

1. For the overwhelming importance of art in the lives of the Heian aristocracy, see Ivan Morris, *The World of the Shining Prince: Court Life in Ancient Japan* (Harmondsworth: Peregrine, 1985), pp. 183–210. See also G. B. Sansom's dictum about Heian aristocratic court life: "religion became an art and art a religion"; *Japan: A Short Cultural History* (Stanford: Stanford University Press, 1978), p. 241.

2. Helen McCullough, "Social and Psychological Aspects of Heian Ritual and Ceremony," in Ōta Saburō and Fukuda Rikutarō, eds., *Studies on Japanese Culture* (Tokyo: Japan PEN Club, 1973), 2:278. The phrase "rule of taste" is Sir George Sansom's; see the title of his ninth chapter (about Heian court culture) in *A History of Japan to 1334* (Stanford: Stanford University Press, 1958).

3. In the *Kojiki,* the deity Izanagi descends to the underworld of Yomi to bring back his sister and wife Izanami. As in the Greek myth of Orpheus and Euridice, however, the impatient glimpse stolen despite the conditions set for the release of the dead beloved ruins the heroic effort. If one can speak of a mythic paradigm of *kaimami* in this example, as Hirota Osamu has, then the forbidden act entails not only a male violation of the female sphere but violent female retribution against the male. See Hirota, "*Genji monogatari* ni okeru yōshiki to shite no kaimami," in Tsuchihashi Yutaka and Hirokawa Katsumi, eds., *Kodai bungaku no yōshiki to kinō* (Ōfūsha, 1988), p. 178.

4. William H. McCullough devotes barely two pages to the important issue of incest in his extensive study "Japanese Marriage Institutions in the Heian Period," *Harvard Journal of Asiatic Studies* 27 (1967):135–136. The regulations drawn up in the *Engi-shiki* (927; Procedures of the Engi Era, 901–922) in response to the eighth-century Taihō and Yōrō civil and penal codes mention under "earthly offenses *(kuni-tsu-tsumi)*" the "offense of violating one's own mother, offense of violating one's child." To this Felicia Gressitt Bock adds "incest between children of the same mother, though marriage of children of different mothers but one father was not taboo"; Bock, trans., *Engi-shiki: Procedures of the Engi Era. Books I–IV* (Tokyo: Sophia University, 1970), p. 3. See also Donald L. Philippi, trans., *Kojiki* (Tokyo: Princeton University Press and University of Tokyo Press, 1969), p. 213, n. 1; p. 259, n. 8; p. 333, n. 2. Karl Florenz also lists under "earthly

offences" in ancient ritual prayers *(norito)* the "offence of [the father's] cohabitation with his stepdaughter" and "the offence of [a man's] cohabitation with his mother-in-law"; "Ancient Japanese Rituals," *Transactions of the Asiatic Society of Japan* 27(1) (1899):61. See also Donald L. Philippi, trans., *Norito: A Translation of the Ancient Japanese Ritual Prayers* (Princeton: Princeton University Press, 1990), p. 46. Concerning "the looseness observed in many Heian marriage ties" and the "ease and informality of Heian divorce," see W. H. McCullough, "Japanese Marriage Institutions in the Heian Period," pp. 124, 139.

5. I am indebted to Robert J. Smith for his epistolary insights.

6. I am grateful to the anthropological internet of Deborah B. Gewertz—especially to Denise O'Brien and Paul B. Roscoe for their detailed and helpful comments.

7. Wakita Haruko has emphasized the "human anguish," emotional "insecurity," and "anxiety" caused women by polygyny; Wakita, "Marriage and Property in Premodern Japan: From the Perspective of Women's History," *Journal of Japanese Studies* 10(1) (Winter 1984):84.

8. In Sung China, as in Heian Japan, jealousy was perceived to be an "illness or possession." Patricia Buckley Ebrey, *The Inner Quarters: Marriage and the Lives of Chinese Women in the Sung Period* (Berkeley: University of California Press, 1993), pp. 166, 263. Unlike Heian women, however, Sung women had no literature comparable to Heian women's diaries or *monogatari* to consult for soothing their emotional turmoil. Ebrey points out that, in order to control domestic conflict, Confucian-minded men tolerated their jealousy-stricken wives' Buddhist leanings; ibid., pp. 170–171.

9. Hitomi Tonomura points out that Mujū Ichien's *Tsuma kagami* (Mirror for Women; 1300) ranks jealousy second among a woman's seven vices, based on a seventh-century Chinese text; see Tonomura, "Black Hair and Red Trousers: Gendering the Flesh in Medieval Japan," *American Historical Review* 99(1) (February 1994):140, n. 47.

10. Susan R. Bordo, "The Body and the Reproduction of Femininity: A Feminist Appropriation of Foucault," in Alison M. Jaggar and Susan R. Bordo, eds., *Gender/Body /Knowledge: Feminist Reconstructions of Being and Knowing* (New Brunswick: Rutgers University Press, 1989), p. 21.

11. For a discussion of "The Diaristic Form of Female Discontent" with focus on Lady Nijō's *Towazugatari* (The Unrequested Story; late thirteenth century), see Michele Marra, *The Aesthetics of Discontent: Politics and Reclusion in Medieval Japanese Literature* (Honolulu: University of Hawai'i Press, 1991), pp. 101–126.

12. The title of *kitamandokoro* was used in lieu of *kitanokata* for the wives of *sesshō* (regent) or *kampaku* (chancellor); see W. H. McCullough, "Japanese Marriage Institutions in the Heian Period," p. 129.

13. H. Paul Varley takes a different view of the author of the *Kagerō*

*nikki:* she is "driven to a neurotic outpouring of self-pity and absorption with her own grievances to the exclusion of any consideration for the feelings of others." Varley, *Japanese Culture: A Short History* (New York: Holt, Rinehart & Winston, 1977), p. 45.

14. Edward Seidensticker, trans., *The Gossamer Years (Kagerō Nikki): The Diary of a Noblewoman of Heian Japan* (Tokyo: Tuttle, 1988), p. 118; NKBT 20:251. Sonja Arntzen has prepared a new translation that tries to capture "a woman's syntax, a distinctive structure for a woman's voice"; Arntzen, "Translating Difference in the *Kagerō Nikki,*" *Japan Foundation Newsletter* 21(3) (November 1993):16.

15. Seidensticker, trans., *The Gossamer Years,* p. 33. The translator has chosen italics to set off the detached voice of the opening statement from the more intimate tone of the rest of the journal; NKBT 20:109.

16. Ibid., p. 69. The last sentence quoted refers to the title by which the journal is known; NKBT 20:170–171.

17. Ibid., p. 33; (my roman). NKBT 20:109.

18. The etymology of the term *"monogatari"* is given in H. Richard Okada, *Figures of Resistance: Language, Poetry, and Narrating in The Tale of Genji and Other Mid-Heian Texts* (Durham, N.C.: Duke University Press, 1992), p. 295, n. 3. Specifically, he notes that in the *Genji* the term "is employed strategically to articulate the seemingly 'marginal' aspects of life." See also Takahashi Tōru, *Monogatari to e no enkinhō* (Perikansha, 1991), p. 308.

19. Michitsuna no haha herself was stricken with *mono no ke* at least once. See Seidensticker, trans., *The Gossamer Years,* p. 50; NKBT 20:137.

20. Haruo Shirane, *The Bridge of Dreams: A Poetics of "The Tale of Genji"* (Stanford: Stanford University Press, 1987), p. 30.

21. Ibid., p. 114. These emotions, Shirane goes on to say, are aroused mainly by "jealousy and the resentment caused by polygamy," that is, polygyny; see my note 24 below.

22. See Takahashi, *Monogatari to e no enkinhō,* pp. 348–352.

23. Susan Bordo, *Unbearable Weight: Feminism, Western Culture, and the Body* (Berkeley: University of California Press, 1993), p. 141.

24. More often than not, the Heian marital system is mistakenly defined by the term "polygamy," referring to marriages in which either sex may have more than one spouse. Polygyny, by contrast, refers to men's exclusive privilege of having more than one female spouse at one time. The Japanese term for polygyny is *ippu tasai:* literally, one husband, many wives.

25. See Ioan Myrddin Lewis, *Ecstatic Religion: An Anthropological Study of Spirit Possession and Shamanism* (Harmondsworth: Penguin, 1971), p. 176.

26. Ibid., p. 32.

27. See Victor Turner, "Liminality and the Performative Genres," in

John J. MacAloon, ed., *Rite, Drama, Festival, Spectacle: Rehearsals Toward a Theory of Cultural Performance* (Philadelphia: Institute for the Study of Human Issues, 1984), pp. 19–41, with specific reference to the *Genji monogatari*. See also Victor Turner, *The Ritual Process: Structure and Anti-Structure* (Chicago: Aldine, 1969), pp. 166–203.

28. See Victor Turner, *On the Edge of the Bush: Anthropology as Experience,* ed. L. B. Turner (Tucson: University of Arizona Press, 1985), p. 292.

29. As one anthropologist reports about the Sri Lankan pattern of alternatives to spirit possession, the "continued use of repression . . . leads to certain expectable character traits in the female population: a propensity to hysteria, anorexia, widespread hypochondriacal tendencies, and somatization of conflicts. . . . If some of the modal psychological problems are intensified, or new stresses have to be coped with, then I believe conditions favorable to spirit possession may arise." Gananath Obeyesekere, "Psychocultural Exegesis of a Case of Spirit Possession in Sri Lanka," in Vincent Crapanzano and Vivian Garrison, eds., *Case Studies in Spirit Possession* (New York: Wiley, 1977), p. 243.

30. Lewis, *Ecstatic Religion,* p. 86: "Neither sex loses face and the official ideology of male supremacy is preserved." Note also Clifford Geertz on the aspect of the "status bloodbath" symbolized by Balinese cockfighting: "*But no one's status really changes.*" Geertz, "Deep Play: Notes on the Balinese Cockfight," in *The Interpretation of Cultures: Selected Essays by Clifford Geertz* (New York: Basic Books, 1973), pp. 436, 443.

31. "Ritual is transformative, ceremony confirmatory." Victor Turner, *The Forest of Symbols: Aspects of Ndembu Ritual* (Ithaca: Cornell University Press, 1981), p. 95.

32. In antiquity, possession was considered mysterious, but the possessed person was not deemed abnormal. As one classicist has noted, a possessed person "might act very strangely and display a kind of *mania,* but was neither regarded as simply 'crazy' nor dismissed as incapable of functioning within ancient Greek society." Plato and Socrates appear to have derived a sense of "heightened awareness and eloquence" as well as unusual forms of "insight" from their possessions. See W. R. Connor, "Seized by the Nymphs: Nympholepsy and Symbolic Expression in Classical Greece," *Classical Antiquity* 7(2) (October 1988):156–157, 158, 159. Antiquity was undoubtedly more open-minded toward altered states of consciousness and more tolerant of the frenzy sometimes associated with possessions than was medieval Europe. It was not until the late nineteenth century that J.-M. Charcot, acquitting the possessed of accusations of madness, diagnosed their emotional disorder as neurosis. See Clarke Garrett, *Spirit Possession and Popular Religion: From the Camisards to the Shakers* (Baltimore: Johns Hopkins University Press, 1987), p. 3. The consensus among anthropologists and psychologists is that spirit possession is neither a primitive practice of superstitious peoples nor a symptom of psychosis.

33. Morris, *The World of the Shining Prince,* p. 147, n. 18; p. 147.

34. Arthur Waley, "Review of *Ivan Morris's The World of the Shining Prince,*" in Ivan Morris, ed., *Madly Singing in the Mountains: An Appreciation and Anthology of Arthur Waley* (New York: Walker & Co., 1970), pp. 375–376.

35. Raymond H. Prince refers to spirit possession as "closely akin to . . . modern psychotherapy"; see his "Foreword" to Crapanzano and Garrison, eds., *Case Studies in Spirit Possession,* p. xiii. Prince also notes the shortcomings of exorcism and psychoanalysis as therapeutic methods.

36. Morris, *The World of the Shining Prince,* pp. 148–149.

37. William H. McCullough, "Spirit Possession in the Heian Period," in Ōta Saburō and Fukuda Rikutarō, eds., *Studies on Japanese Culture* (Tokyo: Japan PEN Club, 1973), 1:97–98. McCullough defines etiological possession as "possession, or spirit intrusion, as a cause of disease. . . . Some or all kinds of disease are identified etiologically as originating in spirit possession, whose only principal observable effect is the disease itself"; ibid., p. 94.

38. Ibid.

39. Although *mono no ke* do not appear in the Japanese myths, there is trance behavior originating in divine possession. This phenomenon bears no trace of mental or physical illness. The first *mono no ke*—recorded in Chinese—appear in one of the *rikkokushi* (Six National Histories): the *Shoku Nihon kōki* (Later Records of Japan Continued; 869), covering Nimmyō's reign (833–850). Closer to shamanism than to spirit possession, the patterns of altered states of consciousness dramatized in Japanese myth foreshadowed the literary narratives of male/female conflict between Heian courtiers and their screened and closeted wives. In the myth, Amaterasu, the sun goddess, is driven into a cave by the insults of her younger brother Susanoo and the entire world is cast into darkness. Ama no Uzume's divinely inspired erotic dance, which brings the goddess out of darkness, resembles the medium's trance. In this sense, the interplay between Amaterasu Ōmikami and Ama no Uzume constitutes the *Ur-Szene* of an indigenous Japanese response to spirit possession, one that employs female mediums in the tradition of Japanese shamanism rather than Buddhism's male exorcists. See Allan Grapard, "Visions of Excess and Excesses of Vision—Women and Transgression in Japanese Myth," *Japanese Journal of Religious Studies* 18(1) (March 1991):13.

40. Janice Boddy, *Wombs and Alien Spirits: Women, Men, and the Zār Cult in Northern Sudan* (Madison: University of Wisconsin Press, 1989), p. 140.

41. See Carmen Blacker, *The Catalpa Bow: A Study of Shamanistic Practices in Japan* (London: Allen & Unwin, 1975), p. 313.

42. Jane Belo, *Trance in Bali* (New York: Columbia University Press, 1960), p. 6. See also *Trance and Dance in Bali,* filmed by Gregory Bateson and Margaret Mead between 1936 and 1939 and released in 1952 by New York University. For the symbolic associations of the *kris* or *keris* with male

power, see Clive S. Kessler, "Conflict and Sovereignty in Kelantanese Malay Spirit Seances," in Crapanzano and Garrison, *Case Studies in Spirit Possession,* pp. 309–310.

43. Ioan Myrddin Lewis, *Social Anthropology in Perspective: The Relevance of Social Anthropology* (Harmondsworth: Penguin, 1976), p. 89.

44. Lewis, *Ecstatic Religion,* p. 118.

45. Blacker, *The Catalpa Bow,* p. 57.

46. This fundamental difference in the Japanese leniency to the possessor has been noted and used to explain, for example, Genji's continuing (and surprisingly good) relations with Rokujō no miyasudokoro, whose living spirit is generally assumed to be responsible for Aoi's death, sometimes also for Yūgao's death.

47. See Blacker, *The Catalpa Bow,* chap. 15, "Exorcism." For the overwrought argument that the *Genji monogatari* is an expression of indigenous shamanism, with the hero on an ill-fated "Seelenreise," see Wilhelm E. Mühlmann, *Die Metamorphose der Frau: Weiblicher Schamanismus und Dichtung* (Berlin: Dietrich Reimer Verlag, 1984), p. 186; see also pp. 183–198.

48. See Lewis, *Ecstatic Religion,* pp. 49–57.

49. Female shamans in Japan acted as both diviners and healers; see Kyoko Motomochi Nakamura, trans., *Miraculous Stories from the Japanese Buddhist Tradition: The Nihon ryōiki of the Monk Kyōkai* (Cambridge, Mass.: Harvard University Press, 1973), p. 83.

50. See Gary L. Ebersole, *Ritual Poetry and the Politics of Death in Early Japan* (Princeton: Princeton University Press, 1989), p. 145.

51. To the present day, this tradition lives on through the blind mediums *(itako)* who gather at Osorezan in northern Honshu for the July Jizō-bon, dedicated to memorial services *(kuyō)* for the dead, especially for dead children *(mizuko)*. Another group akin to *miko* was the *bikuni*, female troupes of wandering professional entertainers who originally specialized in a mixture of religious and amorous behavior in the Kamakura and Muromachi periods. The tradition of female shamanism expired when the *bikuni* turned increasingly to prostitution in the Edo period. See Barbara Ruch, "Medieval Jongleurs and the Making of a National Literature," in John Whitney Hall and Toyoda Takeshi, eds., *Japan in the Muromachi Age* (Berkeley: University of California Press, 1977), pp. 279–309.

52. For the declining influence of *miko* and their gradual marginalization, indeed their ostracism, beginning as early as the tenth century, see Wakita, "Marriage and Property in Premodern Japan," pp. 94–95; Nakamura cites the *Shoku Nihongi* (The Nihongi Continued; national history covering 697–791) for the exile of seventeen diviners; see *Miraculous Stories,* p. 83, n. 124.

53. Traugott Konstantin Oesterreich, *Possession, Demoniacal and Other, among Primitive Races, in Antiquity, the Middle Ages and Modern Times,*

trans. D. Ibberson (New Hyde Park: University Books, 1966); originally published in 1921.

54. In Heian Japan, physical exertion, especially in pregnancy and childbirth, could easily precipitate possession; see McCullough, "Spirit Possession in the Heian Period," p. 94. For similar connections between social customs, psychological stress, and nutritional deficiencies, see Judith D. Gussler, "Social Change, Ecology, and Spirit Possession Among the South African Nguni," in Erika Bourguignon, ed., *Religion, Altered States of Consciousness and Social Change* (Columbus: Ohio State University Press, 1973), pp. 88–126.

55. The classic texts by Michel Foucault are *Histoire de la Folie à l'âge classique* (Paris: Gallimard, 1972) and *Surveiller et Punir: naissance de la prison* (Paris: Gallimard, 1975).

56. In Edward G. Seidensticker's translation of the *Genji*, the woman traditionally known as "Yūgao" appears as "Evening Faces."

57. Donald Harper, for example, notes that "incantatory name-calling" or "simply knowing a demon's name and shouting it [served as] the most common magical device" in the third-century B.C. Shui-hu-ti demonography as well as the Six Dynasties *Pai tse t'u*. Harper, "A Chinese Demonography of the Third Century B.C.," *Harvard Journal of Asiatic Studies* 45(2) (December 1985):494.

58. Erika Bourguignon names three kinds of societies that broadly define the possible evaluation and treatment of possession: "(1) societies where the behavior is desired and often intentionally induced, (2) societies where the behavior is feared and vigorous efforts are made to drive out the spirit supposed to be in residence (often with physical violence) and (3), perhaps most interesting, societies where the initial, spontaneous behavior is considered deviant and perhaps sick, and where a cure involves bringing about possession trance in a controlled setting." Bourguignon, *Possession* (San Francisco: Chandler & Sharp, 1976), p. 9. The third category applies to spirit possession in the *Genji*. For a more detailed study of the sociopolitical context of spirit possession, see Yoshida Teigo, *Nihon no tsukimono: shakai jinruigakuteki kōsatsu* (Chūō Kōronsha, 1972); Hirokawa Katsumi, ed., *Tsukimono—"tatarigami" to majinai* (Sōseki, 1982).

59. The word "drama" is more than a dead metaphor. Indeed, a number of scholars have seen analogies between spirit possession and theatrical performance. A specialist on nympholepsy in ancient Greece cites Xenophon (*Symposium* 1.9.10) in support of the notion that possession, "real or feigned, was often good theater"; Connor, "Seized by the Nymphs," p. 158. A historian of popular religion traces the history of spirit possession from the Camisards of southeastern France to the Shakers of New England and describes the phenomenon as "sacred theater"; Garrett, *Spirit Possession and Popular Religion*, p. 5. Still another scholar likens Japanese *nō* theater to "an ancient shamanistic ritual of ecstasis and possession"; Thomas Immoos, "The Birth of the Jap-

anese Theater," *Monumenta Nipponica* 24(4) (1969):411. Carmen Blacker also agrees that *nō* plays, "in which a supernatural being is manifested, are in themselves concealed shamanic rituals"; Blacker, *The Catalpa Bow*, p. 31. For less religiously motivated individuals, possession is secular theater rather than "sacred theater," but it nonetheless provides a ritualized stage for shared public experience.

60. Walter Burkert has remarked about sacrificial ritual that "the strange and extraordinary events that the participant in the sacrifice is forced to witness are all the more intense because they are left undiscussed"; *Homo Necans*, p. 3.

61. William H. McCullough and Helen Craig McCullough, trans., *A Tale of Flowering Fortunes: Annals of Japanese Aristocratic Life in the Heian Period* (Stanford: Stanford University Press, 1980), pp. 436–437; NKBT 75:369–370. Yorimichi's possession by his beloved wife's father (Prince Tomohira) protests the constraints imposed by hierarchy and arranged marriages following the imperial wish. His target is taboo—namely, the Emperor Sanjō, who wants Yorimichi to marry his daughter Shishi. Spirit possession thus expresses the subordinate Yorimichi's protest against this marriage.

62. In China, as Harper has observed, "disheveled hair was a demonic trait and thus great importance was attached to the binding of the hair." Specifically, in "Han and pre-Han literature . . . long, loose hair . . . is characteristic both of demonic apparitions and of people who are wild or possessed." Harper, "A Chinese Demonography," p. 476 and n. 46. In the *Genji*, more often than not, groaning, wailing, writhing, and flailing emanate from a female medium in trance (as in the mediums attending Aoi and Murasaki) rather than the possessed person proper, but *mono no ke* could also erupt from the possessed person's own body and produce violent trembling (as in Yūgao's case) or speaking in the voice of another (as in the example of Aoi).

63. "The women acting as mediums" in the case of Empress Shōshi's possession are also referred to simply as *"hitobito"* in the *Murasaki Shikibu Nikki;* see Richard Bowring, trans., *Murasaki Shikibu: Her Diary and Poetic Memoirs* (Princeton: Princeton University Press, 1982), pp. 51, 57; NKBT 19:448, 451.

64. *GMH* 7:427. Blacker, relying on Waley's translation (*The Tale of Genji*, pp. 663–665), takes the medium to be a "small boy." Blacker, *The Catalpa Bow*, p. 300.

65. McCullough and McCullough, trans., *A Tale of Flowering Fortunes,* p. 612; NKBT 76:133. Norimichi (996–1075) was the son of Fujiwara Michinaga (966–1027).

66. Vincent Crapanzano sees the spirit's movement as exclusively centripetal; see his informative article on "Spirit Possession" in Mircea Eliade, ed., *The Encyclopedia of Religion* (New York: Macmillan, 1987), 14:14.

67. The collective unconscious I refer to here, unlike Jung's, is the product of the psychological dynamics of a specific situation in a specific culture.

68. It is a striking gender-related feature in the *Genji* that, with arguable exceptions, only women are possessed. Yet it appears that in Heian Japan the subjects of spirit possession were evidently not encouraged by female support groups, as in some other cultures, to join a "cult of affliction" (Turner, *The Ritual Process*) in which possessing spirits could be accommodated, domesticized, or internalized through adorcism, the female therapeutic equivalent to male exorcism. The term "adorcism" is employed by Luc de Heusch, "Cultes de possession et religions initiatiques de salut en Afrique" (1962); quoted in Ioan Myrddin Lewis, "Exorcism and Male Control of Religious Experience," *Ethnos* 55(1–2) (1990):26–27.

69. Ibid., p. 38.

70. Ivan Morris, trans., *The Pillow Book of Sei Shōnagon* (New York: Columbia University Press, 1967), 1:5–6; NKBT 19:48.

71. Ibid., 1:22; NKBT 19:66 (sec. 25 in this edition).

72. In section 155, "People Who Seem to Suffer" *(kurushige naru mono),* the failing exorcist suffers because he fears becoming a laughingstock; see Morris, trans., *The Pillow Book of Sei Shōnagon,* 1:161; NKBT 19:209–210 (sec. 157 in this edition).

73. *Gohō dōji* are often regarded as "anonymous guardian spirits personally attached to priests and hermits who have acquired power and holiness through the practice of austerities"; see Carmen Blacker, "The Divine Boy in Japanese Buddhism," *Asian Folklore Studies* (Tokyo) 22 (1963):77. Blacker also compares these spirit boys to the Siberian and Eskimo shaman's animal familiars. She furthermore suggests that their magic efficacy derives from being "converted demons [according to] the Lotus Sutra"; *The Catalpa Bow,* p. 180.

74. Blacker refers to this section as an unusual instance in which "the evil being was expelled not so much by the power of the priest and his spells as by the *gohō,* which the priest commanded to possess the patient and so displace the malignant influence"; "The Divine Boy," p. 81. Morris refers to *gohō dōji* as the "Guardian Demon of Buddhism"; Morris, trans., *The Pillow Book of Sei Shōnagon,* 1:22; 2:28, n. 106.

75. The preferred female gender configuration in works by women writers is not necessarily representative of the Heian period. The anonymous author of the late Heian historical narrative *Ōkagami* (The Great Mirror; undated), for example, describes Retired Emperor Kazan's (968–1008) "impressive supernatural powers" acquired through the *gohō dōji* of an ascetic monk. See Helen Craig McCullough, trans., *Ōkagami: The Great Mirror; Fujiwara Michinaga (966–1027) and His Times* (Princeton: Princeton University Press, 1980), p. 150.

76. Morris, trans., *The Pillow Book of Sei Shōnagon,* 1:264–265; NKBT 19:326–328 (sec. ippon 23).

77. The only *mono no ke* to appear in the *Yamato monogatari* (Tales of

Yamato; tenth century) becomes the cause of a powerful erotic attraction between an exorcist and a woman in trance. In episode 105 (see also episode 42), the possessed Daughter of Nakaki and the Priest Jōzō are rumored to be in love, as they indeed are. In protest of "such a society," Jōzō sequesters himself in the holy Kurama mountain but cannot shake his longing despite his austerities. Miraculously, a poem-letter from his beloved appears by his bedside. The outcome of their poetry exchange about denied love is uncertain. Yet it is unlikely to be happy, since, as "a result of this disgraceful affair," the young woman has been abandoned by her father. See Mildred M. Tahara, trans., *Tales of Yamato: A Tenth-Century Poem-Tale* (Honolulu: University Press of Hawai'i, 1980), pp. 63–64; NKBZ 8:344–345.

78. For another description of the same historic event in the *Eiga monogatari*, see McCullough and McCullough, trans., *A Tale of Flowering Fortunes*, pp. 270–273; NKBT 75:259–262.

79. Abe Toshiko has listed all the occurrrences of *"onmono no ke"* and *"mono no ke"* in the *Genji monogatari* and speculates on the reasons for honorific versus nonhonorific usage. One hypothesis about the use of an honorific prefix is to suggest the possessed person's identification with the possessor; without the honorific, illness is thought to be the cause of spirit possession. See Abe, *"Genji monogatari* no 'mono no ke,'" part 2, *Kokugo kokubun ronshū* 7 (March 1978):1–4 (list); 4–20.

80. Bowring, trans., *Murasaki Shikibu: Her Diary and Poetic Memoirs,* p. 57; NKBT 19:450–451. For this element of audience participation, as documented in the *Eiga monogatari*, see W. H. McCullough, "Spirit Possession in the Heian Period," pp. 95–96. For the debate about whether the defeated is an exorcist or a medium, see Bowring, trans., *Murasaki Shikibu: Her Diary and Poetic Memoirs*, p. 54, n. 13, on "He was thrown to the ground by evil spirits."

81. Sei Shōnagon also exposes the exorcist's vanity and self-congratulatory manner in section 178, entitled "People Who Look Pleased with Themselves" *(shitari kao naru mono):* "An exorcist who has succeeded in bringing a very stubborn spirit under control." Morris, trans., *The Pillow Book of Sei Shōnagon,* 1:183; NKBT 19:235 (sec. 185 in this edition).

82. For the exact prescription to combat demonic afflictions through "a type of recipe literature," see Harper, "A Chinese Demonography," p. 494.

83. Ibid., pp. 478–479. Prophylactic body postures and gestures are described on pp. 483–490.

84. W. H. McCullough, "Spirit Possession in the Heian Period," p. 98.

85. A history of important public figures' evil spirits is given in Herbert E. Plutschow, *Chaos and Cosmos: Ritual in Early and Medieval Japanese Literature* (Leiden: Brill, 1990), pp. 203–216.

86. See Alvin P. Cohen, "Completing the Business of Life: The Vengeful Dead in Chinese Folk Religion," in *Folk Culture: Folkways in Religion, Gods,*

*Spirits, and Men* (Cuttack, India: Institute of Oriental and Orissan Studies, 1983), 2:59–66.

87. Fear of incomplete pacification of Michizane's angry spirit kept the Kitano shrine from formal recognition by the government for forty years; for a detailed account of Michizane's transformation into a deity *(tenjin)*, see Robert Borgen, *Sugawara no Michizane and the Early Heian Court* (Cambridge, Mass.: Harvard University Press, 1986), pp. 308–325.

88. Morris, *The World of the Shining Prince*, p. 152. Similarly, Seidensticker, in the Introduction to his "retranslation" of the tenth-century *Kagerō Nikki*, ridicules the syncretism of Heian aristocrats who "found it not in the least uncomfortable to harbor a most incoherent mishmash of Shinto, Buddhism, Confucianism, necromancy, and witchcraft"; Seidensticker, trans., *The Gossamer Years*, p. 17.

89. Blacker, *The Catalpa Bow*, p. 33.

90. See Cohen, "The Avenging Ghost," pp. 102–111.

91. For a meticulous history of *mono no ke*, their absence and their presence, in early Japanese literature, see Abe, "*Genji monogatari* no 'mono no ke,' " part 1, *Kokugo kokubun ronshū* 6 (February 1977):24–36.

92. Ebersole, *Ritual Poetry and the Politics of Death in Early Japan*, p. 159. See also Tanigawa Ken'ichi, "Yōkai kigen kō," in Tanigawa Ken'ichi, ed., *Nihon no yōkai*, Bessatsu taiyō, no. 57 (Heibonsha, Spring 1987), p. 19.

93. This information about *mono* and *mono no ke* has been gleaned from the entries in dictionaries as well as special *Kokubungaku* issues about the *Genji monogatari*. A most useful and elaborate genealogy of *mono no ke* in the *Genji* and other works, including the variant spellings connoting different meanings, can be found in Fujio Tomoko, "Mono no ke no keifu," in Kokugo goishi kenkyūkai, ed., *Kokugo goishi no kenkyū* (Osaka: Izumi shoin, 1981), 2:73–100.

94. See Tanaka Sumie, "Kodai no yami ni chōryō suru: yōkai, mono no ketachi," in Tanigawa, *Nihon no yōkai*, p. 59; Kim Soon-Hee, "Murasaki Shikibu ni okeru 'mono no ke' no sekai," *Kokubungaku: kaishaku to kanshō* 53(9) (September 1988):105–109.

95. Seizures by *oni-yōkai* are referred to as *tsukimono;* for a detailed etymological discussion of this term, see Komatsu Kazuhiko, *Hyōrei shinkōron* (Arina shobō, 1984), pp. 19–29.

96. Mori Masato makes the argument that one purpose of the *setsuwa* collection was to "overwhelm the supernatural," referred to as *mono*, by calling it "by its proper name." Mori, "*Konjaku Monogatari-shū:* Supernatural Creatures and Order," trans. W. Michael Kelsey, *Japanese Journal of Religious Studies* 9(2–3) (June–September 1982):166. The classified list of demons and spirits in the *Konjaku* XXVII (secular Japanese stories about supernatural creatures) does not include *mono no ke;* see Mori, ibid., p. 162. Tonomura notes the presence of *oni* in the *Konjaku Monogatari-shū* as "liminal and

ambiguous figures, who usually appear at the borders between this and other worlds or at the boundary between night and day." Tonomura, "Black Hair and Red Trousers," p. 145.

97. See, for example, story 2:3 of *Kankyo no tomo* (A Companion in Solitude; 1222), attributed to Priest Keisei (1189–1268), translated by Rajyashree Pandey in "Women, Sexuality, and Enlightenment: *Kankyo no Tomo*," *Monumenta Nipponica* 50(3) (Autumn 1995):339–340.

98. Takahashi, *Monogatari to e no enkinhō*, p. 25; see also p. 333. Takahashi's argument first appeared in his *Genji monogatari no taii-hō* (Tōkyō Daigaku shuppankai, 1982), p. 226.

99. Fujii Sadakazu, "The Relationship Between the Romance and Religious Observances: *Genji Monogatari* as Myth," trans. W. Michael Kelsey, *Japanese Journal of Religious Studies* 9(2–3) (June–September 1982):131–133.

100. Sigmund Freud, "The Uncanny" (1919), in *The Standard Edition of the Complete Psychological Works of Sigmund Freud,* trans. James Strachey with Anna Freud (London: Hogarth Press and Institute of Psycho-Analysis, 1955), 17:224; Sigmund Freud, *Gesammelte Werke* (Frankfurt: S. Fischer, 1972), 12:235.

101. Freud, "The Uncanny," SE 17:234; *Gesammelte Werke,* 12:246.

102. Boddy cites numerous anthropologists who see possession trance as a text; see *Wombs and Alien Spirits,* pp. 148–149.

103. W. H. McCullough, "Spirit Possession in the Heian Period," p. 94.

104. Ibid., p. 96.

105. See Jean-Michel Oughourlian, *The Puppet of Desire: The Psychology of Hysteria, Possession, and Hypnosis,* trans. Eugene Webb (Stanford: Stanford University Press, 1991), pp. 145–187.

106. Boddy, *Wombs and Alien Spirits,* pp. 254–255.

107. Since the phenomenon of spirit possession can be seen as a dissociation of the self or a merging of selves, it is extremely ambiguous. As a female strategy corresponding to the male technique of substitution, spirit possession disguises the frightening spectacle of the self becoming two selves in one by displacing this transformation in a medium who represents the possessed person.

108. Richard Bowring has emphasized that the *Murasaki Shikibu shū* should be seen as "a literary work, a fictionalized life portrait"; Bowring, trans., *Murasaki Shikibu: Her Diary and Poetic Memoirs,* p. 210.

109. In her translation of the prose preface to sections 44–45, Janet Goff carefully omits all markers identifying the observer of the painting; see Goff, *Noh Drama and The Tale of Genji: The Art of Allusion in Fifteen Classical Plays* (Princeton: Princeton University Press, 1991), p. 51.

110. Goff, *Noh Drama and The Tale of Genji,* p. 51; Bowring, trans., *Murasaki Shikibu: Her Diary and Poetic Memoirs,* p. 231. For the Japanese text of sections 44–45 of the *Murasaki Shikibu shū,* see Hasegawa et al., eds., *Tosa nikki, Kagerō nikki, Murasaki Shikibu nikki, Sarashina nikki,* SNKBT

24:338. All other quotations from section 44 are from this page. The expression *"minikuki kata"* might also imply that the possessed person is drawn in an indecipherable manner; see Takeuchi Michiyo, *Murasaki Shikibu shū hyōshaku* (Ōfūsha, 1969), p. 107.

111. The editors of the SNKBT edition of the *Murasaki Shikibu shū* speculate that the author of the reply may be an older lady-in-waiting or a wet nurse; see Hasegawa et al., eds., SNKBT 24:338, n. 6.

112. Norma Field, *The Splendor of Longing in The Tale of Genji* (Princeton: Princeton University Press, 1987), p. 63.

113. Marian Ury, "A Heian Note on the Supernatural," *Journal of the Association of Teachers of Japanese* 22(2) (November 1988):189.

114. It is interesting to note that the Chinese had not only articulated a sophisticated demonology long before the Japanese but that they also engaged in indeterminable debates about the existence of spirits, as is evident in Ji Yun's (1724–1805) *Yuewei caotang biji,* a collection of tales about supernatural encounters that served "to bolster belief." Leo Tak-hung Chan, "Narrative as Argument: The *Yuewei caotang biji* and the Late Eighteenth-Century Elite Discourse on the Supernatural," *Harvard Journal of Asiatic Studies* 53(1) (June 1993):43.

115. Similarly, Donald Keene's insistence on Murasaki Shikibu's and her contemporaries' belief "in the literal existence of such spirits," apparently intended to depreciate a variety of approaches, does not further our understanding of what such beliefs might have meant. Keene softens his categorical statement by acknowledging Murasaki Shikibu's skepticism concerning the supernatural as presented in earlier Heian literary works. See Keene, *Seeds in the Heart: Japanese Literature from Earliest Times to the Late Sixteenth Century* (New York: Holt, 1993), p. 487.

116. Since there has been no challenge to the traditional view, there is no point in naming all the critics who have ever written about *mono no ke* in the *Genji*. I will cite specific critics as their views become relevant in my discussion of the major cases of spirit possession in the *Genji*. Suffice it to say for now that even Fujimoto Katsuyoshi's recent comprehensive study, *Genji monogatari no "mono no ke": bungaku to kiroku no hazama* (Kasama shoin, 1994), does not change the prevailing focus on the possessing spirit even though the critic acknowledges the necessity of paying attention to the possessed person as well as to the audience.

117. For a description of the "Azumaya I" scene, see Julia Meech-Pekarik, "The Artist's View of Ukifune," in Andrew Pekarik, ed., *Ukifune: Love in The Tale of Genji* (New York: Columbia University Press, 1982), pp. 176–178. For *Genji* illustrations generally, see Akiyama Ken and Taguchi Eiichi, eds., *Gōka "Genji-e" no sekai: Genji monogatari* (Gakken, 1988); Miyeko Murase, *Iconography of The Tale of Genji: Genji Monogatari Ekotoba* (New York: Weatherhill, 1983); Akiyama Terukazu, *Genji monogatari emaki,* in

Tanaka Ichimatsu, ed., *Shinshū Nihon emakimono zenshū*, vol. 2 (Kadokawa shoten, 1975); and Akiyama Terukazu, *Genji-e*, Nihon no Bijutsu 4.119 (Shibundō, 1976). Takahashi Tōru has explored the dynamic between *emaki* and *monogatari* perspectives in *Monogatari to e no enkinhō*.

118. In Seidensticker's translation, "The princess took out illustrations to old romances" (S:958), but the *Genji* does not specify the age of the illustrated text; it merely refers to *"e nado"* (6:66) or "paintings and such."

119. In his analysis of the "Azumaya II" scene of this scroll, Takahashi emphasizes that *nyōbō* are like shamanesses *(miko)* or *mono no ke* in their imaginative power and that Heian literature was not simply women's literature *(joryū bungaku)* but ladies-in-waiting literature *(nyōbō bungaku)*; see *Monogatari to e no enkinhō*, p. 26; see also p. 25.

120. Akiyama Terukazu has suggested that some of the artists of the twelfth-century *Genji monogatari emaki* may have been women, probably *nyōbō*; see Akiyama, "Women Painters at the Heian Court," translated and adapted by Maribeth Graybill, in Marsha Weidner, ed., *Flowering in the Shadows: Women in the History of Chinese and Japanese Painting* (Honolulu: University of Hawai'i Press, 1990), pp. 172–176.

121. Episode 147 of the *Yamato monogatari* (Tales of Yamato; ca. 950), anticipating in a curious way Ukifune's unhappy dilemma between two lovers, is quite explicit about the intense empathy between audience and fictional characters: "Someone depicted this tragic tale of long ago [about the Ikutagawa maiden] in a detailed painting and presented it to the late Empress [Fujiwara no Onshi (872–907)]. Everyone present tried to imagine themselves in the place of one of the three tragic people and composed a number of poems." Tahara, trans., *Tales of Yamato*, p. 95; see NKBZ 8:385.

122. For Ukifune's exceptional role in creating "uncommunicated poetry," see Earl Miner, "The Art of Life in the *Genji monogatari*," unpublished paper, prepared for the "World of Genji" conference (Bloomington, Indiana University, 1982), p. 36.

123. In reference to the twelfth-century *Genji monogatari emaki*, Rosenfield notes the artists' preference for a "monoscenic system of narration, the simple illustration of a single event accompanied by a section of explanatory text." John M. Rosenfield, Fumiko E. Cranston, and Edwin A. Cranston, *The Courtly Tradition in Japanese Art and Literature: Selections from the Hofer and Hyde Collections* (Tokyo: Kodansha International, 1973), p. 265.

124. Murase, *Iconography of The Tale of Genji*, p. 24. Julia Meech-Pekarik, however, cautions us not to overrate the influence of the manual on painters; see "The Artist's View of Ukifune," pp. 194–195.

### Yūgao

1. The earliest record of a *Genji-e* is found in the diary, the *Chōshū ki* (1119), by Minamoto Moritoki (1077–1136). See Miyeko Murase, *Iconogra-*

*phy of The Tale of Genji: Genji Monogatari Ekotoba* (New York: Weatherhill, 1983), p. 10; Julia Meech-Pekarik, "The Artist's View of Ukifune," in Andrew Pekarik, ed., *Ukifune: Love in The Tale of Genji* (New York: Columbia University Press, 1982), pp. 173–174.

2. The literal meaning of the term denoting a softly curved, flowing script may have involved some initial gender stereotyping. In fact, male authors and poets writing in the Japanese—as opposed to the Chinese—mode wrote in *onna-de* as well. For a succinct description of "Japanese Language and Calligraphy," see John M. Rosenfield, Fumiko E. Cranston, and Edwin A. Cranston, *The Courtly Tradition in Japanese Art and Literature: Selections from the Hofer and Hyde Collections* (Tokyo: Kodansha International, 1973), pp. 14–24.

3. See Murase, *Iconography of The Tale of Genji*. The iconographic canon did not go undisputed, however, as is documented in the thirteenth-century *Genji-e chinjō* (Genji Painting Defense). For a hilarious account of the fastidious debate, see Meech-Pekarik, "The Artist's View," pp. 181–182.

4. Yūgao's attendant Ukon is not to be confused with Nakanokimi's Ukon, mentioned in the previous chapter, "Enter *mono no ke*," section "Text and Picture: *emakimono.*"

5. In the *Genji* text, Yūgao's possessing spirit is referred to as *mono* rather than *mono no ke*. Since there is, in this context, essentially no difference in meaning between the two terms, I shall refer to Yūgao's *mono* as *mono no ke* in order to avoid confusion.

6. Murase, *Iconography of The Tale of Genji*, p. 23. Actually, of these unique paintings, the "Azumaya I" scene is "included in the Osaka manual, but the Heian fragment is the only known example of a painting illustrating this scene"; ibid.

7. It is a striking fact that the twelfth century saw not only the pinnacle of elegance in the *Genji monogatari emaki* but also the vigorous plunge into the seething cauldron of ordinary life fired by intense passions and fears. Lower-class life was portrayed with a penchant for fantasy, as in the *Shigisan-engi;* power struggles erupted into violence, as in the *Ban-dainagon-ekotoba;* humanized animals were outlined in lively caricaturistic brush strokes in the *Chōjū-giga*. Perhaps the ultimate contrast to *Genji-e* was the didactic depiction of demon- and disease-infested hells, as in the *Jigoku-zōshi, Gaki-zōshi,* and *Yamai-no-sōshi*.

8. See Tanaka Sumie, "Kodai no yami ni chōryō suru: yōkai, mono no ketachi," in Tanigawa Ken'ichi, ed., *Nihon no yōkai*, Bessatsu taiyō, no. 57 (Heibonsha, Spring 1987), pp. 59–62.

9. Andrew L. Markus, "Representations of *Genji Monogatari* in Edo Period Fiction," unpublished paper, prepared for the "World of Genji" Conference (Bloomington, Indiana University, 1982), p. 39.

10. The *Ise monogatari* was parodied by Ueda Akinari in his *Kuse*

*monogatari* (1791) and in the *kanazōshi* ingeniously called *Nise monogatari,* formerly attributed to Karasuma Mitsuhiro (1579–1630).

11. See Markus, "Representations," pp. 31–55; Andrew Lawrence Markus, *The Willow in Autumn: Ryūtei Tanehiko, 1783–1842* (Cambridge, Mass.: Council on East Asian Studies, Harvard University, 1992), pp. 119–158.

12. Kondo Eiko sets off the Masanobu illustration for the Yūgao possession scene in *Wakakusa Genji* (1738), which features an anthropomorphic ghost, against the Tanehiko-Kunisada realistic rendering of this scene a century later. See Kondo, "Inaka Genji Series," in Matthi Forrer, ed., *Essays on Japanese Art Presented to Jack Hillier* (London: Sawers, 1982), p. 81, figs. 5 and 6.

13. Sebastian Izzard, *Kunisada's World* (New York: Japan Society, in collaboration with the Ukiyo-e Society of America, 1993), pp. 14, 30–35, 168–171; see especially p. 169, plate 84a. Andrew L. Markus has defined modern *Genji-e* as "the literally thousands of *nishiki-e* polychrome prints, a whole subgenre of works, based directly or indirectly on Kunisada's illustrations to *Inaka Genji* and produced between about 1830 and 1890"; Markus, *The Willow in Autumn,* p. 151.

14. For an erotic print of Genji's night with Yūgao at the deserted villa, once removed from the original by Tanehiko's late Edo version, see Utagawa Kunisada's woodblock print "Mitsuiji and Tasogare in a Ruined Temple," from the erotic book *Shō-utsushi aioi Genji,* ca. 1852; in Izzard, *Kunisada's World,* p. 169, plate 84b.

15. For Kunisada's prints based on a *kabuki* play (probably *Higashiyama sakura sōshi:* The Story of the Cherry Blossoms on Higashiyama; 1851), see Kondo, "Inaka Genji Series," p. 83, fig. 10, and Izzard, *Kunisada's World,* p. 169, plate 84. The prints show the scene at the dilapidated temple where Shinonome (Tasogare's mother) threatens to kill Mitsuuji, as described in Tanehiko's novel.

16. Following Tanehiko's recasting of the Yūgao tragedy and Kunisada's illustrations, it is hardly surprising that Yoshitoshi's own attempt at recasting through *nō* conventions introduced further distortions concerning the original *Genji* episode; the Hannya mask in Yoshitoshi's triptych recalls not a *nō* play about Yūgao but *Aoi no ue,* the *nō* play about the woman who becomes possessed after Yūgao.

17. In the design of his print, Yoshitoshi followed Kunisada (see Izzard, *Kunisada's World,* p. 169, plates 84–84a; see also Kondo, "Inaka Genji Series," p. 83, fig. 11 and p. 84, fig. 13) and his teacher Kuniyoshi; for Kuniyoshi's rendering of the same scene, see Kondo, "Inaka Genji Series," p. 84, fig. 12. Kondo demonstrates another instance of anthropomorphic representation versus the invisibility of *mono no ke* in the scene of "Mitsuuji's Flight with Tasogare." The scene departs from the original in that the lovers are threatened by a *mono no ke* not in the deserted villa but rather on their flight from it. In Kunisada's illustration for Tanehiko's novel, a ghostly straw-hatted

creature vaguely hovers near the fleeing lovers, but in his later triptych, signed Toyokuni III, the living spirit of Akogi appears as a woman threatening Mitsuuji while the straw figure stands tall above a prostrate Tasogare; in Kuniyoshi's and Yoshitoshi's depiction of the same scene, the *mono no ke* is invisible. See Kondo, "Inaka Genji Series," p. 85, figs. 16–19.

18. For a color reproduction of the woodblock print by Ebina Masao, private collection, see Enchi Fumiko, *Genji monogatari*, Nihon no koten 5 (Gakken, 1979), pp. 30–31.

19. Haruo Shirane emphasizes the "significant economic and social gap between the woman and the hero" in *The Bridge of Dreams: A Poetics of "The Tale of Genji"* (Stanford: Stanford University Press, 1987), p. 49. Indeed, he insinuates that aside from her "delicate character," her "precarious social circumstances" kill her in the form of an "evil spirit (presumably that of the proud and strong-willed Rokujō lady)"; ibid., p. 68.

20. See Janet Goff, *Noh Drama and The Tale of Genji: The Art of Allusion in Fifteen Classical Plays* (Princeton: Princeton University Press, 1991), pp. 67–78, 102–110.

21. Incestuous affairs in the *Genji* are—as will be demonstrated in subsequent cases of spirit possession—so well hidden by lesser transgressions, such as adultery or other forms of betrayal, that they easily go unrecognized. This blind spot concerning the incest taboo may or may not reflect the historical reality. Although Fujii Sadakazu has examined the possibility of incest in Genji's affair with Fujitsubo, he rejects the idea that a man's sexual relations with his stepmother violated the taboo of incest; see Fujii, *Monogatari no kekkon* (Sōjusha, 1985), p. 56 and chart 2, p. 57. William H. McCullough states that step-relationships were "disapproved"; "Japanese Marriage Institutions in the Heian Period," *Harvard Journal of Asiatic Studies* 27 (1967):135. For a debate of the issue, see Doris G. Bargen, "The Problem of Incest in *The Tale of Genji*," in Edward Kamens, ed., *Approaches to Teaching Murasaki Shikibu's The Tale of Genji* (New York: MLA, 1993), pp. 115–123.

22. The intriguing blank concerning the beginning of the Genji–Fujitsubo affair has, like similar gaps in the *Genji*, stirred the imagination about unrecounted secret meetings before Reizei was conceived and has even led to speculations about a missing chapter "Kagayaku hi no miya"; for details on the "centuries-old dispute," see Norma Field, *The Splendor of Longing in the Tale of Genji* (Princeton: Princeton University Press, 1987), p. 313, n. 8. It is only in the year following Yūgao's death, in "Wakamurasaki" (S: "Lavender"), that we learn that the Genji–Fujitsubo affair has been consummated and borne fruit. Although the Genji–Fujitsubo affair thus does not chronologically intersect with the Genji–Yūgao affair, the energy required to initiate the hero's forbidden affair with his ideal woman is gathered through his intense experience with Yūgao.

23. Shi no kimi, Tō no Chūjō's principal wife, may have resented the fact

that Yūgao preceded her in giving birth; see Kurosu Shigehiko, *Genji monogatari shiron: Yūgao no maki o chūshin to shite* (Kasama shoin, 1990), p. 167. Shi no kimi later gives birth to Kashiwagi, Kōbai, and Kokiden no nyōgo.

24. Genji's political marriage to the four-years-older Aoi is such a mismatch; it is the antithesis of Genji's spontaneous and intense romance with Yūgao. Similarly, Tō no Chūjō's marriage into the Kokiden faction represents an upwardly mobile political match that has its romantic counterpart in "Tokonatsu" as concubine.

25. Arthur Waley suspects in his translation that Fujitsubo is the basis for such rumors; see Waley, trans., *The Tale of Genji: A Novel in Six Parts by Lady Murasaki* (New York: Modern Library, 1960), p. 38. Although the original itself is vague, the Shōgakukan *Genji* commentary confirms Waley's interpretation; see 1:171, n. 18: *Fujitsubo e no rembo o sasu.*

26. Bargen, "The Problem of Incest in *The Tale of Genji*," p. 118. Interestingly, the "Yūgao" chapter ends with remembrances of Utsusemi; Genji returns the robe as the adamant lady of the locust shell leaves with her husband for the provinces.

27. See Aileen Gatten, "The Order of the Early Chapters in the *Genji monogatari*," *Harvard Journal of Asiatic Studies* 41(1) (June 1981):5–46.

28. Gatten argues that Genji's ideal lady in "Hahakigi" (S: "The Broom Tree") and "Utsusemi" (S: "The Shell of the Locust") cannot be clearly identified as Fujitsubo except through "hindsight" provided by later chapters: "If it was Fujitsubo all along, why have we been told only now? Is this an effective technique, an effect willed by the author"? Gatten, "The Order of the Early Chapters," p. 23. Gatten may underestimate the narrative strategy of delay, especially as it relates to the taboo nature of Genji's love for his stepmother.

29. What Gatten refers to as a "poorly introduced" character (Gatten, "The Order of the Early Chapters," p. 23), Waley recognized as a device that anticipates Marcel Proust by nine centuries (Waley, trans., *The Tale of Genji*, p. 39, n. 1). After first arguing that there is nothing in the "Yūgao" chapter to prove that Rokujō watari is identical with Rokujō no miyasudokoro, Gatten (pp. 23, 25) implies that there is little purpose in distinguishing between the two. For a detailed discussion of the terms "Rokujō watari" and "Rokujō no miyasudokoro," see Hirokawa Katsumi, "Monogatari to shite no chimei: Rokujō watari no mono no ke," in Nanba Hiroshi and Hirokawa Katsumi, eds., *Genji monogatari: chimei to hōhō* (Ōfūsha, 1990), pp. 239–240.

30. Hagiwara Hiromichi (1813–1863) is generally credited with noting this flower's unusually ominous qualities. They are used metaphorically throughout the "Yūgao" chapter; *"ayashi"* means strange, suspicious, plain, humble, vulgar, unsightly, absurd; it is noteworthy that the *ke* of *mono no ke* is also read *ayashi*. The flower's metaphorical qualities can best be traced

through the fate of the woman who is intimately associated with it; see Takahashi Tōru, *Monogatari to e no enkinhō* (Perikansha, 1991), pp. 49, 185–186.

31. For an intriguingly similar story, see Mildred M. Tahara, trans., *Tales of Yamato: A Tenth-Century Poem-Tale* (Honolulu: University Press of Hawai'i, 1980), episode 173.

32. Field, *The Splendor of Longing*, p. 90; see also Mori Ichirō, *Genji monogatari seiseiron: kyokumen shūchū to keikiteki tenkai* (Sekai shisōsha, 1986), pp. 31, 34–35.

33. The *nō* play *Hajitomi* focuses on Genji's encounter of Yūgao at Gojō; for an analysis and translation, see Goff, *Noh Drama and The Tale of Genji*, pp. 76–78, 102–107, 111–114.

34. For the religious and secular meanings of the fan on which the *yūgao* flower is offered, see Haraoka Fumiko, *Genji monogatari ryōgi no ito: jinbutsu, hyōgen o megutte* (Yūseidō, 1991), pp. 40–46.

35. Ibid., p. 48.

36. The commentators are divided over whether it is Yūgao or Genji who makes the overture. See Janet Emily Goff, "*The Tale of Genji* as a Source of the Nō: *Yūgao* and *Hajitomi*," *Harvard Journal of Asiatic Studies* 42(1) ( June 1982):197–198.

37. The term "breast brother" is used by Jennifer Brewster, trans., *The Emperor Horikawa Diary, by Fujiwara no Nagako, Sanuki no Suke Nikki* (Honolulu: University Press of Hawai'i, 1977), pp. 31, 34; see also p. 129, n. 95.

38. This peculiar *kaimami* variant appears to match the sustained incognito of the lovers. It originated in Genji's first glimpse at the beginning of the "Yūgao" chapter, when he peeped through an opening from within his unpresuming carriage through an opening in the blinds covering Yūgao's "temporary shelter." What was first a double barrier becomes a mediated one.

39. See Kurosu Shigehiko, *Yūgao to iu onna* (Kasama shoin, 1975). See also Hinata Kazumasa, "Yūgao maki no hōhō," in Hinata, *Genji monogatari no ōken to sasurai* (Shintensha, 1989), pp. 85–102. This theory has been questioned by Inukai Kiyoshi, "Yūgao to no deai," *KGMS* 1:185–197.

40. The novelist and *Genji* translator Enchi Fumiko especially relishes the idea of Yūgao as a courtesan-like, seductive woman. The imagery of the half-raised latticed shutters is part of *emaki* iconography of the life of courtesans; see Enchi, *Genji monogatari shiken* (Shinchōsha, 1974), p. 23.

41. This much debated view is most extensively explored by Haraoka, *Genji monogatari ryōgi no ito*, pp. 33–53.

42. See, for example, the reference to "ren'ai gēmu" in Mori, *Genji monogatari seiseiron*, p. 30.

43. See Haraoka, *Genji monogatari ryōgi no ito*, pp. 53–55; Mitani Eiichi, "Yūgao monogatari to kodenshō," *KGMS* 1:213–215; Takahashi Tōru, *Monogatari bungei no hyōgenshi* (Nagoya: Nagoya Daigaku shuppankai,

1987), pp. 273–276. By contrast, Hirokawa Katsumi attributes the anonymity of the lovers to urban legends rather than the Miwayama myth; see "Monogatari to shite no chimei," p. 228.

44. The less well known type is the "*ninuriya* or red arrow type." See Carmen Blacker, *The Catalpa Bow: A Study of Shamanistic Practices in Japan* (London: Allen & Unwin, 1975), pp. 116–117.

45. Intent on emphasizing Yūgao's shamanistic qualities, Haraoka sees an analogy between Ōmononushi no kami and Genji on the one side and the god's bride *("kami no yome")* and Yūgao on the other. Since a *miko* is thought to be none other than the bride of a *kami*, Yūgao's vocation is confirmed through the Miwayama myth; see Haraoka, *Genji monogatari ryōgi no ito,* p. 54.

46. See Mitani Eiichi, "Yūgao monogatari to kodenshō," *KGMS* 1:214.

47. For the extensive Japanese fox lore and its Chinese origins, see Greg Gubler, "Kitsune: The Remarkable Japanese Fox," *Southern Folklore Quarterly* 38 (1974):121–134.

48. Traditionally, the fifteenth of the eighth lunar month, or September 15; *jūgoya.*

49. As one scholar, struggling to decide whether Yūgao is a pleasure woman *(yūjo)* or a shamaness *(miko),* points out, Genji's Buddhist pledge clashes here with her Shinto role; see Haraoka, *Genji monogatari ryōgi no ito,* p. 50.

50. The site of Minamoto Tōru's villa is in Kyōto-shi, Shimogyō-ku, Honshiogama-chō, Tomikōji dōri, Gojō sagaru; see Kamiya Jirō, "*Genji monogatari no tabi,*" in Enchi Fumiko, *Genji monogatari,* Nihon no koten 5 (Gakken, 1979), p. 188; Wakashiro Kiiko, *Hikaru Genji no butai* (Asahi shinbunsha, 1992), pp. 24–27, 142. The villa in its heyday is described by Helen Craig McCullough, trans., *Tales of Ise: Lyrical Episodes from Tenth-Century Japan* (Stanford: Stanford University Press, 1968), pp. 236–237; p. 124, n. 1, for episode 81. See also H. Richard Okada, *Figures of Resistance: Language, Poetry, and Narrating in The Tale of Genji and Other Mid-Heian Texts* (Durham, N.C.: Duke University Press, 1992), pp. 141–142. On the link between *"nanigashi no in"* and Kawara-in, see Onitsuka Takaaki, "Rekishi to kyokō to *Genji monogatari:* Yūgao maki no mono no ke ni tsuite," in Murasaki Shikibu Gakkai, ed., *Genji monogatari to nikki bungaku kenkyū to shiryō* (Musashino shoin, 1992), especially pp. 265–277.

51. For this *nō* play, see Kenneth Yasuda, *Masterworks of the Nō Theater* (Bloomington: Indiana University Press, 1989), pp. 463–484. The *nō* plays *Utsusemi* and *Go* also use the setting of Nakagawa; see Goff, *Noh Drama and The Tale of Genji,* pp. 87–101.

52. For a translation of this half-humorous encounter, from *Konjaku monogatari-shū* 27.2, see Helen Craig McCullough, trans., *Ōkagami: The Great Mirror; Fujiwara Michinaga (966–1027) and His Times* (Princeton:

Princeton University Press, 1980), pp. 50–51. See *Yamato monogatari,* episode 61; Mildred M. Tahara, trans., *Tales of Yamato,* pp. 34, 219, n. 61.2 (Retired Emperor Uda is here referred to as Teiji no In). See also *Uji shūi monogatari* 151; D. E. Mills, trans., *A Collection of Tales from Uji: A Study and Translation of Uji Shūi Monogatari* (Cambridge: Cambridge University Press, 1970), pp. 368–369.

53. See Onitsuka, "Rekishi to kyokō to *Genji monogatari,*" pp. 267–272, 277.

54. Kurosu calls attention to the fact that Tō no Chūjō (as we refer to him throughout) is not promoted to the rank Yūgao's father held (Sanmi no Chūjō) until the "Aoi" chapter; see Kurosu, *Genji monogatari shiron,* pp. 165–166.

55. Incest rules are cultural constructs corresponding to sociopolitical strictures. In Sung China, for example, incest rules were much stricter than in Heian Japan—partly because of different living arrangements, partly because of the greater hold of Confucian morals on family relationships. According to the Sung penal code, a man's sexual relations with his father's concubine were considered incestuous and carried the death penalty. See Patricia Buckley Ebrey, *The Inner Quarters: Marriage and the Lives of Chinese Women in the Sung Period* (Berkeley: University of California Press, 1993), p. 252.

56. Although there are numerous hints about Fujitsubo's importance in Genji's mind, there are no scenes depicting an encounter until after Yūgao's death.

57. See Takahashi, *Monogatari to e no enkinhō,* p. 265.

58. For the argument that Fujitsubo lurks behind the *mono no ke,* see Takahashi, "Yūgao no maki no hyōgen," in Takahashi, *Monogatari bungei no hyōgenshi,* pp. 286, 300, 305; Mori, *Genji monogatari seiseiron,* pp. 33, 49; Shinohara Shōji, "Hai-in no ke," *KGMS* 1:258.

59. Unlike Seidensticker (S:71) and Benl (*Die Geschichte vom Prinzen Genji,* 1:111), Waley in his translation downplays the notion that the hero might be affected to the point of believing himself possessed: "Thinking that this was *some nightmare or hallucination,* he roused himself and sat up. The lamp had gone out. *Somewhat* agitated he drew his sword . . . " (W:67; my italics).

60. The commentaries link this line of thought (1:243; see n. 18: *kakaru suji*) to another affair, namely the unnarrated Fujitsubo affair. Takahashi argues that Genji's conscience acknowledges his punishment for an inappropriate, forbidden love (1:243: *ōkenaku arumajiki kokoro*), that is, Fujitsubo; see *Monogatari to e no enkinhō,* p. 264; see also Takahashi, *Monogatari bungei no hyōgenshi,* p. 286. Other critics have also noted the undercurrent role of Fujitsubo in the Yūgao affair; see, for example, Mori, *Genji monogatari seiseiron,* pp. 33, 49, 54; Shinohara, "Hai-in no ke," *KGMS* 1:257–258.

61. Field, *The Splendor of Longing,* p. 90.

62. See Shinohara, "Hai-in no ke," *KGMS* 1:258.

63. As Hinata Kazumasa has pointed out, Yūgao begins to conceal her perspective from Genji by lowering the latticed shutters after their first *waka* exchange; see Hinata, *Genji monogatari no ōken to sasurai*, p. 90.

64. For critical opinion on this matter, see Haraoka, *Genji monogatari ryōgi no ito*, pp. 31–33; Inukai, "Yūgao to no deai," *KGMS* 1:185–197.

65. Taya Raishun briefly touches on the question of who the *mono* might be from Yūgao's standpoint; but as there seems no reason for anyone to resent her, this pioneering critic moves on to the question of how *mono* and *mono no ke* are different. See Taya, *Genji monogatari no shisō* (Kyoto: Hōzō-kan, 1952), p. 94.

66. For the three extratextual contexts of the Yūgao episode, see Taka-hashi, *Monogatari bungei no hyōgenshi*, pp. 269–309.

67. Komashaku Kimi draws flawed conclusions from this aspect of posses-sion trance. Having argued—on the basis of the *Murasaki Shikibu shū* 44–45—that Murasaki Shikibu did not believe in *mono no ke*, the feminist critic emphasizes that *mono no ke* do not actually appear in the *Genji*, except in the perception of those attending to a woman in crisis. For Komashaku, Yūgao's *mono no ke* is simply a product of Genji's sinful consciousness. See Komashaku, *Murasaki Shikibu no messēji* (Asahi shinbunsha, 1991), pp. 93–94.

68. For similar imagery in Ukifune's case, see S:993; 6:146.

69. Yoshitoshi's print, dated 1886, is from his series "Tsuki hyakushi" (One Hundred Aspects of the Moon). See Eric van den Ing and Robert Schaap, eds., *Beauty and Violence: Japanese Prints by Yoshitoshi 1839–1892* (Bergeyk, Netherlands: Society for Japanese Arts, 1992), p. 74; John Steven-son, *Yoshitoshi's One Hundred Aspects of the Moon* (Redmond, Wash.: San Francisco Graphic Society, 1992), dust jacket and no. 29, n. p. Stevenson notes "how little the Moon Series is concerned with demons and monsters. . . . In his maturity Yoshitoshi seems to have regarded ghosts and demons as figments of the imagination rather than as real"; ibid., p. 55.

70. Hans Peter Duerr, "Die Angst vor dem Leben und die Sehnsucht nach dem Tode," in Duerr, ed., *Der Wissenschaftler und das Irrationale* (Frankfurt am Main: Syndikat, 1981), 1:621–647.

71. Norma Field, a critic who deserves much credit for emphasizing fem-inist issues in *Genji*, sees women in crisis (referring to Yūgao, Murasaki, Tamakazura, Ukifune) as "victims [who] rarely protest [for] they cannot, either from ignorance or from the knowledge that life offers them no suitable alternatives. A profound passivity characterizes these women at such junc-tures." Field, *The Splendor of Longing*, p. 167.

72. It is interesting to note the parallel roles of Koremitsu and Ukon as the children of the protagonists' nurses. This Ukon is the daughter of Yūgao's wet nurse and, after her mother's death, was raised by Yūgao's father (see S:79–80); see Akiyama Ken, ed., *Genji monogatari jiten* (Gakutōsha, 1989), p. 273.

73. Ivan Morris, *World of the Shining Prince: Court Life in Ancient Japan* (Harmondsworth: Peregrine, 1985), pp. 223, 222. However, Mimi Hall Yiengpruksawan questions the historicity of Morris' and other scholars' notions about the way of life at the Heian court; see Yiengpruksawan, "What's in a Name? Fujiwara Fixation in Japanese Cultural History," *Monumenta Nipponica* 49(4) (Winter 1994):426–427, 452. It is nonetheless intriguing to think that Heian women writers themselves may have contributed to or largely invented this historically inaccurate but highly effective literary conceptualization of the closeted feminine condition.

74. For an extensive discussion of male cases of spirit possession in historic narratives, such as the *Eiga monogatari, Ōkagami, Shōyūki,* and *Midō Kanpakuki,* see Fujimoto Katsuyoshi, *Genji monogatari no "mono no ke": bungaku to kiroku no hazama* (Kasama shoin, 1994), chaps. 6–9.

75. Tamakazura, the sobriquet for Yūgao's daughter, refers to a jeweled wreath that "serves as a *katami,* an object that is used both to recall the deceased to mind for the living and, more important, as a repository for the deceased's *tama.*" Gary L. Ebersole, *Ritual Poetry and the Politics of Death in Early Japan* (Princeton: Princeton University Press, 1989), p. 165.

76. See Taya, *Genji monogatari no shisō,* pp. 87–89.

77. See Shinohara Shōji, "Mono no ke," *Kokubungaku* 28(16) (December 1983):126–129.

78. For a narratological analysis of this passage, see Amanda Mayer Stinchecum, *Narrative Voice in The Tale of Genji* (Urbana, Ill.: Center for East Asian and Pacific Studies, 1985), pp. 10–11. From a deconstructionist approach, the passage pinpoints "the storyteller's dilemma: to speak the truth is to reveal secrets for which the narrator will be subject to punishment; but not to do so and not to be taken seriously would be worse"; Okada, *Figures of Resistance,* p. 342, n. 6.

79. *GMH* 1:98.

80. See Murase, *Iconography of The Tale of Genji,* sec. 5: Lavender, pp. 58–65; Genji's secret meeting with Fujitsubo is omitted. By contrast, the genres of comics *(manga)* and animation know no artistic discretion in the sexy depiction of this scene; see Tsuboi Kou *(manga)* and Shimizu Yoshiko, ed., *Genji monogatari eigohan: The Illustrated Genji monogatari* (Shinjinbutsu Ōraisha, 1989), pp. 62–63; see also Sugii Gisaburō (director), Tsutsui Tomomi (script), and Hosono Haruomi (music), *Murasaki Shikibu: Genji monogatari* (animation), Asahi Video Library, n. d.

81. See Okada, *Figures of Resistance,* p. 358, n. 45; see also p. 261.

82. Ibid., p. 195.

83. Ibid., p. 262: "The child that she [Fujitsubo] bears is marked as a 'big secret' of the text, a secret suggestive of taboo and transgression although, strictly speaking, no sociopolitical taboos have been broken."

84. Field, *The Splendor of Longing,* p. 315, n. 19.

85. Okada emphasizes the responsibility of the lovers' attendants—Fujitsubo's Ōmyōbu and Genji's Koremitsu—for the practical arrangements of the affair; see *Figures of Resistance*, pp. 261, 263. Like Koremitsu for Genji, Ōmyōbu seems to have been for Fujitsubo a *menotogo*, or wet nurse's child, that is, a surrogate sibling; see Field, *The Splendor of Longing*, p. 31. That these intimates fulfilled their masters' innermost desires by securing the safety of the encounters does not exonerate the lovers—as they themselves demonstrate in their feelings of guilt.

86. Genji too is terrified. He had been suffering from an old childhood malaise resembling malaria since the middle of the Third Month, but whether the fever inspired his first encounter with Fujitsubo or was a guilty reaction to it is unclear. In any event, the second meeting with the allegedly ailing Fujitsubo becomes inevitable after Genji, cured of his illness, returns from Kitayama invigorated by a powerful impulse from his first glimpse *(kaimami)* of Fujitsubo's young niece Murasaki. Okada has suggested that the terms decribing Genji's "malaria" (S:84; 1:273: *warawayami*) and Fujitsubo's illness (S:98; 1:305: *nayami*) go far beyond denoting purely physical ailments; see *Figures of Resistance*, pp. 250, 260. Just as the extraordinary second meeting with Fujitsubo is inspired by Genji's discovery of Murasaki, so this most risky affair finds an intriguing echo seven years later. Then twenty-five years old, the hero feels compelled to repeat his earlier transgression against his imperial father with Oborozukiyo, the intended of the new emperor, Genji's half-brother Suzaku. It is already the lovers' second encounter, dramatized by a thunderstorm, but it ends in nightmarish discovery by Oborozukiyo's father. In this botched episode, the woman's pretense of "malaria" is exposed as something else by the puzzled father: "My, but you do look strange. It's not just malaria, it's some sort of evil spirit, I'm sure of it, a very stubborn one. We should have kept those priests at it" (S:212; 2:137).

87. The uncoordinated timing of Fujitsubo's withdrawal from court and the announcement of her pregnancy did not conform to custom. To avoid a possible defilement of the palace, imperial consorts were expected to move to their family's residence upon announcing their third month of pregnancy. The *Eiga monogatari* (ca. 1092) records the anomalous case of the Junior Consort Kishi (d. 985), whom Emperor Kazan (r. 984–986) loved so madly that he detained her until her fifth month, only to reclaim her from her father for a while. Kishi died in her eighth month, leaving Emperor Kazan crazed with grief; see William H. McCullough and Helen Craig McCullough, trans., *A Tale of Flowering Fortunes: Annals of Japanese Aristocratic Life in the Heian Period* (Stanford: Stanford University Press, 1980), pp. 128–131; NKBT 75:94–98.

88. Tamagami Takuya suggests that after the second meeting Fujitsubo's despair is close to suicidal but that suicide was unthinkable because Buddhism

considered it a major sin; see *GMH* 2:107. Just before her delivery, Fujitsubo fears discovery of the secret and considers the possibility of her death as retribution for her sin; see *GMH* 2:279.

89. Death in pregnancy or in childbirth meant, according to Buddhist belief, that a woman left this world in a state of defilement that would result in adverse karma for her next life. The pollution from death during pregnancy or in childbirth could also threaten others, according to Shinto belief. Finally, within the Confucian system of conduct, the woman who died in this manner could not perform her duty as a mother toward the child; if the child died with her, she had failed in her filial and uxorial duties to produce offspring to continue the family line and perform ancestral rites. For dramatic examples of this problem in the lives of *Genji* women, see my chapters "Aoi" and "The Third Princess."

90. Field, *The Splendor of Longing*, p. 24; see also Doris G. Bargen, "The Search for Things Past in the *Genji monogatari*," *Harvard Journal of Asiatic Studies* 51(1) ( June 1991):225. In this article, based on a paper delivered at the "World of Genji" conference at Indiana University in 1982, I describe Fujitsubo as a "primary substitute" for Genji's mother, as opposed to other women placed in the role of "secondary substitutes."

91. Taya, *Genji monogatari no shisō*, p. 85.

92. There is a third theory, proposed by the anonymous author of an early critical appreciation of the *Genji* and other works, the *Mumyōzōshi* (The Untitled Book; ca. 1196–1202). Called the tree-spirit theory *(kodama setsu)*, it is based on the belief that spirits could reside in trees, especially trees distinguished by their age, and threaten passersby; see *GMH* 1:479.

93. The Rokujō *ikisudama* theory was modified in 1937 by Shimazu Hisamoto as the *"miyasudokoro onnen setsu"* or the Rokujō grudge theory. See Shinohara, "Hai-in no ke," *KGMS* 1:247, 250.

94. Taya, *Genji monogatari no shisō*, p. 153.

95. See Arthur Waley, trans., *The Nō Plays of Japan* (New York: Grove Press, 1957), p. 179. Ivan Morris does not explicitly mention Yūgao; see *The World of the Shining Prince*, p. 145, p. 260, n. 88, p. 151. See also Edwin A. Cranston, "Aspects of *The Tale of Genji*," *Journal of the Association of Teachers of Japanese* 11(2–3) (1976):190; Earl Miner, "Some Thematic and Structural Features of the *Genji Monogatari*," *Monumenta Nipponica* 24(1–2) (1969):10; and Richard Bowring, *Murasaki Shikibu: The Tale of Genji* (Cambridge: Cambridge University Press, 1988), p. 28, who adds that Rokujō attacks Yūgao instead of her real target, Genji; p. 29.

96. Haruo Shirane tentatively leans toward the Rokujō theory; *The Bridge of Dreams*, p. 68.

97. Field, *The Splendor of Longing*, p. 47; see also pp. 90–91.

98. Ibid., p. 47.

99. Ibid., pp. 47, 90.

100. See Gatten, "The Order of the Early Chapters," pp. 5–46.

101. Takahashi, *Monogatari bungei no hyōgenshi*, p. 300.

102. See Shinohara, "Hai-in no ke," *KGMS* 1:248.

103. Although the latter two collections of *setsuwa* postdate the *Genji monogatari* by about one hundred or two hundred years, respectively, they are based on an oral tradition that went back to an unspecifiable past.

104. See Onitsuka, "Rekishi to kyokō to *Genji monogatari*," p. 281.

105. Onitsuka suggests that the woman in Genji's dream is, in Jungian terms, his anima; see "Rekishi to kyokō to *Genji monogatari*," pp. 279–280.

106. When Genji, still hoping against hope that Yūgao is not really dead, thinks of Fujiwara Tadahira (880–949), who escaped this fate after crossing the path of a devil *(oni)* in the Shishinden (Nanden; 1:242, n. 1), he is representing the Heian obsession with "demons in human form [who] were believed to frequent abandoned dwellings." H. C. McCullough, trans., *Tales of Ise*, p. 226, n. 4 to episode 58.

107. See Kurosu, *Genji monogatari shiron*, pp. 161–165.

108. This second dream vision not only serves Genji as a confirmation of the first; by closely identifying it with the deserted villa, Genji also revitalizes the legend of the place. As William A. Christian, Jr., has remarked about apparitions in Spain, "the sacralization of a place or the revitalization of a sacred place was one critical purpose of an apparition." Christian, *Apparitions in Late Medieval and Renaissance Spain* (Princeton: Princeton University Press, 1981), p. 212.

109. Shinohara refers to the dreamlike superimposition of Rokujō's shadow and the spirit of the villa as a double exposure *(nijū utsushi)*; see "Hai-in no ke," *KGMS* 1:248. For a similar argument, see Takahashi, *Monogatari bungei no hyōgenshi*, p. 300.

110. According to Hirokawa, the secret location of the unnamed villa in the middle of the capital indicates the transcendence of ordinary space and the exposure of humans to strange creatures. See "Monogatari to shite no chimei," in Nanba and Hirokawa, eds., *Genji monogatari: chimei to hōhō*, p. 229.

111. *Genji* characters are frequently referred to by their residence, title, or rank. The character I refer to simply as Rokujō makes her first appearance at the beginning of the "Yūgao" chapter, as Rokujō watari ("in the vicinity of sixth avenue"). Later she becomes known by her residence cum title, as Rokujō no miyasudokoro (the title "miyasudokoro" refers to the mother of an imperial prince or princess). "Rokujō watari" may refer to nothing more than a location but it can also refer to the woman who lives there. "Rokujō no miyasudokoro" always refers to the woman. For a discussion of Rokujō watari, and a map, see Hirokawa Katsumi, *Shinsō no tennō: Genji monogatari no kokyō* ( Jinbun shoin, 1990), pp. 48–56, 49 (map), 108–113.

112. Hirokawa, "Monogatari to shite no chimei," p. 248.

113. Fujii Sadakazu, *Genji monogatari no shigen to genzai* (Tōjusha, 1980), p. 158.

114. Hirokawa, "Monogatari to shite no chimei," p. 250.

115. See H. C. McCullough, trans., *Ōkagami,* pp. 93–94.

116. Haraoka's statement that the image of aimless wandering ("atedo nai sasurai no imēji") is continued with the move to the villa is flawed in that Yūgao's homelessness is aimless only in its geography but otherwise self-inflicted, or rather self-chosen, until the forced move to the villa. See Haraoka, *Genji monogatari ryōgi no ito,* p. 38.

117. Fujitsubo may have tried to escape Genji after the "first secret meeting" by withdrawing from court to her family's residence. Unlike Yūgao, however, Fujitsubo is on her own territory when Genji pursues her there in the "second secret meeting."

118. In 1930 the *nō* scholar Nogami Toyoichirō reformulated this well-known distribution of roles by proclaiming the principle that *nō* has only one main actor ("nō no shuyaku ichinin shugi"); cited in Mae J. Smethurst, *The Artistry of Aeschylus and Zeami: A Comparative Study of Greek Tragedy and Nō* (Princeton: Princeton University Press, 1989), p. 64. It must be emphasized, however, that the *waki* sometimes takes the principal role.

119. Cited in Goff, *Noh Drama and The Tale of Genji,* p. 33. Goff's translation is based on Omote Akira and Katō Shūichi, eds., *Zeami, Zenchiku* (Iwanami shoten, 1974), pp. 137–138. Goff does not question Zeami's aestheticized notion of spirit possession; see ibid., pp. 34, 49.

120. There is also a play about Yūgao's daughter, called *Tamakazura,* by Komparu Zenchiku (1405–?). For a discussion and translation of all three plays, see Goff, *Noh Drama and The Tale of Genji,* pp. 67–78, 102–124.

121. Ibid., pp. 8, 11–29.

122. Ibid., p. 70.

123. Goff's speculation that the "ambiguity" of the possession scene and "the endless conjecture" about the identity of the possessing spirit lead to the avoidance of the theme—altogether in *Hajitomi* and partially in *Yūgao*—is unconvincing. See Goff, *Noh Drama and The Tale of Genji,* p. 52.

### Aoi

1. Since, in contrast to Yūgao, Aoi speaks in a different voice, her case of possession might be referred to as "spirit mediumship": "Spirit possession . . . does not necessarily include the ability to coherently communicate a spoken message, whereas this is the major emphasis in spirit mediumship." Irving I. Zaretsky and Cynthia Shambaugh, "Introduction" to *Spirit Possession and Spirit Mediumship in Africa and Afro-America: An Annotated Bibliography* (New York: Garland, 1978), p. xvii. Nevertheless, to avoid confusing spirit mediumship with shamanism, I have retained the term "spirit possession" for

the discussion of Aoi's case. In no other case in the *Genji* does the possessed person herself communicate the spirit's message.

2. Haruo Shirane, *The Bridge of Dreams: A Poetics of "The Tale of Genji"* (Stanford: Stanford University Press, 1987), p. 149.

3. For a concise description of the post of *saiin*, see Edward Kamens, *The Buddhist Poetry of the Great Kamo Priestess: Daisaiin Senshi and Hosshin Wakashū* (Ann Arbor: Center for Japanese Studies, University of Michigan, 1990), pp. 50–58.

4. Shirane has gone so far as to assert that Aoi is "more a symbol of her social position than a full-fledged character"; *The Bridge of Dreams,* p. 49.

5. Aoi is not named in this context, but it is she rather than Rokujō whom Genji refers to as jealous, and it is Aoi whom he is obliged to visit after this exchange with young Murasaki. Arthur Waley emphasizes Genji's worst fears of Aoi's wrath—directed not only at Murasaki but at himself as well—by footnoting this passage: "That hate kills is a fundamental thesis of the book" (W:139). For a complementary view on Waley's famous statement, see Edwin A. Cranston, "Aspects of *The Tale of Genji,*" *Journal of the Association of Teachers of Japanese* 11(2–3) (1976):190–192.

6. Stephen Kern, *The Culture of Love: Victorians to Moderns* (Cambridge, Mass.: Harvard University Press, 1992), p. 280.

7. There is no precedent for the *saigū* to be accompanied to Ise by her mother; see Sakamoto Kazuko, "Rokujō Miyasudokoro no Ise gekō to onryō shutsugen," *Bungaku Gogaku* 72 (August 1974):90.

8. For details on political configurations, see Haruo Shirane, "The Aesthetics of Power: Politics in *The Tale of Genji,*" *Harvard Journal of Asiatic Studies* 45(2) (December 1985):619.

9. The two quarrels occur en route to Kiyomizudera and at the Kamo Festival; see Wilfred Whitehouse and Eizo Yanagisawa, trans., *Ochikubo Monogatari—The Tale of the Lady Ochikubo: A Tenth Century Japanese Novel* (Garden City, N.Y.: Doubleday Anchor, 1971), pp. 123–130, 151–156.

10. The *Eiga monogatari* (ca. 1092) tells of several crises in pregnancy and childbirth that raise similar concerns about the mother's karma; see, for example, William H. McCullough and Helen Craig McCullough, trans., *A Tale of Flowering Fortunes: Annals of Japanese Aristocratic Life in the Heian Period* (Stanford: Stanford University Press, 1980), pp. 131, 235, 682, 695–697; NKBT 75:97–98, 221; NKBT 76:221–222, 241–245. The postpartum possession and death in 1024 of a wife of Fujiwara Michinaga's son Norimichi (996–1075) greatly resembles Aoi's case; ibid., pp. 610–617; NKBT 76:131–139. The case of Empress Anshi (927–964), ibid., pp. 84–88; NKBT 75:41–46, is discussed below; see pp. 88, 303 nn. 31–32.

11. Despite the indisputable chronological sequence of the Yūgao and Aoi possessions, Aileen Gatten, inspired by the theory of Abe Akio, has

argued that the "Aoi" chapter ought to precede the "Yūgao" chapter so that the admittedly unidentified spirit who possesses Yūgao can be interpreted by the reader to be Rokujō's. Assuming that Yūgao's possession cannot be governed by factors other than jealousy, Gatten writes: "The 'Yūgao' episode could have been the first statement of the powerful theme that jealousy—in the form of the Rokujō lady—kills." Gatten, "The Order of the Early Chapters in the *Genji monogatari*," *Harvard Journal of Asiatic Studies* 41(1) (June 1981):25; see also p. 32.

12. Ioan Myrddin Lewis, "Witchcraft Within and Without," in Lewis, *Religion in Context: Cults and Charisma* (Cambridge: Cambridge University Press, 1986), p. 55.

13. Janet Emily Goff quotes Zeami (Omote and Katō, eds., *Zeami, Zenchiku,* pp. 137–138), who refers to *yūgen* in "Lady Rokujō's possession of Aoi no ue, Yūgao's possession by a malign spirit, and Ukifune's possession." Goff, "*The Tale of Genji* as a Source of the Nō," *Harvard Journal of Asiatic Studies* 42(1) (June 1982):181 and n. 6. Thomas Blenman Hare cites the passage from Zeami in English; see Hare, *Zeami's Style: The Noh Plays of Zeami Motokiyo* (Stanford: Stanford University Press, 1986), p. 132. In the Heian period, however, *yūgen* was not yet a prominent aesthetic concept.

14. Norma Field, *The Splendor of Longing in The Tale of Genji* (Princeton: Princeton University Press, 1987), p. 50.

15. Hirota Osamu calls attention to the convention of linking *Genji* characters with *waka;* see "*Genji monogatari* ni okeru *waka* no denshōsei: Rokujō Miyasudokoro no mono no ke no baai," *Nihon Bungaku* 31 (May 1982):57.

16. Citing the *Murasaki Shikibu nikki* and the *Eiga monogatari,* Hirota has pointed out that such a combination was unprecedented, at least in the Heian literature that has survived. It is therefore all the more remarkable that in the *Genji* as many as two of the five major *mono no ke* speak in *waka* (S:168; 2:33 and S:618; 4:227). As Hirota has further demonstrated, these two *waka* distinguish themselves from other *waka* in the *Genji* by their lack of natural imagery, the prominence of the speaker, and a remarkable affinity to the imperative diction and imagery of magic spells and folk beliefs. See Hirota, "*Genji monogatari* ni okeru *waka* no denshōsei," pp. 54, 56–62.

17. Field, *The Splendor of Longing,* p. 50; Field follows the headnote to the *Genji* text in NKBZ 2:33, n. 32.

18. The *waka* of Aoi's *mono no ke* has been loosely compared to the *waka* in episode 110 of the *Ise monogatari,* in which a secret lover's poem emphasizes the amorous intent of his lonely spirit and implores the woman: "If you should see it later on,/Pray cast a spell and catch it." Helen Craig McCullough, trans., *Tales of Ise: Lyrical Episodes from Tenth-Century Japan* (Stanford: Stanford University Press, 1968), p. 143; NKBZ 8:226. Yet the two episodes are fundamentally different in that the "Aoi" chapter places the

*waka* in the context of spirit possession whereas the *Ise monogatari* centers on a dream. While the Aoi possession scene dramatizes the conflict between two persons, implicating a third in the form of a *mono no ke,* the woman's dream of her secret lover in the *Ise* episode is lacking the third, distinctly different, figure of the possession triad. Michael Lambek has emphasized that "the triad is the irreducible minimal structure of possession. That is to say, communication entails a minimum of three figures—sender, receiver, and intermediary, or, in other terms, the host (the subject out of trance), the spirit (the subject in trance), and the person or persons with whom the spirit converses. . . . A spirit that arises in a host always does so in order to make its presence known to a third party, that is, in order to speak *to* someone." Lambek, *Human Spirits: A Cultural Account of Trance in Mayotte* (Cambridge: Cambridge University Press, 1981), p. 73. Since the spirits of those appearing to others in their dreams were thought to have wandered loose, thereby constituting separate entities, the analogy to spirit possession is tempting, despite the different motivations for the straying of souls. Moreover, in the *Ise* episode, the mood expressed appears confessional rather than confrontational. See H. C. McCullough, trans., *Tales of Ise,* p. 143; NKBZ 8:226. The comparison of the two episodes serves mainly to demonstrate the intense emotional appeal and lyricism as well as the prevalence of the folk belief about hemming in vagrant spirits. See Hirota, "*Genji monogatari* ni okeru *waka* no denshōsei," p. 61.

19. Takie Sugiyama Lebra has noted reciprocity as well as status reversal in the complementary roles of the possessed, the possessor, and the mediator *(chūkaisha)* of Japan's contemporary "Salvation Cult"; see *Japanese Patterns of Behavior* (Honolulu: University of Hawai'i Press, 1976), pp. 240–241.

20. Bennett Simon, *Mind and Madness in Ancient Greece: The Classical Roots of Modern Psychiatry* (Ithaca: Cornell University Press, 1978), p. 252.

21. Lewis, "Preface" to *Religion in Context,* p. vii.

22. "The woman is absolved from the responsibility for her actions." Gananath Obeyesekere, "Psychocultural Exegesis of a Case of Spirit Possession in Sri Lanka," in Vincent Crapanzano and Vivian Garrison, eds., *Case Studies in Spirit Possession* (New York: Wiley, 1977), p. 252. See also Yoshida Teigo, "Mystical Retribution, Spirit Possession, and Social Structure in a Japanese Village," *Ethnology* 6 (1967):250–251: "*Ikiryoo* possession proper does not involve a deliberate plan to harm others. . . . The woman suspected as a witch . . . did not know what she had done, and was not openly accused."

23. William H. McCullough has noted the importance of "anger and resentment" as a general motive of possessing spirits, also known as "angry spirits" *(onryō).* See McCullough, "Spirit Possession in the Heian Period," in Ōta Saburō and Fukuda Rikutarō, eds., *Studies on Japanese Culture* (Tokyo: Japan PEN Club, 1973), 1:93.

24. In his *setsuwa* collection *Kankyo no Tomo* (A Companion in Solitude;

1222), Priest Keisei (1189–1268) relates the hair-raising story of "How a Deeply Jealous Woman Turned into a Demon While Still Alive" (2.3); for a translation, see Rajyashree Pandey, "Women, Sexuality, and Enlightenment: *Kankyo no Tomo*," *Monumenta Nipponica* 50(3) (Autumn 1995):339–340.

25. The former wife's new-wife bashing is known as *uwanari uchi*. Fujimoto Katsuyoshi cites numerous examples from historical and fictional narratives; see *Genji monogatari no "mono no ke": bungaku to kiroku no hazama* (Kasama shoin, 1994), pp. 38–40. For Fujimoto's argument that the wives' quarrel *(tsuma arasoi)* became Murasaki Shikibu's foundation for creating Rokujō's *ikiryō* incident, see Fujimoto, ibid., p. 42. Murasaki Shikibu depicted such a *tsuma arasoi* rather critically in her poetry collection (*Murasaki Shikibu shū* 44).

26. See Fujimoto, *Genji monogatari no "mono no ke,"* pp. vii, 46–47. Fujimoto develops his *ikiryō* thesis in the first two chapters of his study.

27. Fujimoto may agree that one should not ignore Murasaki Shikibu's intentions—especially her view of *mono no ke* as the projection of a tormented conscience *(kokoro no oni)*—and that one should take a close look at the emotional situation of the *"hihyōsha,"* the victim of spirit possession. See Fujimoto, *Genji monogatari no "mono no ke,"* pp. 25–26. While Fujimoto analyzes the author's position and Rokujō's psychology of jealousy and humiliated pride in detail, he is silent on Aoi's psychology and her role in the possession, except to suggest that she too, like Genji and Rokujō, is suffering from *kokoro no oni;* ibid., p. 28.

28. See Herbert E. Plutschow, *Chaos and Cosmos: Ritual in Early and Medieval Japanese Literature* (Leiden: Brill, 1990), p. 210.

29. There is also a popular linguistic association of heartvine *(aoi)* with meeting *(au)*.

30. Hilary Graham, "The Social Image of Pregnancy: Pregnancy as Spirit Possession," *Sociological Review* (May 1976):297.

31. See McCullough and McCullough, *A Tale of Flowering Fortunes,* pp. 84–88; NKBT 75:41–46.

32. Akazome Emon's historical text identifies the possessing spirit as a *shiryō* belonging to Major Counselor Motokata (888–953) and explains his motives as exclusively political. Although Motokata's daughter Sukehime (d. 967) had borne the emperor his first son, the boy (Prince Hirohira, 950–971) was not designated crown prince. Instead he was almost instantly displaced by Anshi's son, Prince Norihira (950–1011), who, after Emperor Murakami's death in 967, succeeded to the throne as Emperor Reizei. Politics play a role in Aoi's possession too, as is indicated in the court's speculation about Rokujō's father, the late minister, who had been disappointed in his hopes that one day his daughter would become empress.

33. For the analogy between spirit and fetus, see Graham, "The Social Image of Pregnancy," pp. 297–298.

34. Clive S. Kessler describes the symbolism underlying Kelantanese spirit seances that are based on "psychosocial stress illness," mostly by women, and aim at the restoration of the afflicted individual's "sovereignty." The patient is likened to a "battlefield" or an "arena of conflict." The body politic thus resembles that of the patient. See Kessler, "Conflict and Sovereignty in Kelantanese Malay Spirit Seances," in Vincent Crapanzano and Vivian Garrison, eds., *Case Studies in Spirit Possession* (New York: Wiley, 1977), pp. 316, 319–320.

35. In Enchi Fumiko's modern fictional adaptation of Heian supernatural material—especially from the *Genji monogatari*, which the author has translated into modern Japanese—spirit possession functions both as plot line and as critical reflection or metafictional discourse. In *Onnamen* (Shinchōsha, 1966), the thesis is that the possessor and the possessed (Mieko and her widowed daughter-in-law Yasuko) are suspected of having homoerotic relations; see Enchi, *Masks*, trans. Juliet Winters Carpenter (New York: Aventura-Vintage, 1983). For translation/original, see pp. 61ff./80ff.; 79/102; 88–90/113–115; 95/121; 99/126; 119/153; 126/164; 132/171.

36. See, for example, Shirane, *The Bridge of Dreams*, pp. 124–125. Lambek has made similar observations about the impact of female trance on conjugal relations in Mayotte; see *Human Spirits*, pp. 81, 83.

37. See S:168; 2:32: ohara wa imijū takōte fushitamaeru sama, yosobito dani mitatematsuramu ni kokoro midarenubeshi. . . . kō te koso rōtage ni namamekitaru kata soite okashikarikere to miyu.

38. Jeannette H. Henney has linked the development of dissociational states to the sexual response cycle; see "Sex and Status: Women in St. Vincent," in Erika Bourguignon, ed., *A World of Women: Anthropological Studies of Women in the Societies of the World* (New York: Praeger, 1980), pp. 161–183. See also Melford E. Spiro, *Burmese Supernaturalism: A Study in the Exploration and Reduction of Suffering* (Englewood Cliffs, N.J.: Prentice-Hall, 1967), pp. 122, 157–163, 166, 219–221. In *Onnamen* (1958; Masks), Enchi draws on Rokujō and spirit possession as it relates to erotic passion. See especially the lecture on spirit possession in the Heian period by Ibuki Tsuneo: "The state of inspiration itself is intensely physical, heightening a person's sensuality to the furthest degree (unlike intellectual labor, which diminishes sexuality), so that the body of a medium in a trance comes to seem the very incarnation of sex"; *Masks*, p. 77; *Onnamen*, p. 100.

39. See Sigmund Freud, *Gesammelte Werke*, 5:187.

40. Victor Turner, "Liminality and the Performative Genres," in John J. MacAloon, ed., *Rite, Drama, Festival, Spectacle: Rehearsals Toward a Theory of Cultural Performance* (Philadelphia: Institute for the Study of Human Issues, 1984), pp. 22, 26.

41. Clifford Geertz, "Deep Play: Notes on the Balinese Cockfight," in *The Interpretation of Cultures: Selected Essays by Clifford Geertz* (New York:

Basic Books, 1973), p. 447. Geertz's reference to an "animal mask" suggests that the dramatization of Rokujō as possessing spirit is captured in the *nō* theater by the demonic mask called Hannya ("enlightenment"). For contemporary Japan, Ian Buruma has pointed out the significance of the subculture powerfully expressed in the popular performing genres that he interprets to represent "the violent fantasies of a people forced to be gentle. What one sees on the screen, on stage or in the comic-books is usually precisely the reverse of normal behaviour. The morbid and sometimes grotesque taste that runs through Japanese culture—and has done for centuries—is a direct result of being made to conform to such a strict and limiting code of normality. The theatrical imagination, the world of the bizarre is a parallel, or rather the flipside of reality, as fleeting and intangible as a reflection in the mirror." Buruma, *Behind the Mask: On Sexual Demons, Sacred Mothers, Transvestites, Gangsters, Drifters and Other Japanese Cultural Heroes* (New York: Pantheon, 1984), p. 225. See also Lebra, *Japanese Patterns of Behavior,* p. 246: "Possession by a spirit legitimizes taking the roles suppressed or prohibited by the cultural norms." And see Brenda Jordan, "*Yūrei:* Tales of Female Ghosts," in Stephen Addiss, ed., *Japanese Ghosts & Demons: Art of the Supernatural* (New York: Braziller, 1985), p. 32.

42. Geertz, "Deep Play," p. 449. See also Winston Davis' reference to "dissociation *in service of the ego*" in *Dojo: Magic and Exorcism in Modern Japan* (Stanford: Stanford University Press, 1980), p. 136.

43. "If peripheral possession is . . . a gesture of defiance, it is also one of hopelessness"; Ioan Myrddin Lewis, *Ecstatic Religion: An Anthropological Study of Spirit Possession and Shamanism* (Harmondsworth: Penguin, 1971), p. 33.

44. The postbirth spirits could be associated simply with the pollution of childbirth and afterbirth. See Arnold van Gennep, "Pregnancy and Childbirth," in *The Rites of Passage,* trans. Monika B. Vizedom and Gabrielle L. Cafee (Chicago: University of Chicago Press, 1960), p. 43.

45. William E. Naff, personal communication.

46. Shirane has noted that "the Rokujō lady feels little hostility toward Aoi . . . and makes every attempt to accommodate her"; *The Bridge of Dreams,* p. 114.

47. By contrast, Tamagami Takuya supports the commonly held view that Rokujō's living spirit, along with all the other *mono no ke,* played an important part in Aoi's demise: "Miyasudokoro no ikisudama ya mono no ke wa, kyū ni mōi o furuu koto ni natta no de arō to sōzō suru no ga tadashii yomikata to omowareru." *GMH* 2:427.

48. Ibid.

49. Field, *The Splendor of Longing,* p. 51.

50. Approaching the age of thirty—which, as Fujii Sadakazu has shown citing episode 142 of the *Ise monogatari,* is a turning point crucial to securing a woman's marital status—Rokujō has failed in her wife competition (*tsuma*

*arasoi)* with Aoi. Fujii compares Rokujō's crisis to the later crises of Murasaki, Genji's favorite wife, who must yield her position to the Third Princess, and to Kumoinokari, Yūgiri's principal wife, who feels threatened when her husband marries Ochiba (S: the Second Princess). See Fujii, *Monogatari no kekkon* (Sōjusha, 1985), pp. 45–49.

51. Whether or not sexual intercourse nonetheless occurred is irrelevant. Here, as in Genji's pursuit of Utsusemi, it is the woman's forceful resistance that counts.

52. According to Waley, Genji consciously feels guilty: "He knew that it was his neglect that had forced this parting upon them . . . brooding disconsolately upon a turn of affairs for which, as he well knew, he alone was responsible" (W:194, 197).

53. Ōasa Yūji has underlined Genji's poignant choice of Murasaki, rather than Rokujō, as his late principal wife Aoi's replacement; see "Rokujō Miyasudokoro no kunō," *KGMS* 3:30.

54. For a brief discussion of Genji's dream of an angry Fujitsubo, see my chapter "Murasaki," p. 119. Field notes that the Japanese puts Genji in a dreamlike state or "what might have been a dream *(yume to mo naku)*"; *The Splendor of Longing,* p. 44.

55. Fujii has noted that Rokujō takes the tonsure not only because she has fallen critically ill but because she necessarily neglected Buddhism during her six years at the great Shinto shrine at Ise. Her motivation for taking religious vows differs from the motivations of other major female protagonists (Fujitsubo, Utsusemi, the Third Princess, Oborozukiyo, and Ukifune) who were implicated in sexual transgressions. See Fujii, *Monogatari no kekkon,* pp. 54, 56.

56. Seidensticker's rendering of Rokujō's last words (2:303: *sari tomo to tanomoshiku namu*) as "I am no longer afraid to die" (S:286; see also *GMH* 3:341; NKBZ 2:302–303, n. 14) differs from that of others who have interpreted the phrase to indicate Rokujō's confidence in Genji's guardianship; see W:301; Oscar Benl, trans., *Genji-Monogatari: Die Geschichte vom Prinzen Genji* (Zürich: Manesse, 1966), 1:472; NKBT 2:126–127, n. 8; *GMH* 3:342. Read as a whole, however, Seidensticker's sentence also tentatively implies the latter meaning: "I have been able to tell you a little of what has been on my mind, *and* I am no longer afraid to die" (S:286; my italics). Which alternative one accepts depends on the degree one believes Rokujō to be skeptical or deluded about Genji's ability to keep the promise. Unknown to Rokujō, Genji on his part calculates about regaining political leverage by keeping the chaste *saigū* in reserve (*GMH* 3:343: *jibun no mochigoma to shite*) for imperial consort *(kōkyū)* to his son by Fujitsubo. The prospect of a secretive father-son rivalry is as forbidding as it is tempting—and a fitting continuation of the hero's predilection for the agony of love.

57. For text editions of *Nonomiya,* see Koyama, Satō, and Satō, eds.,

*Yōkyoku shū,* NKBZ 33, 1:280–290; Yokomichi and Omote, eds., *Yōkyoku shū,* NKBT 41, 2:318–322. For English translations, see Monica Bethe, "Nonomiya," *Kobe College Studies* 22(3) (1976):237–273 (a useful literal translation or "meta-phrase"); Janet Goff, *Noh Drama and The Tale of Genji: The Art of Allusion in Fifteen Classical Plays* (Princeton: Princeton University Press, 1991), pp. 140–145; Shimazaki Chifumi, trans., *The Noh,* vol. 3, bk. 1: *Woman Noh* (Tokyo: Hinoki shoten, 1976), pp. 35–59; H. Paul Varley, trans., *"The Shrine in the Fields (Nonomiya),"* in Donald Keene, ed., *Twenty Plays of the Nō Theatre* (New York: Columbia University Press, 1970), pp. 179–191; Kenneth Yasuda, *Masterworks of the Nō Theater* (Bloomington: Indiana University Press, 1989), pp. 42–59.

58. For text editions of *Aoi no ue,* see Koyama, Satō, and Satō, eds., *Yōkyoku shū,* NKBZ 34, 2:223–233; Yokomichi and Omote, eds., *Yōkyoku shū,* NKBT 40, 1:124–130. For English translations, see Goff, *Noh Drama and The Tale of Genji,* pp. 134–139; Nippon Gakujutsu Shinkōkai, trans., *Japanese Noh Drama: Ten Plays* (Tokyo: Nippon Gakujutsu Shinkōkai, 1959), 2:85–102; Arthur Waley, trans., *The Nō Plays of Japan* (New York: Grove Press, 1957), pp. 145–152.

59. See Goff, *Noh Drama and The Tale of Genji,* p. 125. There is a third play about Rokujō, *Shikimi tengu,* which I discuss briefly in my chapter "The Third Princess," p. 174.

60. Yasuda, *Masterworks of the Nō Theater,* p. 36. See also Goff, *Noh Drama and The Tale of Genji,* p. 129; Varley, *"The Shrine in the Fields,"* pp. 180–181.

61. If the synopsis of the "Sakaki" chapter in the *Hikaru Genji ichibu renga yoriai no koto* is any indication of the inaccuracy of manuals, then the playwright of *Nonomiya* proves his critical ability and knowledge of the original source by correcting such mistakes as the day of Genji's visit, which was the seventh day, and not the sixteenth day, of the Ninth Month. For a translation of this section of the undated linked-verse *(renga)* handbook, see Goff, *Noh Drama and The Tale of Genji,* pp. 78–79.

62. For details on the unverifiable authorship of *Nonomiya,* see Goff, *Noh Drama and The Tale of Genji,* p. 127.

63. Bethe has minutely examined "how the literary fabric is woven into the structural skeleton" in her "meta-phrase" of the text, given also in *kanji* and *rōmaji;* see *"Nonomiya,"* pp. 237–273.

64. On the role of the fan in the *nō,* see Monica Bethe and Karen Brazell, *Dance in the Nō Theater* (Ithaca: Cornell University Press, 1982), 1:71–74.

65. The well-known reference to the objective correlative is from T. S. Eliot on *Hamlet* in *The Selected Essays* (New York: Harcourt, Brace, 1950), pp. 121–126.

66. According to Goff, the use of the carriage as a prop in the second part of *Nonomiya* was abandoned in the seventeenth century and survives

only as a "variant style of performance"; see *Noh Drama and The Tale of Genji*, p. 129. For a photograph of a contemporary performance with the carriage prop, see Koyama, Satō, and Satō, eds., *Yōkyoku shū*, NKBZ 33, 1:280.

67. In its reversible meaning of both shelter and confinement, the carriage is, like the robe, symbolic of the state of spirit possession. If Rokujō's carriage represents her social status and functions as a physical extension of herself, then her fortified prestigious body is seized, displaced by Aoi's carriage, and usurped to Aoi's advantage at the carriage incident. When Rokujō vividly recalls the dramatic encounter and calls Aoi by name, it is as if Aoi were present on stage.

68. A translation of Zeami's *Sarugaku dangi,* from notes by Hata no Motoyoshi, is available in J. Thomas Rimer and Yamazaki Masakazu, trans., *On the Art of the Nō Drama: The Major Treatises of Zeami* (Princeton: Princeton University Press, 1984), "An Account of Zeami's Reflections on Art *(Sarugaku dangi),*" pp. 172–256. For the first known reference to a performance of *Aoi no ue,* see pp. 176–177.

69. Benito Ortolani, *The Japanese Theatre: From Shamanistic Ritual to Contemporary Pluralism* (Leiden: Brill, 1990), p. 87; see also pp. 90–92. Thomas Immoos has pointed out that "more than half [of 233 plays] contain this basic pattern of possession by a spirit or a god"; Immoos, "The Birth of the Japanese Theater," *Monumenta Nipponica* 24(4) (1969):412.

70. That *Aoi no ue,* unlike other *Genji* plays, uses very little material from its source is illustrated in Goff's translation through her use of italics for borrowed passages and words. See Goff, *Noh Drama and The Tale of Genji*, pp. 125, 128, 134–139.

71. Liza Crihfield Dalby, *Kimono: Fashioning Culture* (New Haven: Yale University Press, 1993), p. 222. Ordinarily, only sleeves or hems were revealed.

72. The commentator of the Nippon Gakujutsu Shinkōkai observes that the "*kosode* may be regarded as one of the *dramatis personae* who never speaks, and when it is carried from the Mirror Room on to the stage by a stage-attendant, the Curtain is often raised just as in the case of actors"; *Japanese Noh Drama*, 2:90.

73. Disembodied robes play a significant role in other *nō* plays, such as *Matsukaze,* text by Kan'ami (1333–1384), revised by Zeami (1363–1443). In this play, dramatizing the unrequited love of two fishergirls for the poet Ariwara no Yukihira (818–893) who left them his robe and court hat (*eboshi*) as a memento, one of the sisters, Matsukaze, first dances with the robe and hat and, thus entranced, dons them to be united with her lover. She in effect becomes other, as she is possessed by Yukihira's spirit through his robe and hat. In *Sotoba Komachi,* attributed to Kan'ami, revised by Zeami, Ono no Komachi (fl. ca. 833–857) can experience Fukakusa's unrequited love for her only by becoming Fukakusa through the transformative power of his dress:

"To represent Fukakusa externally, Komachi dons the white trousers, the formal headgear, and the hunting robe of the courtier." Etsuko Terasaki, "Images and Symbols in *Sotoba Komachi:* A Critical Analysis of a Nō Play," *Harvard Journal of Asiatic Studies* 44(1) ( June 1984):178.

74. The complete traditional classification of *Aoi no ue* is that of a fourth-category *(yobanmemono)* contemporary, madwoman play *(genzainō, kyō-jomono, onryō-mono)*; Bethe and Brazell follow the classification of *Aoi no ue* as a fourth-category play but modify it as a ghost play *(shūnen mono)* leaning toward fifth-category demon plays. They argue that the exorcism *(inori)* is "performed in a realistic action piece" *(hataraki)*. Bethe and Brazell, *Dance in the Nō Theater,* 2:100; see also 2:255. For the classification of *Aoi no ue* as an *"onryō-mono"* of the fourth category, see Nippon Gakujutsu Shinkōkai, trans., *Japanese Noh Drama,* 2:89.

75. Goff opens up the possibility of *mugen nō* by suggesting that *Aoi no ue* "has the aura of a dream . . . since the spirit is seen only by the sorceress"; *Noh Drama and The Tale of Genji,* p. 56. Yokomichi Mario and Omote Akira, the NKBT editors of *Yōkyoku shū,* 1:124, classify *Aoi no ue* as a *"jun-mugen nō,"* a quasi-dream *nō,* meaning that the action is dreamlike and the *shite* living rather than dead as in *mugen nō* proper.

76. For the mutual influence of *kagura* and *nō,* see Frank Hoff, *Song, Dance, Storytelling: Aspects of the Performing Arts in Japan* (Ithaca: Cornell University Press, 1978), pp. 165 passim.

77. Because of the syncretic origins of the Shugendō sect of esoteric Buddhism, *yamabushi* are perfectly suited to perform ancient shamanistic Shinto rituals in order to achieve Buddhist enlightenment.

78. The robe in *Aoi no ue* is usually understood to represent the ailing Aoi possessed by the jealous Rokujō; see, for example, Carmen Blacker, *The Catalpa Bow: A Study of Shamanistic Practices in Japan* (London: Allen & Unwin, 1975), p. 19; Waley, *The Nō Plays of Japan,* p. 180; Yasuda, *Masterworks of the Nō Theater,* p. 39.

79. It is remarkable that, for all his admittedly limited knowledge about the *Genji* and the *nō,* Ezra Pound interpreted "the concrete figure on the stage [as] a phantom or image of Awoi no Uye's own jealousy. That is to say, Awoi is tormented by her own passion, and this passion obsesses her first in the form of a personal apparition of Rokujo, then in demonic form." In their shared passion of jealousy, Pound sees Aoi and Rokujō as virtually interchangeable, but he emphasizes that "the whole play is a dramatization, or externalization, of Awoi's jealousy [which] makes her subject to the demon-possession." Pound arrives at this unusual view from his knowledge of modern Western drama, in particular Ibsen's psychological character portrayals. Ezra Pound and Ernest Fenollosa, trans., *The Classic Noh Theatre of Japan* (New York: New Directions, 1959), pp. 114–115.

80. William H. Matheson, "Madness in Literature: Reading the 'Heart-

vine' Chapter and Its Descendants," in Edward Kamens, ed., *Approaches to Teaching Murasaki Shikibu's The Tale of Genji* (New York: MLA, 1993), p. 166.

81. Matheson tentatively expresses the idea that the living Rokujō's dream in the *Genji* is transformed in *Aoi no ue* into the dead Rokujō's performance of the living Rokujō's dream: "The living spirit of the Rokujō lady (or the now dead spirit of the Rokujō lady *as* the Rokujō lady?) differs from her manifestation as a demon as one view of time differs from another." "Madness in Literature," p. 166.

82. Goff, *Noh Drama and The Tale of Genji*, p. 53. The text referred to here is the *Genji*, not the *nō* text.

83. See Saeki Shōichi, Donald Keene, Muramatsu Takeshi, and Tanaka Miyoko, eds., *Mishima Yukio Zenshū* (Shinchōsha, 1974), 21:33–53.

84. Donald Keene sees Mishima's nurse as "the counterpart of the priest who exorcises the living phantasm of Rokujō." Keene, trans., *Five Modern Nō Plays by Yukio Mishima* (New York: Knopf, 1957), p. xiv.

85. Ibid., p. xii; for Mishima's *The Lady Aoi*, see pp. 144–171.

86. Ibid., p. 152; *Mishima Yukio Zenshū*, 21:40.

87. By translating Mishima's invisible *bouquet* of pain *("mienai hanataba"; "kutsū no hanataba")* as "invisible. Flowers of pain," Keene brilliantly captures the foreign associations of *"hanataba"* and gives them the French scent of *"fleurs du mal."* Keene, trans., *Five Modern Nō Plays by Yukio Mishima*, p. 153; *Mishima Yukio Zenshū*, 21:40.

88. Keene, trans., *Five Modern Nō Plays by Yukio Mishima*, pp. 160, 156; *Mishima Yukio Zenshū*, 21:45, 42.

89. Keene, trans., *Five Modern Nō Plays by Yukio Mishima*, p. 160; *Mishima Yukio Zenshū*, 21:45.

90. Keene sees the sailboat as Mishima's transformation of the carriage in the *kuruma arasoi* scene in the *Genji*; see Keene, trans., *Five Modern Nō Plays by Yukio Mishima*, p. xiv.

91. Keene, trans., *Five Modern Nō Plays by Yukio Mishima*, p. 167; *Mishima Yukio Zenshū*, 21:50.

92. Keene, trans., *Five Modern Nō Plays by Yukio Mishima*, p. 171; *Mishima Yukio Zenshū*, 21:52: *ikiryō*.

93. Jay Rubin, "The Art of the Flower of Mumbo Jumbo," *Harvard Journal of Asiatic Studies* 53(2) (December 1993):521.

94. Matheson has raised the question of "the liberating role played by lyricism, particularly, indeed, the nurse's 'Ode to the Night'." "Madness in Literature," p. 167.

95. Cited by Henry Scott-Stokes, *The Life and Death of Yukio Mishima* (New York: Farrar, Straus & Giroux, 1974), p. 205.

96. Nancy J. Barnes, "Lady Rokujō's Ghost: Spirit Possession, Buddhism, and Healing in Japanese Literature," *Literature and Medicine* 8 (1989):119.

97. Matheson, "Madness in Literature," p. 166.

98. Mishima Yukio, *Sun & Steel,* trans. John Bester (Tokyo: Kodansha International, 1970), p. 54. In her analysis of Mishima's modern *nō* play *Genji kuyō* (A Genji Requiem), Linda M. Sylte points out that the excruciating pain of Murasaki Nozoe's uterine cancer proves her supreme existence and that, according to Mishima, "words are merely a pathetic attempt to resist death and oblivion." Sylte, "Zenchiku's 'A Genji Requiem' and Mishima's Modern Adaptation," unpublished M.A. thesis, (Washington University, 1980), p. 16.

## Murasaki

1. William H. McCullough has contested the view that the alleged provincial status of Murasaki's maternal relatives disqualified her from becoming Genji's principal wife. McCullough notes that Murasaki's mother was "not the daughter of a provincial official, but of a Great Counselor *(dainagon).*" Moreover, Murasaki's maternal grandfather held the same title of *azechi dainagon* as Genji's own maternal grandfather. See McCullough, "Japanese Marriage Institutions in the Heian Period," *Harvard Journal of Asiatic Studies* 27 (1967):138; 165, n. 276. Norma Field, on the other hand, insists that the textual references to Murasaki as Genji's *kita no kata* cannot be taken at face value because they come either from politically motivated characters (Higekuro and his wife) or occur at a time that requires symbolic honorific treatment (Murasaki's charge of the Akashi daughter's entry into the crown prince's household); see Field, *The Splendor of Longing in The Tale of Genji* (Princeton: Princeton University Press, 1987), p. 172. Murasaki's honorific title of *ue* is associated but not identical with *kita no kata.*

2. In contrast to myths and old narratives, *kaimami* in *monogatari* are controlled by court etiquette that conceals the taboo behind an elegant activity. For a lucid discussion of the evolution of *kaimami* from myth to the *Genji monogatari* and for the structural varieties of *kaimami,* see Hirota Osamu, "*Genji monogatari* ni okeru yōshiki to shite no kaimami," in Tsuchihashi Yutaka and Hirokawa Katsumi, eds., *Kodai bungaku no yōshiki to kinō* (Ōfūsha, 1988), pp. 169–186.

3. Haruo Shirane has pointed out that the "competition inherent in polygamous marriage demanded that women bear children"; *The Bridge of Dreams: A Poetics of "The Tale of Genji"* (Stanford: Stanford University Press, 1987), p. 54.

4. Field has gone so far as to characterize Murasaki, from the "Aoi" (S: "Heartvine") to the "Wakana" (S: "New Herbs") chapters, as "idealized, static, and—uninteresting." Field, *The Splendor of Longing,* p. 174.

5. The Genji–Murasaki relationship is dominated by a profound irony generated by the stepmother complex. For a discussion of step-relationships, see Shirane, *The Bridge of Dreams,* pp. 88–103. For the stepmother as a liter-

ary archetype, see Marian Ury, "Stepmother Tales in Japan," *Children's Literature* 9 (1981):62–63, 66–68.

6. For the complexities of Japanese adoption practices, especially among the modern nobility, see Takie Sugiyama Lebra, *Above the Clouds: Status Culture of the Modern Japanese Nobility* (Berkeley: University of California Press, 1993), pp. 106–129, 211–214, 240–241, 336–337.

7. The Mother of Michitsuna (dates uncertain; married 954) was competing against her husband Kaneie's principal wife Tokihime (d. 980), who was the mother of three known sons (including Fujiwara Michinaga [966–1027]) and two daughters (Chōshi [d. 982] and Senshi [962–1002]) who became imperial consorts and the mothers of emperors.

8. Edward Seidensticker, trans., *The Gossamer Years (Kagerō Nikki): The Diary of a Noblewoman of Heian Japan* (Tokyo: Tuttle, 1988), p. 130; NKBT 20:268.

9. Field argues that Yūgiri's restrained incestuous peeping at Murasaki in "Nowaki" (S: "The Typhoon") "breathe[s] life into Murasaki's abstract idealization." Field, *The Splendor of Longing*, p. 180.

10. Shirley M. Loui, who has sensitized readers to Akashi's drama rather than Murasaki's, writes: "Our sense of injustice and fair play aroused, we do not particularly care that Murasaki's jealousy of the Akashi Lady is thus [through the adoption] assuaged, nor that she is delighted with the child, nor that she is finally able to give expression to her maternal instincts." Loui, *Murasaki's Genji and Proust's Recherche: A Comparative Study* (Lewiston/Queenston/Lampeter: Edwin Mellen Press, 1991), pp. 161–162.

11. Readers should bear in mind that Murasaki's age is calculated on the basis of Genji's and therefore cannot be given with any precision.

12. Kimura Masanori has noted that Murasaki turns to Akashi for an ally to distract herself from her anxiety over the Third Princess; see "Wakamiya tanjō: Akashi ichizoku no shuku-un," *KGMS* 6:152–153.

13. Shirane has pointed out that Murasaki Shikibu "avoids the conventional image of the wicked stepmother. Being a stepmother herself, the author may have disliked the idea." Shirane, *The Bridge of Dreams*, p. 89.

14. This new mistress resembles Murasaki in that she has two politically powerful fathers: her neglectful biological father Tō no Chūjō and her caring foster father Genji. This paternal excess compensates for not having any maternal backing since Tamakazura's mother (Yūgao), like Murasaki's mother, died when she was an infant. Their situation stands in contrast to the Akashi daughter's position, which is strengthened by two mothers in addition to Genji's proud fatherhood.

15. Through this connection, the Rokujō-in intertextually reverberates with Yūgao's spirit possession, as discussed earlier.

16. See Hirota Osamu, "Rokujō-in no kōzō: Hikaru Genji monogatari

no keisei to tenkan," in Hirokawa Katsumi, ed., *Shinwa, kinki, hyōhaku: monogatari to setsuwa no sekai* (Ōfūsha, 1976), pp. 122, 131–132, passim.

17. Ibid., p. 121.

18. See Fujii Sadakazu, *Genji monogatari no shigen to genzai* (Tōjusha, 1980), pp. 157–159. This old mansion was located on Rokujō near the Eastern Hills (Higashiyama); see S:288; 2:307. It had fallen into ruins after Rokujō's death.

19. Field, *The Splendor of Longing*, p. 57.

20. Fujii, *Genji monogatari no shigen to genzai*, p. 158.

21. To readers of Waley's translation of the *Genji*, the Third Princess (Onna san no miya) is known as Nyosan.

22. See Takahashi Tōru, *Genji monogatari no taii-hō* (Tōkyō Daigaku shuppankai, 1982), p. 115.

23. Shirane, *The Bridge of Dreams*, p. 116.

24. Ibid., p. 114.

25. Ibid., pp. 115–116. The critic alludes to Sandra Gilbert and Susan Gubar, *The Madwoman in the Attic* (New Haven: Yale University Press, 1979) but distances himself from the applicability of the feminists' thesis to the *Genji*.

26. Field, *The Splendor of Longing*, p. 62; see also Fukazawa Michio, "Rokujō Miyasudokoro akuryō jiken no shudaisei ni tsuite," in Murasaki Shikibu Gakkai, ed., *Genji monogatari to sono eikyō: kenkyū to shiryō* (Musashino shoin, 1978), p. 85.

27. Field, *The Splendor of Longing*, p. 60.

28. See Sakamoto Kazuko, "Hikaru Genji no keifu," *Kokugakuin Zasshi* 76 (December 1975), cited in Field, *The Splendor of Longing*, p. 320, n. 59; Fujii Sadakazu, lecture at Amherst, Five Colleges, March 6, 1993; Field, *The Splendor of Longing*, pp. 61, 79. For a genealogical chart linking the Kiritsubo and Akashi lines, see Shirane, *The Bridge of Dreams*, p. 74.

29. The critics' exposure of the blood link between Kiritsubo and Akashi suggests a distant echo of blood incest in Genji's Akashi affair that parallels his forbidden affair with his stepmother. Genji fathers royal progeny through incestuous relations with both his paternal and maternal line. Rokujō, who is aware neither of Reizei's identity nor of the Akashi daughter's existence or family background, has no reason to be jealous of the mothers of these children.

30. See Fujii Sadakazu, "Rokujō Miyasudokoro no mono no ke," *KGMS* 7:45.

31. See H. Richard Okada, *Figures of Resistance: Language, Poetry, and Narrating in The Tale of Genji and Other Mid-Heian Texts* (Durham, N.C.: Duke University Press, 1992), pp. 276, 363, n. 48; see also p. 285.

32. Field has noted that "Higekuro's wife's suffering foreshadows

Murasaki's agony in the 'New Herbs' chapters." *The Splendor of Longing*, p. 146; see also pp. 149–159.

33. Higekuro's wife was in an especially painful situation because Higekuro not only visited Tamakazura according to common duolocal marriage practice but also intended to bring Tamakazura into his household, thereby threatening his principal wife with loss of status. W. H. McCullough has pointed out that instances of a secondary wife living under the same roof with the main wife were "rare." See McCullough, "Japanese Marriage Institutions in the Heian Period," p. 135.

34. Higekuro's suit was apparently helped along by Bennomoto (see S:491, 627; 3:341, 4:251), in attendance to the unwilling Tamakazura. See Field, *The Splendor of Longing*, pp. 145–146. It is also important that Tamakazura's half-brother Kashiwagi, buffooned in his own courtship of Tamakazura by Genji's incest game, becomes Higekuro's intermediary (see S:488; 3:334).

35. It appears that, more often than not, painters of *Genji-e* prefer a quiet, static rendering of this most dynamic expression of physical violence in the *Genji*. In the Freer Mitsunori album, for example, Higekuro is seated in front of a folding screen with the censer between him and his wife. The arrangement makes it difficult to imagine how Higekuro's wife could possibly have picked up the censer and stepped behind Higekuro without arousing his suspicion. For this image, see Miyeko Murase, *Iconography of The Tale of Genji: Genji Monogatari Ekotoba* (New York: Weatherhill, 1983), p. 175, plate 31–1. For a rare dynamic depiction of this scene, see Yamamoto Shun-shō's woodblock print (1650) in the Mary and Jackson Burke Collection (S:496).

36. Field, *The Splendor of Longing*, p. 151.

37. Fujimoto Katsuyoshi, who regards the medium *(yorimashi)* as essential for a successful Heian exorcism, attributes the failure of Higekuro's wife's possession to her usurpation of the medium's role; see *Genji monogatari no "mono no ke": bungaku to kiroku no hazama* (Kasama shoin, 1994), pp. 116–120.

38. By the Western count, the Third Princess is thirteen and Genji thirty-nine at the time of their marriage. Although it must be remembered that in Heian times the Third Princess' age was not uncommonly young for marriage, her disposition was considered immature and continued to be, with few exceptional moments, a permanent feature of her character.

39. Field, *The Splendor of Longing*, p. 186.

40. Shirane, *The Bridge of Dreams*, p. 115.

41. Shinohara Shōji, for example, cites the appearance of the Kiritsubo Emperor's dead spirit *(goryō)* in Genji's and the Suzaku Emperor's dreams; see "Mono no ke," *Kokubungaku* 28(16) (December 1983):127. Fujimoto also discusses the Suzaku Emperor's dream visitation by the Kiritsubo

Emperor in terms of spirit possession; see *Genji monogatari no "mono no ke,"* pp. 111–113.

42. Genji had several other haunting dreams—most notably of his late father at Suma and of the late Fujitsubo—that similarly compelled him to alleviate his bad conscience. Such a motivation, however, plays no role in spirit possession.

43. Shirane, *The Bridge of Dreams,* p. 53.

44. There is, furthermore, an association in Genji's mind between Oborozukiyo and Tamakazura (Genji's incestuously desired foster daughter): the former served Suzaku as his *naishi no kami,* or chief lady of the palace attendants office, and the latter chose not to become Reizei's *naishi no kami* but to marry Higekuro instead; see Field, *The Splendor of Longing,* p. 151.

45. Ibid., p. 32.

46. The Third Princess is promoted to Princess of the Second Rank (see S:597; 4:169) by the Kinjō Emperor, her half-brother.

47. See Field, *The Splendor of Longing,* pp. 189–190.

48. Jane Tibbetts Schulenburg, "The Heroics of Virginity: Brides of Christ and Sacrificial Mutilation," in Mary Beth Rose, ed., *Women in the Middle Ages and the Renaissance* (Syracuse: Syracuse University Press, 1986), p. 41.

49. The phrase is from Schulenburg, "The Heroics of Virginity," p. 40.

50. See Shirane, *The Bridge of Dreams,* p. 111. Field, on the other hand, has called attention to an "insistent religious streak" in Murasaki; see *The Splendor of Longing,* p. 190.

51. Fujimoto cites historical narratives such as Fujiwara Michinaga's (966–1027) *Midō kanpakuki* and Fujiwara Sanesuke's (957–1046) *Shōyūki* as evidence for the belief that chest pains were caused by *mono no ke* or *zake;* in the *Genji monogatari* this causal connection is made in Murasaki's case, which succeeds Aoi's. See Fujimoto, *Genji monogatari no "mono no ke,"* pp. 53–54.

52. Field, *The Splendor of Longing,* p. 190.

53. Fujimoto, *Genji monogatari no "mono no ke,"* pp. 66–67, 76.

54. See, for example, Sakamoto Kazuko, "Rokujō Miyasudokoro no Ise gekō to onryō shutsugen," *Bungaku Gogaku* 72 (August 1974):98. Sakamoto cautions that the famous conversation between Genji and Murasaki may merely be a pretext *("kōjitsu")* for the appearance of Rokujō's angry family spirit *("onryō");* instead, the critic suggests, without elaborating, that the Third Princess' secret affair with Kashiwagi may be the chief cause; ibid., p. 99. William H. McCullough argues that Rokujō's "resentment of Genji's defamatory remarks" is the "basic motive" for Murasaki's possession. McCullough, "Spirit Possession in the Heian Period," in Ōta Saburō and Fukuda Rikutarō, eds., *Studies on Japanese Culture* (Tokyo: Japan PEN Club, 1973), p. 93.

55. Shirane, *The Bridge of Dreams,* p. 115; see also Komachiya Teruhiko,

"Murasaki no ue no kunō: Murasaki no ue ron (3)," *KGMS* 6:93–109; especially pp. 96, 98, 100, 102.

56. In her brief scanning of Murasaki's possession, Komashaku Kimi asserts that Genji perceives Murasaki, trained not to express her jealousy openly, as the victim and exact opposite of Rokujō, whom he continues to fear because of her intense pride and strong ego. See Komashaku, *Murasaki Shikibu no messēji* (Asahi shinbunsha, 1991), pp. 147–148.

57. Fujimoto, however, argues that Genji identifies Murasaki's possessing spirit as Rokujō because of his pangs of conscience about Aoi's possession by Rokujō's *ikiryō* in the distant past; see *Genji monogatari no "mono no ke,"* p. 67.

58. Although W. H. McCullough recognizes Murasaki's delicate condition at the time of her spirit possession, the critic interprets her case mainly as Rokujō's rage over Genji's defamatory remarks, thus making Murasaki almost incidental to their conflict. McCullough notes that "the spirit's spleen was not always vented directly upon the person who had committed the wrong [that is, Genji]." McCullough, "Spirit Possession in the Heian Period," p. 93.

59. See Enchi Fumiko, *Genji monogatari shiken* (Shinchōsha, 1974), pp. 133, 146; see also Doris G. Bargen, "Twin Blossoms on a Single Branch: The Cycle of Retribution in *Onnamen*," *Monumenta Nipponica* 46(2) (Summer 1991):155.

60. Enchi Fumiko, *Masks,* trans. Juliet Winters Carpenter (New York: Aventura-Vintage, 1983), p. 57; Enchi Fumiko, *Onnamen* (Shinchōsha, 1966), p. 76.

61. It is interesting to note that there appears to be no *nō* play specifically devoted to Murasaki's spirit possession.

62. Adorcism refers to a form of exorcism that aims at the accommodation of the possessing spirits rather than their expulsion: "Spirit accommodation or internalisation (termed 'adorcism' by de Heusch 1962, 1971) . . . cultivates the power of the invasive, peripheral spirits, with the formation of what are essentially women's cults which have a subversive potential." Ioan Myrddin Lewis, "Exorcism and Male Control of Religious Experience," *Ethnos* 55(1–2) (1990):26–27.

63. See Fujimoto, *Genji monogatari no "mono no ke,"* pp. 60–63.

64. For other interpretations of this passage, see Field, *The Splendor of Longing,* p. 198; Shirane, *The Bridge of Dreams,* p. 118.

65. Susan R. Bordo, "The Body and the Reproduction of Femininity: A Feminist Appropriation of Foucault," in Alison M. Jaggar and Susan R. Bordo, eds., *Gender /Body /Knowledge: Feminist Reconstructions of Being and Knowing* (New Brunswick: Rutgers University Press, 1989), pp. 20–22.

### The Third Princess

1. Concerning the evolution from mythic taboo violation through *kaimami* to the increasingly indirect, sometimes symbolic, violation depicted in

*monogatari,* see Hirota Osamu, "*Genji monogatari* ni okeru yōshiki to shite no kaimami," in Tsuchihashi Yutaka and Hirokawa Katsumi, eds., *Kodai bungaku no yōshiki to kinō* (Ōfūsha, 1988), pp. 175–180.

2. It will be recalled that Rokujō's hopes were pinned on Crown Prince Zenbō and the hopes of the Third Princess' mother on Suzaku.

3. The Suzaku Emperor did not seem to have designated one of his wives as empress. His high consort Jōkyōden, the sister of Higekuro, provided the crown prince who married the Akashi daughter (fig. 3 in App. B).

4. In the heyday of Fujiwara regent *(sekkan)* rule through their daughters, it had become all but impossible for a princess to "assume the position of a high imperial consort, not to mention that of empress." As has been furthermore pointed out in the effort to correlate fact and fiction, the Third Princess is caught in the middle between Fujitsubo's successful rise to empress and the dreadful uncertainties of the Uji princesses. See Haruo Shirane, *The Bridge of Dreams: A Poetics of "The Tale of Genji"* (Stanford: Stanford University Press, 1987), p. 134; see also pp. 135, 137–139. Norma Field quotes the marriage statistics (provided in 4:23, n. 25) for princesses of the blood *(naishinnō)* during the Fujiwara period (781–986) as 15 percent. See Field, *The Splendor of Longing in The Tale of Genji* (Princeton: Princeton University Press, 1987), pp. 340–341, n. 24.

5. Ellen Peel has been misled by Western notions of incest to describe Genji's marriage to his half-brother's daughter as "literal inbreeding." Peel, "Mediation and Mediators: Letters, Screens, and Other Go-Betweens in *The Tale of Genji,*" in Edward Kamens, ed., *Approaches to Teaching Murasaki Shikibu's The Tale of Genji* (New York: MLA, 1993), p. 110.

6. The phrase "*murasaki no yukari,*" or purple connection, metaphorically expresses through a wide range of hues a person's court rank, the degree of kinship to another, as well as the (sometimes illicit) transference of feelings of affinity from one person to another. For an extensive discussion, see Field, *The Splendor of Longing,* pp. 161–166. See also Shirane, *The Bridge of Dreams,* pp. 46–47, and H. Richard Okada, *Figures of Resistance: Language, Poetry, and Narrating in The Tale of Genji and Other Mid-Heian Texts* (Durham, N.C.: Duke University Press, 1992), p. 264. On the whole spectrum of purple hues, see Liza Crihfield Dalby, *Kimono: Fashioning Culture* (New Haven: Yale University Press, 1993), pp. 235–237, 246–247, 251, 254–261. It should be noted that the Third Princess is not metaphorically linked to Fujitsubo (*"fuji"* means wisteria) and Murasaki (*"murasaki"* means lavender). Despite her high rank and her intimate kinship ties to Fujitsubo and Murasaki, Genji is unable to form the erotic link essential to *murasaki no yukari.*

7. For an analysis of this phrase, see Field, *The Splendor of Longing,* p. 336, n. 17.

8. Ibid., p. 234.

9. John J. Winkler, *The Constraints of Desire: The Anthropology of Sex and Gender in Ancient Greece* (New York: Routledge, 1990), p. 106.

10. Field, *The Splendor of Longing,* p. 234.

11. See Akiyama Ken, "Kemari no hi: Kashiwagi tōjō," *KGMS* 6:158.

12. Field, *The Splendor of Longing,* p. 315, n. 22.

13. Lady Nijō describes an unusual women's *kemari* scene conceived as a reenactment of the *Genji* incident involving the Third Princess; see Karen Brazell, trans., *The Confessions of Lady Nijō* (Stanford: Stanford University Press, 1973), pp. 92–95.

14. Victor Turner observes that *kemari* functions as a carnival festival making the audience receptive to the liminal by shifting the locus of the stage from the grounds of play to the veranda; see "Frame, Flow and Reflection: Ritual and Drama as Public Liminality," *Japanese Journal of Religious Studies* 6(4) (December 1979):486, 488.

15. The *kemari* scene in this more representative form, attributed to a follower of Tosa Mitsuyoshi, is luxuriously reproduced in Miyeko Murase, *Masterpieces of Japanese Screen Painting: The American Collections* (New York: Braziller, 1990), pp. 154–155.

16. The Third Princess' spontaneous attempt to rescue her Chinese cat run wild bears an uncanny resemblance to young Murasaki's frustration over her playmate Inuki's error in letting her baby sparrow(s) escape. In analogy to their own liminal transition from childhood to adulthood, they are engaged in domesticating their animal pets. While both are scolded for their unrestrained outbursts, the Third Princess is considered past the age when childishness could still be considered natural in Heian culture. Furthermore, young Murasaki, who unwittingly becomes subject to the convention of *kaimami,* cannot be accused of allowing herself to be seen.

17. Norma Field recognizes that the cat substitutes for the Third Princess, but she describes this case as "a parodic extreme [of the logic of substitution] were it not for the intensity verging on madness." Field, *The Splendor of Longing,* p. 168. Similarly, Haruo Shirane holds that "both the cat and the sister [Ochiba] function as substitute figures" and that Kashiwagi's pursuit of the cat and marriage to Ochiba "reflect the ludicrous degree to which he is ruled by his attachment to Genji's wife." Shirane, *The Bridge of Dreams,* p. 178.

18. The formation of court football families *(kemaridō ke)* had evolved soon after the importation of *kemari* from China in the seventh century. The Fujiwara family in particular became well known for its secret teachings about the ceremonial rules of the game. See Jörg Möller, *Spiel und Sport am Japanischen Kaiserhof im 7. bis 14. Jahrhundert* (München: Iudicium, 1993), pp. 94–95.

19. For details on children of wet nurses *(menotogo),* see Shirane, *The Bridge of Dreams,* p. 145; Saigō Nobutsuna, "Jōji to menotogo," in *Genji monogatari o yomu tame ni* (Heibonsha, 1983), pp. 69–76.

20. Examples are numerous. For the *Genji,* the "Aoi" episode, for example, expresses the *mono no ke*'s plea of binding her wandering spirit in the hem of the robe (see S:168; 2:33). See also *Ise monogatari,* episode 110.

21. Hirota Osamu traces the history of the Chinese koto *(kin)* among *Genji* characters—from Kaoru and the Third Princess to Genji, Hotaru, and Onna ichi no miya (Genji's older siblings) to Kiritsubo-in. See Hirota, "*Genji monogatari* ni okeru ongaku to keifu," in *Genji monogatari no tankyū: dai jū-san shū* (Kazama shobō, 1988), pp. 265–272.

22. Shirane, *The Bridge of Dreams,* p. 172.

23. Field, *The Splendor of Longing,* p. 28.

24. William H. McCullough does not comment upon a man's affair with his wife's half-sister; see "Japanese Marriage Institutions in the Heian Period," *Harvard Journal of Asiatic Studies* 27 (1967):135–136. Fujii Sadakazu claims that marriage with half-sisters of different mothers was not considered taboo in Heian society; see *Genji monogatari no shigen to genzai* (Tōjusha, 1980), p. 236. It seems to me, however, that Murasaki Shikibu problematizes such relationships, albeit through fiction, when they became intertwined with adultery. See note 49 below and my chapter "Ukifune," pp. 212, 216–266.

25. In the *Utsubo monogatari* (The Tale of the Hollow Tree; second half of the tenth century) Fujimoto Katsuyoshi has found a rare literary precedent for Kashiwagi's alleged possession by a woman's spirit. It features Nakazumi's fantasy of adultery and sibling incest with Atemiya, followed by his possession by a female spirit. See Fujimoto, *Genji monogatari no "mono no ke": bungaku to kiroku no hazama* (Kasama shoin, 1994), pp. 104–106. For a translation of this part of the *Utsubo monogatari,* see Edwin A. Cranston, "Atemiya: A Translation from the *Utsubo monogatari,*" *Monumenta Nipponica* 24(3) (1969):289–314.

26. Field, *The Splendor of Longing,* p. 256.

27. Shirane, *The Bridge of Dreams,* p. 178.

28. Edward Kamens cites the similar case of Sonshi (965?–985), an imperial princess who took religious vows in 982, which led Fujiwara Sanesuke (957–1046) in his diary, *Shōyūki,* to note rumors that this step "was the work of an evil spirit in possession of her." In the eyes of others, such as Yoshishige Yasutane (d. 1002), Sonshi's tonsure happened as a result of her "long-nurtured intention." See Kamens, *The Three Jewels: A Study and Translation of Minamoto Tamenori's Sanbōe* (Ann Arbor: Center for Japanese Studies, University of Michigan, 1988), pp. 8, 11. Fujimoto suggests that Murasaki Shikibu may have had Sonshi's family background and the rare, shocking incident of her tonsure in mind as a model for the Third Princess; see *Genji monogatari no "mono no ke,"* pp. 85–86.

29. Hirota Osamu, "*Genji monogatari* ni okeru waka no denshōsei: Rokujō Miyasudokoro no mono no ke no baai," *Nihon Bungaku* 31 (May 1982):55.

30. The process is thought to be analogous to the ritual of becoming a shamaness *(miko)*; see Fujii Sadakazu, "Tsuku bungaku: *Genji monogatari* ron no tame ni," *Bungaku* 50 (November 1982):110, 113.

31. Fujimoto, *Genji monogatari no "mono no ke,"* pp. 83–84.

32. Takahashi Tōru, *Genji monogatari no taii-hō* (Tōkyō Daigaku shup-pankai, 1982), p. 116.

33. Hasegawa Masaharu, for example, has noted that Rokujō's spirit not only possesses Genji's wives but also drives them to their death or into taking the tonsure; see "Onna san no miya shukke," *KGMS* 7:33. Takahashi sees Rokujō's increasing obnoxiousness as *mono no ke* in direct correspondence to Genji's decline as hero; Takahashi, *Genji monogatari taii-hō,* p. 116.

34. Hirota, "*Genji monogatari* ni okeru waka no denshōsei," p. 56.

35. Taya Raishun, recognizing that Rokujō's spirit has no connection to the Third Princess, modifies the identity of the *mono no ke* as vaguely combin-ing the features of an evil spirit ("akuma-teki") and Rokujō ("Miyasudokoro-teki"); see Taya, *Genji monogatari no shisō* (Kyoto: Hōzōkan, 1952), p. 134; see also p. 163.

36. Mae Michiko, "Tod als Selbstverwirklichung in einem Leben ohne Liebe: Drei Frauengestalten in der japanischen Literatur," in Renate Berger and Inge Stephan, eds., *Weiblichkeit und Tod in der Literatur* (Köln / Wien: Böhlau Verlag, 1987), p. 44.

37. Saigō, *Genji monogatari o yomu tame ni,* p. 131.

38. Field, *The Splendor of Longing,* p. 60.

39. Janet Goff, *Noh Drama and The Tale of Genji: The Art of Allusion in Fifteen Classical Plays* (Princeton: Princeton University Press, 1991), p. 49.

40. For a definition of *tengu* and an illustration, see Goff, *Noh Drama and The Tale of Genji,* pp. 48, 54, 130, and 131 (fig. 7). Goff does not con-nect the play's raucous laughter to the possession of the Third Princess. Rather she associates Rokujō's "frenzied state" in *Shikimi tengu* with her sim-ilarly tortured appearance in Murasaki's spirit possession. Goff also sees a "slender link" between the play's hellish smoke and Akikonomu's concerns about her mother's wanderings in the "smokes of hell" (S:674–675; 4:376). See Goff, *Noh Drama and The Tale of Genji,* pp. 132, 54.

41. Ibid., p. 149; for a complete translation of this play, see pp. 146–149.

42. Haraoka Fumiko, "Rokujō Miyasudokoro o megutte," *Nihon Bungaku* 36 (March 1971):36–38.

43. Taya, *Genji monogatari no shisō,* p. 140 passim. While noting that the Third Princess' *mono no ke* successfully resists exorcism by Buddhist rituals, Fujii Sadakazu has not pursued this insight in order to question the spirit's received identity as Rokujō. See Fujii, "Rokujō Miyasudokoro no mono no ke," *KGMS* 7:41–42.

44. See Abe Toshiko, "*Genji monogatari* no 'mono no ke,'" *Kokugo kokubun ronshū* 6 (February 1977):35–36.

45. Helen Hardacre notes an interesting departure from the interdependent ritual functions of *yamabushi* and *miko* in Nakayama Miki's (1798–1887) possession by a male deity. By enacting both *yamabushi* and *miko* roles herself, the founder of the New Religion of Tenrikyō changed the Shugendō male construction of gender and left the "males on the losing side . . . humiliatingly 'feminized' as a result of their defeat." Hardacre, "Conflict Between Shugendō and the New Religions of Bakumatsu Japan," *Japanese Journal of Religious Studies* 21(2–3) ( June–September 1994):155.

46. Walter Burkert notes that "in ethology, even laughter is thought to originate in an aggressive display of teeth." Burkert, *Homo Necans: The Anthropology of Ancient Greek Sacrificial Ritual and Myth,* trans. Peter Bing (Berkeley: University of California Press, 1983), p. 24. Catharina Blomberg, who holds that the Heian custom of blackening teeth *(hagurome)* was done for "cosmetic purposes and considered as an embellishment," cites the story of "Mushi mezuru himegimi" (The Lady Who Admired Vermin) from the *Tsutsumi Chūnagon monogatari* (The Tale of the Tsutsumi Middle Counselor; late Heian) as an example of a flagrant violation of this custom. See Blomberg, "'A Strange White Smile': A Survey of Tooth-Blackening and Other Dental Practices in Japan," *Japan Forum* 2(2) (November 1990):245. The noblewoman's radical subversion of the courtly ideal of femininity—by refusing, among other things, to blacken her teeth—can also be seen as her liberation from cultural constraints and her recovery of repressed emotions, such as aggression, by flashing gleaming white dental bones at the man intent on ridiculing her eccentricities. Michele Marra has called the story "a manifesto of firm opposition to the court's code of refinement and a denunciation of its rules." Marra, *The Aesthetics of Discontent: Politics and Reclusion in Medieval Japanese Literature* (Honolulu: University of Hawai'i Press, 1991), p. 65; see also pp. 68–69.

47. Edward Kamens has suggested that Kaoru, in contemplating his mother's religious commitment, does not understand her motivations and "condescends, and dismisses her," partly because of the Five Obstructions *(itsutsu no sawari; goshō)* that denigrate women and their prospects for enlightenment. See Kamens, "Dragon-Girl, Maidenflower, Buddha: The Transformation of a Waka Topos, 'The Five Obstructions'," *Harvard Journal of Asiatic Studies* 53(2) (December 1993):393. However, Kaoru does not seem to worry so much about whether or not she, as a woman, can overcome the Five Obstructions. His strikingly nonchalant reference to the religious topos as "itsutsu no nanigashi" (5:18)—in Kamens' rendering "the five something-or-other" or "the five-what-you-may-call-its" (p. 390)—hardly assigns much relevance to his mother's future religious welfare. Rather, he is driven to learn the causes of her religious step. He is mystified because he suspects that it was not pure religious intent that led her to take the tonsure but "that some horrible surprise had overtaken her, something that had shaken her to

the roots of her being" (S:738; 5:18). In this contemplative scene Kaoru is beginning to associate his youthful mother's withdrawal from the world with Kashiwagi's premature death.

48. For the provenance and legacy of this flute, from the Yōzei Emperor to Kaoru, see Hirota, "*Genji monogatari* ni okeru ongaku to keifu," pp. 250–259. Kaoru eventually comes in possession of the flute (see S:929; 5:469).

49. Ochiba is extremely troubled by incestuous fears of stealing her sister-in-law Kumoinokari's husband and by the shameful ostracism to be expected from Kashiwagi's in-laws for marrying his sister's husband.

50. The "Yūgiri" scene is captured by the artists of the *Genji monogatari emaki* (Gotō Art Museum, Tokyo). The scene graces the cover of Field's *The Splendor of Longing;* see also the unnumbered illustration in Shirane, *The Bridge of Dreams.*

51. Fujimoto argues that Ichijō's death, which need not be seen in connection with her spirit possession, became inevitable when Yūgiri was able to claim Ochiba, Ichijō's raison d'être *("ikigai");* see *Genji monogatari no "mono no ke,"* p. 129.

52. Erika Bourguignon has noted that it "is indeed striking that children are hardly ever seen to experience possession trance and that the phenomenon is relatively rare in older people. To the extent that it occurs in young people, it is part of learning the appropriate cult-related roles and part of learning adult secular roles as well." Bourguignon, *Possession* (San Francisco: Chandler & Sharp, 1976), p. 39.

53. See Goff, *Noh Drama and The Tale of Genji*, pp. 45, 169; for a translation of *Darani Ochiba*, see pp. 176–181.

54. For a translation of *Ochiba*, see Goff, *Noh Drama and The Tale of Genji*, pp. 171–175.

55. For the debate about the structural and thematic placement of the "Yūgiri" chapter, see Shirane, *The Bridge of Dreams*, p. 238, n. 18.

## Ukifune

1. For Uji place-name associations—in linguistic as well as poetic resonances, geographic symbolism, and the succession dispute among the three sons of Emperor Ōjin (r. 270–310), as recounted in the *Kojiki* (712), the *Nihon shoki* (720), and the *Fudoki* (713)—see Norma Field, *The Splendor of Longing in The Tale of Genji* (Princeton: Princeton University Press, 1987), pp. 218–221, and Haruo Shirane, *The Bridge of Dreams: A Poetics of "The Tale of Genji"* (Stanford: Stanford University Press, 1987), pp. 186–187.

2. Shirane, *The Bridge of Dreams*, p. 151.

3. Field, *The Splendor of Longing*, p. 222.

4. For an extensive discussion of this coinage, see Field, *The Splendor of Longing*, pp. 223–225 and pp. 338–339, n. 9 and n. 12.

5. See Leon Hurvitz, trans., *Scripture of the Lotus Blossom of the Fine*

*Dharma (The Lotus Sutra). Translated from the Chinese of Kumārajīva* (New York: Columbia University Press, 1976), pp. 64–71.

6. In his famous essay "Das Unheimliche" ("The Uncanny"; 1919), Sigmund Freud criticized as limited E. Jentsch's 1906 treatise about the origins of the uncanny in an "intellektuellen Unsicherheit" (*Gesammelte Werke,* 12:231; *Standard Edition,* 17:221: "intellectual uncertainty"). Freud elaborated on the concept of the uncanny by pointing first to the paradox at the core of the word *"unheimlich,"* which implies the frightful aspects of the seemingly familiar rather than the unfamiliar. He then analyzed E.T.A. Hoffmann's "Der Sandmann" (1816) to go beyond Jentsch's notion of intellectual uncertainty toward childhood castration fears and adult neuroses as expressed in sexual inhibition and the death wish.

7. Although Kaoru is not in fact the Eighth Prince's nephew, he is related to him through his maternal grandfather Suzaku. The Eighth Prince is Kaoru's granduncle. Moreover, through Shi no kimi, his paternal grandmother and sister of Kokiden, Kaoru becomes genealogically implicated in a distasteful tradition of failed political schemes. Kaoru's ancestors have, to some degree, forged the Eighth Prince's sad destiny.

8. See Doris G. Bargen, "The Search for Things Past in the *Genji monogatari,*" *Harvard Journal of Asiatic Studies* 51(1) (June 1991): 211 and 211, n. 21. The original version of this article was presented in 1982 at the "World of Genji" conference at Indiana University at Bloomington. Paul G. Schalow has expanded upon my thesis of homoerotic bonding between Kaoru and the Eighth Prince in his paper " 'Bridging' as a Mechanism of Male Homosocial Desire in *The Tale of Genji,*" presented at the annual meeting of the Association for Asian Studies in Honolulu on April 13, 1996.

9. Komashaku Kimi has noted the Eighth Prince's motherly role in raising his two legitimate daughters after the death of his wife; see Komashaku, *Murasaki Shikibu no messēji* (Asahi shinbunsha, 1991), p. 164.

10. Esperanza Ramirez-Christensen has described Bennokimi as "a sorcerer figure and medium of fate [who] mesmerizes Kaoru with stories of the past." Ramirez-Christensen, "The Operation of the Lyrical Mode in the *Genji Monogatari,*" in Andrew Pekarik, ed., *Ukifune: Love in The Tale of Genji* (New York: Columbia University Press, 1982), p. 35.

11. By contrast, no such religious piety stood in the way of another parent-child pair: Genji and Reizei achieved a tacit understanding in their nonverbal communication—rendered best, that is, without actual words, through the painterly medium by the artists of the *Genji monogatari emaki* ("Suzumushi II," Gotō Museum, Tokyo). For a description of this delicate scene, see Miyeko Murase, *Emaki: Narrative Scrolls from Japan* (New York: Asia Society, 1983), pp. 64–70; color illus. front cover and p. 38 (detail); full monochrome illus., p. 64.

12. Freud citing Schelling, in "The Uncanny," *Standard Edition,* 17:

224 (my roman); see also *Standard Edition,* 17:225, 241; *Gesammelte Werke,* 12:235, 236, 254.

13. The original frequently uses the expression *"monogatari"* (see, for example, 5:220, 222, 227) or commonly used verbs for speaking and listening.

14. See Hasegawa Masaharu, "Uji jūjō no sekai: Hachi no miya no yuigon no jubakusei," in *Genji monogatari IV* (Yūseidō, 1982), p. 140.

15. Scholars' understanding of the Kaoru–Ōigimi "affair" is generally based on the premise that the two have fallen in love but deviate curiously from courtship convention. See Ramirez-Christensen, "The Operation of the Lyrical Mode," pp. 31, 33, 55–56.

16. The scene recalls most vividly Genji's night with Utsusemi's step-daughter (Nokiba no ogi), as has frequently been pointed out; see, for example, Field, *The Splendor of Longing,* p. 244.

17. Just as the sisters represent two sides of their father, so Kaoru and Niou here incorporate the Eighth Prince's spirituality and carnality. More typically, Kaoru and Niou are interpreted to represent pale shadows of a divided Genji; see, for example, Haruo Shirane, "The Uji Chapters and the Denial of Romance," in Andrew Pekarik, ed., *Ukifune: Love in The Tale of Genji* (New York: Columbia University Press, 1982), pp. 126–128, 130.

18. Caroline Walker Bynum, *Holy Feast and Holy Fast: The Religious Significance of Food to Medieval Women* (Berkeley: University of California Press, 1987), especially chap. 6.

19. The custom reached its first peak during the late Heian period and was largely the domain of the male mountain priests *(yamabushi)* of the eclectic Shugendō sect. The bizarre practice culminated in the extraordinary ascetic feat of producing Japanese mummies *(miira)* through a gruesome process of "self-mummification."

20. Yūgiri's wife Kumoinokari is an exception to this pattern: her breast-feeding and general intimacy with her many children appear rather boorish, except when she turns to breastfeeding to dispel her jealousy and as a strategy to elicit her husband's sympathy. Miyeko Murase notes that this domestic scene is excluded from the Osaka manual; its depiction by the atelier of the *Genji monogatari emaki* ("Yokobue," Tokugawa Reimeikai Foundation) is therefore "the most unexpected scene in the *Genji* paintings of the Heian period." Murase, *Iconography of The Tale of Genji: Genji Monogatari Ekotoba* (New York: Weatherhill, 1983), p. 23; fig. 6, p. 24. By contrast, Murasaki's offering of her small breast to the newly adopted Akashi daughter (Plate 2.5) is moving precisely because it can only be a symbolic gesture (see S:337; 2:430).

21. William H. McCullough and Helen Craig McCullough, *A Tale of Flowering Fortunes: Annals of Japanese Aristocratic Life in the Heian Period* (Stanford: Stanford University Press, 1980), p. 297, n. 158.

22. Ramirez-Christensen, "The Operation of the Lyrical Mode," p. 59.

For an exploration of Ōigimi's death scene in terms of the aesthetic significance of emaciation, see Aileen Gatten, "Death and Salvation in *Genji Monogatari*," in Aileen Gatten and Anthony Hood Chambers, eds., *New Leaves: Studies and Translations of Japanese Literature in Honor of Edward Seidensticker* (Ann Arbor: Center for Japanese Studies, University of Michigan, 1993), pp. 11–13; Shirane, *The Bridge of Dreams,* pp. 124, 190. Writing about European Romanticism, Elisabeth Bronfen has stated that "a feminisation of death occurs even as the body is desexualised. It is an aesthetically pleasing corpse. . . . Its beauty marks the purification and distance from two moments of insecurity—female sexuality and decay." Bronfen, *Over Her Dead Body: Death, Femininity and the Aesthetic* (New York: Routledge, 1992), p. 11.

23. Fujimura Kiyoshi interprets Ōigimi's inability to dream of her father as her lack of a bad conscience, while in Nakanokimi's case the Eighth Prince is seen as a source of anxiety. See Fujimura, "Hachi no miya no yuigon," *KGMS* 8:116–117. To put the matter differently, it is Ōigimi who actively desires to dream of her father but cannot ("usetamaite nochi, ika de yume ni mo mitatematsuramu to omou o, sara ni koso mitatematsurane"; 5:302; see also 5:301). Nakanokimi, however, being less obsessed, dreams of him spontaneously.

24. This meant that his marital residence had not been decided; if named crown prince, Niou could have a virilocal marriage (the wife enters the husband's household) and exercise a privilege that was "normally reserved for emperors and heirs apparent." Peter Nickerson, "The Meaning of Matrilocality: Kinship, Property, and Politics in Mid-Heian," *Monumenta Nipponica* 48(4) (Winter 1993):459; see also p. 462. William H. McCullough categorizes Niou's final marriage arrangement with Nakanokimi as "neolocal"; "Japanese Marriage Institutions in the Heian Period," *Harvard Journal of Asiatic Studies* 27 (1967):117.

25. See chapter 12 of the Lotus Sutra, called "Devadatta," in Hurvitz, trans., *Scripture of the Lotus Blossom,* pp. 195–201. The *Ōjōyōshū* (Essentials for Rebirth in the Pure Land; 985) by the priest Genshin (942–1017) also promises salvation to women through the practice of evoking the Buddha's name *(nenbutsu).*

26. In his note (S:1016) Seidensticker expresses surprise not only at the sibling blood tie between the abbot and nurse but also at nurse's "close ties with Uji." Yet this connection makes eminent sense in view of the abbot's role in the Eighth Prince's life.

27. The specific term of *amakakerite* is reminiscent of Rokujō's restless dead spirit (see S:618; 4:227).

28. It is interesting to note that the Osaka manual for painters *(Genji monogatari ekotoba)* omits the entire narrative complex culminating in Ōigimi's death.

29. Fujimoto Katsuyoshi, *Genji monogatari no "mono no ke": bungaku to*

*kiroku no hazama* (Kasama shoin, 1994), p. 92. Fujimoto cites Mitani Eiichi (*"Genji monogatari* ni okeru minkan shinkō"; 1971) as noting a contradiction between Ōigimi's nonpossession and her apparent death by the evil spirit of a priest who later possesses Ukifune; ibid., p. 93.

30. Susan R. Bordo has pointed to the "ingenious literalism" with which modern female disorders such as anorexia and agoraphobia carry male constructs of femininity to their logical extreme. Bordo, "The Body and the Reproduction of Femininity: A Feminist Appropriation of Foucault," in Alison M. Jaggar and Susan R. Bordo, eds., *Gender/Body/Knowledge: Feminist Reconstructions of Being and Knowing* (New Brunswick: Rutgers University Press, 1989), p. 17.

31. Bronfen, *Over Her Dead Body,* p. 102.

32. Mae Michiko has compared Ōigimi and Rokujō in their attempt to find self-realization ("Selbstverwirklichung") in the interstice ("Zwischenraum") between life and death; Mae, "Tod als Selbstverwirklichung in einem Leben ohne Liebe: Drei Frauengestalten in der japanischen Literatur," in Renate Berger and Inge Stephan, eds., *Weiblichkeit und Tod in der Literatur* (Köln / Wien: Böhlau Verlag, 1987), p. 48.

33. Bronfen, *Over Her Dead Body,* p. 120.

34. This relatively minor character is known after her residences, first as Reikeiden, then as Fujitsubo nyōgo (see 5:363, n. 2). To avoid confusion with Genji's stepmother Fujitsubo and with the Third Princess' mother Fujitsubo nyōgo, she is here referred to only as Reikeiden. She becomes possessed apparently as a result of frantic preparations for her only daughter's initiation ceremonies. Echoing Ichijō's fatal anxiety over Ochiba, Reikeiden dies from *mono no ke* (see S:886; 5:364). Otherwise, not enough is known about Reikeiden to warrant a more substantial discussion of her case of spirit possession and death.

35. Some scholars have been led by the unconventionality of both Kashiwagi's and Kaoru's courtship to interpret their amorous episodes as not merely eccentric but laughable. It appears that Norma Field especially has been tempted to describe Kaoru's approach to Ōigimi, and even her death, as a trifle comic. See Field, *The Splendor of Longing,* pp. 246, 248–249, 256.

36. For Ōigimi's own unorthodox concept of substitution, see Hirota Osamu, "*Genji monogatari* ni okeru 'yukari' kara tasha no hakken e," *Chūko bungaku* 20 (October 1978):28–38.

37. Bronfen's analysis of Poe's "The Oval Portrait" (1842) demonstrates that the artist's desire to create "the perfect resemblance" leads to the experience of the uncanny, which, following Freud's essay on the topic (*Standard Edition,* 17:217–256), produces a profound uncertainty ("Unsicherheit") as to "whether something is animate (alive) or inanimate (dead), whether something is real or imagined, unique, original or a repetition, a copy." Bronfen, *Over Her Dead Body,* pp. 112–113.

38. The Iwanami *Kogo jiten* cites this example from "Yadorigi" under the *"henge"* entry.

39. Although Ukifune's mother here flatters Nakanokimi by addressing her as *kita no kata*, it is as doubtful as in Murasaki's case that Nakanokimi could ever officially claim the title in the absence of family backing and the presence of a powerful female rival.

40. For an elaboration on reader participation in producing meaning in the *Genji*, see Lynne K. Miyake, "The Narrative Triad in *The Tale of Genji*," in Edward Kamens, ed., *Approaches to Teaching Murasaki Shikibu's The Tale of Genji* (New York: MLA, 1993), especially pp. 79–80, 85.

41. En route between her current residence in the capital and Hatsuse she stops each way at Uji (see S:935; 5:482: *nakayadori*) to pay her respects at the Eighth Prince's grave, an ancestral site that is, unlike the two extreme poles of her journey, neither secular nor religious. Uji perfectly reflects the Eighth Prince's existential condition as *zoku hijiri*.

42. Ukifune's stepfather is actually referred to as the Governor of Hitachi, but since such a position could be held only by imperial princes, he was no more than vice-governor of that remote province (to the northeast of modern Tokyo, in Ibaraki prefecture). Like the "governor's" pretentious title, the status of his favorite daughter, known as "Himegimi" (princess), is similarly misleading. The fact that he is merely Ukifune's stepfather further underlines the pattern of manipulated social status and analogous relationships.

43. Ukifune is not as fortunate as Murasaki and Kumoinokari, who were raised by grandparents who shielded them from conflict with a stepparent over competing with the stepparent's children.

44. Chūjō's arrangement for her troubled daughter produces an anomalous situation within the Heian pattern of separate postmarital residences for sisters, which points to male ego/ wife's sister sexual relations being inappropriate. W. H. McCullough does not rule out that sisters could both be married uxorilocally, but he indicates that considerations of space made it necessary for either the parents or one of the two daughters to live in a neolocal residence; "Japanese Marriage Institutions in the Heian Period," p. 117.

45. For a description of this scene, see my chapter "Enter *mono no ke*," pp. 28–31.

46. The Kinjō Emperor worries about his daughter being controlled by her husband's mother rather than her parents who would customarily have provided the uxorilocal or neolocal residence (see S:927; 5:464). W. H. McCullough does not discuss Kaoru's marriage to the Second Princess, but he classifies Kaoru's earlier marriage plan for Ōigimi, whom Kaoru also intended to install at his mother's rebuilt residence, in terms of a "neolocal" arrangement because the Sanjō residence originally was the property of the Third Princess' father. McCullough explains "that marriage residence among aristocrats in the Heian period was consistently either uxorilocal, duolocal, or

neolocal, and equally important, that it was never virilocal." McCullough, "Japanese Marriage Institutions in the Heian Period," pp. 115, 105. Virilocal marital residence was the privilege of emperors and heirs apparent; see Nickerson, "The Meaning of Matrilocality," p. 453 and n. 75.

47. Seidensticker notes that this critical sentence is "missing from numbers of texts" (S:945 n.).

48. This Uji Ukon (fig. 7 in App. B) is not to be confused with Nakanokimi's Ukon. For a detailed argument distinguishing these two characters named Ukon, see Aileen Gatten, "Three Problems in the Text of 'Ukifune'," in Andrew Pekarik, ed., *Ukifune: Love in The Tale of Genji* (New York: Columbia University Press, 1982), pp. 102–108.

49. For an illustration and description of this painting, see Julia Meech-Pekarik, "The Artist's View of Ukifune," in Andrew Pekarik, ed., *Ukifune: Love in The Tale of Genji* (New York: Columbia University Press, 1982), fig. 3 and pp. 182–185. The art historian notes that the sewing scene "is obviously related to the illustration of the 'Sawarabi' (S: 'Early Ferns') chapter in the Heian *Genji* scroll [*Genji monogatari emaki*] in which Nakanokimi's ladies sew garments in preparation for her move to the capital"; ibid., p. 184. The Seidensticker translation (see S:879) of this passage does not make explicit the reference to sewing in the original text (see 5:350).

50. To be gruesomely precise, the heavenly weaving maiden "struck her genitals against the shuttle and died." Donald L. Philippi, trans., *Kojiki* (Tokyo: Princeton University Press and University of Tokyo Press, 1969), p. 80. In some accounts of the *Nihon shoki* it is Amaterasu ōmikami herself who is "alarmed and injured"; ibid., n. 9.

51. Seidensticker supplies a kinship term where there is none in the original; but then "Heian aristocrats, despite the importance of descent and affinity in social and political life, seem to have used kin terms sparingly, to the extent that actual usage is reflected in Heian literature." Nickerson, "The Meaning of Matrilocality," p. 449, n. 62.

52. The problem of incest in Heian society and literature deserves much more study than it has so far received—especially in light of recent research on the fairly unexplored area of illicit sexual relationships and/or marital ties between in-laws. Only now is a terminology being developed for "affinal" incest, see Paul B. Roscoe, "Amity and Aggression: A Symbolic Theory of Incest," *Man* (n.s.) 29 (March 1994):69–70; for "secondary" incest, see Françoise Héritier, *Les deux soeurs et leur mère: anthropologie de l'inceste* (Paris: Éditions Odile Jacob, 1994), pt. 3. I am grateful to Deborah B. Gewertz and Bruce Knauft for calling these recent publications to my attention.

53. The combination of a man's sexual relations with his wife's sister and marriage after the wife's death seems especially problematic. According to historic precedent recorded in the *Eiga monogatari*, Emperor Murakami (926–967; r. 946–967) first courted his brother Prince Shigeakira's wife Tōshi with the assistance of her own sister, Murakami's favorite wife Anshi.

Although Murakami, as emperor, was officially beyond criticism, this unusual romantic arrangement soon overtaxed all its participants: "The Empress [Anshi] flew into a rage, the Emperor lost his nerve, Tōshi quaked with fear, and the affair ended." McCullough and McCullough, *A Tale of Flowering Fortunes,* p. 81; NKBT 75:38. It is only after Anshi's death, precipitated by a difficult childbirth and spirit possession, that Murakami actually married Tōshi, who continued to live in fear of the spirits of her dead sister and her dead husband; ibid., pp. 88–90; NKBT 75:46–48.

54. The First Princess (Onna ichi no miya) is the daughter of the Kinjō Emperor and the Akashi Empress. She was raised together with Niou by Murasaki, her mother's foster mother. Fujimura Kiyoshi has observed that none of the First Princesses in the *Genji* is the subject of an extensively developed *monogatari*. Another notably obscure First Princess is the presumed daughter of the Reizei Emperor—generally thought to have produced no offspring—by the Kokiden nyōgo, a daughter of Tō no Chūjō and Shi no kimi. See Fujimura, "Onna ichi no miya," *KGMS* 9:167–168, 173–174. Kojima Naoko has attributed Kaoru's superior interest in the Kinjō Emperor's First Princess to the fact that her mother is an empress, unlike the mother of the Second Princess or the mother of the Reizei Emperor's only daughter; see "Onna ichi no miya monogatari no kanata e: *Genji monogatari* 'fu' no jikan," *Kokugo to kokubungaku* 58 (August 1981):23–37. The possibility of a connection between sibling incest and spirit possession is dramatized in the *Utsubo monogatari* (The Tale of the Hollow Tree; second half of the tenth century) in which the lovesick Nakazumi, who has been wooing his full sister Atemiya, is suspected of suffering from "a woman's disembodied spirit." Edwin A. Cranston, "Atemiya: A Translation from the *Utsubo monogatari,*" *Monumenta Nipponica* 24(3) (1969):300. By contrast, in the *Genji* it is not the suitor-brother Niou but the wooed First Princess who becomes possessed by *mono no ke.*

55. In the literary precedents for Ukifune's plan to commit suicide, however, it is the women (the maiden Unai and the maiden Tekona) who, intending to forestall male aggression, direct violence at themselves. They commit suicide in the river, which in the case of Unai is followed by the suicide of her unhappy suitors. See Mildred M. Tahara, trans., *Tales of Yamato: A Tenth-Century Poem-Tale* (Honolulu: University Press of Hawai'i, 1980), episode 147, pp. 93–98; Nippon Gakujutsu Shinkōkai, trans., *The Manyōshū* (New York: Columbia University Press, 1965), nos. 674–676 (Maiden Unai of Ashinoya); nos. 575–577 and 672–673 (Maiden Tekona of Mama); nos. 823–824 (Sakura-ko). It is interesting to note that in the legend of Sakura-ko the heroine tries to prevent violence among her two suitors by hanging herself from a tree. Together with Unai's suicide in the Ikutagawa and Tekona's at the river's mouth, these various grim solutions anticipate Ukifune's fate. For a version of the legend of Unai-otome, see the *nō* drama *Motomezuka.*

56. Bronfen, *Over Her Dead Body,* p. 119.

57. Since Niou has long coveted his sister, the element of homoeroticism is also present in Kaoru's interest in the First Princess. Furthermore, the connection between the plots concerning the First Princess and Ukifune has not been adequately understood. The critical debate has centered on the structural integration of the Onna ichi no miya *monogatari*—speculated to have been abandoned as the original sequel to the Genji–Murasaki plot line—into the Uji chapters and the question whether the First Princess foreshadows Ukifune's story or whether hers is merely a fragmented tale; see Fujimura, "Onna ichi no miya," *KGMS* 9:169–172, 174–176. However, a close examination of Ukifune's crisis between men and her spirit possession can shed significant light on the cryptic First Princess.

58. After all, the Akashi Empress is told not of an ordinary matter but a "curse" (S:1034; 6:248: *odoro odoroshiku ozoki yō nari tote*).

59. Why would the empress and other representatives of the Heian aristocracy have felt an aversion to a man's sexual relations with his wife's half-sister? In polygynous societies, half-sisters are more likely to share a father than a mother. Half-sisters were raised by different mothers and their families. Since the Heian marital system was uxorilocal, duolocal, or neolocal, the man would not normally see his wife's half-sister under her roof. In a duolocal marriage arrangement a man might find his wife's sister under the same roof (as at Uji) but not her half-sister (who would be living with her mother). (According to W. H. McCullough, full sisters were frequently separated in the postmarital arrangement of establishing the older uxorilocally and the younger in a neolocal residence; "Japanese Marriage Institutions in the Heian Period," p. 117.) The anomalous situation Niou finds at his Nijō-in, where Ukifune in an emergency has sought shelter with her half-sister, is even more unexpected than if Nakanokimi had been a full sister. Since it is easy to see why a man's sexual interest in his wife's sisters may have caused considerable strain among the sisters (as it did at Uji even between the unmarried Nakanokimi and Ōigimi), it makes sense for the prohibition rule to be extended to the man's sister-in-law, if half-sisters were for some extraordinary reason to live under the same roof.

60. Kaoru's indeterminacy concerning Ōigimi and Ukifune has been widely misunderstood as a weakness of character. His intellectual and emotional courage to confront the difference between model and copy (between Genji and Kashiwagi, Kashiwagi and the Eighth Prince, the Eighth Prince and Ōigimi, and, finally, Ōigimi and Ukifune) has, to my mind, been greatly underrated. Kaoru similarly posits himself against his "double" Niou and generates yet another sequence of model/copy pairs, such as Niou and the First Princess or the First and Second Princesses.

61. Chikamatsu Monzaemon's (1653–1725) *jōruri* manifesto was transmitted in 1738 by his friend, Hozumi Ikan (1692–1769), in *Naniwa Miyage* (A Present from Naniwa); cited in Donald Keene, ed., *Anthology of Japanese*

*Literature: From the Earliest Era to the Mid-Nineteenth Century* (New York: Grove Press, 1955), p. 390.

62. Ikeda Kazuomi has contrasted the phrase "ito kiyoge naru otoko" (6:284) with the phrase "ito okashige naru onna" (1:238) in the "Yūgao" chapter. Ikeda, "Tenarai maki mono no ke kō: Ukifune monogatari no shudai to kōzō," in Chūko Bungaku Kenkyūkai, ed., *Genji monogatari no jinbutsu to kōzō* (Kasama shoin, 1982), p. 164. It is significant to note, however, that the afflicted Ukifune herself perceives her abductor in these terms, whereas in the "Yūgao" chapter it is Genji who has a vision of Yūgao's *mono no ke* as "an exceedingly beautiful woman" (S:71).

63. Field, *The Splendor of Longing,* pp. 280–281.

64. Niou did not abandon Ukifune, but Ukifune finally rejected Niou.

65. It is a place previously unmentioned, and the NKBZ commentary (6:268, n. 9) merely indicates that the late Suzaku Emperor is Genji's older half-brother whose year of death is not told; it is further suggested that possibly the reference is to the historic Suzaku-in (923–952) or, according to old commentaries, such as the *Kakaishō* of 1364, Emperor Uda (Suzaku-in). Unfortunately, this footnote information does not help us understand the symbolic meaning of the locus classicus for Ukifune's rescue from certain death. See also Teramoto Naohiko, *Genji monogatari ronkō: kochūshaku, juyō* (Kazama shobō, 1989), pp. 238–247.

66. Ikeda, "Tenarai maki mono no ke kō," pp. 163–164.

67. See Edward Kamens, "Genshin's 'Shadow'," in Edward Kamens, ed., *Approaches to Teaching Murasaki Shikibu's The Tale of Genji* (New York: MLA, 1993), pp. 132–141.

68. Seidensticker quotes Ukifune as saying that she wants to be "thrown back in the river" (S:1047; see 1049), but there is no indication in the original that she wants to be thrown *back* in the river (see 6:276, 279).

69. Although a depiction of Ukifune's exorcism exists in a private collection (see Akiyama and Taguchi, eds., *Gōka "Genji-e" no sekai,* p. 242), neither this exorcism nor the Third Princess' is mentioned in the *Genji monogatari ekotoba.* The omission is important. Moreover, since not all artists followed this Osaka manual, the neglect of these two possession scenes in the work of artists following different painterly traditions is difficult to explain except as a reluctance to deal with subversive episodes.

70. See Shirane, *The Bridge of Dreams,* pp. 161–163, 194–199.

71. Kamens portrays critics engaged in the continuing and somewhat suspect search for historic models of the Yokawa no Sōzu; see "Genshin's 'Shadow'," p. 139.

72. There are but few Japanese studies, cited below in notes 75, 78, 80–83. Of the recent monographs on *Genji* in English, only Field has analyzed Ukifune's possession. My thesis about Ukifune's possession by the spirit of her dead father was first proposed in a comparative paper delivered at "The

World of Genji" conference at Indiana University (August 17–21, 1982); for a revised version of this paper, see Bargen, "The Search for Things Past in the *Genji monogatari*."

73. Field, *The Splendor of Longing,* pp. 280–281.

74. Ibid., p. 282.

75. Fujimoto questions Ukifune's possession because she has no awareness of it; all she can remember is her abduction by Niou. See *Genji monogatari no "mono no ke,"* pp. 99–101. However, it is a well-known fact that the possessed are in a trance and have no memory of it.

76. Field, *The Splendor of Longing,* p. 281.

77. See Bargen, "The Search for Things Past in the *Genji monogatari,*" pp. 199–232. See also Field, *The Splendor of Longing,* p. 279; in a footnote Field points out other male spirits, albeit "of a different order," such as Rokujō's father in Aoi's case and Kashiwagi in Yūgiri's dream about the flute; ibid., p. 345, n. 62.

78. See Mitani Kuniaki, "*Genji monogatari* daisanbu no hōhō: chūshin no sōshitsu aruiwa fuzai no monogatari," *Bungaku* 50 (August 1982):101–103.

79. *GMH* 12:376.

80. See Ikeda, "Tenarai maki mono no ke kō," p. 164.

81. Ikeda notes the similarity in the description of the slight grudge concerning the Eighth Prince's appearance in the Uji *azari*'s dream just before Ōigimi's death (see S:863; 5:310) and Ukifune's *mono no ke* (see S:1050; 6:283); "Tenarai maki mono no ke kō," p. 166.

82. Fujimoto speculates that the Sōzu's disciples interpret the "house full of beautiful girls" as a reference to their master's broken Buddhist precepts; *Genji monogatari no "mono no ke,"* p. 98. Of the two women Ukifune's possessing spirit specifically mentions, only the one who died has been identified as Ōigimi. See Earl Miner, "The Heroine: Identity, Recurrence, Destiny," in Andrew Pekarik, ed., *Ukifune: Love in The Tale of Genji* (New York: Columbia University Press, 1982), p. 69. See also 6:283, nn. 19–20, and *GMH* 12:375–376.

83. Yanai Shigeshi has pointed out that in the Miraculous Tales of the Bodhisattva Kannon *(Kannon reigen tan)* the Hatsuse Kannon sometimes appears in the guise of a priest *(ubasoku)* to save others. He follows the traditional view that the Kannon leads the Sōzu and his sister to rescue Ukifune from the bothersome dead spirit *(bōrei)* of the possessing priest. Yanai, "Hatsuse no Kannon no reigen," *KGMS* 9:199.

84. Earl Miner prefers to read *"tenarai"* as "Poetic Composition" rather than as the English translators' "writing practice"; Miner, "The Art of Life in the *Genji monogatari,*" unpublished paper, prepared for the "World of Genji" conference (Bloomington, Indiana University, 1982), p. 33. See also Miner, "The Heroine," p. 73: "Ukifune's poetic acts . . . share something of

the restraint of copying apposite poems by others and something of the originality of writing one's own poems."

85. Scroll VI, section 11 (Tenarai), of the *Hakubyō Genji monogatari
emaki,* dated 1554, by Keifuku-in Gyokuei (the daughter of Konoe Taneie
[1502–1566]), in the Spencer Collection of the New York Public Library
appears to fuse (or confuse) the scenes of Ukifune's taking of religious vows
and her poetry practice. Sarah E. Thompson notes that the presence of the
Sōzu at Ukifune's writing practice suggests that the "writing box is a mistaken interpretation of the comb box, with the scissors needed for hair-cut-
ting." Thompson, "A *Hakubyō Genji Monogatari Emaki* in the Spencer
Collection," unpublished M.A. thesis (Columbia University, 1983), p. 104.

86. Ukifune composes 26 poems, of which an astonishing 11 poems are
solitary, an equal number are in answer to somebody, and 4 poems are
intended to be sent but only 1 of these is in fact sent. The transformative
chapter of "Tenarai" (S: "At Writing Practice") contains 9 of the 11 solitary
poems, none sent, and only 3 answers, showing Ukifune's increasing resolve
to live the life of a poetic recluse. By comparison, Yūgao's 6 poems divide into
0 solitary, 2 sent, and 4 answers. Aoi does not compose poetry, except when
inspired by *mono no ke.* (This poem is ordinarily attributed to Rokujō's
*ikisudama.*) Rokujō is credited with 11 poems, 2 of which are solitary, 5 of 7
sent (of these one is recited by her *ikisudama* [see Aoi] and another by her
*shiryō* [see Murasaki]), and 2 answers. Of the women involved in the experience of possession Murasaki scores highest with 23 poems, 2 of which are solitary, 10 sent, 9 answers, 2 as part of a poetry gathering involving at least two
other poets. The Third Princess' 7 poems divide into 0 solitary, 2 sent, and 5
answers. These poetry statistics are derived from Suzuki, "*Genji monogatari*
sakuchū waka ichiran" (*Genji,* NKBZ 17), 6:517–549. Gotō Shōko has high-
lighted Ukifune's exceptional poetic preference by comparing her 42 percent
solitary poems *(dokueika)* to Genji's 23 percent and Kaoru's 30 percent.
Gotō, "Tenarai no uta," *KGMS* 9:224.

87. Hirokawa Katsumi has carefully delineated the transformation of
Ukifune's "persona" from an ascribed identity, that of *hitogata,* to a religious
vocation, reflecting the construction of a peripheral cyclical topos. Hirokawa,
"Ukifune shukke no isō: Ukifune ron (3)," *KGMS* 9:239–256.

88. Hirokawa Katsumi has argued that Ukifune's motivation for taking
the tonsure is to escape the entanglements of aristocratic life; the problem of
her religious salvation therefore lies not so much in the Sōzu's Buddhist con-
victions as in Heian social conditions. Hirokawa, "Ukifune saisei to Yokawa
no sōzu," in Taya Raishun, ed., *Bukkyō bungaku kenkyū* (Kyoto: Hōzōkan,
1966), pp. 53, 62.

89. The details about the spirit possession of the First Princess are not,
and need not be, revealed because her case almost precisely mirrors Ukifune's
in terms of forbidden kinship entanglements. Both Niou, her brother, and

Kaoru, her half-sister's husband, had occasionally approached the First Princess as a surrogate for their frustrating Uji adventures. The mere fact that she has been seized by spirits signals an analogy to Ukifune's conflict between (the same) two men. Although the First Princess firmly rejects the forbidden suitors and appears unmoved by them, her possession episode hints at unresolved and unacknowledged conflict. Ukifune's relations with the husband (Niou) and the intended (Kaoru) of her two half-sisters are complicated by her greater social insecurity and emotional vulnerability.

90. There is no connection between the old Ono nun's grandson and Utsusemi's stepson, both of whom are referred to by their office of Governor of Kii.

91. Ukifune is frequently compared to Kaguyahime from the *Taketori monogatari* (The Tale of the Bamboo Cutter; early to mid-tenth century); the moon princess was expelled from her heavenly realm for an unspecified crime but is finally reclaimed by heavenly beings. For an extended discussion of this analogy, see Field, *The Splendor of Longing*, p. 284; Shirane, *The Bridge of Dreams*, p. 199.

92. See Janet Goff, *Noh Drama and The Tale of Genji: The Art of Allusion in Fifteen Classical Plays* (Princeton: Princeton University Press, 1991), p. 182.

93. For further details on the textual history of *Kodama Ukifune*, see Goff, *Noh Drama and The Tale of Genji*, pp. 186–187.

94. *Ukifune*, in Sanari Kentarō, ed., *Yōkyoku taikan* (Meiji shoin, 1931–1933), 1:320.

95. Ibid., 1:323.

96. Goff nonetheless asserts that in the *nō* drama *Ukifune* "a handsome man she [Ukifune] took to be Niou lifted her in his arms and took her away"; *Noh Drama and The Tale of Genji*, p. 183.

97. Ibid., p. 80.

98. *Hajitomi*, however, does not deal with Yūgao's spirit possession, as does *Yūgao*, attributed to Zeami; see Goff, *Noh Drama and The Tale of Genji*, p. 107.

99. Ibid., p. 195. Due to the inaccessibility of the text of *Kodama Ukifune*, my interpretation relies on Goff's translation, pp. 193–197.

100. Ibid., p. 196.

101. Ibid., p. 185.

102. The *shite* can appear in a variety of transformations. In the *nō* drama *Fujito*, for example, the *shite* in the first part is a mother mourning her slain son and in the second part the ghost of the son. In *Kodama Ukifune*, the *shite* dyad consists of daughter and father.

103. Ibid., p. 196. I have rendered Goff's translation without the italics she uses to mark citations from the *Genji*.

104. Goff believes the "man of great learning" to be the Eighth Prince; see *Noh Drama and The Tale of Genji*, p. 196; see p. 273, n. 63.

105. Ibid., p. 196.
106. Ibid., p. 83.
107. Ibid., p. 197.

### Exit *mono no ke*

1. Gotō Shōko, however, has suggested that Rokujō, who is frequently perceived as avenging her father's shattered ambitions, acts as an angry spirit under a family curse *(tatari)* spanning generations. See Gotō, "Rokujō Miyasudokoro wa naze mono no ke ni nari tsuzukeru no ka," *Kokubungaku* 25(6) (May 1980):118–121.

2. See Joy Hendry, *Wrapping Culture: Politeness, Presentation and Power in Japan and Other Societies* (Oxford: Clarendon Press, 1993), especially chap. 4, "Wrapping of the Body," pp. 70–97, and chap. 5, "The Wrapping of Space," pp. 98–122. The principle of enclosure is carried to its logical extreme in some African *zār* cults, as in Northern Sudan, where the wall-enclosed house is "symbolic of the womb" and women endure pharaonic circumcision, or infibulation, "figuratively representing interiority." Janice Boddy, *Wombs and Alien Spirits: Women, Men, and the Zār Cult in Northern Sudan* (Madison: University of Wisconsin Press, 1989), pp. 73–74.

3. Boddy, *Wombs and Alien Spirits,* p. 121.

4. For an enlightening examination of the topos of the Five Obstructions, with references to the *Genji,* see Edward Kamens, "Dragon-Girl, Maiden-enflower, Buddha: The Transformation of a Waka Topos, 'The Five Obstructions'," *Harvard Journal of Asiatic Studies* 53(2) (December 1993):389–442.

5. Michael Lambek, *Human Spirits: A Cultural Account of Trance in Mayotte* (Cambridge: Cambridge University Press, 1981), p. 79.

6. Ibid., pp. 6, 41, 73.

7. Helen McCullough, "Social and Psychological Aspects of Heian Ritual and Ceremony," in Ōta Saburō and Fukuda Rikutarō, eds., *Studies on Japanese Culture* (Tokyo: Japan PEN Club, 1973), 2:278.

# Bibliography

THE PLACE of publication of all items in Japanese is Tokyo unless otherwise noted.

Abe Akio. *Genji monogatari: tsukuribanashi to shijitsu.* Iwanami shoin, 1985.

———. *Genji monogatari no honbun.* Iwanami shoin, 1986.

———. *Hikaru Genji ron: hosshin to shukke.* Tōkyō Daigaku shuppankai, 1989.

Abe Akio, Akiyama Ken, and Imai Gen'e, eds. *Genji monogatari.* NKBZ 12–17. Shōgakukan, 1970–1976.

Abe Toshiko. "*Genji monogatari* no 'mono no ke.'" Part 1. *Kokugo kokubun ronshū* 6 (February 1977):24–36.

———. "*Genji monogatari* no 'mono no ke.'" Part 2. *Kokugo kokubun ronshū* 7 (March 1978):1–20.

Ablon, Steven Luria. "The Usefulness of Dreams During Pregnancy." *International Journal of Psycho-Analysis* 75 (April 1994):291–299.

Addiss, Stephen, ed. *Japanese Ghosts & Demons: Art of the Supernatural.* New York: Braziller, 1985.

Akiyama Ken, ed. *Genji monogatari hikkei.* Gakutōsha, 1967.

———, ed. *Genji monogatari hikkei I.* Bessatsu kokubungaku, no. 1. Gakutōsha, 1978.

———. "Kemari no hi: Kashiwagi tōjō." *KGMS* 6:157–176.

———, ed. *Genji monogatari hikkei II.* Bessatsu kokubungaku, no. 13. Gakutōsha, 1982.

———, ed. *Genji monogatari jiten.* Bessatsu kokubungaku, no. 36. Gakutōsha, 1989.

———. *Genji monogatari no joseitachi.* Shōgakukan, 1991. Originally published in 1987.

Akiyama Ken and Taguchi Eiichi, eds. *Gōka "Genji-e" no sekai: Genji monogatari.* Gakken, 1988.

Akiyama Ken, Kimura Masanori, and Shimizu Yoshiko, eds. *Kōza Genji monogatari no sekai.* 9 vols. Yūhikaku, 1980–1984.

Akiyama Terukazu. *Genji monogatari emaki.* In Tanaka Ichimatsu, ed., *Shin-shū Nihon emakimono zenshū,* vol 2. Kadokawa shoten, 1975.

———. *Genji-e.* Nihon no Bijutsu 4(119). Shibundō, 1976.

———. "Women Painters at the Heian Court," pp. 159–184. Translated and adapted by Maribeth Graybill. In Marsha Weidner, ed., *Flowering in the Shadows: Women in the History of Chinese and Japanese Painting.* Honolulu: University of Hawai'i Press, 1990.

Algarin, Joanne P., ed. *Japanese Folk Literature.* New York: Bowker, 1982.

Arntzen, Sonja. "Translating Difference in the *Kagerō Nikki.*" *Japan Foundation Newsletter* 21(3) (November 1993):16–19, 28.

Baba Akiko. *Oni no kenkyū.* Chikuma shobō, 1988.

Baba Ichijirō, ed. *Genji monogatari e-maki gojūyon jō.* Bessatsu taiyō, no. 3. Heibonsha, 1973.

Bargen, Doris G. "Yūgao: A Case of Spirit Possession in *The Tale of Genji.*" *Mosaic: A Journal for the Interdisciplinary Study of Literature* 19(3) (Summer 1986):15–24.

———. "Spirit Possession in the Context of Dramatic Expressions of Gender Conflict: The Aoi Episode of the *Genji monogatari.*" *Harvard Journal of Asiatic Studies* 48(1) (June 1988):95–130.

———. "The Search for Things Past in the *Genji monogatari.*" *Harvard Journal of Asiatic Studies* 51(1) (June 1991):199–232.

———. "Twin Blossoms on a Single Branch: The Cycle of Retribution in *Onnamen.*" *Monumenta Nipponica* 46(2) (Summer 1991):147–171.

———. "The Problem of Incest in *The Tale of Genji,*" pp. 115–123. In Edward Kamens, ed., *Approaches to Teaching Murasaki Shikibu's The Tale of Genji.* New York: MLA, 1993.

———. "Translation and Reproduction in Enchi Fumiko's 'A Bond for Two Lifetimes—Gleanings.'" In Paul G. Schalow and Janet A. Walker, eds., *The Woman's Hand: Gender and Theory in Japanese Women's Writing.* Stanford: Stanford University Press, 1996.

Barnes, Nancy J. "Lady Rokujō's Ghost: Spirit Possession, Buddhism, and Healing in Japanese Literature." *Literature and Medicine* 8 (1989):106–121.

Bateson, Gregory, and Margaret Mead. *Trance and Dance in Bali.* Filmed between 1936 and 1939. Released in 1952 by New York University. 20 min.; black and white.

Beattie, J., and J. Middleton, eds. *Spirit Mediumship and Society in Africa.* London: Routledge & Kegan Paul, 1969.

Bell, Rudolph. *Holy Anorexia.* Chicago: University of Chicago Press, 1985.

Belo, Jane. *Trance in Bali.* New York: Columbia University Press, 1960.

Benl, Oscar, trans. *Genji-Monogatari: Die Geschichte vom Prinzen Genji.* 2 vols. Zürich: Manesse, 1966.

Berger, Renate, and Inge Stephan, eds. *Weiblichkeit und Tod in der Literatur.* Köln/Wien: Böhlau Verlag, 1987.

Bethe, Monica. *"Nonomiya." Kobe College Studies* 22(3) (1976):237–273.

Bethe, Monica, and Karen Brazell. *Dance in the Nō Theater.* 3 vols. Cornell University East Asia Papers, no. 29. Ithaca: Cornell University, 1982.

Blacker, Carmen. "The Divine Boy in Japanese Buddhism." *Asian Folklore Studies* (Tokyo) 22 (1963):77–88.

———. "Supernatural Abduction in Japanese Folklore." *Asian Folklore Studies* (Tokyo) 26(2) (1967):111–148.

———. *The Catalpa Bow: A Study of Shamanistic Practices in Japan.* London: Allen & Unwin, 1975.

Blomberg, Catharina. " 'A Strange White Smile': A Survey of Tooth-Blackening and Other Dental Practices in Japan." *Japan Forum* 2(2) (November 1990):243–251.

Bock, Felicia Gressitt, trans. *Engi-Shiki: Procedures of the Engi Era. Books I–IV.* Tokyo: Sophia University, 1970.

Boddy, Janice. *Wombs and Alien Spirits: Women, Men, and the Zār Cult in Northern Sudan.* Madison: University of Wisconsin Press, 1989.

Bordo, Susan R. "The Body and the Reproduction of Femininity: A Feminist Appropriation of Foucault," pp. 13–33. In Alison M. Jaggar and Susan R. Bordo, eds., *Gender/Body/Knowledge: Feminist Reconstructions of Being and Knowing.* New Brunswick: Rutgers University Press, 1989.

———. *Unbearable Weight: Feminism, Western Culture, and the Body.* Berkeley: University of California Press, 1993.

Borgen, Robert. *Sugawara no Michizane and the Early Heian Court.* Cambridge, Mass.: Harvard University Press, 1986.

———. "Ōe no Masafusa and the Spirit of Michizane." *Monumenta Nipponica* 50(3) (Autumn 1995):357–384.

Bourguignon, Erika, ed. *Religion, Altered States of Consciousness and Social Change.* Columbus: Ohio State University Press, 1973.

———. *Possession.* San Francisco: Chandler & Sharp, 1976.

———, ed. *A World of Women: Anthropological Studies of Women in the Societies of the World.* New York: Praeger, 1980.

Bowring, Richard, trans. *Murasaki Shikibu: Her Diary and Poetic Memoirs.* Princeton: Princeton University Press, 1982.

———. *Murasaki Shikibu: The Tale of Genji.* Landmarks of World Literature. Cambridge: Cambridge University Press, 1988.

Brazell, Karen, trans. *The Confessions of Lady Nijō.* Stanford: Stanford University Press, 1973.

Brewster, Jennifer, trans. *The Emperor Horikawa Diary, by Fujiwara no Nagako, Sanuki no Suke Nikki.* Honolulu: University Press of Hawai'i, 1977.

Bronfen, Elisabeth. *Over Her Dead Body: Death, Femininity and the Aesthetic.* New York: Routledge, 1992.

Buell, Pamela. *Genji: The World of a Prince—Sketches from the Tale.* Bloomington: Indiana University Art Museum, 1982.

Burkert, Walter. *Homo Necans: The Anthropology of Ancient Greek Sacrificial Ritual and Myth*. Translated by Peter Bing. Berkeley: University of California Press, 1983. Originally published in 1972.

Buruma, Ian. *Behind the Mask: On Sexual Demons, Sacred Mothers, Transvestites, Gangsters, Drifters and Other Japanese Cultural Heroes*. New York: Pantheon, 1984.

Bynum, Caroline Walker. *Holy Feast and Holy Fast: The Religious Significance of Food to Medieval Women*. Berkeley: University of California Press, 1987.

Casal, U.A. "The Goblin Fox and Badger and Other Witch Animals of Japan." *Folklore Studies* 18 (1959):1–94.

Chan, Leo Tak-hung. "Narrative as Argument: The *Yuewei caotang biji* and the Late Eighteenth-Century Elite Discourse on the Supernatural." *Harvard Journal of Asiatic Studies* 53(1) (June 1993):25–62.

Christian, William A., Jr. *Apparitions in Late Medieval and Renaissance Spain*. Princeton: Princeton University Press, 1981.

Chūko Bungaku Kenkyūkai, ed. *Genji monogatari no jinbutsu to kōzō*. Kasama shoin, 1982.

Cohen, Alvin P. "The Avenging Ghost: Moral Judgement in Chinese Historical Texts." Ph.D. dissertation, University of California at Berkeley, 1971.

———. "Completing the Business of Life: The Vengeful Dead in Chinese Folk Religion," pp. 59–66. In *Folk Culture*, vol. 2: *Folkways in Religion, Gods, Spirits, and Men*. Cuttack, India: Institute of Oriental and Orissan Studies, 1983.

Connor, W.R. "Seized by the Nymphs: Nympholepsy and Symbolic Expression in Classical Greece." *Classical Antiquity* 7(2) (October 1988): 155–189.

Cranston, Edwin A. *The Izumi Shikibu Diary: A Romance of the Heian Court*. Cambridge, Mass.: Harvard University Press, 1969.

———. "Atemiya: A Translation from the *Utsubo monogatari*." *Monumenta Nipponica* 24(3) (1969):289–314.

———. "Murasaki's Art of Fiction." *Japan Quarterly* 2 (April–June 1971):207–213.

———. "Aspects of *The Tale of Genji*." *Journal of the Association of Teachers of Japanese* 11(2–3) (1976):183–199.

Crapanzano, Vincent. "Spirit Possession," 14:12–19. In Mircea Eliade, ed., *The Encyclopedia of Religion*. 16 vols. New York: Macmillan, 1987.

Crapanzano, Vincent, and Vivian Garrison, eds. *Case Studies in Spirit Possession*. New York: Wiley, 1977.

Dalby, Liza Crihfield. *Kimono: Fashioning Culture*. New Haven: Yale University Press, 1993.

Davis, Winston. *Dojo: Magic and Exorcism in Modern Japan*. Stanford: Stanford University Press, 1980.

Dorson, Richard M., ed. *Studies in Japanese Folklore*. Bloomington: Indiana University Press, 1963.

Duerr, Hans Peter. "Die Angst vor dem Leben und die Sehnsucht nach dem Tode," 1:621–647. In Hans Peter Duerr, ed., *Der Wissenschaftler und das Irrationale*. Frankfurt am Main: Syndikat, 1981.

Duerr, Hans Peter, ed. *Der Wissenschaftler und das Irrationale*. Vol. 1: *Beiträge aus Ethnologie und Anthropologie*. Frankfurt am Main: Syndikat, 1981.

———. *Traumzeit: Über die Grenzen zur Wildnis und Zivilisation*. Frankfurt am Main: Syndikat, 1983.

———. *Dreamtime: Concerning the Boundary Between Wilderness and Civilization*. Translated by Felicitas D. Goodman. New York: Basil Blackwell, 1985.

Dykstra, Yoshiko Kurata. "Tales of the Compassionate Kannon: The *Hasedera Kannon genki*." *Monumenta Nipponica* 31(2) (Summer 1976): 113–143.

Ebersole, Gary L. *Ritual Poetry and the Politics of Death in Early Japan*. Princeton: Princeton University Press, 1989.

Ebrey, Patricia Buckley. *The Inner Quarters: Marriage and the Lives of Chinese Women in the Sung Period*. Berkeley: University of California Press, 1993.

Eder, Matthias. "Schamanismus in Japan." *Paideuma* 7(7) (1958):367–380.

Eliade, Mircea. "Recent Works on Shamanism: A Review Article." *History of Religions* 1(1) (Summer 1961):152–186.

———. *Shamanism: Archaic Techniques of Ecstasy*. Princeton: Princeton University Press, 1964. Originally published in 1951.

———. *Occultism, Witchcraft and Cultural Fashions: Essays in Comparative Religions*. Chicago: University of Chicago Press, 1976.

———, ed. *The Encyclopedia of Religion*. 16 vols. New York: Macmillan, 1987.

Eliot, T. S. *The Selected Essays*. New York: Harcourt, Brace, 1950.

Ellenberger, Henri F. *The Discovery of the Unconscious*. New York: Basic Books, 1970.

Enchi Fumiko. *Onnamen*. Shinchōsha, 1966. Originally published in 1958.

———. *Genji monogatari no sekai: Kyōto*. Heibonsha, 1974.

———. *Genji monogatari shiken*. Shinchōsha, 1974.

———. *Genji monogatari*. Gendai goyaku: Nihon no koten 5. Gakken, 1979.

———. *Masks*. Translated by Juliet Winters Carpenter. New York: Aventura-Vintage, 1983.

Enchi Fumiko et al. *Genji monogatari*. Gakken no jitsuyō tokusen shiriizu. Gakken, 1986.

Fairchild, William P. "Shamanism in Japan." *Folklore Studies* 21 (1962):1–122.

Field, Norma. *The Splendor of Longing in the Tale of Genji*. Princeton: Princeton University Press, 1987.

Finucane, R. C. *Appearances of the Dead: A Cultural History of Ghosts.* Buffalo, N.Y.: Prometheus Books, 1984.

Florenz, Karl. "Ancient Japanese Rituals." *Transactions of the Asiatic Society of Japan* 27(1) (1899):1–112.

*Folk Culture.* Vol. 2: *Folkways in Religion, Gods, Spirits, and Men.* Cuttack, India: Institute of Oriental and Orissan Studies, 1983.

Forrer, Matthi, ed. *Essays on Japanese Art Presented to Jack Hillier.* London: Sawers, 1982.

Foucault, Michel. *Histoire de la folie à l'âge classique.* Paris: Gallimard, 1972.

———. *Surveiller et punir: naissance de la prison.* Paris: Gallimard, 1975.

Fox, Robin. *Kinship and Marriage: An Anthropological Perspective.* Harmondsworth: Penguin, 1967.

———. *The Red Lamp of Incest: An Enquiry into the Origins of Mind and Society.* Notre Dame: University of Notre Dame Press, 1983. Originally published in 1980.

Freud, Sigmund. "Das Unheimliche," 12:227–268. *Gesammelte Werke: Chronologisch Geordnet.* London: Imago, 1947. Reprinted Frankfurt: S. Fischer, 1972.

———. "The Uncanny (1919)," 17:217–256. *The Standard Edition of the Complete Psychological Works of Sigmund Freud.* Translated by James Strachey with Anna Freud. London: Hogarth Press and Institute of Psycho-Analysis, 1955.

———. *Gesammelte Werke: Chronologisch Geordnet.* 18 vols. London: Imago, 1940–1968. Reprinted Frankfurt: S. Fischer, 1972.

———. *The Standard Edition of the Complete Psychological Works of Sigmund Freud.* Translated by James Strachey with Anna Freud. 24 vols. London: Hogarth Press and Institute of Psycho-Analysis, 1953–1974.

Fujii Sadakazu. *Genji monogatari no shigen to genzai.* Tōjusha, 1980.

———. "*Genji monogatari* ron: shamanizumu yōso." *Yuriika* 12 (December 1980):142–155.

———. "Rokujō Miyasudokoro no mono no ke." *KGMS* 7:36–51.

———. "The Relationship Between the Romance and Religious Observances: *Genji Monogatari* as Myth." Translated by W. Michael Kelsey. *Japanese Journal of Religious Studies* 9 (2–3) (June–September 1982): 127–146.

———. "Tsuku bungaku: *Genji monogatari* ron no tame ni." *Bungaku* 50 (November 1982):100–116.

———. *Monogatari no kekkon.* Sōjusha, 1985.

———. "Katashiro no hito." *Kokubungaku* 32(13) (November 1987):130–134.

———. "*Genji monogatari* seikatsu jiten." Entry 8: "Tōbyō seikatsu to mono no ke," pp. 104–106. In Akiyama Ken, ed., *Genji monogatari jiten.* Gakutōsha, 1989.

Fujikōge Toshiaki. "Yūgao," pp. 89–99. In *Monogatari o orinasu hitobito*. Vol. 2 of *Genji monogatari kōza*. Benseisha, 1991.

———. "Yūgao maki no senshō ni tsuite: *Genji monogatari* to shite no kakuritsu," pp. 215–247. In Murasaki Shikibu Gakkai, ed., *Genji monogatari to nikki bungaku kenkyū to shiryō*. Musashino shoin, 1992.

Fujimoto Katsuyoshi. "Rokujō Miyasudokoro no shiryō to Kamo matsuri: mono no ke chōryō to shinji." 2:65–84. In Ōchō monogatari kenkyūkai, ed., *Genji monogatari to sono zengo*. Shintensha, 1991.

———. "Yūgao." *Kokubungaku* 36(5) (May 1991):120–121.

———. *Genji monogatari no "mono no ke": bungaku to kiroku no hazama*. Kasama shoin, 1994.

Fujimura Kiyoshi. "Hachi no miya no yuigon." *KGMS* 8:100–117.

———. "Onna ichi no miya." *KGMS* 9:167–176.

———. *Genji gakujosetsu*. Kasama shoin, 1987.

Fujio Tomoko. "Mono no ke no keifu," pp. 73–100. In Kokugo goishi kenkyūkai, ed., *Kokugo goishi no kenkyū*, vol. 2. Osaka: Izumi shoin, 1981.

Fukasawa Michio. *Genji monogatari no keisei*. Ōfūsha, 1972.

———. "Rokujō Miyasudokoro akuryō jiken no shudaisei ni tsuite," pp. 49–98. In Murasaki Shikibu Gakkai, ed., *Genji monogatari to sono eikyō: kenkyū to shiryō*. Musashino shoin, 1978.

Garrett, Clarke. *Spirit Possession and Popular Religion: From the Camisards to the Shakers*. Baltimore: Johns Hopkins University Press, 1987.

Gatten, Aileen. "A Wisp of Smoke: Scent and Character in *The Tale of Genji*." *Monumenta Nipponica* 32(1) (Spring 1977):35–48.

———. "The Order of the Early Chapters in the *Genji monogatari*." *Harvard Journal of Asiatic Studies* 41(1) (June 1981):5–46.

———. "Supplementary Narratives to *The Tale of Genji*: 'Yamaji no tsuyu,' 'Kumogakure Rokujō,' and 'Tamakazura.'" Unpublished paper, prepared for the "World of Genji" conference, Bloomington, Indiana University, 1982.

———. "Three Problems in the Text of 'Ukifune'," pp. 83–111. In Andrew Pekarik, ed., *Ukifune: Love in The Tale of Genji*. New York: Columbia University Press, 1982.

———. "Weird Ladies: Narrative Strategy in the *Genji Monogatari*." *Journal of the Association of Teachers of Japanese* 20(1) (April 1986):29–48.

———. "Death and Salvation in *Genji Monogatari*," pp. 5–27. In Aileen Gatten and Anthony Hood Chambers, eds., *New Leaves: Studies and Translations of Japanese Literature in Honor of Edward Seidensticker*. Ann Arbor: Center for Japanese Studies, University of Michigan, 1993.

Gatten, Aileen, and Anthony Hood Chambers, eds. *New Leaves: Studies and Translations of Japanese Literature in Honor of Edward Seidensticker*. Ann Arbor: Center for Japanese Studies, University of Michigan, 1993.

Gay, Suzanne. "Introduction," pp. 73–76. In Wakita Haruko, "Marriage and

Property in Premodern Japan: From the Perspective of Women's History." *Journal of Japanese Studies* 10(1) (Winter 1984):73–99.

Geertz, Clifford. "Deep Play: Notes on the Balinese Cockfight." *Daedalus* 101 (1972):1–37; rpt. *The Interpretation of Cultures: Selected Essays by Clifford Geertz,* pp. 412–453.

———. *The Interpretation of Cultures: Selected Essays by Clifford Geertz.* New York: Basic Books, 1973.

*Genji monogatari kōza: Monogatari o orinasu hitobito.* Benseisha, 1991.

*Genji monogatari no tankyū: dai jū-san shū.* Kazama shobō, 1988.

*Genji monogatari o dō yomu ka. Kokubungaku* 28(16) (December 1983).

*Genji monogatari IV.* Nihon bungaku kenkyū shiryō series. Yūseidō, 1982.

Gennep, Arnold van. *The Rites of Passage.* Translated by Monika B. Vizedom and Gabrielle L. Cafee. Chicago: University of Chicago Press, 1960. Originally published in 1909.

Goff, Janet Emily. "*The Tale of Genji* as a Source of the Nō: *Yūgao* and *Hajitomi.*" *Harvard Journal of Asiatic Studies* 42(1) ( June 1982):177–229.

———. *Noh Drama and The Tale of Genji: The Art of Allusion in Fifteen Classical Plays.* Princeton: Princeton University Press, 1991.

Goodman, Felicitas D. *How About Demons? Possession and Exorcism in the Modern World.* Bloomington: Indiana University Press, 1988.

Goodman, Felicitas D., Jeannette H. Henney, and Esther Pressel. *Trance, Healing, and Hallucination: Three Field Studies in Religious Experience.* New York: Wiley, 1974.

Goody, Jack. "A Comparative Approach to Incest and Adultery." *British Journal of Sociology* 7 (1956):286–305.

Gotō Shōko. "Rokujō Miyasudokoro wa naze mono no ke ni nari tsuzukeru no ka." *Kokubungaku* 25(6) (May 1980):118–121.

———. "Tenarai no uta." *KGMS* 9:224–238.

———. "Sei Shōnagon ni tsuku omokage." *Kokubungaku: kaishaku to kanshō* 53(9) (September 1988):100–104.

Graham, Hilary. "The Social Image of Pregnancy: Pregnancy as Spirit Possession." *Sociological Review* (May 1976):291–308.

Grapard, Allan G. "Visions of Excess and Excesses of Vision—Women and Transgression in Japanese Myth." *Japanese Journal of Religious Studies* 18(1) (March 1991):3–22.

Grim, John A. *The Shaman: Patterns of Siberian and Ojibway Healing.* Norman: University of Oklahoma Press, 1983.

Gubler, Greg. "Kitsune: The Remarkable Japanese Fox." *Southern Folklore Quarterly* 38 (1974):121–134.

Gussler, Judith D. "Social Change, Ecology, and Spirit Possession Among the South African Nguni," pp. 88–126. In Erika Bourguignon, ed., *Religion, Altered States of Consciousness and Social Change.* Columbus: Ohio State University Press, 1973.

Hall, John Whitney, and Jeffrey P. Mass, eds. *Medieval Japan: Essays in Insti-*

*tutional History*. Stanford: Stanford University Press, 1988. Originally published in 1974.

Hall, John Whitney, and Toyoda Takeshi, eds. *Japan in the Muromachi Age*. Berkeley: University of California Press, 1977.

Haraoka Fumiko. "Rokujō Miyasudokoro o megutte." *Nihon Bungaku* 36 (March 1971):17–39.

———. "Ukifune," pp. 362–378. In *Monogatari o orinasu hitobito*. Vol. 2 of *Genji monogatari kōza*. Benseisha, 1991.

———. *Genji monogatari ryōgi no ito: jinbutsu, hyōgen o megutte*. Yūseidō, 1991.

Hardacre, Helen. "Conflict Between Shugendō and the New Religions of Bakumatsu Japan." *Japanese Journal of Religious Studies* 21(2–3) ( June–September 1994):137–166.

Hare, Thomas Blenman. *Zeami's Style: The Noh Plays of Zeami Motokiyo*. Stanford: Stanford University Press, 1986.

Harper, Donald. "A Chinese Demonography of the Third Century B.C." *Harvard Journal of Asiatic Studies* 45(2) (December 1985):459–498.

Harper, J. Thomas. "Motoori Norinaga's Criticism of the *Genji Monogatari*: A Study of the Background and Critical Content of His *Genji Monogatari Tama no Ogushi*." Ph.D. dissertation, University of Michigan, 1971.

Hasegawa Masaharu. "*Genji monogatari* no sasurai no keifu." *Nihon bungaku ronkyū* 14 (November 1980):33–41.

———. "Uji jūjō no sekai: Hachi no miya no yuigon no jubakusei." In *Genji monogatari IV*. Nihon bungaku kenkyū shiryō series, pp. 135–144. Yūseidō, 1982. Originally published in 1970.

———. "Onna san no miya no shukke." *KGMS* 7:22–35.

Hasegawa Masaharu, Imanishi Yūichirō, Itō Hiroshi, and Yoshioka Hiroshi, eds. *Tosa nikki, Kagerō nikki, Murasaki Shikibu nikki, Sarashina nikki*. SNKBT 24. Iwanami shoten, 1989.

Hayashida Takakazu. *Genji monogatari no hassō*. Ōfūsha, 1980.

———. "Tsuki no bi." *KGMS* 2:256–269.

Hendry, Joy. *Wrapping Culture: Politeness, Presentation and Power in Japan and Other Societies*. Oxford: Clarendon Press, 1993.

Henney, Jeannette H. "Sex and Status: Women in St. Vincent," pp. 161–183. In Erika Bourguignon, ed., *A World of Women: Anthropological Studies of Women in the Societies of the World*. New York: Praeger, 1980.

Héritier, Françoise. *Les deux soeurs et leur mère: anthropologie de l'inceste*. Paris: Éditions Odile Jacob, 1994.

Hinata Kazumasa. "*Genji monogatari* no shi to saishō: Ukifune o chūshin ni." *Kokubungaku: kaishaku to kanshō* 53(9) (September 1988):48–53.

———. *Genji monogatari no ōken to sasurai*. Shintensha, 1989.

Hirokawa Katsumi. "Ukifune saisei to Yokawa no sōzu," pp. 33–63. In Taya Raishun, ed., *Bukkyō bungaku kenkyū*. Kyoto: Hōzōkan, 1966.

————, ed. *Shinwa, kinki, hyōhaku: monogatari to setsuwa no sekai.* Ōfūsha, 1976.

————. "Mumyō no haihansha: Onna san no miya, Kashiwagi monogatari," pp. 123–141. In Chūko bungaku kenkyūkai, ed., *Genji monogatari no kyōgen to kōzō.* Kasama shoin, 1979.

————, ed. *Tsukimono—"tatarigami" to majinai.* Sōseki, 1982.

————. "Ukifune shukke no isō: Ukifune ron (3)." *KGMS* 9:239–256.

————. *Monogatari kenkyū josetsu: denshōshiteki hōhōron.* Ōfūsha, 1985.

————. *Okashi to ijin: mukashibanashi no kisō.* Jinbun shoin, 1986.

————. "Monogatari to shite no chimei: Rokujō watari no mono no ke," pp. 219–253. In Nanba Hiroshi and Hirokawa Katsumi, eds., *Genji monogatari: chimei to hōhō.* Ōfūsha, 1990.

————. *Shinsō no tennō: Genji monogatari no kokyō.* Jinbun shoin, 1990.

Hirota Osamu. "Rokujō-in no kōzō: Hikaru Genji monogatari no keisei to tenkan," pp. 121–132. In Hirokawa Katsumi, ed., *Shinwa, kinki, hyōhaku: monogatari to setsuwa no sekai.* Ōfūsha, 1976.

————. "*Genji monogatari* ni okeru 'yukari' kara tasha no hakken e." *Chūko bungaku* 20 (October 1978):28–38.

————. "*Genji monogatari* ni okeru waka no denshōsei: Rokujō Miyasudokoro no mono no ke no baai." *Nihon Bungaku* 31 (May 1982):54–63.

————. "*Genji monogatari* no 'ōken' to sono denshōsei." *Nihon Bungaku* 31 (December 1982):12–21.

————. "*Genji monogatari* ni okeru ongaku to keifu," pp. 245–277. In *Genji monogatari no tankyū: dai jū-san shū.* Kazama shobō, 1988.

————. "*Genji monogatari* ni okeru yōshiki to shite no kaimami," pp. 169–186. In Tsuchihashi Yutaka and Hirokawa Katsumi, eds., *Kodai bungaku no yōshiki to kinō.* Ōfūsha, 1988.

Hochstedler, Carol, trans. *The Tale of Nezame: Part Three of Yowa no Nezame Monogatari.* Ithaca: Cornell University Press, 1979.

Hoff, Frank. *Song, Dance, Storytelling: Aspects of the Performing Arts in Japan.* Ithaca: Cornell University Press, 1978.

Hori Ichirō. "On the Concept of Hijiri (Holy Man)." *Numens* 5 (1958):128–160; 199–232.

————. *Folk Religion in Japan: Continuity and Change.* Translated by Joseph M. Kitagawa and Alan L. Miller. Chicago: University of Chicago Press, 1968.

Horton, H. Mack. "In the Service of Realism and Rhetoric: The Function and Development of the Lady-in-Waiting Character in *The Tale of Genji.*" *Phi Theta Papers* 16 (1984):102–136. Revised as "They Also Serve: Ladies-in-Waiting in *The Tale of Genji*," pp. 95–107. In Edward Kamens, ed., *Approaches to Teaching Murasaki Shikibu's The Tale of Genji.* New York: MLA, 1993.

Huntington, Richard, and Peter Metcalf. *Celebrations of Death: The Anthro-*

*pology of Mortuary Ritual.* Cambridge: Cambridge University Press, 1979.

Hurst, G. Cameron III. "The Structure of the Heian Court: Some Thoughts on the Nature of 'Familial Authority' in Heian Japan," pp. 39–59. In John W. Hall and Jeffrey P. Mass, eds., *Medieval Japan: Essays in Institutional History.* Stanford: Stanford University Press, 1988. Originally published in 1974.

Hurvitz, Leon, trans. *Scripture of the Lotus Blossom of the Fine Dharma. Translated from the Chinese of Kumārajīva.* New York: Columbia University Press, 1976.

Ii Haruki. "Aoi no ue," pp. 71–79. In *Monogatari o orinasu hitobito.* Vol. 2 of *Genji monogatari kōza.* Benseisha, 1991.

Ike Kōzō. *Genji monogatari: sono sumai no sekai.* Chūō kōronbijutsu, 1989.

Ikeda Kazuomi. "Tenarai maki mono no ke kō: Ukifune monogatari no shudai to kōzō," pp. 163–184. In Chūko Bungaku Kenkyūkai, ed., *Genji monogatari no jinbutsu to kōzō.* Kasama shoin, 1982.

Ikeda Kikan, ed. *Genji monogatari taisei.* 8 vols. Chūō Kōronsha, 1953–1956.

———. *Genji monogatari jiten.* 2 vols. Tōkyōdō, 1960.

Ikeda Kikan, Kishigami Shinji, and Akiyama Ken, eds. *Makura no sōshi, Murasaki Shikibu nikki.* NKBT 19. Iwanami shoten, 1958.

Ikeda Setsuko. "Onna san no miya," pp. 253–265. In *Monogatari o orinasu hitobito.* Vol. 2 of *Genji monogatari kōza.* Benseisha, 1991.

Imai Gen'e. *Genji monogatari no shinen.* Kasama shoin, 1987.

Imai Takuji, Onitsuka Takaaki, Gotō Shōko, and Nakano Kōichi, eds. *Genji monogatari kōza.* 10 vols. Benseisha, 1991–1993.

Imanishi Yūichirō. "Rokujō Miyasudokoro." *Kokubungaku* 36(5) (May 1991):127–131.

Immoos, Thomas. "The Birth of the Japanese Theater." *Monumenta Nipponica* 24(4) (1969):403–414.

Inaga Keiji, ed. *Imagawa Norimasa: Genji monogatari teiyō.* Vol. 2 of *Genji monogatari kochū shūsei.* Ōfūsha, 1978.

———. *Genji monogatari no uchi to soto.* Kazama shobō, 1987.

Ing, Eric van den, and Robert Schaap, eds. *Beauty and Violence: Japanese Prints by Yoshitoshi 1839–1892.* Bergeyk, Netherlands: Society for Japanese Arts, 1992.

Inukai Kiyoshi. "Yūgao to no deai." *KGMS* 1:185–197.

Ishida Jōji. "Onna to shite no Fujitsubo." *KGMS* 2:77–96.

———. *Genji monogatari kō sono ta.* Kasama shoin, 1989.

Ishihara Shōhei. "Michitsuna no haha no reikon kankaku." *Kokubungaku: kaishaku to kanshō* 53(9) (September 1988):90–94.

Itō Hiroshi. *Genji monogatari no genten.* Meiji shoin, 1980.

Iwai Yoshio. *Genji monogatari gohōkō.* Kasama shoin, 1976.

Iwase Hōun. *Genji monogatari to bukkyō shisō.* Kasama shoin, 1972.

Izzard, Sebastian. *Kunisada's World.* Exhibition catalog. New York: Japan Society, in collaboration with the Ukiyo-e Society of America, 1993.

Jaggar, Alison M., and Susan R. Bordo, eds. *Gender/Body/Knowledge: Feminist Reconstructions of Being and Knowing.* New Brunswick: Rutgers University Press, 1989.

Jordan, Brenda. "Yūrei: Tales of Female Ghosts," pp. 25–33. In Stephen Addiss, ed., *Japanese Ghosts & Demons: Art of the Supernatural.* New York: Braziller, 1985.

Kahan, Gail Capitol. "As a Driven Leaf: Love and Psychological Characterization in the *Tale of Genji.*" *Occasional Papers of the Center for Japanese Studies* (Michigan University), no. 11 (1969):155–173.

Kamens, Edward. *The Three Jewels: A Study and Translation of Minamoto Tamenori's Sanbōe.* Ann Arbor: Center for Japanese Studies, University of Michigan, 1988.

———. *The Buddhist Poetry of the Great Kamo Priestess: Daisaiin Senshi and Hosshin Wakashū.* Ann Arbor: Center for Japanese Studies, University of Michigan, 1990.

———. "Genshin's 'Shadow'," pp. 132–141. In Edward Kamens, ed., *Approaches to Teaching Murasaki Shikibu's The Tale of Genji.* New York: MLA, 1993.

———, ed. *Approaches to Teaching Murasaki Shikibu's The Tale of Genji.* New York: MLA, 1993.

———. "Dragon-Girl, Maidenflower, Buddha: The Transformation of a Waka Topos, 'The Five Obstructions.' " *Harvard Journal of Asiatic Studies* 53(2) (December 1993):389–442.

Kamiya Jirō. "*Genji monogatari* no tabi," pp. 188–191. In Enchi Fumiko, *Genji monogatari.* Gendai goshaku: Nihon no koten 5. Gakken, 1979.

Kaneda Motohiko. *Genji monogatari shiki.* 2 vols. Kazama shobō, 1989–1990.

Kapferer, Bruce. *A Celebration of Demons: Exorcism and the Aesthetics of Healing in Sri Lanka.* Bloomington: Indiana University Press, 1983.

———. "The Ritual Process and the Problem of Reflexivity in Sinhalese Demon Exorcisms," pp. 179–207. In John J. MacAloon, ed., *Rite, Drama, Festival, Spectacle: Rehearsals Toward a Theory of Cultural Performance.* Philadelphia: Institute for the Study of Human Issues, 1984.

Katagiri Yōichi, Fukui Teisuke, Takahashi Shōji, and Shimizu Yoshiko, eds. *Taketori monogatari, Ise monogatari, Yamato monogatari, Heichū monogatari.* NKBZ 8. Shōgakukan, 1972.

Kawasaki Noboru. "Rokujō Miyasudokoro no shinkōteki haikei." *Kokugakuin zasshi* (September 1967):13–23.

Keene, Donald, ed. *Anthology of Japanese Literature: From the Earliest Era to the Mid-Nineteenth Century.* New York: Grove Press, 1955.

———, trans. *Five Modern Nō Plays by Yukio Mishima*. New York: Knopf, 1957.

———, ed. *Twenty Plays of the Nō Theatre*. New York: Columbia University Press, 1970.

———. *Seeds in the Heart: Japanese Literature from Earliest Times to the Late Sixteenth Century*. New York: Holt, 1993.

Kendall, Laurel. *Shamans, Housewives, and Other Restless Spirits: Women in Korean Ritual Life*. Honolulu: University of Hawai'i Press, 1985.

Kern, Stephen. *The Culture of Love: Victorians to Moderns*. Cambridge, Mass.: Harvard University Press, 1992.

Kessler, Clive S. "Conflict and Sovereignty in Kelantanese Malay Spirit Seances," pp. 295–331. In Vincent Crapanzano and Vivian Garrison, eds., *Case Studies in Spirit Possession*. New York: Wiley, 1977.

Kifune Shigeaki. "Uji Hachi no miya no sōzō to zōkei: *Genji monogatari* no hyōgen to hōhō." *Kokugo to kokubungaku* 53(10) (1976):27–41.

Kiley, Cornelius J. "State and Dynasty in Archaic Yamato." *Journal of Asian Studies* 33(1) (November 1973):25–49.

Kim Soon-Hee. "Murasaki Shikibu ni okeru 'mono no ke' no sekai." *Kokubungaku: kaishaku to kanshō* 53(9) (September 1988):105–109.

Kimura Masanori. "Yūgao no onna." *KGMS* 1:220–234.

———. "Wakamiya tanjō: Akashi ichizoku no shuku-un." *KGMS* 6:136–156.

Kinoshita Masao. *Genji monogatari yōgo sakuin*. 2 vols. Kokusho Kankōkai, 1974.

Kitayama Keita. *Genji monogatari jiten*. Heibonsha, 1957.

Kojima Naoko. "Onna ichi no miya monogatari no kanata e: *Genji monogatari* 'fu' no jikan." *Kokugo to kokubungaku* 58 (August 1981):23–37.

*Kokugo kokubungaku kenkyūshi taisei*. Compiled by Zenkoku Daigaku Kokugo Kokubun Gakkai. 15 vols. Sanseidō, 1965–1969.

Komachiya Teruhiko. "Murasaki no ue no kunō: Murasaki no ue ron (3)." *KGMS* 6:93–109.

Komashaku Kimi. *Murasaki Shikibu no messēji*. Asahi shinbunsha, 1991.

———. "A Feminist Reinterpretation of *The Tale of Genji:* Genji and Murasaki." Translated by Yoda Tomiko. *U.S.–Japan Women's Journal: English Supplement* No. 5 (1993):28–51. Modified version of "Murasaki no Ue: aidentiti sōshitsu no higeki," pp. 107–153. In Komashaku Kimi, *Murasaki Shikibu no messēji*. Asahi shinbunsha, 1991.

Komatsu Kazuhiko. *Hyōrei shinkōron*. Arina shobō, 1984.

Kondo Eiko. "Inaka Genji Series," pp. 78–93. In Matthi Forrer, ed., *Essays on Japanese Art Presented to Jack Hillier*. London: Sawers, 1982.

Koyama Hiroshi, Satō Kikuo, and Satō Ken'ichirō, eds. *Yōkyoku shū*. 2 vols. NKBZ 33–34. Shōgakukan, 1973–1975.

Koyama Toshihiko. *Genji monogatari o jiku to shita ōchō bungaku sekai no kenkyū*. Ōfūsha, 1982.

Krauss, Ellis S., Thomas P. Rohlen, and Patricia G. Steinhoff, eds. *Conflict in Japan*. Honolulu: University of Hawai'i Press, 1984.

Krohn, Alan. *Hysteria: The Elusive Neurosis*. New York: International University Press, 1978.

Kumano Ken'ichi. *Genji monogatari: sono hijiri to zoku*. Hōsei Daigaku shuppankyoku, 1989.

Kurosu Shigehiko. *Yūgao to iu onna*. Kasama shoin, 1975.

———. *Genji monogatari shiron: Yūgao no maki o chūshin to shite*. Kasama shoin, 1990.

Kuwabara Hiroshi. "*Genji monogatari* no mono no ke ni tsuite: Hikaru Genji no seishin sayō to shite," 2: 47–64. In Ōchō monogatari kenkyūkai, ed., *Genji monogatari to sono zengo*. Shintensha, 1991.

Kyōto Kokuritsu Hakubutsukan. *Genji monogatari no bijutsu*. Exhibition catalog. Kyoto: Nihon keizai shinbunsha, 1975.

Lambek, Michael. *Human Spirits: A Cultural Account of Trance in Mayotte*. Cambridge: Cambridge University Press, 1981.

Lebra, Takie Sugiyama. "Spirit Possession: The 'Salvation Cult,'" pp. 232–247. In Takie Sugiyama Lebra, *Japanese Patterns of Behavior*. Honolulu: University of Hawai'i Press, 1976.

———. *Japanese Patterns of Behavior*. Honolulu: University of Hawai'i Press, 1976.

———. *Above the Clouds: Status Culture of the Modern Japanese Nobility*. Berkeley: University of California Press, 1993.

Lévi-Strauss, Claude. *The View from Afar*. Translated by Joachim Neugroschel and Phoebe Hoss. New York: Basic Books, 1985. Originally published as *Le regard éloigné* in French in 1983.

Lewis, Ioan Myrddin. *Ecstatic Religion: An Anthropological Study of Spirit Possession and Shamanism*. Harmondsworth: Penguin, 1971.

———. *Social Anthropology in Perspective: The Relevance of Social Anthropology*. Harmondsworth: Penguin, 1976.

———. *Religion in Context: Cults and Charisma*. Cambridge: Cambridge University Press, 1986.

———. "Exorcism and Male Control of Religious Experience." *Ethnos* 55(1–2) (1990):26–40.

Loui, Shirley M. *Murasaki's Genji and Proust's Recherche: A Comparative Study*. Lewiston/Queenston/Lampeter: Edwin Mellen Press, 1991.

Mack, John E. "Other Realities: The 'Alien Abduction' Phenomenon." *Noetic Sciences Review*, no. 73 (Autumn 1992):5–11.

Mae Michiko. "Tod als Selbstverwirklichung in einem Leben ohne Liebe: Drei Frauengestalten in der japanischen Literatur," pp. 35–68. In Renate Berger and Inge Stephan, eds., *Weiblichkeit und Tod in der Literatur*. Köln/Wien: Böhlau Verlag, 1987.

Maraini, Fosco. Review of *Il corpo e il paradiso: Esperienze ascetiche in Asia*

*Orientale,* by Massimo Raveri. Venice: Marsilio Editori, 1992. In *Monumenta Nipponica* 48(2) (Summer 1993):276–278.

Markus, Andrew L. "Representations of *Genji Monogatari* in Edo Period Fiction." Unpublished paper, prepared for the "World of Genji" Conference, Bloomington, Indiana University, 1982.

———. *The Willow in Autumn: Ryūtei Tanehiko, 1783–1842.* Cambridge, Mass.: Council on East Asian Studies, Harvard University, 1992.

Marra, Michele. *The Aesthetics of Discontent: Politics and Reclusion in Medieval Japanese Literature.* Honolulu: University of Hawai'i Press, 1991.

Maruyama Kiyoko. *Genji monogatari no bukkyō: sono shūkyōsei no kōsatsu to gensen to naru kyōsetsu ni tsuite no tankyū.* Sōbunsha, 1985.

*Masterpieces from the Shin'enkan Collection: Japanese Painting of the Edo Period.* Los Angeles: Los Angeles County Museum of Art, 1986.

Masuda Katsumi. *Kazan rettō no shisō.* Chikuma shobō, 1983. Originally published in 1968.

Matheson, William H. "Madness in Literature: Reading the 'Heartvine' Chapter and Its Descendants," pp. 162–167. In Edward Kamens, ed., *Approaches to Teaching Murasaki Shikibu's The Tale of Genji.* New York: MLA, 1993.

Matisoff, Susan. *The Legend of Semimaru: Blind Musician of Japan.* New York: Columbia University Press, 1978.

Matsumura Hiroji and Yamanaka Yutaka, eds. *Eiga monogatari.* 2 vols. NKBT 75–76. Iwanami shoten, 1964–1965.

McCullough, Helen Craig, trans. *Tales of Ise: Lyrical Episodes from Tenth-Century Japan.* Stanford: Stanford University Press, 1968.

———. "Social and Psychological Aspects of Heian Ritual and Ceremony," 2: 275–279. In Ōta Saburō and Fukuda Rikutarō, eds., *Studies on Japanese Culture.* Tokyo: Japan PEN Club, 1973.

———, trans. *Ōkagami: The Great Mirror; Fujiwara Michinaga (966–1027) and His Times.* Princeton: Princeton University Press, 1980.

McCullough, William H. "Japanese Marriage Institutions in the Heian Period." *Harvard Journal of Asiatic Studies* 27 (1967):103–167.

———. "Spirit Possession in the Heian Period," 1: 91–98. In Ōta Saburō and Fukuda Rikutarō, eds., *Studies on Japanese Culture.* Tokyo: Japan PEN Club, 1973.

McCullough, William H., and Helen Craig McCullough, trans. *A Tale of Flowering Fortunes: Annals of Japanese Aristocratic Life in the Heian Period.* 2 vols. Stanford: Stanford University Press, 1980.

Meech-Pekarik, Julia. "The Artist's View of Ukifune," pp. 173–215. In Andrew Pekarik, ed., *Ukifune: Love in The Tale of Genji.* New York: Columbia University Press, 1982.

Mergé, Salvatore. "Demonologia nipponica: l'*oni.*" *Monumenta Nipponica* 2 (1939):276–280.

Mills, D. E., trans. *A Collection of Tales from Uji: A Study and Translation of Uji Shūi Monogatari*. Cambridge: Cambridge University Press, 1970.

Miner, Earl. "Some Thematic and Structural Features of the *Genji Monogatari*." *Monumenta Nipponica* 24(1–2) (1969):1–19.

————. "The Heroine: Identity, Recurrence, Destiny," pp. 63–81. In Andrew Pekarik, ed., *Ukifune: Love in The Tale of Genji*. New York: Columbia University Press, 1982.

————. "The Art of Life in the *Genji monogatari*." Unpublished paper, prepared for the "World of Genji" conference, Bloomington, Indiana University, 1982.

————, ed. *Principles of Classical Japanese Literature*. Princeton: Princeton University Press, 1985.

————. *Comparative Poetics: An Intercultural Essay on Theories of Literature*. Princeton: Princeton University Press, 1990.

Mischel, Walter, and Francis Mischel. "Psychological Aspects of Spirit Possession." *American Anthropologist* 60 (1958):249–260.

Mishima Yukio. *Sun & Steel*. Translated by John Bester. Tokyo: Kodansha International, 1970.

Mitani Eiichi. *Nihon bungaku no minzokugakuteki kenkyū*. Yūseidō, 1960.

————. *Genji monogatari jiten*. Yūseidō, 1973.

————. *Monogatari bungaku no sekai*. Yūseidō, 1975.

————. "Yūgao monogatari to kodenshō." *KGMS* 1:198–219.

Mitani Kuniaki. "*Genji monogatari* daisanbu no hōhō: chūshin no sōshitsu aruiwa fuzai no monogatari." *Bungaku* 50 (August 1982):76–104.

————. *Monogatari bungaku no hōhō*. 2 vols. Yūseidō, 1989.

Mitoma Kōsuke. *Genji monogatari no minzokugakuteki kenkyū*. Ōfūsha, 1980.

————. *Genji monogatari no kodai to bungaku*. Ōfūsha, 1985.

Miyake, Lynne K. "The Narrative Triad in *The Tale of Genji*: Narrator, Reader, and Text," pp. 77–87. In Edward Kamens, ed., *Approaches to Teaching Murasaki Shikibu's The Tale of Genji*. New York: MLA, 1993.

————. "*The Tosa Diary*: In the Interstices of Gender and Criticism." In Paul G. Schalow and Janet A. Walker, eds., *The Woman's Hand: Gender and Theory in Japanese Women's Writing*. Stanford: Stanford University Press, 1996.

Möller, Jörg. *Spiel und Sport am Japanischen Kaiserhof im 7. bis 14. Jahrhundert*. München: Iudicium, 1993.

Mori Ichirō. *Genji monogatari seiseiron: kyokumen shūchū to keikiteki tenkai*. Sekai shisōsha, 1986.

————, ed. *Genji monogatari 1: Nihon bungaku kenkyū taisei*. Kokusho kankōkai, 1988.

Mori Masato. "*Konjaku monogatari-shū*: Supernatural Creatures and Order." Translated by W. Michael Kelsey. *Japanese Journal of Religious Studies* 9(2–3) (June–September 1982):147–170.

Moritō Tadako. *Genji monogatari: onnatachi no shukuse*. Ōfūsha, 1984.

Morris, Ivan, trans. *The Pillow Book of Sei Shōnagon*. 2 vols. New York: Columbia University Press, 1967.

———, trans. *The Life of an Amorous Woman and Other Writings by Ihara Saikaku*. New York: New Directions, 1969. Originally published in 1963.

———, ed. *Madly Singing in the Mountains: An Appreciation and Anthology of Arthur Waley*. New York: Walker & Co., 1970.

———. *The World of the Shining Prince: Court Life in Ancient Japan*. Harmondsworth: Peregrine, 1985. Originally published in 1964.

Morris, Ivan, and Andrew Pekarik. "Deception and Self-Deception," pp. 139–151. In Andrew Pekarik, ed., *Ukifune: Love in The Tale of Genji*. New York: Columbia University Press, 1982.

Morris, Mark. "Desire and the Prince: New Work on *Genji monogatari*—a Review Article." *Journal of Asian Studies* 49(2) (May 1990):291–304.

Mühlmann, Wilhelm E. *Die Metamorphose der Frau: Weiblicher Schamanismus und Dichtung*. 2nd ed. Berlin: Dietrich Reimer Verlag, 1984. Originally published in 1981.

Murasaki Shikibu Gakkai, ed. *Genji monogatari to sono eikyō: kenkyū to shiryō*. Musashino shoin, 1978.

———. *Genji monogatari to nikki bungaku kenkyū to shiryō*. Musashino shoin, 1992.

*Murasaki Shikibu shū*. See Hasegawa Masaharu et al., eds. SNKBT 24, 1989.

Murase, Miyeko. *Emaki: Narrative Scrolls from Japan*. New York: Asia Society, 1983.

———. *Iconography of The Tale of Genji: Genji Monogatari Ekotoba*. New York: Weatherhill, 1983.

———. *Masterpieces of Japanese Screen Painting: The American Collections*. New York: Braziller, 1990.

Nakai Kazuko. *Genji monogatari: iro, nioi, oto*. Osaka: Izumi shoin, 1991.

Nakamura, Kyoko Motomochi, trans. *Miraculous Stories from the Japanese Buddhist Tradition: The Nihon ryōiki of the Monk Kyōkai*. Cambridge, Mass.: Harvard University Press, 1973.

Nakamura Yoshio. *Ōchō no fūzoku to bungaku*. Hanawa shobō, 1962.

Nakashima Ayako. "Yūgao kō," pp. 27–37. In Imai Gen'e, ed., *Genji monogatari to sono shū'en*. Osaka: Izumi shoin, 1989.

Nanba Hiroshi and Hirokawa Katsumi, eds. *Genji monogatari: chimei to hōhō*. Ōfūsha, 1990.

Narahara Shigeko. "Rokujō Miyasudokoro," 2:100–110. In *Genji monogatari kōza: Monogatari o orinasu hitobito*. Benseisha, 1991.

Nickerson, Peter. "The Meaning of Matrilocality: Kinship, Property, and Politics in Mid-Heian." *Monumenta Nipponica* 48(4) (Winter 1993): 429–467.

*Nihon bungaku kenkyū shiryō sōsho.* 50 vols. Yūseidō, first series, 1970–1975; second series, 1977–.

Nippon Gakujutsu Shinkōkai, trans. *Japanese Noh Drama: Ten Plays.* Vol. 2. Nippon Gakujutsu Shinkōkai, 1959.

———. *The Man'yōshū.* New York: Columbia University Press, 1965. Originally published in 1940.

Norbeck, Edward, and Margaret Lock. *Health, Illness, and Medical Care in Japan: Culture and Social Dimensions.* Honolulu: University of Hawai'i Press, 1987.

Ōasa Yūji. "Rokujō Miyasudokoro no kunō." *KGMS* 3:12–30.

Obayashi Taryo. "*Uji* Society and *Ie* Society from Prehistory to Medieval Times." *Journal of Japanese Studies* 11(1) (Winter 1985):3–27.

Obeyesekere, Gananath. "Psychocultural Exegesis of a Case of Spirit Possession in Sri Lanka," pp. 235–294. In Vincent Crapanzano and Vivian Garrison, eds., *Case Studies in Spirit Possession.* New York: Wiley, 1977.

Ōchō monogatari kenkyūkai, ed. *Genji monogatari to sono zengo.* 2 vols. Shintensha, 1990–1991.

Oesterreich, Traugott Konstantin. *Possession, Demoniacal and Other, Among Primitive Races, in Antiquity, the Middle Ages and Modern Times.* Translated by D. Ibberson. New Hyde Park: University Books, 1966. Originally published in 1921.

Oka Kazuo. *Genji monogatari jiten.* Shunjūsha, 1964.

———, ed. *Heianchō bungaku jiten.* Tōkyōdō shuppan, 1972.

Okada, H. Richard. *Figures of Resistance: Language, Poetry, and Narrating in The Tale of Genji and Other Mid-Heian Texts.* Durham, N.C.: Duke University Press, 1992.

Okada Shachihiko. *Genji monogatari satsujin jiken.* Ōbunsha, 1980.

Okazaki Kazuko. *Heianchō josei no monomōde.* Kyoto: Hōzōkan, 1967.

Omote Akira and Katō Shūichi, eds. *Zeami, Zenchiku.* Nihon shisō taikei 24. Iwanami shoten, 1974.

Onitsuka Takaaki. "Rekishi to kyokō to *Genji monogatari*: Yūgao maki no mono no ke ni tsuite," pp. 249–283. In Murasaki Shikibu Gakkai, ed., *Genji monogatari to nikki bungaku kenkyū to shiryō.* Musashino shoin, 1992.

Ōno Susumu et al. *Kogo jiten.* Iwanami shoten, 1974.

Ortolani, Benito. *The Japanese Theatre: From Shamanistic Ritual to Contemporary Pluralism.* Leiden: Brill, 1990.

Ōta Saburō and Fukuda Rikutarō, eds. *Studies on Japanese Culture.* 2 vols. Tokyo: Japan PEN Club, 1973.

Oughourlian, Jean-Michel. *The Puppet of Desire: The Psychology of Hysteria, Possession, and Hypnosis.* Translated by Eugene Webb. Stanford: Stanford University Press, 1991. Originally published as *Un mime nommé désir: hystérie, transe, possession, adorcisme* in French in 1982.

Owen, A.R.G. *Hysteria, Hypnosis, and Healing: The Work of J.-M. Charcot.* New York: Garrett, 1975.

Pandey, Rajyashree. "Women, Sexuality, and Enlightenment: *Kankyo no Tomo.*" *Monumenta Nipponica* 50(3) (Autumn 1995):325–356.

Peel, Ellen. "Mediation and Mediators: Letters, Screens, and Other Go-Betweens in *The Tale of Genji*," pp. 108–114. In Edward Kamens, ed., *Approaches to Teaching Murasaki Shikibu's The Tale of Genji.* New York: MLA, 1993.

Pekarik, Andrew, ed. *Ukifune: Love in The Tale of Genji.* New York: Columbia University Press, 1982.

Philippi, Donald L., trans. *Kojiki.* Tokyo: Princeton University Press and University of Tokyo Press, 1969.

———, trans. *Norito: A Translation of the Ancient Japanese Ritual Prayers.* Princeton: Princeton University Press, 1990. Originally published in 1959.

Plutschow, Herbert E. *Chaos and Cosmos: Ritual in Early and Medieval Japanese Literature.* Leiden: Brill, 1990.

Pollack, David. "The Informing Image: 'China' in *Genji Monogatari.*" *Monumenta Nipponica* 38(4) (Winter 1983):360–375.

Pound, Ezra, and Ernest Fenollosa, trans. *The Classic Noh Theatre of Japan.* New York: New Directions, 1959. Originally published in 1917.

Prince, Raymond H. "The Problem of 'Spirit Possession' as Treatment for Psychiatric Disorders." *Ethos* 2 (1974):315–333.

———. "Foreword," pp. xi–xvi. In Vincent Crapanzano and Vivian Garrison, eds., *Case Studies in Spirit Possession.* New York: Wiley, 1977.

Ramirez-Christensen, Esperanza. "The Operation of the Lyrical Mode in the *Genji Monogatari*," pp. 21–61. In Andrew Pekarik, ed., *Ukifune: Love in The Tale of Genji.* New York: Columbia University Press, 1982.

Reynolds, Frank E., and Earle H. Waugh, eds. *Religious Encounters with Death: Insights from the History and Anthropology of Religions.* University Park: Pennsylvania State University Press, 1977.

Rimer, J. Thomas, and Yamazaki Masakazu, trans. *On the Art of the Nō Drama: The Major Treatises of Zeami.* Princeton: Princeton University Press, 1984.

Rohlich, Thomas H., trans. *A Tale of Eleventh-Century Japan: Hamamatsu Chūnagon Monogatari.* Princeton: Princeton University Press, 1983.

Roscoe, Paul B. "Amity and Aggression: A Symbolic Theory of Incest." *Man* (n.s.) 29 (March 1994):49–76.

Rose, Mary Beth, ed. *Women in the Middle Ages and the Renaissance.* Syracuse: Syracuse University Press, 1986.

Rosenfield, John M., Fumiko E. Cranston, and Edwin A. Cranston. *The Courtly Tradition in Japanese Art and Literature: Selections from the Hofer and Hyde Collections.* Fogg Art Museum Catalog, Harvard University. Tokyo: Kodansha International, 1973.

Rubin, Jay. "The Art of the Flower of Mumbo Jumbo." *Harvard Journal of Asiatic Studies* 53(2) (December 1993):513–541.

Ruch, Barbara. "Medieval Jongleurs and the Making of a National Literature," pp. 279–309. In John Whitney Hall and Toyoda Takeshi, eds., *Japan in the Muromachi Age*. Berkeley: University of California Press, 1977.

Saegusa Hideaki. "Tsumi no hitobito: Kashiwagi, Murasaki no ue, Kaoru no tsumi, shukuse, shūkyō ni tsuite." 2: 145–202. In Ōchō monogatari ken-kyūkai, ed., *Genji monogatari to sono zengo*. Shintensha, 1991.

Saeki Shōichi, Donald Keene, Muramatsu Takeshi, and Tanaka Miyoko, eds. *Mishima Yukio Zenshū*. Vol. 21. Shinchōsha, 1974.

Saigō Nobutsuna. *Shi no hassei: bungaku ni okeru genshi, kodai no imi*. Rev. ed. Miraisha, 1964.

———. *Genji monogatari o yomu tame ni*. Heibonsha, 1983.

Saitō Akiko. *Genji monogatari no bukkyō to ningen*. Ōfūsha, 1989.

Sakamoto Kazuko. "Rokujō Miyasudokoro no Ise gekō to onryō shutsugen." *Bungaku Gogaku* 72 (August 1974):90–100.

———. "Hikaru Genji no keifu." *Kokugakuin Zasshi* 76 (December 1975): 33–43.

Sakamoto Noboru. *Genji monogatari kōsōron*. Meiji shoin, 1981.

———. "Rokujō Miyasudokoro," pp. 135–138. In Akiyama Ken, ed., *Genji monogatari hikkei II*. Gakutōsha, 1982.

———. "Onna ichi no miya: 'Kagerō'." *Kokubungaku* 32(13) (November 1987):135–137.

Sakurai Tokutarō. *Reikonkan no keifu: rekishi minzokugaku no shiten*. Kōdansha, 1989.

———. *Minkan shinkō no kenkyū*. Yoshikawa kōbunkan, 1990.

Sanari Kentarō, ed. *Yōkyoku taikan*. 7 vols. Meiji shoin, 1931–1933. Reprinted in 1964 and 1982.

Sansom, G.B. *A History of Japan to 1334*. Stanford: Stanford University Press, 1958.

———. *Japan: A Short Cultural History*. Rev. ed. Stanford: Stanford University Press, 1978. Originally published in 1931.

Schalow, Paul G. " 'Bridging' as a Mechanism of Male Homosocial Desire in *The Tale of Genji*." Unpublished paper, presented at the annual meeting of the Association for Asian Studies, Honolulu, 1996.

Schalow, Paul G., and Janet A. Walker, eds. *The Woman's Hand: Gender and Theory in Japanese Women's Writing*. Stanford: Stanford University Press, 1996.

Schechner, Richard. *Between Theater and Anthropology*. Philadelphia: University of Pennsylvania Press, 1985.

Schechner, Richard, and Willa Appel, eds. *By Means of Performance: Intercultural Studies of Theatre and Ritual*. Cambridge: Cambridge University Press, 1989.

Schulenburg, Jane Tibbetts. "The Heroics of Virginity: Brides of Christ and Sacrificial Mutilation," pp. 29–72. In Mary Beth Rose, ed., *Women in the Middle Ages and the Renaissance*. Syracuse: Syracuse University Press, 1986.

Scott-Stokes, Henry. *The Life and Death of Yukio Mishima*. New York: Farrar, Straus & Giroux, 1974.

Sedgwick, Eve Kosofsky. *Between Men: English Literature and Male Homosocial Desire*. New York: Columbia University Press, 1985.

Segi Shin'ichi. *Yoshitoshi: The Splendid Decadent*. Translated by Alfred Birnbaum. Tokyo: Kodansha International, 1985.

Seidensticker, Edward G., trans. *The Tale of Genji*. 2 vols. New York: Knopf, 1976.

———. *The Gossamer Years (Kagerō Nikki): The Diary of a Noblewoman of Heian Japan*. Tokyo: Tuttle, 1988. Originally published in 1964.

Sekine Kenji. *Monogatari bungaku ron: Genji monogatari zengo*. Ōfūsha, 1980.

———. *"Genji monogatari* ni okeru shamanizumu yōso." *Kokubungaku: kaishaku to kanshō* 46 (May 1981):63–67.

———. "Fusha to bungaku: shinwa to shamanizumu." *Kokubungaku: kaishaku to kanshō* 53(9) (September 1988):25–35.

Sharf, Robert H. "The Idolization of Enlightenment: On the Mummification of Ch'an Masters in Medieval China." *History of Religions* 32(1) (1992):1–31.

Shell, Marc. *The End of Kinship: 'Measure for Measure,' Incest, and the Ideal of Universal Siblinghood*. Stanford: Stanford University Press, 1988.

Shigematsu Nobuhiro. *Genji monogatari no kokoro*. Kōsei shuppansha, 1990.

Shimazaki Chifumi, trans. *The Noh*. Vol. 3, bk. 1: *Woman Noh*. Tokyo: Hinoki shoten, 1976.

Shimazu Hisamoto, Yamagishi Tokuhei, and Ikeda Kikan, eds. *Genji monogatari kenkyū*. Yūseidō, 1970.

Shimizu, Yoshiaki, and Susan E. Nelson. *Genji: The World of a Prince*. Bloomington: Indiana University Art Museum, 1982.

Shimizu Yoshiko. *Genji no onnagimi*. Hanawa shobō, 1967.

———. *Genji monogatari no buntai to hōhō*. Tōkyō daigaku shuppankai, 1980.

Shinohara Shoji. "Hai-in no ke." *KGMS* 1:246–258.

———. "Mono no ke." In *Genji monogatari o dō yomu ka*. *Kokubungaku* 28(16) (December 1983):126–129.

———. "Rokujō Miyasudokoro to Fujitsubo." *Kokubungaku* 32(13) (November 1987):52–55.

Shirane, Haruo. "The Uji Chapters and the Denial of the Romance," pp. 113–138. In Andrew Pekarik, ed., *Ukifune: Love in The Tale of Genji*. New York: Columbia University Press, 1982.

————. "The Aesthetics of Power: Politics in *The Tale of Genji*." *Harvard Journal of Asiatic Studies* 45(2) (December 1985):615–647.

————. *The Bridge of Dreams: A Poetics of "The Tale of Genji"*. Stanford: Stanford University Press, 1987.

Simon, Bennett. *Mind and Madness in Ancient Greece: The Classical Roots of Modern Psychiatry*. Ithaca: Cornell University Press, 1978.

Smethurst, Mae J. *The Artistry of Aeschylus and Zeami: A Comparative Study of Greek Tragedy and Nō*. Princeton: Princeton University Press, 1989.

Smith, Robert J. *Ancestor Worship in Contemporary Japan*. Stanford: Stanford University Press, 1974.

Smith-Rosenberg, Carroll. *Disorderly Conduct: Visions of Gender in Victorian America*. New York: Knopf, 1985.

Sonoda, Kyoichi. *Health and Illness in Changing Japanese Society*. Tokyo: University of Tokyo Press, 1988.

Spanos, Nicholas P., and Jack Gottlieb. "Demonic Possession, Mesmerism, and Hysteria: A Social Psychological Perspective on Their Historical Interrelations." *Journal of Abnormal Psychology* 88(5) (1979):527–546.

Spiro, Melford E. *Burmese Supernaturalism: A Study in the Exploration and Reduction of Suffering*. Englewood Cliffs, N.J.: Prentice-Hall, 1967.

Stevenson, John. *Yoshitoshi's One Hundred Aspects of the Moon*. Redmond, Wash.: San Francisco Graphic Society, 1992.

Stinchecum, Amanda Mayer. "Who Tells the Tale? 'Ukifune': A Study in Narrative Voice." *Monumenta Nipponica* 35(4) (1980):375–405.

————. *Narrative Voice in The Tale of Genji*. Illinois Papers in Asian Studies 5. Urbana, Ill.: Center for East Asian and Pacific Studies, 1985.

Sugii Gisaburō (director), Tsutsui Tomomi (script), and Hosono Haruomi (music). *Murasaki Shikibu: Genji monogatari*. Animation. Asahi Video Library, n. d.

Suzuki Hideo. "*Genji monogatari* sakuchū waka ichiran." NKBZ 17; *Genji monogatari* 6:517–549.

————. "Hikaru Genji no onnagimitachi," pp. 100–150. In Murasaki Shikibu Gakkai, ed., *Genji monogatari to sono eikyō: kenkyū to shiryō*. Musashino, 1978.

————. "*Genji monogatari* toshidate," pp. 127–137. In Akiyama Ken, ed., *Genji monogatari hikkei I*. Bessatsu kokubungaku, no. 1. Gakutōsha, 1978.

Suzuki Kazuo. "*Genji monogatari* nenpu /keizu," pp. 376–394. In Akiyama Ken, ed., *Genji monogatari jiten*. Bessatsu kokubungaku, no. 36. Gakutōsha, 1989.

Suzuki Tomotarō, Kawaguchi Hisao, Endō Yoshimoto, and Nishishita Kyōichi, eds. *Tosa nikki, Kagerō nikki, Izumi Shikibu nikki, Sarashina nikki*. NKBT 20. Iwanami shoten, 1957.

Sylte, Linda M. "Zenchiku's 'A Genji Requiem' and Mishima's Modern Adaptation." Unpublished M.A. thesis, Washington University, 1980.

Tahara, Mildred M., trans. *Tales of Yamato: A Tenth-Century Poem-Tale.* Honolulu: University Press of Hawai'i, 1980.

Takagi Sōkan. *Genji monogatari to bukkyō.* Ōfūsha, 1991.

Takahashi Kazuo. *Genji monogatari no shudai to kōsō.* Ōfūsha, 1971.

———. "Rokujō-in no zōei: otome." *Nihon bungaku* 32(13) (November 1987):72–75.

Takahashi Tōru. *Genji monogatari no taii-hō.* Tōkyō Daigaku shuppankai, 1982.

———. *Monogatari bungei no hyōgenshi.* Nagoya: Nagoya Daigaku shuppan-kai, 1987.

———. *Monogatari to e no enkinhō.* Perikansha, 1991.

Takehara Hiroshi. "Ōigimi no kekkon kyohi tsuikō: Uji jūjōron josetsu," pp. 171–191. In Murasaki Shikibu Gakkai, ed., *Genji monogatari no shisō to hyōgen: kenkyū to shiryō.* Musashino shoin, 1989.

Takemoto Mikio. "*Genji monogatari* to yōkyoku." *Kokubungaku: kaishaku to kanshō* 48(10) (July 1983):123–128.

Takeuchi Michiyo. *Murasaki Shikibu shū hyōshaku.* Ōfūsha, 1969.

Tamagami Takuya, ed. *Genji monogatari hyōshaku.* 12 vols. Kadokawa shoten, 1964–1968.

———. "*Genji monogatari* no Rokujō-in," pp. 49–61. In Oboroya Hisashi et al., eds., *Heiankyō no teidai.* Kyoto: Bōryōsha, 1987.

Tanabe Seiko. *Genji monogatari no otokotachi: misutā Genji no seikatsu to iken.* Iwanami shoten, 1990.

Tanaka Ichimatsu, ed. *Shinshū Nihon emakimono zenshū.* Vol. 2. Kadokawa shoten, 1975.

Tanaka Sumie. "Kodai no yami ni chōryō suru: yōkai, mono no ketachi," pp. 59–62. In Tanigawa Ken'ichi, ed., *Nihon no yōkai.* Bessatsu taiyō, no. 57. Heibonsha, Spring 1987.

Tanaka Tsunemasa. *Genji monogatari no kenkyū: Utsusemi, Uji no Ōigimi, Ukifune monogatari no kōsei.* Kasama shoin, 1991.

Tanigawa Ken'ichi, ed. *Nihon no yōkai.* Bessatsu taiyō, no. 57. Heibonsha, Spring 1987.

Taya Raishun. *Genji monogatari no shisō.* Kyoto: Hōzōkan, 1952.

———, ed. *Bukkyō bungaku kenkyū.* Kyoto: Hōzōkan, 1966.

Teramoto Naohiko. *Genji monogatari ronkō: kochūshaku, juyō.* Kazama shobō, 1989.

Terasaki Etsuko. "Images and Symbols in *Sotoba Komachi:* A Critical Analysis of a Nō Play." *Harvard Journal of Asiatic Studies* 44(1) (June 1984): 155–184.

Thompson, Sarah E. "A *Hakubyō Genji Monogatari Emaki* in the Spencer Collection." Unpublished M.A. thesis, Columbia University, 1983.

Tonomura, Hitomi. "Black Hair and Red Trousers: Gendering the Flesh in Medieval Japan." *American Historical Review* 99(1) (February 1994): 129–154.

Tsuboi Kou (*manga* artist) and Shimizu Yoshiko, ed. *Genji monogatari eigo-han: The Illustrated Genji monogatari*. Shinjinbutsu Ōraisha, 1989.

Tsuchihashi Yutaka and Hirokawa Katsumi, eds. *Kodai bungaku no yōshiki to kinō*. Ōfūsha, 1988.

Turner, Victor. *The Ritual Process: Structure and Anti-Structure*. Chicago: Aldine, 1969.

———. "Social Dramas and Ritual Metaphors," pp. 23–59. In *Dramas, Fields, and Metaphors: Symbolic Action in Human Society*. Ithaca: Cornell University Press, 1974.

———. "Frame, Flow and Reflection: Ritual and Drama as Public Liminality." *Japanese Journal of Religious Studies* 6(4) (December 1979):465–499. Originally published in 1977.

———. *The Forest of Symbols: Aspects of Ndembu Ritual*. Ithaca: Cornell University Press, 1981. Originally published in 1967.

———. "Liminality and the Performative Genres," pp. 19–41. In John J. MacAloon, ed., *Rite, Drama, Festival, Spectacle: Rehearsals Toward a Theory of Cultural Performance*. Philadelphia: Institute for the Study of Human Issues, 1984.

———. *On the Edge of the Bush: Anthropology as Experience*. Edited by L. B. Turner. Tucson: University of Arizona Press, 1985.

Uesaka Nobuo. *Genji monogatari no shii, josetsu: kodai monogatari no kenkyū*. Kasama shoin, 1982.

Ury, Marian. "Virtue Rewarded and Evil Scourged: Tales from the *Nihon Ryōiki*." *California Quarterly* 2 (Summer 1972):51–59.

———, trans. *Tales of Times Now Past: Sixty-Two Stories from a Medieval Japanese Collection*. Berkeley: University of California Press, 1979.

———. "Stepmother Tales in Japan." *Children's Literature* 9 (1981):61–72.

———. "A Heian Note on the Supernatural." *Journal of the Association of Teachers of Japanese* 22(2) (November 1988):189–194.

Varley, H. Paul, trans. *"The Shrine in the Fields (Nonomiya),"* pp. 179–192. In Donald Keene, ed., *Twenty Plays of the Nō Theatre*. New York: Columbia University Press, 1970.

———. *Japanese Culture: A Short History*. Expanded ed. New York: Holt, Rinehart & Winston, 1977.

Veith, Ilza. *Hysteria: The History of a Disease*. Chicago: University of Chicago Press, 1965.

Wakashiro Kiiko. *Hikaru Genji no butai*. Asahi shinbunsha, 1992.

Wakita Haruko. "Marriage and Property in Premodern Japan: From the Perspective of Women's History." *Journal of Japanese Studies* 10(1) (Winter 1984):73–99.

Waley, Arthur, trans. *The Nō Plays of Japan*. New York: Grove Press, 1957.

———, trans. *The Tale of Genji: A Novel in Six Parts by Lady Murasaki*. New York: Modern Library, 1960.

————. "Review of Ivan Morris's *The World of the Shining Prince: Court Life in Ancient Japan*" (1964), pp. 375–378. In Ivan Morris, ed., *Madly Singing in the Mountains: An Appreciation and Anthology of Arthur Waley*. New York: Walker & Co., 1970.

Walker, D. P. *Unclean Spirits: Possession and Exorcism in France and England in the Late Sixteenth and Early Seventeenth Centuries*. Philadelphia: University of Pennsylvania Press, 1981.

Washiyama Shigeo. *Genji monogatari shudairon: Uji jūjō no sekai*. Hanawa shobō, 1985.

Watanabe Minoru. *Heianchō bunshōshi*. Tōkyō Daigaku shuppankai, 1981.

Weidner, Marsha, ed. *Flowering in the Shadows: Women in the History of Chinese and Japanese Painting*. Honolulu: University of Hawai'i Press, 1990.

Whitehouse, Wilfred, and Eizo Yanagisawa, trans. *Ochikubo Monogatari—The Tale of the Lady Ochikubo: A Tenth Century Japanese Novel*. Garden City, N.Y.: Doubleday Anchor, 1971. Originally published in 1965.

Wilson, Peter. "Status Ambiguity and Spirit Possession." *Man: The Journal of the Royal Anthropological Institute* 2 (1967):366–378.

Winkler, John J. *The Constraints of Desire: The Anthropology of Sex and Gender in Ancient Greece*. New York: Routledge, 1990.

Wolf, Arthur P., ed. *Religion and Ritual in Chinese Society*. Stanford: Stanford University Press, 1974.

Wood, Ann Douglas. "The Fashionable Diseases: Women's Complaints and Their Treatment." *Journal of Interdisciplinary History* 4(1) (Summer 1973):25–52.

Yamada Katsumi. " 'Mono no ke' gengi kō." *Jōchi Daigaku kokubungaku ronshū* 1 (March 1968):15–42.

Yamagishi Tokuhei and Oka Kazuo, eds. *Genji monogatari kōza*. 8 vols. Yūseidō, 1971–1972.

Yamaguchi Takeshi. "*Genji monogatari* kenkyū: Yūgao no maki ni arawaretaru 'mono no ke' ni tsuite," pp. 172–195. In *Genji monogatari III: Nihon bungaku kenkyū shiryō sōsho*. Yūseidō, 1971.

Yanai Shigeshi. "Hatsuse no Kannon no reigen." *KGMS* 9:193–204.

————. "Tenarai no kimi." *Kokubungaku* 32(13) (November 1987):138–141.

Yasuda, Kenneth. *Masterworks of the Nō Theater*. Bloomington: Indiana University Press, 1989.

Yiengpruksawan, Mimi Hall. "What's in a Name? Fujiwara Fixation in Japanese Cultural History." *Monumenta Nipponica* 49(4) (Winter 1994):423–453.

Yokomichi Mario and Omote Akira, eds. *Yōkyoku shū*. 2 vols. NKBT 40–41. Iwanami shoten, 1960–1963.

Yoshida Teigo. "Mystical Retribution, Spirit Possession, and Social Structure in a Japanese Village." *Ethnology* 6 (1967):237–262.

————. *Nihon no tsukimono: shakai jinruigakuteki kōsatsu.* Chūō Kōronsha, 1972.

————. "Spirit Possession and Village Conflict," pp. 85–104. In Ellis S. Krauss, Thomas P. Rohlen, and Patricia G. Steinhoff, eds., *Conflict in Japan.* Honolulu: University of Hawai'i Press, 1984.

Yotsutsuji Yoshinari. *Kakaishō* [ca. 1364]. In Tamagami Takuya, Yamamoto Ritatsu, and Ishida Jōji, eds., *Shimeishō, Kakaishō.* Kadokawa shoten, 1968.

Zaretsky, Irving I., and Cynthia Shambaugh. *Spirit Possession and Spirit Mediumship in Africa and Afro-America: An Annotated Bibliography.* New York: Garland, 1978.

# Index

# About the Author

DORIS G. BARGEN is currently visiting assistant professor of Japanese literature at the University of Massachusetts at Amherst. She received her doctorate from the Universität Tübingen in Germany. Her study of spirit possession in *The Tale of Genji* has been supported by grants from the National Endowment for the Humanities and the Social Science Research Council. Her first article on *The Tale of Genji* was published in *Mosaic* (1986), followed by two articles in the *Harvard Journal of Asiatic Studies* (1988 and 1991) and another in *Approaches to Teaching Murasaki Shikibu's The Tale of Genji,* edited by Edward Kamens (New York: MLA, 1993). She has also published articles on Enchi Fumiko in *Monumenta Nipponica* (1991) and Kawabata Yasunari in the *Japanese Journal of Religious Studies* (1992). Another article on Enchi appears in *The Woman's Hand: Gender and Theory in Japanese Women's Writing,* edited by Paul G. Schalow and Janet A. Walker (Stanford: Stanford University Press, 1996).